Nationalism, Ethnicity
and the State

Nationalism, Ethnicity and the State

Making and breaking nations

John Coakley

Los Angeles | London | New Delhi
Singapore | Washington DC

Los Angeles | London | New Delhi
Singapore | Washington DC

SAGE Publications Ltd
1 Oliver's Yard
55 City Road
London EC1Y 1SP

SAGE Publications Inc.
2455 Teller Road
Thousand Oaks, California 91320

SAGE Publications India Pvt Ltd
B 1/I 1 Mohan Cooperative Industrial Area
Mathura Road
New Delhi 110 044

SAGE Publications Asia-Pacific Pte Ltd
3 Church Street
#10-04 Samsung Hub
Singapore 049483

Editor: Natalie Aguilera
Editorial assistant: James Piper
Production editor: Imogen Roome
Marketing manager: Sally Ransom
Cover design: Francis Kenny
Typeset by: C&M Digitals (P) Ltd, Chennai, India
Printed in India at Replika Press Pvt Ltd

Cover image: annual bonfire celebrating victory of Protestant King William over Catholic King James at the Battle of the Boyn (1690), Annadale Embankment, Belfast, 11 July 2011.

Library of Congress Control Number: 2011945431

British Library Cataloguing in Publication data

A catalogue record for this book is available from the British Library

ISBN 978-1-4462-4742-6
ISBN 978-1-4462-4743-3(pbk)

CONTENTS

LIST OF TABLES

LIST OF FIGURES

PREFACE

The rapidly growing range of books and articles on nationalism raises the question as to why yet another book on the subject is needed. Those familiar with this vast literature, however, will be aware that, for all its extent and quality, it is overwhelmingly dominated by case studies, with theoretical analyses occupying a respectable niche, and just a tiny number of comparative works.

There have been notable efforts to synthesise the huge body of writing that has emerged in recent decades, and impressive strides have been made in the domain of sociological theories of nationalism. Nevertheless, this still leaves a gap: the need for further broad comparative study of this powerful force. The present book tries to respond to this need, though necessarily subject to two important restrictions. First, this multi-faceted phenomenon clearly requires interdisciplinary analysis; but the present study reflects the perspective of the political scientist. Second, the reach of nationalism is global; but few scholars can claim familiarity with all zones of the world, and the European bias of this book must be acknowledged.

The book seeks, then, to offer an overview of nationalism characterised by a comparative historical approach that combines an attempt to synthesise the existing literature on the concomitants of nationalism with theoretical speculation regarding the path that it typically follows. The book rests on analysis of a large number of case studies of very different kinds, an approach that relies on the generous assistance of many people and institutions.

I would like in the first place to record my gratitude to the many libraries in which it was my privilege and pleasure to work. The libraries of University College Dublin and Queen's University Belfast have been of particular assistance, but it has been a rewarding experience to work also in so many other university libraries (with that of the London School of Economics as the richest in resources in this area) and national libraries (with the National Library of Ireland and the British Library as those on which I have relied most). The eccentricities of national library culture are, indeed, almost as intriguing as nationalism itself, with only experienced practitioners having the capacity to penetrate unwritten norms to ensure that books are not only ordered but are likely to be delivered. The extremes are represented by the openness of the Library of Congress system (sadly limited in recent years by security considerations) and the eccentric and often frustrating unpredictability of the old German *Staatsbibliothek* in East Berlin and its unique relationship with its West Berlin counterpart during the years of the cold war.

The gigantic expansion in availability of data that was ushered in by the information technology revolution makes it necessary also to acknowledge the invaluable assistance of other institutions. These include national statistical databases (notably, central statistics offices), but also, in particular, data archives which have made important datasets available. Among these, I am grateful to ARK-Northern Ireland Life and Times Survey, Centro de Investigaciones Sociológicas in Madrid, DANS in the Netherlands, GESIS – Leibniz Institute for the Social Sciences in Germany, the Inter-University Consortium for Political and Social Research at the University of Michigan, the Irish Social Science Data Archive at University College Dublin, the Norwegian Social Science Data Services at the University of Bergen (for the European Social Survey), Réseau Quetelet in Paris, the United Kingdom Data Archive at the University of Essex, and the World Values Survey network.

My thanks are due also to the several institutions that have hosted sabbatical visits over the years, including the Free University of Berlin, the Fondation Nationale des Sciences Politiques in Paris, the University of Helsinki, the Woodrow Wilson Center in Washington, DC, and Australian National University. Warm thanks are due to friends and colleagues who read one or more chapters of the book or assisted in other ways: Stefan Auer, Joe Brady, Steve Bruce, Linda Cardinal, Walker Connor, John Edwards, Bryan Fanning, Yvonne Galligan, Tom Garvin, Adrian Guelke, Katy Hayward, Michael Holmes, Iseult Honohan, Derek Hutcheson, Jean Laponce, Wolfgang Marx, Stephen Mennell, Gerald Mills, Brendan O'Leary, Pascal Pragnere, Joe Ruane, Claudia Saba, Bill Safran and Tobias Theiler. I am particularly indebted to Siniša Malešević and Jennifer Todd, who read all, or almost all, of the text. Finally, I am grateful to the staff of Sage Publications, including Natalie Aguilera, Patrick Brindle, David Mainwaring, James Piper, Imogen Roome and their colleagues, for their work at various stages in ensuring the publication of this book.

INTRODUCTION

1

THE STUDY OF NATIONALISM

INTRODUCTION

'Nationalism is an infantile sickness. It is the measles of the human race' – this was the verdict attributed to Albert Einstein on the force that had so profound an impact on the Europe of his middle years (Dukas and Hoffman, 1979: 38). This judgement of a theoretical physicist briefly turned political commentator was, if anything, milder than the assessments of later analysts of nationalism, many of whom would have used the metaphor of a much more deadly disease than measles. One distinguished scholar alleged that it has 'created new conflict, exacerbated tensions, and brought catastrophe to numberless people innocent of all politics' (Kedourie, 1993: 134). Others have pointed to its potential for generating hatred, civil unrest, violence, war and political instability (Kellas, 1998: 11–12; Poole, 1999: 9; Joireman, 2003: 1). There is, however, agreement on its huge importance in contemporary societies, with Greenfeld (1992: 3) seeing nationalism 'at the basis' of the world in which we live, Hechter (2000: 3) taking the view that 'nationalism and its close cousin, ethnicity, currently are the most potent political forces in the world', Puri (2004: 3) seeing the crisis of September 11, 2001, in the USA as revealing the force of nationalism in various ways (in particular, through the vigour of the American popular response), and Roshwald (2006: 1) drawing attention to its pervasiveness in the post-Cold War world.

As a political force, nationalism is very broad in its reach, and hard to pin down. It is conventionally seen as finding expression in an extraordinarily wide range of phenomena – war in Afghanistan, rebellion in Chechnya, unrest in Ukraine, instability in Belgium, and many other expressions of dissent at the polling booth or in the streets (for other examples, see Hearn, 2006: 1–3). Together, these examples illustrate the complexity and elusiveness of nationalism, whose very ubiquity makes studying it a huge challenge. It appears to have no borders: we can see nationalism almost everywhere, and the word is used in a bewildering variety of ways, and to convey sharply conflicting judgements. For some it is one of the most progressive forces in history, while for others it is a dangerous stage just short of authoritarianism; for some it liberates people, for others it enslaves them – in short, for some it is a sacred force, and for others a curse.

Analyzing nationalism may not be easy, but it is nevertheless important. The object of this book is to offer an approach to this complex but vibrant topic. In doing so, it aims to strike a balance between two very widely adopted perspectives. The first is the empirical analysis of particular forms of nationalism (to which may be added a small number of comparative studies based on similar cases). The second is the theoretical discussion of nationalism as a distinctive political phenomenon, a discussion which often remains at the level of the general and abstract, using limited illustrative material. Finding a middle ground between these approaches is not easy, but the present chapter indicates how this will be attempted.

There is one important respect in which the study of nationalism diverges from many other subfields of the social sciences: it lacks an agreed terminology. Since there is no escaping this problem, it is addressed in the first main section of this chapter. But there are other respects in which the study of nationalism resembles other subfields: it is possible to make the same kind of distinction between normative and analytical approaches as is made in the study of, say, democracy. One set of questions is evaluative: whether the phenomenon under study is in general a 'positive' feature of political life, and whether it is more or less appropriate in particular configurations of circumstances – a set of essentially prescriptive issues. The second addresses the actual nature of this phenomenon: in which circumstances it occurs, what its characteristics are, what its consequences are, and so on – a range of questions implying description and explanation. This book focuses on the second set of questions, but it is rarely possible in social analysis to make a hard-and-fast distinction between analysis and evaluation. In any case, even if we were to succeed in doing so, we would still find that the distinction is ignored in large bodies of research – perhaps for very good reasons. This chapter therefore continues in the second section by outlining briefly the big literature that assesses or passes judgement on nationalism as a force in modern politics, before going on in the third section to outline the manner in which the book will address the core matters of description and explanation that are its central concern.

MATTERS OF DEFINITION

The exceptional difficulty of establishing an agreed terminology in nationalism studies has long been recognized. It is now almost a century since the author of an article on nationalism suggested, in effect, that an international assembly of scholars was needed – 'a sort of Nicene Council on the terminology used in connection with the social sciences' (Handman, 1921: 104n). More than 30 years later, Louis Snyder, one of the founding fathers of nationalism studies, concluded that the term 'nationalism' had baffled several generations of scholars, who had 'not been able to achieve unanimity of definition' (Snyder, 1954: 4). Since then, efforts on the part of various bodies and individuals to plot a path forward have had little impact on everyday usage by scholars. Examples of such worthwhile efforts include the compilation by Unesco of a glossary in the area of 'ethnic questions' (Unesco, 1977), a similar initiative by the Research Committee on Conceptual and Terminological Analysis of the International Social Science Council (Riggs, 1985), and parallel efforts by a long-standing student of nationalism, Thomas Spira (1999). The words of one specialist in the 1920s have, unfortunately, been echoed many times since then: scholars recognize there is a problem but have been unable to come up with a solution, and many of them 'set out by alluding to the embarrassment occasioned by the use of different terms such as "nationality" and "nationalism" in the same sense, and end up by confounding the terms themselves' (Joseph, 1929: 18).

This confusion over terminology explains why so many texts dealing with nationalism begin with a long discussion of matters of definition. The tradition had already been established in the late nineteenth century, when Julius Neumann (1888: 1–31) engaged on a study of this issue in Germany. But the older literature in other languages displays a similar preoccupation. Thus, we find extended discussions of terminology in Hungarian (Elekes, 1940), Finnish (Kemiläinen, 1964), Czech (Kořalka, 1969) and Russian (Bromley, 1974). In English, the word 'ethnic' poses a similar challenge (McKay and Lewins, 1978), and Walker Connor (1978) gave his celebrated article documenting this confusion the paradoxical title 'a nation is a nation, is a state, is an ethnic group, is a …'.

As well as difficulties within languages, various problems exist between them. Conventional translations may in reality have different meanings in two languages (Polakovič, 1985), and it has long been acknowledged that 'nation' in English, the same term in French, *Nation* in German, *nación* in Spanish and *nazione* in Italian all have slightly different meanings (Royal Institute for International Affairs, 1939: xvi–xx). The reality here is that 'nation' as understood in English cannot be precisely translated into the languages of central and eastern Europe. As one of the dominant figures in European nationalism studies observed, 'I have no problems speaking about a Flemish nation in Czech or German, but I understand that English speakers have difficulties doing so' (Hroch, 2010: 883). This discussion of definition continues in the more recent literature in English (see for example, Kellas, 1998: 2–6; Puri, 2004: 22–37; Hearn, 2006: 3–5), and a full volume in French addresses terminology in this area (Rémi-Giraud and Rétat, 1996). This rest of this section therefore explores the manner in which these terms are used in the existing literature, and continues with an indication of how they will be employed elsewhere in this book.

Terminological confusion

Since the central concern of this book hinges on the relationship between state and nation, it is obviously vital to arrive at a relatively clear understanding of what these terms mean. But the problem does not end there. Other terms in this same area, ranging from 'ethnic' to 'nationalism' itself, are also lacking in an agreed meaning. A set of terms that illustrate the variety of approaches to definition is reported in Table 1.1. The reader will notice that there is an alarming continuum here that illustrates the great difficulties that impede progress in this area: the definitions overlap, especially on the boundaries between the five sections into which the table is divided. Thus, the first definition of 'nation' (by Friedrich) overlaps with the opening definition of 'state', and this overlap continues between the other categories.

State. Of the terms that are central in the study of nationalism, 'state' presents fewest difficulties. One classical definition is presented in Table 1.1. For Max Weber – though

Table 1.1   Issues of definition: examples

STATE

A compulsory political organisation with continuous operations will be called a '**state**' insofar as its administrative staff successfully upholds the claim to the monopoly of the legitimate use of physical force in the maintenance of its order (Weber, 1968 [1922]: 54).

NATION

[A **nation** is] any cohesive group possessing 'independence' within the confines of the international order as provided by the United Nations, which provides a constituency for a government effectively ruling such a group and receiving from that group the acclamation which legitimizes the government as part of the world order (Friedrich, 1966: 27–32).

A **nation** [is] a named human population sharing an historic territory, common myths and historical memories, a mass, public culture, a common economy and common legal rights and duties for all members (A. D. Smith, 1991: 14).

A **nation** is a historically constituted, stable community of people, formed on the basis of a common language, territory, economic life and psychological makeup manifested in a common culture (Stalin, 1953 [1913]: 306).

A **nation** is a body of men inhabiting a definite territory, who normally are drawn from different races, but possess a common stock of thoughts and feelings acquired and transmitted during the course of a common history; who on the whole and in the main, though more in the past than in the present, include in that stock a common religious belief; who generally and as a rule use a common language as a vehicle for their thoughts and feelings; and who, besides common thoughts and feelings, also cherish a common will, and accordingly form, or tend to form, a separate state for the expression of that will (Barker, 1927).

NATIONALITY

A portion of mankind may be said to constitute a **nationality**, if they are united among themselves by common sympathies, which do not exist between them and any others – which make them cooperate with each other more willingly than with other people, desire to be under the same government, and desire that it should be government by themselves or a portion of themselves, exclusively (Mill, 1861: 287).

ETHNIC GROUP

Ethnic groups are fundamental units of social organization which consist of members who define themselves, or are defined, by a sense of common historical origins that may also include religious beliefs, a similar language, or a shared culture (Stone and Piya, 2007).

An **ethnic group** is ... a collectivity within a larger society having real or putative common ancestry, memories of a shared historical past, and a cultural focus on one or more symbolic elements defined as the epitome of their peoplehood (Schermerhorn, 1970: 12).

We shall call '**ethnic groups**' those human groups that entertain a subjective belief in their common descent because of similarities of physical types or of customs or both, or because of memories of colonisation and migration; this belief must be important for the propagation of group formation; conversely, it does not matter whether or not an objective blood relationship exists (Weber, 1968 [1922]: 389).

RACE

We can define a **race** ... as a human group defined by itself or others as distinct by virtue of perceived characteristics that are held to be inherent. A race is a group of human beings socially defined on the basis of physical characteristics (Cornell and Hartmann, 1998: 24).

his definition at first sight seems oblique and unnecessarily complex – the state can only be territorially defined, and those within its borders are governed by an agency which exists continuously over time. While these characteristics apply to many different types of administrative district, the crucial defining characteristic is the last one: the governing agency 'successfully upholds the claim to the monopoly of the legitimate use of physical force in the maintenance of its order', a feature that might otherwise be described as the possession of sovereignty. As Weber further put it,

> The primary formal characteristics of the modern state are as follows: it possesses an administrative and legal order subject to change by legislation, to which the organised activities of the administrative staff, which are also controlled by regulations, are oriented. This system of order claims binding authority, not only over the members of the state, the citizens, most of whom have obtained membership by birth, but also to a very large extent over all action taking place in the area of its jurisdiction. It is thus a compulsory organisation with a territorial basis. Furthermore, the use of force is regarded as legitimate only so far as it is either permitted by the state or prescribed by it. ... The claim of the modern state to monopolise the use of force is as essential to it as its character of compulsory jurisdiction and of continuous operation (Weber, 1968 [1922]: 56).

This feature – the capacity ultimately to ensure that its writ runs, if necessary by force – clearly sets the governing agency of a state apart from other such agencies. It also makes it relatively easy to operationalize this term: we can ask of a particular territory whether it constitutes a 'state' in Weber's sense, and in most cases come up with a clear answer: 'no' in the case of Yorkshire, Wales or the European Union (at least, at present); 'yes' in the case of the United Kingdom, Norway or Russia. The value of the definition is illustrated by the extent to which it matches conventional usage, at least in Europe. The decision by the international community in 1992 to recognize Bosnia as one of its members rested precisely on an assessment that its government was able, more or less, to exercise jurisdiction over its territory, just as in the mid-nineteenth century it took civil wars in Switzerland (1847) and the USA (1861–65) to determine that these territories were indeed 'states' in the sense that Weber meant: it was established beyond doubt that when the centre clashed with the component units its will would prevail. The extent to which – by contrast to the term 'nation' – there is agreement on the term 'state' will be clear from the many studies in the area which begin by explicitly taking Weber's definition as a starting point (see for example, Pierson, 2004: 5–9; Hay and Lister, 2006: 4–13).

But the American example draws attention to a major dilemma. The 'states' that make up the USA do not match Weber's definition. Each may have its own police, and even its own military in the shape of the National Guard. However, as the term is used here, American 'states' are in fact substate entities, lacking the crucial feature of sovereignty: they may not secede, and do not have the military capacity to rival that which exists at federal level (even the National Guard has an important federal function, in its reserve military role). Because of the ubiquity of this terminology in North America, the term 'state' has acquired a much more general meaning, except among specialists: it refers to one of the territorial components of the US federation, one possessing its own institutions of government, but lacking sovereignty. We need, therefore, to be mindful of the confusion generated by this use of a term that in Europe has a decidedly stronger meaning.

This much less demanding use of the term 'state' has important consequences. If the United 'States' are the entities which have come together as the USA, how is the whole American collectivity to be named? In American usage, there is an agreed term: 'nation'. The word is thus used in precisely the sense in which Weber used 'state' – and in addition to its application to the USA, American political scientists commonly use it to refer to states all over the world. This has extended to general political usage, so that, for example, the terms 'United Nations' and 'League of Nations' refer in fact to organizations of states. Some researchers have tried to resolve this by moving towards a more general conception of statehood, using the term 'governance unit' (defined as the territorial unit responsible for providing the bulk of social order and other collective goods; Hechter, 2000: 9–10), but this term is not widely used. Philip Roeder (2007: 12), similarly, tries to sidestep the distinction between the central state and its component parts (where they exist) by labelling the former 'common-state' and the latter 'segment-state'.

Nation. Since the word 'nation' has commonly been used to describe an entity identical to the state, it is not surprising that we can easily find definitions of nation that reflect this usage. The first such definition in Table 1.1, by Carl Friedrich, reflects precisely this usage (an ironic one, since Friedrich was a German scholar who moved to the USA early in his academic career, but would have also been profoundly familiar with Weber's understanding of the term 'state'). We will find other such definitions of 'nation' by American scholars in particular. As one scholar summed up the position, 'in prevailing usage in English and other languages, a "nation" is either synonymous with a state and its inhabitants or else it denotes a human group bound together by common solidarity – a group whose members place loyalty to the group as a whole over any conflicting loyalties' (Rustow, 1968: 7). Through a process of semantic change, the meaning of 'nation' seems to have been transformed over the centuries, from divisions within the medieval university to groups within modern society (Greenfeld, 1992: 8–9).

Yet, especially in Europe and among those who specialize in the study of nationalism, there is strong pressure to reserve the term 'nation' for another type of collectivity – one that is much more difficult to describe and define. The remaining definitions in this part of Table 1.1 illustrate three different approaches, and are selected from a much wider number of definitions. For Anthony Smith, there must be a shared culture, historical consciousness and common name, but there is also a more 'objective' dimension: the possession of common legal rights and duties. The next definition, by Joseph Stalin, presents itself as 'objective', with its emphasis on the possession of a common language and other structural characteristics, but there is also a subjective component: the emphasis on a common 'psychological makeup'. The last definition, by Ernest Barker, is social psychological in its emphasis on a 'common will' as a defining characteristic, though it also stresses the dependence of this feature on quasi-objective factors, such as language and religion. It will be noticed that Barker's definition is very similar to Mill's definition of a related term, 'nationality': this, too, rests on the notion of an entity united by the collective desire for self-determination. Both of these are close to the classic definition by Ernest Renan, who defined a nation as 'a living soul, a spiritual principle' that depended on two features: 'the possession of a rich heritage of memories' and 'the desire to live together, the will to preserve worthily the undivided inheritance which has been handed down' (Renan, 1896: 80).

Though differing in content, all of these definitions apart from Friedrich's are hard to operationalize. By contrast to the relative clarity of Weber's definition of 'state', it is very difficult to give a straightforward answer to the question of whether a particular population group constitutes a 'nation' in the sense of any of these three definitions. In some cases, such as the Czechs, the Norwegians and the French, the answer will be 'yes'; in others, such as the Belgians, the Canadians, the British and the English, we may find it difficult (for varying reasons) to give a clear-cut answer. Yet there are circumstances where an answer *must* be found. Implementing the principle of 'national self-determination' obviously depends on defining the boundaries of the nation. In communist-run countries (of which only a few survived after 1989), 'nationalities policy' generally rested on Stalin's definition of 'nation'. In the Soviet Union, each person's ethnic nationality was recorded on his or her 'internal passport', essentially an identity document (Simonsen, 2005). The discrediting of Stalin in 1956 (when, three years after his death, Communist leader Khrushchev denounced his harsh, despotic rule) did not lead to the displacement of the old communist policy on the national question. Instead, it continued to determine policy on granting certain institutional privileges to designated 'nations' in the Soviet Union and elsewhere, as will be seen in Chapter 10. Moving to the present, China operates on similar principles; by 1990 it had formally recognized 55 national minorities (Hoddie, 1998: 124).

Other terms. 'Nation' and 'nationality' are not the only problematic terms in the vocabulary of nationalism. Many scholars use the terms 'nation' and 'ethnic group' interchangeably, but Table 1.1 suggests that – while definitions of 'ethnic group' overlap with those of 'nation' in certain of their features – the latter is usually perceived in more political terms. The two words which occupy so prominent a place in the literature derive from the Latin *natio* (deriving from *nascio*, to be born) and the Greek *ethnos* (a 'nation'), but over time they have acquired rather different connotations. Indeed, Weber's definition of 'ethnic group' refers to possible similarities in physical characteristics, taking us close to the concept of 'race'. To what extent is an ethnic group distinct from a 'race', or racial grouping? As the definition of race offered here shows, there is some overlap in the subjective domain: a race is defined not just by its physical distinctiveness, but also by people's consciousness of this.

Soviet scholars recognized a hierarchy of social organizational forms in this area (Connor, 1984b: 217–39). This began at the top with *nation* (using the word in the sense described by Stalin; the Russians and Georgians are examples), and this was followed by *nationality* (a less mature version of the nation; the Abkhazians were an example), *ethnic group* (a small-scale group, less developed than the nationality, for example the Aleuts of Siberia) and *ethnographic*

9

group (similar to ethnic group, but in the process of being absorbed by another nation or nationality, as in the case of the Latgalians who were absorbed by the Latvians). The term *national group* was reserved to refer to a fragment of an external nation or nationality, such as the Koreans of the Soviet Union (Fedoseyev et al., 1977: 17–50). This classification was not of mere academic interest: nations were entitled to the status of union republic, or constitutive member of the Soviet Union, while ethnographic groups were not entitled to any autonomy, with groups of intermediate status entitled to appropriate intermediate levels of autonomy (see Chapter 10). Communist-run Yugoslavia made a similar distinction between nations (such as the Serbs, Croats or Slovenes, each of which had a republic) and nationalities or national minorities (such as the Albanians and Hungarians who were given autonomous status within Serbia; see Ramet, 1984: 58–63).

So far, we have considered a set of collective nouns that refer to groups of people (Table 1.1 confines itself to such terms). We now need to consider the corresponding set of abstract nouns – terms largely derived from the ones just mentioned, such as 'nationalism', 'ethnicity', 'ethnocentrism' or 'racism'. Three of these terms (the three '–isms') refer to forms of attachment to nations, ethnic groups and races respectively, but have rather different connotations. 'Ethnocentrism' refers to a particular type of excessively positive evaluation of one's own ethnic group; 'racism', by contrast, normally refers to a form of negative evaluation of those who are seen as belonging to 'other races'. The full connotations of each could be explored more extensively, but for our present purposes we shall confine ourselves to the third '–ism', nationalism. Here, perhaps not surprisingly, we find definitions ranging widely. Usage by one author alone illustrates the diversity of the phenomenon: he variously describes nationalism as 'an attempt to make the boundaries of the state and those of the nation coincide', 'a political movement which seeks to attain and defend an objective we may call national integrity', 'a collective grievance against a foreign oppressor', and 'a set of ideas' that are more rhetorical than theoretical (Minogue, 1967: 12, 25, 104, 153). But we find many other definitions of 'nationalism', a central topic of this book to which we must therefore return below.

'Ethnicity' refers to the phenomenon of the division into or relations between ethnic groups, but it may also refer simply to the question of affiliation to a particular ethnic group, as in the survey question 'what is your ethnicity?'[1] 'Nationality' may be seen as having a meaning parallel to 'ethnicity' in this second sense, as in the question 'what is your nationality?'. But there are two serious difficulties here. First, as well as being an abstract noun in this sense, 'nationality' is also a collective noun, with a meaning similar to 'nation', as defined by Mill (see Table 1.1). Second, in its other sense, the meaning of the question 'what is your nationality?' is ambiguous. It is more likely to be interpreted as 'of what state

---

1 In English-speaking countries, questions on ethnicity in the population census vary in approach. For example, the US census of 2010 asks two such questions: 'Is person X of Hispanic, Latino or Spanish origin?' and 'What is person X's race?' (2010.census.gov/2010census/how/interactive-form.php); the English and Welsh census of 2011 asked two similar questions: 'What is your ethnic group?' and 'How would you describe your national identity?' (UK Cabinet Office, 2008: 49–51). Similar difficulties are encountered elsewhere; for a detailed discussion of the issues, and in particular their implications for Australia, see Trewin (2000).

are you a citizen?' than as 'of what nation are you a member?' This arises from the fact that in English, as in French, the noun 'state' has no accepted adjective; instead, 'national' is used (Minogue, 1967: 10), thereby being rendered indistinguishable from the adjective 'national' derived from 'nation'. In many other languages, however, it is much easier to differentiate between membership of a state (citizenship or political nationality) and membership of a nation ('ethnic nationality'). The distinction between *grazhdanstvo* and *natsionalnost'* in Russian is an example, a distinction to be found also in other central and east European languages.

A prescriptive approach

One superficially appealing solution to the problem of terminological ambiguity would be to coin entirely new words. A distinguished Russian expert recommended dropping the term 'nation' altogether, since it was insufficiently distinct from both 'state' and 'ethnic group' (Tishkov, 2000). Efforts have indeed been made to do precisely this: for example, Smith (1971: 187–91) used the word 'ethnie', and van den Berghe (1981a: 22) introduced a similar term, 'ethny'. Such terms never managed to achieve wide usage among scholars, however, and thus have tended to add to the terminological morass rather than helping the position. Neologisms are not always welcome; use of a similar term, '*ethnie*', in French has been described as 'a remedy worse than the disease' (Polakovič, 1985: 114). It is prob-able that the only successful effort to create a new terminology has been Walker Connor's (1994b) coining of the terms 'ethnonational' and 'ethnonationalism', which he designed to resolve the difficulties with 'national' and 'nationalism' already mentioned.

It is not likely that we will be able to abstract any generally agreed definition of the terms discussed above. But approaches to definition need not be 'lexical'– that is, they need not simply try to generalize about conventional usage. For a long time epistemologists have tried to identify an alternative 'prescriptive' or 'stipulative' approach – a (possibly arbitrary) statement that is intended to equate a particular term with a precisely described concept (Abelson, 1967). This approach is adopted here; it rests on a simple statement regarding how a particular term is going to be used, without making any claim as to the level of acceptance of this definition (though obviously the more widely acceptable, the better). In this book, it is proposed we define five key terms as follows.

> **State**. A state is a self-governing territorial entity with a central decision-making agency which possesses a monopoly of the legitimate use of force in ensuring compliance with its decisions on the part of all persons within its borders.
>
> **Racial group**. A racial group is a large collectivity whose members share cer-tain phenotypical characteristics which they or others see as defining a social boundary between members and non-members of the group.
>
> **Ethnic group**. An ethnic group is a large collectivity whose members are linked by certain cultural characteristics – including the sense of sharing a common past – which they and others see as defining a social boundary between members and non-members of the group.

Nation. A nation is an ethnic group whose members are mobilized in the pursuit of political self-determination for that group.

Nationalism. Nationalism is either (a) a form of political mobilization that is directed at rectifying a perceived absence of fit between the boundaries of the nation and the boundaries of the state; or (b) the ideology that justifies this.

The terms 'nation' and 'ethnic group' as defined above are not intended to refer to objective social realities: there is considerable variation in the extent to which individuals identify with such groups and, quite apart from other identities, individuals may have complex allegiances at different geographical levels. These definitions, in other words, do not preclude the existence of multilevel, nested identities. None of these definitions is original, or unproblematic; nor do they cover all of the difficult terms to which attention has been drawn. They build upon and abstract from existing definitions – but, as with the definitions on which they are based, they do not offer any clear-cut criteria that may be used to place collectivities within or beyond the boundaries of a particular definition. How large, for instance, must a collectivity be? What is meant by 'cultural characteristics'? How intense must a particular form of political mobilization be? What does 'self-determination' mean? These questions are not answered by the above definitions; however, these do at least give an indication of how the terms are used in this book, which is necessary as a starting point for the discussion that follows.

The relationship between three of these collective terms is illustrated in Figure 1.1, where the circles refer to terms (not sets of individuals): the grey circle refers to 'racial group', the dotted one to 'ethnic group', and the black one to 'nation'. Area A illustrates a racial group with a low level of group consciousness, thereby falling short of being an ethnic group. In area B, however, the ethnic dimension is present: members of the group are conscious of a shared past. Area E illustrates ethnic groups which do not define themselves in respect of racial group. Finally, areas C and D illustrate the case of ethnic groups which are politically conscious as such, with their identity linked respectively to racial and non-racial features.

Two important matters follow on from this discussion. The first is that definitions often imply classifications, or can at least be used to provide the basis of such classifications, and the analysis of nationalism relies heavily on such typologies. But there is no agreement on how nationalism should be classified (for a range of typologies, see Maxwell, 2010: 867–8). Even a cursory overview of the literature will show that some older typologies are essentially historical, distinguishing evolutionary phases (see for example, Hayes, 1931; Wright, 1942). Others are geographical, identifying 'western' and 'eastern' forms (see for example, Kohn, 1944: 329–33, 574–5; Gellner, 1983: 88–97). More commonly, though, they are thematic, with separation and integration as the two main themes (see for example, Snyder, 1954; Seton-Watson, 1965; Kellas, 1998: 92–5; Hechter, 2000: 15–17), and Gutiérrez (2006: 341) makes a distinction between state- and nation-building forms. Anthony Smith (1971: 211–29) provides the most elaborate classification of all, identifying many different subtypes. This issue will be revisited in Chapter 8 (where another classification will be presented) and Chapter 9 (where the 'east–west' dichotomy will be discussed).

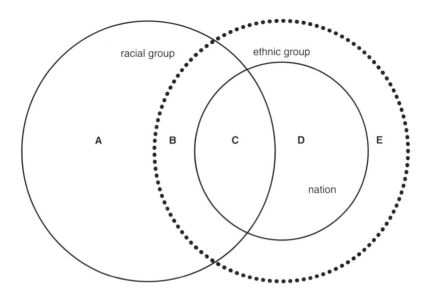

Figure 1.1 Relationship between the terms 'nation', 'ethnic group' and 'racial group'

Note: The circles refer to concepts, not to groups of people.

The second matter is that terms such as 'nation' have been defined here (and are used in this book) with a level of precision which may well be misleading, given the complexity of the phenomenon and the extent to which a scholarly consensus is lacking. Similar caution needs to be exercised in interpreting the word 'identity', a term devoid of conceptual clarity and hugely challenging to operationalize (Malešević, 2006: 13–57). The word 'nation' is used here in an apparently precise sense, but Rogers Brubaker's warning (1996: 13–22) about the danger of slipping into an assumption that this is a concrete, durable phenomenon rather than an amorphous, fluid one needs to be borne in mind continually. There are three concrete difficulties.

First, at any one time, an individual may identify to varying degrees with several groups of which he or she is a member. In the nineteenth century, for example, many people in what is now Slovakia felt to varying degrees Slovak, Czechoslovak, Slav or Hungarian (Maxwell, 2005: 386). In other instances, they identified with no group at all, as in the case of the *tutejszy* in the early twentieth century in what is now Belarus (see Pershai, 2008). Alternatively, they may identify simultaneously with their ethnic group and with a subethnic group, as in the case of the Mordvins in Russia, who are made up of two 'subethnic communities', the Erzia and the Moksha (Iurchenkov, 2001), or the Albanians, who are similarly divided between Ghegs and Tosks.

Second, an individual's patterns of identity may change over time, whether as a consequence of a large-scale boundary shift or because of an incremental boundary modification (Wimmer, 2008). Thus, among many other examples, the Danish identification of the population of southern Sweden was gradually eroded by the eighteenth century (Østergård,

1996 [1992]), and the British identity of the southern Protestant minority in Ireland seems to have been similarly undermined in the twentieth century (Coakley, 1998).

Third, whatever an individual's 'real' identity pattern, this may be distorted in the process of its measurement. It has been argued that 'almost all the official censuses of the pre-1914 empires and post-1919 states exaggerated the demographic dominance of the establishment and minimised the representation of national minorities' (Pearson, 1983: 17), and there are also some more recent examples, as in Kazakhstan (Dave, 2004). But census takers also forced choices on residents, helping to eliminate intermediate groups in Europe (Teleki and Rónai, 1937: 28), to create new minorities in Asia (Anderson, 1998: 318–23; 1997), and to oversimplify the status of such groups as the Métis in Canada (Andersen, 2008: 360). States may also seek to redefine the identity of minorities extending across the border from another state, as in the case of Yugoslavia's short-lived efforts to relabel ethnic Albanians as *Šiptari* rather than *Albanci* (Babuna, 2004: 305–6) and the Soviet Union's similar efforts to differentiate Karelians and Moldovans, respectively, from Finland and Romania.

MATTERS OF EVALUATION

As will be clear, the study of nationalism cannot confine itself to the level of description and explanation. Literature in the area is full of implicit and explicit value judgements. As we have seen, some of these are sweeping as well as explicit. One leading political theorist has described nationalism as 'the starkest political shame of the twentieth century, the deepest, most intractable and yet most unanticipated blot on the political history of the world since the year 1900' (Dunn, 1999 [1979]: 27). It is thus worth exploring the nature of this evaluative perspective before going back to the central issue of this book: the study of nationalism as a political and social phenomenon rather than as an ideology.[2]

What are the normative issues that arise in the study of nationalism? In a general sense, the philosophical analysis of nationalism spans all of the major areas that are covered in this book: the relationship between nationalism and culture, the processes by which nations come into existence, the political demands of nationalist leaders, and the relationship between nations and states (for a useful overview, see Gilbert, 1998). But the debate in this area has tended to cluster around two narrower but overlapping areas. The first has to do with the 'right of self-determination': is this something to which nations are entitled? The second concerns the position of nations or groups which are either denied or do not demand self-determination: to what rights should national minorities be entitled? These are discussed in the two subsections that follow. It is not possible to engage in a further discussion here of the other big normative questions addressed by scholars of nationalism, or certain more specific issues that are less frequently addressed, such as the acceptability of the set of methods that are commonly used in the nation-building process (Norman, 1999: 59–60).

---

2 For a stimulating presentation of the normative debate, in the form of an imaginary dialogue between Herder, Fichte, Mazzini, Mill, Renan, Hitler and Stalin, see Heater (1998). Several excellent collections of texts by leading theorists also cover major topics of the debate; see Couture, Nielsen and Seymour (1996) and Beiner (1999).

The right of self-determination

One of the most characteristic of all demands of nationalists has been the call for a reorganization of states so that they coincide with the boundaries of nations. Nationalists themselves typically express this demand, however, not as a universal principle, but rather as one which applies to their own perceived nation – even if it is presented as a particular application of a wider principle. Thus, the philosopher widely seen as the father of German nationalism, Johann Gottlieb Fichte (1762–1814), argued that

> Those who speak the same language … belong together and are by nature one and an inseparable whole. Such a whole, if it wishes to absorb and mingle with itself any other people of different descent and language, cannot do so without itself becoming confused, in the beginning at any rate, and violently disturbing the even progress of its culture (Fichte, 1922 [1808]: 223–4).

Fichte was concerned in particular with the disunity of his own people, the Germans, but the general implications of his position are clear. As summarized by a leading theorist who was strongly critical of nationalism, 'the doctrine holds that humanity is naturally divided into nations, that nations are known by certain characteristics which can be ascertained, and that the only legitimate type of government is national self-government' (Kedourie, 1993: 1). It is worth considering in turn the further development of this form of *traditional nationalism*; the position opposed to this which might be labelled *anti-nationalism*; and a more recent attempt to present a modified version of the original principle, *liberal nationalism*.

Traditional nationalism.   While it is easy to find articulations of the view that a particular nation should be entitled to self-determination, it is much more difficult to find expressions of this as a universal principle – the argument that each nation should have its own state. While the German philosopher Fichte has already been quoted, his views may be seen as a development of those held by his fellow-German, Johann Gottfried Herder (1744–1803). In Herder's deterministic perspective, language communities were authentic, self-contained groups, which deserved autonomous cultural and political expression. Much later, this point was made more forcefully by nineteenth-century nationalists in respect of their own peoples. For the Hungarian nationalist leader Lajos Kossuth (1802–94), the disappearance of the nations of classical antiquity was a call to defend his own fatherland lest it suffer a similar fate (Kossuth, 1852: 9–16). In the view of his Italian counterpart Giuseppe Mazzini (1805–72), 'nations are the individuals of humanity', and should be so defended (Mazzini, 1887: 241).

This position was also expressed in a much more subtle and more qualified way by John Stuart Mill (1806–73), who defended the right of nations to decide their own future, if necessary by establishing a state of their own. As Mill put it, 'where the sentiment of nationality exists in any force, there is a *prima facie* case for uniting all the members of the nationality under the same government, and a government to themselves apart' (Mill, 1861: 289). This 'principle of national self-determination' found its most famous practical expression in one of the so-called 'fourteen points' enunciated by US President Woodrow Wilson in an address to the US Congress on 8 January 1918, which set the agenda for separatist nationalism in postwar Europe (Manela, 2007: 215–25). Notwithstanding inconsistencies in this position and the scarcity of philosophical justifications for it, the principle has continued ever since to attract strong support among nationalist activists.

The flaws in traditional nationalist ideology are obvious. To start with, even if the principle of national self-determination makes sense in theory, it may be extraordinarily difficult to implement it in practice (Cobban, 1969: 57–97). The root problem lies in identifying which communities possess the right to self-determination on the grounds that they are 'nations'. As Sir Ivor Jennings warned in the mid-twentieth century,

> Nearly forty years ago a Professor of Political Science who was also President of the United States, President Wilson, enunciated a doctrine which was ridiculous, but which was widely accepted as a sensible proposition, the doctrine of self-determination. On the surface it seemed reasonable: let the people decide. It was in fact ridiculous because the people cannot decide until somebody decides who are the people (Jennings, 1956: 55–6).

In other words, we commonly lack the basic evidence as to whether or not a particular group of people indeed constitutes a nation, and it may be by no means clear as to how their 'will' should be tested in, say, a plebiscite; before such a vote, the territory within which the votes will be counted needs to be specified, and this is itself a political decision likely to affect the outcome of the plebiscite. Furthermore, even if a nation and its membership can be clearly identified, it does not follow that they will exclusively inhabit a coherent territory that may realistically become a state. Indeed, as the post-1918 reconfiguration of the map of Europe showed, the problem of intermingling of 'nations' was so great that clear boundaries between them may rarely be drawn, and attempts to consult 'the people' by plebiscite have had an extraordinarily varied history (Qvortrup, 2012).

Anti-nationalism.   There are more profound objections to the 'principle of nationality' than the impracticality of redrawing state borders. For some critics, the more appropriate response to the existence of separate nations is to link them freely within the boundaries of the state so that each will enrich the overall culture. This was the view associated with Mill's critic, Lord Acton (1834–1902), who in 1862 argued that:

> The coexistence of several nations under the same state is ... one of the chief instruments of civilisation; and, as such, it is in the natural and providential order, and indicates a state of greater advancement than the national unity which is the ideal of modern liberalism. The combination of different nations in one state is as necessary a condition of civilised life as the combination of men in society. Inferior races are raised by living in political union with races intellectually superior. Exhausted and decaying nations are revived by the contact of a younger vitality. Nations in which the elements of organisation and the capacity for government have been lost ... are restored and educated anew under the discipline of a stronger and less corrupted race (Acton, 1907 [1862]: 290).

Though the anti-nationalist position underwent a reversal in the early and mid-twentieth century, when the principle of national self-determination and the force of anti-colonialism were in their heyday, profound philosophical objections have continued to be directed at nationalism. Dunn (1999) has already been cited in this respect. Kedourie (1993: 134) argued that nationalism 'has created new conflicts, exacerbated tensions, and brought catastrophe to numberless people innocent of all politics'. Another critic detected a dreadful trend within nationalism, which 'begins as Sleeping Beauty and ends as Frankenstein's monster' (Minogue, 1967: 7). The key objection of these critics has to do with the absence of any general argument that could justify the nationalist position. Thus, for example, Minogue (1967: 153) dismissed nationalism as a set of ideas which in practice amounted 'less to a theory than to a rhetoric, a form of self-expression by which a certain kind of political excitement can be communicated from an elite to the masses'. For Kedourie (1993: 87), nationalist ideology oversimplifies a complex world, displaying 'a contempt of things as they are, of the world as it is', so that it 'ultimately becomes a rejection of life, and a love of death'.

It is easy to see why, whatever the validity of their arguments, some critics of the old principle of national self-determination may be accused of being self-serving and defensive of vested interests. Those hostile to traditional nationalist ideology would themselves commonly represent the interests of established nations, or may be seen as doing so. It is, then, entirely to be expected that English or French intellectuals would criticize nationalism – they are open to the accusation that they are simply defending the hegemony of their own nation, whose right to rule minority national groups within the state it controls they implicitly accept.

Liberal nationalism. More recently, the upsurge in nationalism in the late twentieth century has prompted philosophers and political theorists to seek to transform traditional nationalist arguments by creating a new theory of 'liberal nationalism', though they have typically done this without necessarily acknowledging the extent to which their own positions implicitly accept the logic of nationhood (Canovan, 1996: 5–15). Carefully articulated versions of such a theory have been presented by Neil MacCormick (1999), a Scottish nationalist politician and professor of public law, and Yael Tamir (1993), an Israeli Labour politician and professor of political philosophy. This position aims to steer a middle course between the conservatism and potential for oppression of ideologies that decry nationalism and the impracticality and potential for injustice that are implicit in traditional nationalist ideology by proposing a vision of national self-determination that also protects individual rights. The challenge offered to Canada by Quebec nationalism has also extended to Canadian political theorists and philosophers, who have produced an impressive volume of output that seeks to define a philosophical position for setting political choices in context, and in charting a 'liberal nationalist' course in this respect (discussed in another context below; see also Buchanan, 1991; Miller, 1995; Kymlicka, 2001; Moore, 2001).

The rights of national minorities

Whether or not the secession of smaller nations from the states within which they find themselves located is justifiable, there will always be circumstances in which states will be dominated by a particular nation while containing minorities from one or more others. This raises particular issues of coexistence in the context of the modern state, which places such great value on national unity (Wimmer, 2002: 3–4). These circumstances obviously give rise to debates that overlap with those that arise over the principle of national self-determination: once again, the collective rights of nations are at issue (even if we are now leaving aside consideration of the separatist option). As before, we may identify two polar positions, though contemporary political theorists in reality fall somewhere between the two: the view may be taken that full protection of the *individual rights* of the members of minority groups is adequate (indeed, even the existence of such groups may be denied), or minorities may be seen as being entitled to particular forms of *group rights*.

Individual rights.   A strong regime of protecting individual rights may be reassuring to minorities, but it is not incompatible with policies of assimilation. Elements of this perspective may have already been identified in the thinking of John Stuart Mill. As we have seen, Mill was prepared to concede the principle of self-determination to viable nations, but others faced a future of collective disappearance:

> When the nationality which succeeds in overpowering the other, is both the most numerous and the most improved; and especially if the subdued nationality is small, and has no hope of reasserting its independence; then, if it is governed with any tolerable justice, and if the members of the more powerful nationality are not made odious by being invested with exclusive privileges, the smaller nationality is gradually reconciled to its position, and becomes amalgamated with the larger. No Bas-Breton, nor even any Alsatian, has the smallest wish at the present day to be separated from France. If all Irishmen have not yet arrived at the same disposition towards England, it is partly because they are sufficiently numerous to be capable of constituting a respectable nationality by themselves; but principally because, until of late years, they had been so atrociously governed (Mill, 1861: 295).

There is a certain consistency in this position, which still rests on the notion of conformity between the borders of nations and the borders of states. This conformity, in Mill's view, could be brought about either by adjusting the borders of states or by changing the borders of nations, and the implication of his position was that more developed nations would follow the former course and less developed cultural groups the latter.

But it is a short step to less attractive forms of nationalism, when minorities are deliberately converted to the culture of the majority. As the German nationalist historian Heinrich von Treitschke (1834–96) put it,

> When several nations are united under one state, the simplest relationship is that the one which wields the authority should also be the superior in civilisation. Matters can then develop comparatively peacefully, and when the

blending is complete it is felt to have been inevitable, although it can never be accomplished without endless misery for the subjugated race. The most remarkable fusion took place after this fashion in the colonies of North-East Germany. It was the murder of a people; that cannot be denied, but after the amalgamation was complete it became a blessing. What could the Prussians[3] have contributed to history? The Germans were so infinitely their superiors that to be Germanised was for them as great a good fortune as it was for the Wends (von Treitschke, 1916 [1897]: I: 282–3).

Treitschke extended this logic to groups such as the Jews which, in his view, could not be assimilated (von Treitschke, 1916 [1897]: I: 302). His role as an intellectual ancestor of the more politically explicit Nazi ideology, and its attempts to 'purify' the German nation, is clear.

The outcome need not be this brutal. States can preside over and promote cultural assimilation of minorities while at the same time extending to them an impressive package of individual rights. This was the formula ushered in by the French revolution, where loyalty to the state takes precedence over loyalty to cultural groups within the state – a perspective that may be traced back to the eighteenth-century philosopher from Geneva, Jean-Jacques Rousseau (1712–78). His theory of the state as comprising a 'social contract' between its members rested on the notion of the individual as the primary political actor, and formed a basis for later models of society as comprising a set of individuals whose relations to the central authorities are not mediated by any other group. The French revolution thus sought explicitly to replace the notion of government by corporate bodies (including different gradations of nobility and clergy, as well as the privileged burghers and others of the 'third estate') with the notion of government by 'the people'. This progressive development and its impact on the spread of individual freedom have been seen by many as representing fulfilment of the ultimate goal of democracy, sidelining the rights of groups who were defined not just in traditional socio-legal terms (such as the nobility), but also in cultural terms (such as national minorities). Advocating of policies of 'ethnic blindness' even in multinational societies thus forms one distinctive response to the issue of minority rights (van den Berghe, 1981b). A range of conflict reduction techniques may also be adopted in these circumstances in order to reconcile individual rights with cultural diversity and promote political stability (for an evaluation, see Horowitz, 2000: 563–680).

Group rights. At the opposite extreme is a set of thinkers for whom a full institutional recognition of all significant minorities is important. As discussed in Chapter 10, this

---

3 This is not a reference to the (Germanic) population of the Kingdom of Prussia but to the Old Prussians of Baltic origin, who spoke a Baltic language akin to Latvian and Lithuanian but who had been almost entirely assimilated into German culture by the eighteenth century. The Wends referred to in this extract were a Slavic population that had also substantially assimilated into German culture, but of which a fragment survives around Bautzen and Cottbus in eastern Germany, where they are more commonly known as Sorbs.

may take a number of forms. It may confine itself substantially to the cultural level (with provisions for full linguistic rights for all groups within the public sphere), or it may have a significant political institutional dimension (with provision for political power-sharing between groups of a consociational kind, or devolution of power to these groups, whether on a territorial or a non-territorial basis). Whatever legal expression it takes, though, this approach rests on the assumption that, alongside individual citizens, cultural or national groups are key political actors; society is seen 'both as a community of citizens and a community of communities' (Parekh, 2000: 340).

As already mentioned, recent challenges faced by Canada (confronted with demands of very different types from Quebec, aboriginal peoples and newer immigrant minorities) have given a major impetus to the philosophical study of nationalism and minority rights. One outcome has been the emergence of a distinctive and sophisticated attempt to define a balance between group rights and individual rights. Noting that these may clash (for example, introducing a regime of linguistic autonomy in one area, where a minority language has primary official status, may have implications for the rights of individuals who speak other languages), theorists have developed a new position that allows for a conditional concession of group rights. Thus, for example, Charles Taylor (1994), Will Kymlicka (1995, 2001) and James Tully (1995) have sought to reconcile the kinds of rights demanded by minority groups with what they describe as 'liberal' values.[4]

The issues already discussed (the rights of minorities, extending to the right to self-determination) cover only part – albeit a central part – of the philosophical debate about nationalism. Even within this area, we have glossed over further questions that may arise in respect of minority rights. For example, should all minorities be entitled to rights on the same basis, or should a distinction be made between immigrant minorities and aboriginal peoples? Theorists may well argue that the case for making concessions to immigrant groups (who are present in the state because of a prior decision on their part) is weaker than the case in respect of aboriginal peoples (who did not choose the invasion of their territories by outside peoples, with the resulting suffering and dispossession; see Kymlicka, 1995: 116–20; Poole, 1996). In this book, however, we try to confine ourselves to the empirical aspects of such questions, even though facts commonly have striking implications for values.

MATTERS OF ANALYSIS

Nationalism, as we have seen, is an enormous topic. But does it have core features that may be subject to rigorous examination without requiring us to be experts in the history of the world? This book rests on the assumption that it does. It is possible to begin with an even simpler assumption: that nationalism has to do with the relationship between two central phenomena that will be examined in greater detail later, *nation* and *state*. In fact, this

---

4 The term 'liberal' is used in a very distinctive way in political theory to refer to law-based protection of individuals in a context of political tolerance – very different from its use in southern Europe as a label for a political ideology that is based on defence of the individual against intrusion by church and state (with a consequent right-wing, anti-state programme).

book consists precisely of an examination of this complex relationship. Its goal is an ambitious one: to steer a course between the many studies of nationalism that focus on specific geographical contexts or historical periods on one side, and purely theoretical studies of nationalism on the other. It should be stressed that, although the book's scope is intended to be global, both the type of illustrative data presented and the set of theoretical perspectives discussed tend to focus particularly on one continent, Europe. While their relevance for our understanding of nationalism outside this small area is limited, it nevertheless seems likely that many of the themes will have a resonance in other continents, even if the significance of, say, the African or Asian experience requires a radical revision of the framework presented here. The remainder of this section outlines the approach being taken here and introduces the existing literature in the area.

Outline of this book

The rest of the book is divided into two parts. The first looks at the raw materials out of which nations and nationalism emerge. The second examines the process by which this emergence takes place and explores its political consequences. The last chapter draws together the threads that have been explored in the earlier chapters, provides a synthesis of the arguments presented there, and engages in some speculation about the future of this powerful and remarkable political force.

Nation and society.   Part 1 examines a range of factors that have an impact on national identity. Of these, one of the most difficult is the first. Anyone studying nationalism will quickly discover that many people feel that national identity is 'in the blood' – that it is an inherited characteristic. Chapter 2 explores this myth by looking at the significance of race (and in particular of the manipulation of concepts of race) in identity formation. But 'race' is not the only characteristic that is handed on to us: this chapter also explores the curiously neglected topic of gender and its implications for nationalism. Sex-based differences are of fundamental importance, in that men and women have traditionally been assigned distinctive roles in the nationalist project, and nationalist ideology is full of gendered imagery.

We then go on to look at one of the most widely discussed factors of all of those associated with nationalism. The importance of language for nation formation is widely acknowledged, and early writing on the subject sometimes even equated the nation with a language community. The reasons why this might be the case, and the more general relationship between language and nation, are discussed in Chapter 3.

Especially in the past, though, and in much of the contemporary non-western world, another force has offered itself as a major challenge to language as a force exerting an influence on nationalism: religion. The importance of religion for political mobilization in the Middle East is obvious, and it has sometimes been articulated in the context of a 'war of civilizations' involving the Western Christian and the Muslim worlds, among others (Huntington, 1993, 1996). However, it is easy to find examples of deep divisions within both of these religious groups, from Ireland to Iraq, that have an important bearing on nationalism. Chapter 4 looks at the role religion plays in the creation and reinforcement of national identity – one that is very different from that of language.

Language and religion may well have a big impact on national identity, but they are not simply objective sources of influence. Each may, in its own turn, be subject to influence by nationalist-type forces. Nationalist elites do not simply respond to linguistic and religious realities; they may try to influence them, by shaping the nature and extent of a particular language and the content and geographical reach of religious belief. This is even more true of the next set of influences on nationalism, considered in Chapter 5: historical consciousness. In many ways, this is a defining characteristic of national identity. It is easy to imagine – and to cite many examples of – a nation which does not have a common, distinct language, or a single, unique religion. But it is much harder to find examples of nations which do not possess a shared belief in a common past, even if this is in large measure a creation of nationalist elites rather than an objective background feature.

Nationalist leaders do not seek only to shape people's perceptions of the past. They also see contemporary culture as reflecting national glory, and they typically encourage this association. For this reason, we commonly find a close relationship between nationalism and popular culture (including folklore, folk music and vernacular literature), but 'high' culture (including classical music and the visual arts) may play an important role too. In particular, though, sport is commonly associated with nationalism. These issues are considered in Chapter 6.

Nationalist mobilization. Part 1 offers a largely static picture of the nationalist phenomenon, simply reporting and illustrating relationships between national identity and a range of background factors. But nationalism is far from being a static phenomenon, and its dynamic character is explored in Part 2 of the book, which looks at nationalism as a process. The first sparks in a nationalist revolution are frequently ignited not by cultural renewal (as expressed, for example, in recognition that a particular language community shares a distinctive cultural heritage) but by socioeconomic grievance (such as a perception that one's community – perhaps defined in relation to language – suffers discrimination of a more material kind). The relationship between nationalism and other universal sources of division (such as class and region) that do not of themselves carry any particular nationalist implications is discussed in Chapter 7. This chapter considers in particular not just the overt consequences of these phenomena for nationalism, but also the consequences of socioeconomic dislocation and political displacement in the context of rapid social change.

Chapter 8 draws together more systematically the threads already discussed, looking at the manner in which nationalist movements have conventionally been organized. Here the organizing principle mixes historical with thematic criteria: an effort is made to generalize about the broad span of nationalist movements, from those driving to unify territories in the name of the national principle to those seeking independence in its name, or pursuing other agendas. This generalization builds on material presented in the earlier chapters, and charts a range of different pathways associated with the nationalist process.

Chapter 9 addresses what is in many ways the most demanding and the most difficult question of all: how do nationalist movements arise, and what sustains them? A large literature has been generated in this area, and this chapter seeks to explore the main lines of argument. Rather than concluding that any single approach works, however, the chapter suggests that it is too early to choose between the variety of interpretations that are currently on offer, many of which, in any case, seek only to account for a specific type or phase of nationalism. In this area, as in so many others in the social sciences, there is (at least as yet) no consensus on matters of explanation.

Having looked in some detail at the manner in which elites try to lead nationalist movements in one direction or another, it is important to consider the questions raised by nationalist mobilization from another perspective. Not all nationalist movements succeed in establishing states for their target nations, and some may not even wish to do so. But all of them pose a challenge for existing state authorities. The last main chapter of the book therefore considers the options open to the state in dealing with nationalist demands – and especially with demands from national minorities. Chapter 10 examines the broad range of options open to the state, from the most barbaric and repressive to the most generous and accommodating, and discusses these within the context of a relatively unchanged state structure.

Central themes.   In varying degrees, three themes recur in the chapters that follow, and constitute central arguments of this book. While these are in certain respects commonplace, it is worth highlighting them here, since they also clash with many of the current perspectives on nationalism.

- First, nationalism can almost always been looked at from *two perspectives, not one*: those of the politically dominant group which controls the state, and of the counter-group which wishes to reshape the state in line with its own vision for the nation. It has been argued that nation-state and empire may be seen as alternative expressions of power, in that each has a 'state-bearing' people (Kumar, 2010); and this extends in a modified way to the substate region. From the perspective of 'enlightened' state-builders, opposition comes from 'reactionary' or 'rebellious' nationalists; each group and its supporters project themselves in a positive light and their opponents in a negative light; and each may be located at, above, or below the level of the established state.
- Second, nationalism in principle involves three major sets of actors, not two: it involves *a triangular rather than a bilateral relationship*, with three potentially conflicting sets of actors (a centralizing metropolitan area, a separatist periphery, and another geographically peripheral group facing in several directions). This triangular model (an ideal type, of course) need not always be present, but it constitutes a surprisingly fruitful framework for the analysis of many different types of nationalism.
- Third, it is possible to create a model of *nationalist mobilization as extending over four phases* (cultural exploration, elite politicization, mass mobilization and national consolidation). This template is an ideal type of limited application, and several of the phases will be absent in very many nationalist movements, but it offers a sufficiently rewarding structure to illuminate the path of nationalist mobilization in many cases.

Bibliographical orientation

A book of this kind can do little more than scratch the surface of a phenomenon as complex as nationalism. But this is a very old area of study; already in the late nineteenth century it was attracting the attention of scholars. The chapters that follow offer extensive reference to the big literature that has appeared. Yet attention should also be drawn to a number of general studies that offer useful introductions to the subject (in general, the most recent edition of multi-edition works is cited below). A large volume of additional material is available on the internet.

The English language literature for much of the time lacked the kind of short introductory texts on nationalism that existed in other languages, such as French, where Paul Sabourin's *Les nationalismes européens* (1996), Raoul Girardet's *Nationalismes et nation* (1996), Patrick Cabanel's *La question nationale au XIXᵉ siècle* (1997) and Astrid von Busekist's *Nations et nationalisme: XIXᵉ et XXᵉ siècles* (1998) combine elegant organization with impressive brevity, while also managing to cover the terrain comprehensively. This gap in English language writing has since been rectified by the publication of several useful texts of this kind: for example, Timothy Baycroft's *Nationalism in Europe, 1789–1945* (1998), David Brown's *Contemporary nationalism* (2000), Steven Grosby's *Nationalism: a very short introduction* (2005), Richard Bosworth's *Nationalism* (2007), and Ireneusz Karolewski and Andrzej Suszycki's *The nation and nationalism in Europe: an introduction* (2011). Another very useful historical introduction originally published in German was later made available in English – Peter Alter's *Nationalism* (1994) – while the views of distinguished historians are elaborated in Hugh Seton-Watson's *States and nations* (1977), John Breuilly's *Nationalism and the state* (1993), Eric Hobsbawm's *Nations and nationalism since 1780* (1992), John Hutchinson's *Nations as zones of conflict* (2005) and Paul Lawrence's *Nationalism: history and theory* (2005). The perspectives of the philosopher, the political scientist and the sociologist are illustrated respectively in three highly influential studies – Ernest Gellner's *Nations and nationalism* (2006b), Benedict Anderson's *Imagined communities* (2006) and Rogers Brubaker's *Nationalism reframed* (1996).

Classifying literature in this area by the disciplinary background of its authors is of strictly limited value, since nationalism spans disciplines, but it is useful in giving an indication of the starting point of a particular study. Thus, for example, further sociological perspectives are available in Craig Calhoun's *Nationalism* (1997), David McCrone's *Sociology of nationalism* (1998), Philip Spencer and Howard Wollman's *Nationalism* (2002) and Jonathan Hearn's *Rethinking nationalism* (2006). Political science perspectives will be found in James Kellas's *Politics of nationalism and ethnicity* (1998), Walker Connor's *Ethnonationalism* (1994b), John Hutchinson's *Modern nationalism* (1994) and Montserrat Guibernau's *Nationalisms* (1996). Although its title might initially suggest that it addresses a different topic, Donald Horowitz's *Ethnic groups in conflict* (2000) provides a rich and detailed overview of nationalism in the modern state. The various works of Anthony Smith, such as *Theories of nationalism* (1983) and *Nationalism and modernism* (1998), supply an important theoretical perspective, as do Graham Day and Andrew Thompson's *Theorising nationalism* (2004) and Umut Özkırımlı's *Theories of nationalism* (2010).

In addition to these full-length books, a flavour of the phenomenon of nationalism will be found in a number of collections of essays or classic writings in the area. An early compilation of short extracts of this kind is to be found in Louis Snyder's *The dynamics of nationalism* (1964). Later, several collections of a smaller number of more substantial pieces have appeared, including John Hutchinson and Anthony Smith's collection of readings entitled simply *Nationalism* (1994), and the same editors' similar collection entitled *Ethnicity* (1996); Omar Dahbour and Micheline Ishay's *Nationalism reader* (1995); Stuart Woolf's *Nationalism in Europe* (1996); Geoff Eley and Ronald Suny's *Becoming national* (1996); Montserrat Guibernau and John Rex's *Ethnicity reader* (1997); and Philip Spencer and Howard Wollman's *Nations and nationalism* (2005). There are also some much larger collections of basic literature, such as a reprint of 83 key articles in a five-volume collection by Hutchinson and Smith, *Nationalism* (2000), and of 65 articles in a four-volume collection by Rajat Ganguly, *Ethnic conflict* (2009).

Attention should also be drawn to a number of reference works. These include encyclopedias or dictionaries, of which no fewer than three are entitled *Encyclopaedia of nationalism:* those of Louis Snyder (1990), Alexander Motyl (2001) and Athena Leoussi (2001). In a similarly general mould is Gerard Delanty and Krishan Kumar's *Sage handbook of nations and nationalism* (2006). There are also several valuable reference works with a more specific focus, such as Raymond Pearson's *Longman companion to European nationalism* (1994) and Karl Cordell and Stefan Wolff's *Routledge handbook of ethnic conflict* (2011).

Finally, several journals specialize in this area. One of the oldest was *Nation und Staat* (which began publication in Leipzig in 1927), but this, not surprisingly, fell victim to the excesses of Nazi Germany and ceased publication in 1944. Indeed, this episode discredited the study of nationalism and national minorities, especially in Germany, but a multilingual journal presenting itself as successor to *Nation und Staat* began publication in Vienna in 1961: *Europa Ethnica* (the journal of the Federal Union of European Nationalities). An American organization with a more academic focus, the Association for the Study of Nationalities, launched a new journal in 1972 – the *Nationalities Papers* – which has a particular focus on central and eastern Europe and the former Soviet Union; later, it adopted a second journal, *Ethnopolitics* (formerly *Global Review of Ethnopolitics;* 2001–). The British-based Association for the Study of Ethnicity and Nationalism has published its own journal, *Nations and Nationalism,* since 1995, and in 2001 launched a new periodical that publishes short articles and news, *Studies in Ethnicity and Nationalism.* Other journals in the area include the *Journal of Ethnic and Migration Studies* (1971–), *Canadian Review of Studies in Nationalism* (1973–2005), *Ethnicity* (1974–81), *Ethnic and Racial Studies* (1978–), *Nationalism and Ethnic Politics* (1995–), *Identities: Global Studies in Culture and Power* (1995–), *National Identities* (1999–), *Asian Ethnicity* (2000–) and *Ethnicities* (2001–).

CONCLUSION

The study of nationalism (as with other areas of the social sciences) is, then, very different from the study of, say, astronomy (or other areas of the natural sciences). Natural scientists, unlike their colleagues within many fields of the social sciences, are agreed on basic terminology: it is both easier to define a 'planet' and to recognize one when we see it than it is a 'nation'. For related reasons, natural scientists are then able to agree on descriptive typologies and classification systems, and on procedures for measurement: solar systems may be identified and described with a precision that is lacking when we turn to forms of nationalism. Consequently, natural scientists may realistically seek to generate and test laws about their objects of study; in the analysis of nationalism, the most we can hope for is the formulation of generalizations whose truth is a matter of probability, not certainty. For natural scientists, too, the question of ethics has to do with *how* a particular phenomenon is studied in certain sensitive areas, not with the moral qualities of that phenomenon itself: unlike nationalism, planetary orbits are neither 'good' nor 'bad'.

PART I
NATION AND SOCIETY

2

NATIONALISM, RACE AND GENDER

INTRODUCTION

The election of Barack Obama as President of the United States in November 2008 was greeted by the media as a momentous occasion – as 'a strikingly symbolic moment in the evolution of the nation's fraught racial history', according to the *New York Times* (4 November 2008), which reminded its readers that the election marked 'a new era in a country where just 143 years ago, Mr Obama, as a black man, could have been owned as a slave'. The election represented the collapse of yet another *de facto* barrier to political progress in a country where, as recently as the 1950s, the conventional wisdom was that the election of a Catholic to the presidency would be near-impossible, and the election of an African American would be inconceivable. This drama draws attention to the significance of race in politics and in people's perceptions of their identity, a topic that is the subject of the first half of this chapter. Since, however, it is not a person's physical characteristics that matter but rather the manner in which these are given social and political meaning, we shall consider separately the two topics of race and the manipulation of racial imagery in the creation of national identity, before considering its implications for nationalism.

Race, however, is not the only taboo against which US presidential candidates have had to battle. No woman has ever stood as a presidential candidate for either of the two main American parties (though women were nominated as vice-presidential candidates in 1984 and 2008). Nevertheless, women have for long played a highly visible role at the apex of the American political system, in the White House. But the literature that analyses the position of American 'First Lady' generally takes for granted the subordinate status of this informal office, with perceptions of its role ranging from that of social hostess to informal political advisor to the President (Stooksbury and Edgemon, 2003). The role has been described as follows:

> The First Lady personifies domesticity and traditional womanhood: for example, she must attend to heads of state visiting the executive mansion, care for the home itself, or supervise such activities as the observance of Christmas or Easter on the White House grounds (Williams, 2009: 835).

The challenge posed by Michelle Obama linked race and gender in conflict with this image. While gender is important for politics in general, it is particularly so for the politics of nationalism. Once again, the issue is not so much the difference between the sexes (though this may have particular implications for nationalism) as the social definition of gender roles and their cultural and political expression, topics we consider separately in the last section of this chapter.

RACE AND NATION

The importance of race for national identity and nation formation is clear, given the tendency of nationalist ideology to define the nation as a community of descent. It is reflected in the first instance in issues of terminology. In European languages such as English, it was commonly the case in the past that 'race' and 'nation' were used interchangeably, with many casual references to 'the British race' (for example, Ebbutt, 1920) or to 'the Irish race' (for example, MacManus, 1944). There are many Asian languages in which these words may still not easily be distinguished: Chinese, Korean, Thai and Malay/Indonesian, for example (Reid, 2010: 6–7). The extent to which nationalists borrow the concept of race (with its implications for blood line or descent) requires an explanation of this potential component in the nationalist message. This section considers that role from three perspectives: first, the traditional thinking on race, and the conclusions of scientific researchers on the value of this term; second, the political implications of perceptions of race; and, third, the relationship between race and nationalism (for an overview of recent writing in the area, see Knowles, 2010).

The analysis of race

The European 'Enlightenment' of the eighteenth century, which stimulated curiosity about various aspects of the world, also encouraged speculation about the varieties of humankind. Efforts to classify human population groups were undertaken on a systematic basis, with naturalists attempting to define the border between humans and other species, such as apes, and to devise typologies of humans. These efforts have continued into the present, though with biologists long acknowledging the complexity of this enterprise (Banton, 1983: 32–50, 1998: 17–116). Attempts at classifying people on the basis of phenotypical characteristics (including such visible features as pigmentation, retinal colour, eye shape, hair type, and shape of nose) were pursued vigorously, and reinforced by determined efforts at measurement, notably of stature and of skull shape and size. But, collectively, these indicators failed to coincide sufficiently to define discrete groups. One exhaustive study in the late nineteenth century concluded that 'there is no single European or white race of men', but rather that the population of Europe seemed to be distributed between three distinct 'racial types', Teutonic, Alpine (Celtic) and Mediterranean; that there was no sole 'Aryan race', but that the European races 'show signs of a secondary or derived origin', intermediate between Asiatic and Negro types; and that, in any event, quite apart from inherited characteristics, environmental factors exercise a significant impact on those features commonly attributed to genetic background (Ripley, 1899: 103–30, 457–61, 513–30).

This broad position has not subsequently been dislodged by research on the part of physical anthropologists: miscegenation or interbreeding has been a characteristic of human development, and, together with environmental factors, it conditions physiological characteristics. While the existence of three broad racial categories – Caucasoid, Mongoloid and Negroid – was generally accepted, these, and the subdivisions within them, had little value in explaining the differences between nations (Benedict, 1942: 19–35). As the position was summarized in the mid-twentieth century:

> The lack of any correlation between race and sovereign states is obvious. The individuals who plan the policies of Germany or France or who shout together in the streets over a national victory in war are united not by the similarities of their cephalic indices or by any common family tree, but by the fact that they read the same newspapers and will be called on to die for the same flag (Benedict, 1942: 35).

There are obvious hazards attached to research into race. Those conducting it in the past have come mainly from a continent which in the course of the nineteenth century managed to assert its dominance over much of the rest of the world. The success of the European imperial enterprise was attributed to military, economic, technological and cultural superiority; and it was a short step for many to trace this back also to 'racial' superiority. Arguments of this kind did not just provide an explanation for particular historical realities (such as the apparent invincibility of European empires); they also provided a justification for specific contemporary policies (such as slavery and colonial rule). They could thus be used in defence of European intervention in other continents but also, within particular states, in defence of the white monopoly of political power, as will be seen below.

It was, in other words, a short step from classification to ranking. Efforts to determine systematic differences in body height (with its perceived implications for strength and physical prowess) and in brain capacity (seen as an indicator of intelligence and mental ability) were reinforced by spurious interpretations of history, which purported to identify the superiority of some races over others (Benedict, 1942: 63–88). For many physical anthropologists in the late nineteenth and early twentieth centuries, craniology was seen as key: the study of human skulls, and differences in the size and shape of these, was used by some to prove the 'superior intelligence' of white Europeans. The simple classification of racial groups was transformed into a ranking of these groups, as discussed below.

The kind of 'race science' promoted in Nazi Germany in the 1930s offered a scientific challenge to mainstream physical anthropology, and an ideological challenge to the political world. This was acutely felt in the Soviet Union, committed to the notion of historical materialism – an interpretation that stressed the centrality of sociohistorical forces, not racial ones, in driving human progress. Soviet anthropologists and ethnologists were consequently encouraged to research the sociohistorical origins of peoples, with a view to undermining the sociobiological arguments of the Nazis (Hirsch, 2005: 231–72). This tradition continued after 1945, when research into race in the West had been discredited because of the extent to which it had been apparently 'captured' by the Nazis. It also showed a considerable degree of continuity with the nineteenth-century anthropological tradition. The Soviet official consensus was summed up as follows:

Taking into consideration the basic morphological, physiological, and psychological traits of contemporary humans, the similarity among the races is great, and the differences are insubstantial. There is no factual foundation for reactionary conceptions regarding the existence of 'higher' and 'lower' races and the descent of the races from different species of higher apes. The data of anthropology and other sciences prove that all the races are descended from one species of fossil hominid (Cheboksarov, 1973: 376).

An example of the manner in which Soviet ethnologists classified the races of the world in the mid-1960s is given in Table 2.1. This shows an initial grouping into three 'great races' (Mongoloid, European and Equatorial), with each divided in turn into large 'racial groups'. This was an important component in the construction of a monumental *Atlas of the peoples of the world* (Bruk and Apenchenko, 1964), which continues to be used to the present as an important data source on ethnic diversity. This further broke racial groups down into component races, and it will be of interest to note that the European racial group was divided into three races similar to those identified by Ripley (1899: 103–39), though now labelled simply northern, mixed and southern (Bruk and Apenchenko, 1964: 8–9). This approach was continued in a later major ethnological survey, as part of which a *Handbook of the peoples of the world* summarized racial and other divisions (Bromley, 1988: 573–4).

This approach to race was endorsed by Unesco in its statement on 'the race question' (Unesco, 1950), thereby setting the tone for the international scientific community, and was echoed in subsequent statements by international bodies. More recently, the American Sociological Association (2002) intervened in a debate between social scientists about the merits of collecting data on race through the population census, which some argued 'perpetuates the negative consequences of thinking in racial terms'; it came down decisively in favour of an alternative view – that the collection of such data was necessary in order 'to track disparities and to inform policymaking to achieve greater social justice'.

While the notion of race is still considered central by biologists and physical anthropologists, then, the meaning they attribute to it is entirely removed from that in Germany in the

Table 2.1 Soviet estimates of the size of the world's racial groups, 1964

Great race	Racial group	Population (millions)	Concentration
Mongoloid	Asiatic	558	China
	– mixed with Equatorial	515	Northern India, Japan
	– mixed with European	33	Soviet Union
	American	23	Americas (indigenous peoples)
	– mixed with European	80	Americas (mixed peoples)
European	European	1,426	Europe, South Asia, Americas, North Africa
Equatorial	African	163	Central and Southern Africa
	Oceanic	7	Oceania
	– Asiatic mixed with European	263	South India, East Africa

Source: Derived from Bruk and Apenchenko (1964: 122)

1930s. For decades, as we have seen, it has been clear that attempts to measure racial differences by relying on phenotypical characteristics were doomed to failure. This kind of evidence showed only that, notwithstanding marked physical concentrations of different types, the world's population remained mixed. This has long been established by research into the distribution of blood types (Benedict, 1942: 27–35). More recently, advances in genetic research have allowed distinctive patterns of regional clustering of particular gene types to be mapped, showing the absence of genetic 'purity', with genetic mixing as the norm within spatially defined groups (Hill, Jobling and Bradley, 2000). In other words, as Chris Gilligan (2010: 185) put it, 'races do not exist in any biological sense; they are social constructs'.

The social construction of race

Even the most 'objective' and conscientious forms of scientific enquiry leave themselves open to misrepresentation, especially when their findings are popularized outside the world of research, and this is particularly true of studies of race. As indicated already, it was in the interest of particular groups to assert their primacy over others, and 'race science' proved to be an important tool in this respect. Races were not just different, it was argued; they were inherently unequal. This was the view associated with the French aristocrat, the Comte de Gobineau (1816–82), who accepted the familiar primary division of humankind into three races, based on skin colour and physiognomy; but these were, he argued, fundamentally unequal, with whites being the superior race – superior intellectually, physically, and in other respects (Gobineau, 1970 [1853]: 134–7).

The implicit hierarchy of this approach is illustrated in Figure 2.1, which reproduces a 'family tree' of races by the nineteenth-century anthropologist Augustus Henry Keane. Close to the bottom are the 'Bushman' and 'Hottentot' peoples of southern Africa. At the top are the Anglo-Saxons, including their colonial branches, with other European and Asian peoples ranked lower. Indeed, according to the author, 'all the works of man worthy of record have, with few or doubtful exceptions, emanated from the large and much convoluted brain of the white Homo Caucasicus' (Keane, 1896: 226). The description of four ideal types offered reassuring evidence of the superiority of the European 'Caucasic' peoples, who were compared with three other types in a table that took account of differences in hair, colour, skull, jaws, cheek bone, nose, eyes, teeth, stature, speech and religion. But it was differences in the last feature, 'temperament', that illustrated Caucasian superiority most clearly. The four types were described as follows:

- Negro: sensuous, indolent, improvident; fitful, passionate and cruel, though often affectionate and faithful; little self-respect, hence easy acceptance of the yoke of slavery; science and art undeveloped
- Mongol: sluggish, somewhat sullen, with little initiative, but great endurance; generally frugal, thrifty and industrious, but moral standard low; science slightly, art and letters moderately developed
- [Native] American: moody, taciturn, wary; deep feelings masked by an impassive exterior; indifference to physical pain; science slightly, art moderately, letters scarcely at all developed
- Caucasic: active, enterprising and imaginative; serious, steadfast, solid and stolid [in the North]; fiery, impulsive, fickle [in the South]; science, art and letters highly developed (Keane, 1896: 228).

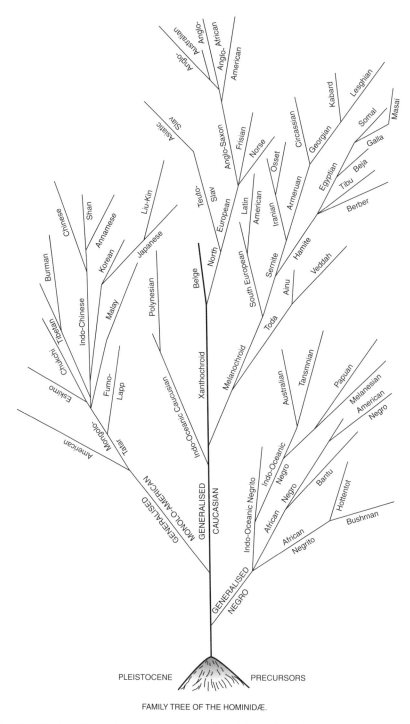

FAMILY TREE OF THE HOMINIDÆ.

Figure 2.1 Nineteenth-century interpretation of racial relationships

Source: Keane, 1896: 224

34

Racism and colonial peoples.   This implicit racial hierarchy had clear implications for relations between colonial powers and 'inferior' peoples, providing an ideological justification for imperialism. It was, in this view, simply an act of responsibility to humanity for enlightened European peoples to try to civilize 'benighted' peoples in Africa, Asia and elsewhere, as the English and French had done earlier in North America and the Spanish and Portuguese in South America. This implied providing good government (through a European proconsular system or by indirect rule), promoting economic development (by encouraging the exploitation of natural resources by European settlers) and saving the souls of the local population (by converting them to Christianity). This 'duty' of empire is well summarized in Rudyard Kipling's poem, 'The white man's burden', in which he urges the Americans to step up to their responsibilities in the Philippines in 1899:

> Take up the White Man's burden—
> Send forth the best ye breed—
> Go bind your sons to exile
> To serve your captives' need;
> To wait in heavy harness
> On fluttered folk and wild—
> Your new-caught, sullen peoples,
> Half-devil and half-child (Kipling, 1912: 323).

Military intervention in remote parts of the world could thus be seen not just as ethically acceptable but as morally required. This clearly feeds into the sense of 'national mission' discussed in Chapter 5, with European powers finding a comforting justification for flexing their military muscle and expanding their colonial reach. The profound link between racist thinking and imperialism justified, however, not only colonial intervention, but also the institution of slavery, with the capture and transportation of African slaves to the Americas as its most terrible expression (Rex, 1983: 32–58).

Racism and domestic minorities.   Racist thinking also served a function in a domestic setting. It offered dominant groups in many societies an important legitimation of their superior status. It also helped to paper over divisions (sometimes deeply rooted class ones) within the dominant group (Day and Thompson, 2004: 139–40). With the transposition of colonialist thinking to domestic contexts, indigenous peoples became the most obvious targets of the racist perspective – to be conquered militarily as 'brutal savages', to be displaced on valuable land since they were 'primitive hunters', and to be converted to Christianity as 'barbaric heathens' (Coates, 2004: 90). This introduced an element of inequality into traditional egalitarian thinking on race based on the Old Testament, in particular the *Book of Genesis*, which traced all of humanity back to the three sons of Noah who survived the deluge: Japheth, ancestor of the peoples of the North; Ham, ancestor of the Africans; and Sem, ancestor of the middle peoples (Ross, 1980).

Thus, for example, the low status of blacks in the United States could be put down not so much to historical disadvantage as to racial inferiority, with biblical justifications for

TIME'S WAXWORKS.

(1881 *JUST ADDED TO THE COLLECTION.*)

Mr. P. "HA! YOU'LL HAVE TO PUT HIM INTO THE CHAMBER OF HORRORS!"

Figure 2.2 Acquisitions of empire: Irish, African and Asian subject races, 1881

Source: Punch, 31 December 1881

slavery reinforced by the notion of Africans as an 'inferior' race. Indeed, by the middle of the nineteenth century even opponents of slavery were agreed on the fundamental, deep-seated inferiority of blacks (Fredrickson, 1987: 320–5). Later in the nineteenth century, it proved possible to mobilize similar arguments against other groups with the potential to challenge white Anglo-Saxon dominance, such as the Irish. In the United Kingdom, similarly, the 'superior' qualities of the English (or British) were extolled in respect not just of distant peoples in Africa and Asia, but in relation to 'white negroes' at home: the Irish. This was expressed in the late nineteenth century in illustrations in popular magazines, attributing simian features to the Irish. But such imagery migrated comfortably across the Atlantic, where the image of the savage Irish peasant was both familiar and frightening to the dominant classes (Curtis, 1997: 29–67). Figure 2.2 (from the satirical London magazine *Punch*) shows echoes of this perspective, with an ape-like Irish revolutionary joining a collection of exotic imperial acquisitions alongside a Zulu warrior. On both sides of the Atlantic, the rehabilitation of the Irish savage, the process by which the Irish 'became white', was a slow one, giving rise to a transition by which 'the Catholic Irish, an oppressed race in Ireland, became part of an oppressing class in America' (Ignatiev, 1995: 1). The Irish were not alone in being classified in effect as 'white negroes'; the Italians in the USA had the same experience (Guglielmo and Salerno, 2003).

As is well known, racial classification and hierarchy proved to be of especial importance in Germany, where a particular role was played by an Austrian/German of British birth, Houston Chamberlain (1855–1927), who helped to pave the way for the racist component in Nazi ideology. He argued that the Jews lay at the lower end of the spectrum of knowledge, civilization and culture, with the Indo-Aryans (who in his eyes had created western civilization) at the higher end; and a particularly elevated status was occupied in the latter group by the Teuton – 'the only human being who can be compared to the Hellenes' (Chamberlain, 1911 [1899]: II: 246–7, 255). This interpretation matched that of certain contemporary German historians such as Heinrich von Treitschke, who took the view that the integrity of the Germans was threatened by the Jews, whose social isolation he called for (von Treitschke, 1916 [1897]: I: 302). Such attitudes were embedded in a long tradition of anti-Semitism in Europe more broadly, derived in part (but by no means exclusively) from elements of Christian belief. Anti-Semitism served the function of defining the 'other', and provided a convenient scapegoat at times of crisis (Weber, 1980). Jews were expelled from particular countries at different points in time, and pogroms or local riots targeted Jewish communities in the nineteenth and early twentieth centuries. This climate prepared the ground for the elaboration by 'race scientists' in post-1918 Germany of more virulent forms of anti-Jewish dogma (see for example Rosenberg, 1966 [1928]).

This trend acquired particular political significance after the Nazi assumption of power in 1933. The new ideology offered not just an analysis of the evolution of the 'Teutonic race' in Germany, but a prescription regarding the way forward: racial purification (Benedict, 1942: 131–5; Burleigh and Wippermann, 1991: 23–73). Jews lost citizenship rights, were barred from the professions and prevented from pursuing certain other occupations, and were discriminated against in various other ways (Angress, 1980). Their status as outcasts was underscored in particular in the 'Nuremberg laws' of 1935, which included measures to prevent marriages that might produce 'offspring likely to be prejudicial to the purity of German blood' (Burleigh and Wippermann, 1991: 49). The events of *Kristallnacht* (so called from the broken glass resulting from attacks on Jewish-owned premises) on 9–10 November 1938 gave a foretaste of what was to come: a wave of Nazi-led attacks on Jewish businesses and synagogues resulted in the deaths of more than 90 Jews. The physical segregation of Jews was followed in many cases by their confinement to ghettoes, the compulsory wearing of a yellow Star of David by all Jews, their imprisonment in concentration camps, and their ultimate extermination (Hilberg, 1980; see also Chapter 10).

Contemporary racism. The collapse of Nazi Germany in 1945 led inevitably to a reaction against racist expressions in political life, with the horrors of the Holocaust leaving a deep impression. The impact of this reaction was, however, slow and uneven, with racial differences continuing to be of substantive significance in the southern United States, South Africa and elsewhere. Indeed, South Africa provided the clearest expression of the formal organization of political life on the basis of race. The fusion of racist ideology with Calvinist theology in the interwar period provided a potent image of difference between the white population (and especially Afrikaners) and what were described as inferior Bantu,

Bushmen and Hottentot peoples. This was followed by the elaboration of an ideology of *apartheid* ('separateness') in the 1950 and 1960s, implemented in policies of near-complete racial segregation (Dubow, 1995: 246–83; Guelke, 2005). The attitudes that drove politics of this kind did not necessarily wither as the policies themselves were discarded. Racist attitudes, sometimes crudely displayed but often only subtly expressed, have survived into the present in varying intensity in western and non-western societies. Expressions of racism are to be found today in European sports, for example, notably in soccer (FRA, 2010), and a particular variant, anti-Semitism, continues to find expression in societies with Jewish populations (see for example annual reports such as Porat and Stauber (2010) and Chanes (2004) for a discussion of the issues).

Furthermore, use of language itself can have racist implications. It is true that the many terms used to describe persons of 'mixed race' (Banton, 1997: 54–5) have substantially disappeared. In racially conscious societies, such terminology sought to define precise genealogical relationships. In the southern United States, for example, a person with one African and one white parent was called a 'mulatto'; a person with one African grandparent and three white grandparents was a 'quadroon'; and a person with one African great-grandparent and seven white great-grandparents was an 'octoroon'. Nazi Germany operated a similar classification in respect of persons of mixed descent: someone with three or four Jewish grandparents was classified as Jewish, someone with two as *Mischling* first class, and someone with one as *Mischling* second class (Burleigh and Wippermann, 1991: 47). But issues of naming remain, and are commonly associated with a political agenda: allocation of names to a subordinate group by a dominant one may be used to delegitimize or marginalize minorities (Safran, 2008b). In China, a northern minority was labelled *xongnu* (implying slave-like people) and a southern one *nanman* (with implications of barbarity; Zhao, 2000: 25–6). Similarly, such terms as 'Lapp', 'Negro' and 'Tinker' came to imply low socioeconomic status and social marginalization, and were replaced by 'Saami', 'Black' or 'African American', and 'Irish Traveller'. Such 'neutral' descriptors can survive, though, only to the extent that these groups shed their image of inferior status; otherwise, the cycle of terminological replacement continues. By contrast, there are also circumstances where the name chosen will have implications for a particular territorial claim or indigenous status (Banton, 1997: 18–24).

Other racist expressions can be subtle, and thus apparently harmless. The phenomenon of the 'ethnic' (or racist) joke is an example: under the cloak of humour, it helps to perpetuate stereotypes. Thus, a genre of jokes dismisses certain peoples as 'stupid'. The jokes are seen as having a particular point precisely because it is claimed that specifically 'backward' traits may be detected among such peoples – and that these are genetically inherent rather than socially conditioned. It may well have been the case that Belgian, Irish, Norwegian or Polish peasants, especially in the past, had difficulty reading public signs in a neighbouring foreign city, that their communication skills in the language of that city were limited, and that navigating the city transport system was a particular challenge; but that was a consequence of geography and life experience, not genetics and blood. The same peasants, faced with the task of recalling local lore in their home villages, mastering the skills of agricultural life and handling complex local social codes, would no doubt display more impressive ability than their urbane, urban counterparts.

Race and nationalism

Although the adjective 'racist' has been extensively used above, the noun 'racism' has not so far been defined. By this is meant, for our present purposes, the view that humanity is divided into races and that these are inherently unequal (usually implying an assumption that the race to which one belongs is superior to those with which it is in contact; see also Benedict, 1942: 96–7; Banton and Miles, 1994). The political significance of race, racism and ethnicity in particular societies has been extensively explored (on the United States, see Schaeffer, 2006; on Great Britain, Law, 2010). But what relation do race and racism bear to nationalism? Broadly speaking, two answers have been offered in this area: that the two phenomena are quite separate, at least conceptually, and that racism is a particular expression of nationalism.

One early study suggested that notwithstanding popular identification of race and nationality with each other, the concepts are quite separate (one referring to natural science, the other to social science). Furthermore, it argued, the modes of mobilization to which they give rise are quite different (Hertz, 1944: 52–77). For Day and Thompson (2004: 132), similarly, while racism and nationalism overlap, they are theoretically quite separate ideologies, in that racism depends on notions of 'inherent and hierarchically organised difference' in a way that nationalism does not. A much sharper distinction between the two was made by Benedict Anderson, who argued that unlike nationalism, racism was concerned with 'blood' and 'breeding':

> The fact of the matter is that nationalism thinks in terms of historical destinies, while racism dreams of eternal contaminations, transmitted from the origins of time through an endless sequence of loathsome copulations … on the whole, racism and anti-semitism manifest themselves, not across national boundaries, but within them. In other words, they justify not so much foreign wars as domestic repression and domination (Anderson, 1983: 136).

The second answer is that racism emerges out of nationalism, stirring the 'racial' ingredient into the complex of phenomena believed to define the nation, and injecting a sense of innate superiority into its members. This is the position taken, for example, by Wimmer (2002: 12–13), who argues that racism is an extreme form of nationalism, and by Jenkins (1997: 84–5), who suggests that nationality may find ideological expression not just through nationalism, but also through racism. The most commonly cited example is that of Germany. Alter (1989: 27–8) has pointed to the common conception that nationalism in Germany culminated in the interwar period in a form of ultranationalism that was itself a type of racism, and Greenfeld (1992: 368–9) interpreted German nationalism in the same way, with its inherently racist basis finding full expression only in the early twentieth century.

It is possible to find some middle ground between these perspectives, which are differentiated from each other in part by different definitional starting points. Already at the end of the nineteenth century, a leading anthropologist warned against 'the error of confusing identity of language with identity of race', since 'nationality may often follow linguistic boundaries, but race bears no necessary relation whatever to them'. Instead, he pointed out, Italy and Germany were racially divided, but this did not prevent the emergence in each of a strong sense of nationality (Ripley, 1899: 17, 214–15). Miles (1993: 56–65) points perceptively to the close similarity between nationalism and racism: each rests on what is seen as an 'objective' boundary defining criterion, used to unify those inside this boundary and to distinguish them from all who are outside it. The two ideologies thus have formal features 'which simultaneously overlap and contrast' (Miles, 1987). Races and nations became synonymous for many in the nineteenth century – though nationalism, unlike racism, had a specific political project. It is clear that, for the most part, nationalism does not depend on race, or on racial perceptions; but this does not mean that racial thinking is of no significance for it. Indeed, precisely because of its role in providing a myth of ancestry, racist thinking and racial concepts are open to exploitation by nationalism. For the purposes of this book, then, the notion of race is of central importance. We may discard its role as an objective determinant of group membership, but we cannot afford to ignore its potential significance as a powerful ingredient in nationalist mobilization.

GENDER AND NATION

Unlike the issue of race, the significance of gender-linked issues for nationalism has been sub-stantially ignored in mainstream writing on the subject. Notwithstanding the predominance of feminine imagery, the ubiquity of the female contribution to patterns of demographic evolu-tion and the distinctive role of women activists in nationalist movements, the issue has attracted relatively little attention. A distinguished scholar in the area, Cynthia Enloe (1993: 230), captured the mood even of women academics in the past, in acknowledging that she herself had been 'remarkably' incurious about gender. Yet, as will be obvious elsewhere in this book and as will emerge in this section, the significance of gender has been central, and subtle. Gender roles (rather than the role of women) are an important object of study in themselves: studying female roles in nationalism helps to make visible the male role, as, for example, in the patriotic duty of the male to respond to military service, and of the female to support this (Nagel, 1998). It thus draws attention to the big impact of a gender-based division of labour in nationalist mobilization.

The existing literature shows little consensus on the range of areas within which the relationship between gender and nationalism works itself out. Blom (2000: 14–17) identi-fies two areas where women have a particular role: public (including the defence of the nation during wartime) and private (producing new members of the nation). Mayer (2000: 6–14) identifies three: as well as the 'private' role, she distinguishes two important aspects of women's public role: representation of the nation (through the creation of an ideal-ized image of its women, and the feminization of the 'motherland'), and protection of its boundaries (in providing criteria for the inclusion or exclusion of members of the nation). Nira Yuval-Davis (1997: 21–5), based on earlier work in a path-breaking contribution with Floya Anthias (Anthias and Yuval-Davis, 1989: 6–12), identifies four major points of inter-section. Three correspond to those already mentioned (the importance of gender in the reproduction of the nation, its cultural contribution, and its role in boundary maintenance); the fourth is the issue of gender roles in patterns of participation in the nationalist move-ment. This framework defines the rest of this section: the role of gender differentiation in the biological reproduction of the nation, its cultural significance (including also its role in boundary maintenance), and its role in political participation.

The reproductive dimension

The most profound expression of gender role differentiation (or, more accurately, of the difference between the sexes) lies in the area of physical reproduction. There is an obvious sense in which, while men cannot practically be dispensed with as agents in securing the biological renewal of the nation, the real burden falls on women. Family size is an important consideration in many situations of ethnic contact: to remain vibrant and continue to grow (or at least not stagnate), a nation will normally need to exceed the birth rate which ensures at least replacement levels (in developed countries at present, this figure is about 2.1 children per woman).

In many cases the issue is seen as being more pressing: communities may be seen as engaging in a form of demographic competition with high stakes. The rapid growth of distinctive populations of recent immigrant origin in West European states, contrasted with the negative growth rate of the long-established population, is likely to profoundly change the character of these states. But particularly intense levels of demographic competition may be characteristic of certain binational relationships. In Fiji, for example, finely balanced competition between the Fijian and Indian populations has helped to determine which community would ultimately control the state. In Northern Ireland, rapid growth in the Catholic population is likely to raise the question as to whether Northern Ireland should remain part of the United Kingdom or be unified with the Republic of Ireland. In Macedonia, the growth of the ethnic Albanian population has been seen as posing a similar challenge (Brunnbauer, 2004: 568). But in Israel the issue has been most fundamental of all, with profound implications for the character of the state. Prime Minister Golda Meir is said to have feared, in the early 1970s, that 'she would have to wake up every morning wondering how many Arab babies have been born during the night' (Yuval-Davis, 1989: 92).

In many cases, the extent of the 'demographic threat' may be deliberately exaggerated by elites as a mechanism for reinforcing their leadership role. Elites may also seek to reshape public policy to meet perceived threats. Thus, the Israeli government responded to demographic challenges in the 1950s by organizing special awards for 'heroine mothers' who had ten children or more, and later offered other incentives, such as housing subsidies for families with more than three children (Yuval-Davis, 1989: 95–6). In Croatia, similarly, the drive to secure the 'biological continuation' of the nation was used by Croatian nationalist leaders in 1992 to promote an agenda that included opposition to abortion, raising of family benefits and encouraging mothers to vacate the workplace (Enloe, 1993: 241–3).

Propagating the nation may not be merely a matter of giving birth: appropriate paternity is also usually an issue. Expectations of endogamy – the notion that women (in particular) should marry within the group – tend to be high. Complex social (or even legal) rules on the status of children may accompany this: offspring from exogamous marriages may be welcomed as members of the group on the basis of the background of one parent, but they may also be rejected for the same reason. There are three broad patterns here. First, where the patrilineal principle applies, the boundary is determined by the group to which the father belongs; the background of the mother is irrelevant (as in many traditional Arab societies, but also in a more restricted way in western societies more generally). Second, more rarely, it is the matrilineal principle that matters: the mother's background is all important, and the father does not count as regards transmission of affiliation (as among Orthodox Jews). Third, more commonly, the child is acknowledged as having a mixed heritage, with affiliation being either divided, or based on contingent rules or customs. In the Soviet Union, 'ethnic nationality', as inscribed on 'internal passports', was determined by individual choice in the case of those with mixed parentage (Simonsen, 2005).

In general, when children are born to linguistically mixed parents, they tend to be brought up in the language of the parent who speaks the more prestigious and more useful language, especially if there is a big status difference between the two (though bilingualism is another possible outcome). Thus, the children of mixed marriages in nineteenth-century Finland were often brought up as speakers of Swedish, the language of prestige; but in the twentieth century they were more commonly brought up as speakers of Finnish, the politically and demographically dominant language. Where the marker of difference is another cultural characteristic, the norms may be different. There was, for example, a convention in eighteenth-century Ireland by which children of mixed marriages were brought up in the religion of the parent of the same sex, a useful formula for maintaining demographic equilibrium.

For similar reasons, there is frequently a strong expectation that sexual relations be confined to members of the group. In such circumstances, rape by members of another group constitutes a very specific form of attack on the community, at once a personal assault and an ethnic affront. In a perceptive, vivid and chilling analysis of a particular kind of war crime, Enloe (2004 [1998]) explores the path that led a Serbian militiaman in Bosnia from an obscure, non-political civilian life to rape and murder for what he saw as the nationalist cause, a bizarre manipulation of masculinity. In Kosovo, allegations of rape of Serbian women by Albanians led to a change in the criminal code in 1986: a new crime of 'nationalist rape', more serious than simple rape, was created (Bracewell, 2000: 579). Nationalist sensitivities may extend further, to the issue of prostitution. Until its closure in 1992, the US naval base at Subic Bay stimulated Filipino nationalism, with the image of local women providing sexual services to American sailors 'at the centre of a nationalist mural of humiliation' (Enloe, 1993: 244–5).

The cultural dimension

In looking at the biological implications of sex difference, we have already strayed into the sociocultural domain. The rearing of children of course only begins at the moment of birth, but a particular burden is subsequently placed on women to continue the process of weaning and teaching the child. Thus, women are commonly seen as primary agents in the socialization of children: in the inculcation of cultural norms and values and, in particular, in the teaching of language. It is not by accident that the language one first learns is generally described as one's 'mother tongue'. This explains why separating children from their mothers has been seen in certain noted cases as an effective mechanism for inducting them into a new culture. The removal of thousands of Australian Aboriginal children from their parents and their placement with foster parents before 1969 is an example of this, one with many counterparts elsewhere.

Women and war.   In many societies, the male role is defined by nationalist leaders as a warrior one: men fight to defend the nation. This ethos is summarized in the official Australian text describing the annual commemoration of the crushing losses of the Australia and New Zealand Army Corps (ANZAC) in Gallipoli in 1915: 'the spirit of ANZAC, with its human qualities of courage, mateship, and sacrifice, continues to have meaning and relevance for our sense of national identity'.[1] Explicit reference to gender may be absent, but the concept of 'mateship' is essentially male, and the war deaths were overwhelmingly so, with women stoically accepting the loss of their menfolk. But the woman's role is seen as supportive, not passive. Women must be prepared for extremes of self-sacrifice, as in the image of the Spartan mother instructing her son to come home from the wars with honour – either victorious or dead. Strikingly, the terracotta image of 'The Greek mother' presented by British artist George Tinworth on the opening of the new (now 'old') Australian parliament building in Canberra in 1927 celebrated the mother enjoining her son to 'either bring this shield back or be brought back upon it'. This traditional view has been challenged by equality policies and by women's involvement in the armed forces – an area where the principle of gender equality was to prove particularly threatening to men, given the masculine ethos of the military (Sparks, 2000: 191–2).

Metaphors of the nation.   The cultural definition of gender roles extends also to that most distinctive of institutions, the family. A comparison of Japan, India, Sweden and Norway suggests that the family plays a central role in national symbolism, which tends to project the nation as resembling the family. The Japanese case differed from the other three in the dominant position of the father, with the mother as a subservient figure, seeing her sons as sons of the Emperor, and if necessary available for sacrifice. The state-supported women's organization, *Aikoku Fujinkai* (Patriotic Women's Association, 1901), served to console women who had lost sons or husbands in war, while 'exorting them to fulfil the ideal of the Japanese mother' (Blom, 2000: 9). In France, Germany and other European countries in the late nineteenth century, too, the image of the nation as a family, with the father at its head, was a powerful one (Caine and Sluga, 2000: 105). The iconic Irish declaration of independence drawn up by radical nationalists in 1916 implied a central role for the nation as a family, with the population referred to as 'children of the nation'. This appeal to traditional bonds of solidarity is to be seen also in Belgium, where there was a saying that sought to emphasize familial unity against the odds: 'Fleming, Walloon are just forenames – Belgian is our family name' (Mellor, 1989: 13).

The metaphor of 'nation as family' is commonly replaced or supplemented by that of 'nation as woman'. The feminized image of the motherland (Britannia, Germania, Helvetia, and their less well-known French sister, Marianne) is a recurring one, even in societies where it is challenged by more warlike male images. This image is commonly maternal, as in Mother Sweden (*Moder Svea*) or Mother Russia (*Matushka Rus'*). Mother Russia, set up as 'the emblem of nation, motherhood, and women', was projected as personally powerless, though a symbol of revolution (Hemenway, 1997: 116). The idea of the Indian nation

---

1 Australian War Memorial, Anzac Day, available www.awm.gov.au/commemoration/anzac/.

as a goddess was advanced in Bengali literature, through the image of 'Mother India' (Bose, 1998). This image, in part derived from the 'British mother goddess', Queen Victoria, was paradoxically mobilized against the male image of the British empire, symbolized by the lion (Sarkar, 1987: 2011). In Mexico, Malinche (an indigenous woman who in the early sixteenth century bore a son to the Spanish *conquistador*, Cortés) has been presented as a mother-figure for the nation, thereby reinforcing its *mestizo* self-image (Gutiérrez, 2006: 342–4, 2007).

Settler societies created by British colonial power tended to retain a strong affection for the 'mother country', and particular ties of 'kith and kin' were boasted about on both sides. This was not enough ultimately to prevent a break-up of the relationship, however, as new 'fatherlands' emerged in the former colonies. The fatherland–motherland dichotomy is an interesting one, and is to be found in different forms in many languages (Edmondson, 2003: 55). It is not clear how far the choice of 'motherland' over 'fatherland' is conscious rather than otherwise, or to what extent it arises from a simple linguistic accident. Use of an internet search to explore the frequency of each of these terms (*in English*) in the same text as particular country names suggests distinctive patterns.[2] In certain Asian and African societies, the use of 'motherland' is clearly predominant (Sri Lanka, Pakistan, Malaysia, Indonesia and Zambia, for example); in European societies such as Poland, the Netherlands, France and Romania, 'fatherland' is preferred, and this is the case also among certain other societies (such as Morocco and Vietnam) and former British colonies (Australia, Canada, New Zealand and the USA). It would be risky to attach too much significance to this, since linguistic norms and simple rules relating to grammatical gender may affect the outcome; but the importance of feminized images of countries that see themselves as vulnerable should not be underestimated. Following the partition of Ireland in 1921, the psychoanalyst Ernest Jones (1964 [1922]) argued that the image of the inviolability of the island of Ireland, imagined as a mother, had a deep impact on the psychology of the Irish, with partition of the island by the British seen as an act of rape.

Elsewhere, the feminine image may be virginal rather than maternal, as in the case of the Maid of Finland (*Suomi-nieto*) or, for the Serbs, the Maid of Kosovo (*Kosovka devojka*) (Edmondson, 2003: 58–60). This found a specific expression in certain Catholic societies, where a *marianismo–machismo* dichotomy has developed (Wilford, 1998: 11). In Ireland, for example, cultivation of the Virgin Mary in the nineteenth and twentieth centuries, expressed *inter alia* in the construction of roadside shrines, served not only to symbolize the nation, but to offer an image of chastity and of endurance of suffering (Cusack, 2000). This pervaded Irish society, extending to the proclamation of the Blessed Virgin as patroness of the Irish defence forces (Turpin, 2003). The image of Mother Ireland was ultimately fused with Catholic imagery of the Blessed Virgin in the shape of Cathleen ni Houlihan, a mythical image who was invoked by radical nationalists in the early twentieth century (Loftus, 1990: 62–4). In Mexico, Malinche was not the only feminine symbol of the nation: the Virgin of Guadeloupe, represented by an icon in the Basilica of Guadeloupe, was another powerful nationalist symbol (Gutiérrez, 2006: 342–4). The Virgin had also been proclaimed Queen

---

2 This refers to the position on 1 July 2010, using Google as the search engine.

of Poland in 1655, and was regarded as the 'protector' of Spain – associations that were to persist for centuries (Edmondson, 2003: 58).

The political dimension

At the more explicitly political level, we may identify two domains in which gender roles need to be assessed: patterns of participation within nationalist movements, and the interaction between feminist and nationalist ideology. Given the overwhelming dominance of men in the political world, looking for a significant contribution by women may at first sight present a formidable challenge; the sheer weight of patriarchy was calculated to crush women's struggles for a political voice (Day and Thompson, 2004: 112–20). Until the twentieth century, after all, women were generally prohibited from voting, sitting in parliament, or participating in any other meaningful way in political life (Randall, 1987). The major exception was royal office holding in those countries which permitted female succession to the throne (some countries retained the Salic law, confining succession to the male line; female succession was permitted in Belgium, for instance, only in 1991). Elsewhere, there were isolated examples of 'women who stepped into the breach when male successors were not available' (Jayawardene, 1986: 258). Joan of Arc, heroine of France's fifteenth-century wars against the English, is one obvious example.

While the weight of law and tradition may have restricted women's political participation, it also opened certain doors to radical movements, such as nationalism and socialism. Discrimination against women could be attributed to alien rule or to the evils of the ruling class, permitting alliances to be forged with activist women. The argument that nationalism was 'modern' could be used to define women's emancipation as part of the broader nationalist struggle, legitimizing the public presence of women. Thus, women were to play a distinctive role in nationalist movements in Palestine, China and Vietnam (de Mel, 2001: 5–9). Women have also become prominently involved in such radical nationalist movements as ETA in the Basque Country, where their role stands in sharp contrast to the masculine role of the security forces (Hamilton, 2007: 176–7). This role has not necessarily been uncontested. It has been alleged that Basque-medium schools perpetuate the role of men as quintessential, 'authentic', Basque speakers (Echeverria, 2001). In many cases, too, the 'support' role of women has been transformed; in Mexico, for instance, female school teachers and instructors played a key role in the nation-building process (Gutiérrez, 2006: 354).

Women have sometimes been more militant, intruding on traditional male domains, especially in revolutionary movements. Following the overthrow of the Russian tsar in 1917, for instance, a former tsarist soldier and intense Russian nationalist, Mariya Bochkareva, organized a women's battalion, the so-called 'battalion of death', one of several that appeared at this time. This battalion, whose members were designed to serve as 'models of military heroism to their male comrades who were to be shamed into remaining in their posts', played a key but ultimately unsuccessful role in defending the Kerensky government in the Winter Palace in Petrograd during the October revolution, but ultimately failed in this (McDermid and Hillyar, 1999: 178–82). Characteristically, Kerensky's reliance on women soldiers was the subject of derision in the masculine culture of the time.

The remarkable comparative study by Kumari Jayawardena (1986) of the role of women in 12 Asian and Middle Eastern societies during the period of nationalist mobilization highlights the extent of female involvement. Capitalist development freed bourgeois women from traditional constraints, but they were overshadowed by men, who laid down the boundaries for female participation, reducing the role of women to a 'contributive' one. The outcome was that once women enjoyed suffrage in a new state, women's movements 'either faded away or degenerated into social welfare organizations concerned with women's education, handicrafts and home care' – with independence, 'male politicians, who had consciously mobilised women in the struggle, pushed them back into their "accustomed place"' (Jayawardena, 1986: 259). This was also the experience of women in Europe, with male nationalist leaders in Italy, France, Germany and Ireland regarding women's issues as distractions from the nationalist cause, at best, arguing that their resolution could wait (Murphy, 1997). Women in the Bolshevik revolution in Russia experienced a similar relegation to support roles (Wilford, 1998: 15; McDermid and Hillyar, 1999: 199–201).

It should not, then, be assumed that mobilization behind issues of gender or class can easily supplant mobilization along lines of national or ethnic identity. Anne McClintock's (1997: 99–108) perceptive analysis of the relationship between women and both Afrikaner and African nationalism illustrates this. Women had great difficulty in the Afrikaner *Broederbond* (the significantly named 'brotherhood') and the African National Congress and its predecessor in occupying anything other than a role that was supportive of men, even when this role was critically important for the nationalist project. Images of Afrikaner women and children incarcerated in concentration camps during the Anglo-Boer War (1899–1902) were important as instruments of propaganda, and later protests by African women against the pass laws that restricted their movement formed part of the African struggle. But this was not an experience of shared suffering by women at the hands of men; through their authority in the household, however limited, white women continued to be able to dominate Africans, women and men alike, leaving African feminists suspicious of the notion of a universal sisterhood (McClintock, 1997: 105). It has similarly been argued that in other struggles between settler and indigenous populations there is an abiding conflict of interest between women on the two sides – between white women and Maori women in New Zealand, for instance, and between white women and native Hawaiian women in Hawaii (Trask, 1997: 194–5). This reflects the reality that feminism, like nationalism itself, takes a range of forms: there are contexts within which it may be progressive, but it may also be imperialist (McClintock, 1997: 109).

From the point of view of the nationalist project, then, engagement with feminism helps both to broaden support and to provide ideological strength (Heng, 1997: 30–34). But the fact that both movements tend to spring from similar social roots sets up a competitive dynamic between them (as it had between nationalism and socialism earlier). The outcome often has been for nationalists to promise major concessions to feminism (or socialism) provided the priority of the national struggle is recognized. But once this struggle has been won, the urgency of commitments in these areas in nationalist eyes commonly evaporates: 'with victory, the practical and strategic interests of women are subordinated to masculinist priorities' (Peterson and Runyan, 1993: 133). Perhaps for this reason, it has been argued that feminism, however defined, only rarely finds itself in alignment with nationalism (Cockburn, 1998: 41–2). Like the perspective of other ideologies, nationalism tends to welcome women, leaving an honoured place for them in the process of mobilization; but it also tends to be successful in securing the priority of what are defined as collective nationalist goals over what may be presented as more 'sectional' gender-based ones, which may easily be deferred until successful attainment of the goals of the nationalist project.

CONCLUSION

As we have seen, then, physical differences may matter from the perspective of nationalist mobilization. Regarding race, there is a scientific consensus on the mixed character of humans, with widely ranging phenotypical characteristics, mixtures of blood types and genetic intermingling. This is not to deny the reality that different parts of the world are characterized by a dominant local physiological type. But this becomes significant for nationalism, and for political mobilization more generally, only when it is endowed with a particular sociocultural significance. Where physical characteristics are used to define the 'other', it may well be the case that this is being used in the same way as such cultural traits as language – to identify intergroup boundaries, in a way that is classically characteristic of nationalism. But where it is seen as having a genetic basis that is linked to a socio-political hierarchy, it becomes a form of racism, one which can often -- but by no means always – have further implications for nationalist mobilization.

Sex differences, however, seem to be of universal importance – not because women and men line up on different sides of nationalist movements, but because of the huge significance of gender roles. The fundamental male–female biological difference has led to a definition of women as givers of life, who bear and nurture the children of the nation, and men as takers of life, prepared to kill to defend the nation and advance its interests. The feminization of the image of the nation adds further depth to this. Such role definitions have important implications for other cultural values and for patterns of political participation. Some of these features have been discussed above, and others will be addressed in other chapters of this book; for example, 'national' costumes, discussed in Chapter 6, were disproportionately used by women, with a tendency for men to prefer business suits, emphasizing their modernity (Blom, 2000: 11–14). But it is important also to watch out for eloquent silences – for the many circumstances in which 'people' might be described more precisely as 'men', in expressions which reflect the reality of women's largely hidden role in this aspect of political life, as in so many others.

3

NATIONALISM AND LANGUAGE

INTRODUCTION

When we meet strangers, among the first clues that we pick up as to their backgrounds are linguistic ones. Language (the actual code spoken, and the manner in which it is articulated) tells us a great deal about other human characteristics. We frequently use it as a short-cut that allows us – fairly or unfairly – to pigeon-hole people whom we have just met, to place them in a category that makes sense to us. In many contexts, it is language that is used to tell friend from foe, to distinguish between members of in- and out-groups. This tendency can be traced back to biblical times, when we find an instance where a particular word, 'shibboleth' (probably meaning a stream), was used by a Semitic tribe, the Gileadites, as a kind of linguistic test to single out their enemies, the defeated and fleeing Ephraimites, who mispronounced the initial 'sh' as 's':

> Gilead then cut Ephraim off from the fords of the Jordan, and whenever Ephraimite fugitives said, 'Let me cross', the men of Gilead would ask, 'Are you an Ephraimite?' If he said, 'No', they then said 'Very well, say Shibboleth'. If anyone said 'Sibboleth', because he could not pronounce it, then they would seize him and kill him at the fords of the Jordan. Forty-two thousand Ephraimites fell on this occasion (Book of Judges, 12: 4–6).

It was not only the Ephraimites that suffered through such mis-articulation of a linguistic password, or 'shibboleth' as it became known generically. This kind of filtering system has been widely utilized in conflict situations throughout history, where groups being hunted down were required to pass a particular phonetic test at which only native speakers of the language of their pursuers were likely to succeed; and the price of failure was death. Thus, efforts were made to identify French soldiers during the Flemish rebellion against the French in Bruges in 1302 by requiring them to say *schilde ende vriend* ('shield a friend'; van den Berghe, 1978: 410, n. 1), and to identify Danish soldiers during the Swedish revolt of the early sixteenth century by requiring them to say *hvit hest i korngulf* ('a white horse in a cornfield'; Haugen, 1968: 275).

Language, then, commonly performs a labelling function: speech acts as a pointer to community. This in itself – the link between language and identity – is worth analyzing further, and is the subject of the last section of this chapter. Before looking at the specific role of language in the definition of identity, however, we need to examine the social and, more specifically, political function of language. But prior to addressing even this, we need to undertake a *tour d'horizon* of the nature of language itself (for a useful overview, see Pei, 1965).

LANGUAGE AND ITS NATURE

While there is a common-sense level at which we feel that we know very well what is meant by language, it is worth exploring this phenomenon more explicitly. Here, we address just two of the several important questions in this area. The first has to do with the origin and nature of language, and its character as a boundary defining mechanism. Second, we need to consider the pattern of competition between languages that results in the survival of some, the disappearance of others, and the transformation of yet others – the general question of the evolution of languages.

Classification of languages

The apparently flippant description of a language as 'a dialect that has an army and navy' (cited in Edwards, 2009: 64) draws attention to an important marker of status as a language – a political one. It is certainly more thought-provoking than the formal definition of language as 'an arbitrary system of vocal (or visual) symbols used by the members of a speech community for the purpose of communication' (Nuessel, 2006: 665). This raises the vital question of boundaries – of a dialect area, or of a speech community – and of the difference between a dialect and a language. A particular speech community may have clearly defined boundaries that enclose a population within which oral communication proceeds easily and comfortably; but it may also be deeply divided by dialect, or its speech form may itself be seen as merely a dialectal variant of a wider speech form. In this, while purely linguistic matters (such as grammar and vocabulary) are important, so too are social and political considerations: a regional speech form may be perceived as essentially the same as that of an adjacent region, or it may be seen as entirely distinct, as a separate language – regardless of the more or less measurable linguistic distance between the two.

When it comes to the classification of languages, scholars agree on the broad outlines of a comprehensive typology. One major project calculated that by 2000 there were more than 7,000 languages in the world, and that these could be grouped into a little more than 100 language families. In addition, there were several language 'isolates', unrelated to any other language, and unclassified languages (Grimes, 2000; Garry and Rubino, 2001; Ethnologue, 2002; for overviews of minorities in Europe with a linguistic base, see Krejčí and Velímský, 1981 and Pan and Pfeil, 2003; for Africa, Unesco, 1981, and Sow and Abdulaziz, 1993; for Asia, Connor, 1979). Major languages, grouped by 'family', are listed in Table 3.1. The first two language families are by far the most important; the great world languages are clustered

Table 3.1 Classification of languages

Family	Examples	Speakers, 1999 (millions)
Indo-European (443)	Hindi	366
	Spanish (Castilian)	358
	English	341
	Portuguese	176
	Russian	167
Sino-Tibetan (365)	Chinese (Mandarin)	874
Niger-Congo (1,489)	Yoruba	20
Austronesian (1,262)	Javanese	76
	Malay	18
Afro-Asiatic (372)	Arabic	150
	Hausa	24
	Hebrew	5
Dravidian (75)	Telugu	70
	Tamil	66
	Kannada	44
	Malayalam	36
Altaic (65)	Turkish	61
	Azerbaijani	31
Japanese (12)	Japanese	125
Austro-Asiatic (168)	Vietnamese	68
Uralic (38)	Hungarian	15
	Finnish	6
	Estonian	1
Nilo-Saharan (199)	Kanuri	4
91 other families (2,413)	Guarani	5
	Georgian	4
	Chechen	1
Language isolates (30)	Korean	78
Creoles (81)	Haitian (French Creole)	7
Pidgins (17)	Liberian English	–

Note: Figures in brackets indicate numbers of languages within each language family. The figure on number of speakers of Arabic has been added by the author.

Source: Based on Ethnologue (2002)

here, and they account for 70% of the world's population (indeed, the first seven language families account for all but 8% of the world's population). A residual category groups a large number of independent language families of greatly varying degrees of significance (the number itself is rather arbitrary, since the number of languages and of language families is continually being revised). In addition, a small number of languages, such as Korean, are not known to have any relatives. Alongside these are two hybrid types, pidgins (simplified colloquial languages that draw on elements of other languages that are in contact) and creoles (more developed pidgins that have been internalized as mother tongues), as well as artificial languages such as Esperanto, a late nineteenth-century invention.

While the languages listed in Table 3.1 are for the most part of considerable significance, most of the world's languages are not, at least from a demographic perspective. The great majority have fewer than one million speakers, with all that that implies for economies of scale (in providing education to the highest level, for example, and in providing a full state service in the language). Indeed, many languages are so small that their continued survival may be in question (see Nettle and Romaine, 2000: 26–49). Even if we confine ourselves to Europe, we find estimates of 50,000 for Faroese, 40,000 for Romansch (an Italic language in Switzerland), 30,000 for Sorbian (an isolated Slavic language in eastern Germany), 20,000 for Agul (a Caucasian language in Russian Dagestan) and 10,000 for Aragonese (a Spanish-related language in northern Spain). But many languages with even smaller numbers of speakers are clearly on the verge of disappearance; indeed, whole language families are in immediate danger, notably among indigenous peoples of the Americas. The survival of the Gaelic-speaking communities of Scotland and Ireland is also in question. Indeed, two of the six Celtic languages that have traditionally been identified have already disappeared, Cornish in the eighteenth century and Manx in the twentieth (Edwards, 1994: 19–23; Nettle and Romaine, 2000: 2–4).

The move from oral to written language imposes an important filtering effect. In practice, written languages require a literate public and, therefore, a minimum degree of standardization, including an agreed spelling system, a common vocabulary and accepted rules of grammar. The number of written languages is therefore much less than the total number of languages – though it still reaches several hundred. Indeed, as we move from simple existence as a written language to the more demanding status of being a language with a substantial scientific literature, the number diminishes further. The extent to which the linguistic marketplace is dominated by a small number of languages will become clear if we consider the case of the English language, which by the end of the twentieth century accounted for approximately 8% of the global population as an oral language, but for 78% of web pages and 83% of scientific writing (Laponce, 2003).

The notion of a language family is a powerful metaphor for the purposes of language classification, implying that each 'family' has a common ancestor. Evidence for this common origin is said to be available in, for example, words used to describe numbers, words expressing family relationships (mother, father, brother, sister) and words used for body parts (such as head, hand, foot). The relationship between selected Indo-European languages is illustrated in this way (in simplified form) in Figure 3.1. This suggests that, like human families, language families are made up of components that may be as closely related as siblings, or more distantly related in the manner of first or second cousins. But this analogy can be dangerous in two key respects. First, languages are not unambiguously identifiable and clearly demarcated phenomena comparable with human beings. The interrelations between the Scandinavian languages, and between German and its various dialects, illustrate this difficulty: we cannot easily answer the question as to how many languages actually exist in these two areas. Does the typical resident of the Swiss capital speak German, or *Schweizerdeutsch*, or Bernese? He or she may indeed be able to switch between (standard) German and a local speech form, but how the latter is classified may not be straightforward.

Second, just as a given individual may resemble her cousin more closely than her sister, so too may a particular language resemble a language from another branch of the same

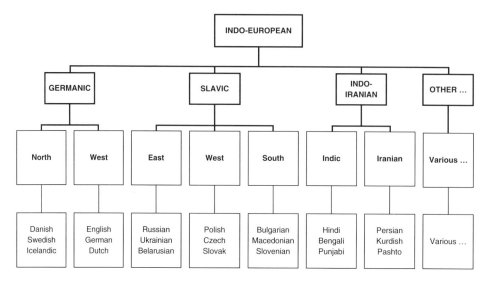

Figure 3.1 Schematic relationship between selected Indo-European languages

family more closely than other languages of the same branch. Close interaction between languages may profoundly influence the character of each, without undermining their syntactical structure. Thus, the basic structure of English may continue to be Germanic, but during its crucial 'middle-English' phase it accepted an estimated 10,000 loan words from French, the language of the ruling classes in the centuries immediately after the Norman conquest of the eleventh century (Crystal, 2002: 184–206). The English language today thus shares more of its vocabulary with its 'cousin', French, than with its 'brother', German. Many other examples of these kinds of hybrid influences could be cited, such as Yiddish (Germanic structure, but with significant imports into its vocabulary from other languages, including Hebrew) and the various pidgins and creoles.

There is another aspect of language that has also acquired political importance: the nature of the script that is used. In addition to the familiar 'Roman' script in which this book is printed, its close relative, the Russian Cyrillic script, is widely used. At a further remove are other scripts, believed to be related, and to be of Semitic origin (the Hebrew, Arabic, Persian, Urdu and Malay scripts, for example). Also sharing a similar origin are the Devangari script, used in the writing of Hindi, and different scripts used by other Indian languages. By contrast to these substantially phonographic scripts (which seek to reproduce sounds), another range of scripts (of which Chinese is an example) are 'logographic' and seek to represent meaning, and thus have a much greater range of characters (see Sampson, 1985; Coulmas, 1989; DeFrancis, 1989; Daniels and Bright, 1996). Scripts may help to differentiate between languages, but they may also draw them closer together; and they can fulfil a not insignificant symbolic role. It has been observed that the many Indian scripts 'are each important symbols of the cultural unity and identity of the groups which employ them', and that most have strong regional, linguistic and religious associations (Coulmas, 1989: 199). Script played a particular role in differentiating between the Hindi- and Urdu-speaking communities (which use respectively the Devanagari and Arabic scripts), and between Serbs and Croats (groups that tend increasingly exclusively to use respectively the Cyrillic and Roman alphabets).

To conclude, then, we need to be conscious that the boundary-defining character of language is complex. The genealogical principle may tell us much about the probability that speakers of two languages will be able to understand each other (though we need to take account also of other linguistic developments, such as patterns of lexical borrowing); and it will certainly give us an idea as to the difficulty that speakers of one language are likely to encounter in learning other languages. For example, a speaker of Swedish will find it very difficult to learn a language from another language family, such as Finnish; considerably easier to learn a language from another branch of the Indo-European family, such as French; much easier to learn other languages from the same Germanic branch of that family, such as English; and easier still to learn adjacent languages such as Danish and Norwegian – so easy, in fact, that learning them as distinct languages may scarcely be necessary. For purposes of intercommunication, Scandinavians typically speak each in his or her own language; thus our hypothetical Swede may well be fluent in English or German, but is unlikely ever to speak in Danish or Norwegian. But the switch to written codes forces people to select a standard, providing a link between adjacent speech forms or driving them further apart; and political considerations may, as we will see below, also play a part.

Evolution of languages

Languages of course evolve organically, in line with broader patterns of social development; but they are also susceptible to influence by human agency, and particularly by political interests. We have already noted the symbolic significance of the scripts whose usage is dictated by elites, and this process can often be driven by a strong political agenda. In the former Soviet Union, for example, conversion to the Russian script was encouraged as 'a factor promoting convergence among Soviet peoples' (Isayev, 1977: 255). Many newly standardized languages in the Soviet Union were originally given scripts of their own, or used the Roman script, but they typically made a transition to the Russian script, a factor that was seen as promoting political unity. Thus, the conversion of Moldovan (seen by many as a dialect of Romanian) from Roman to Russian script served to differentiate it from the language spoken outside the Soviet Union and to link it to other Soviet languages; not surprisingly, Moldovan independence in 1991 was associated with reversion to the Roman script. Elsewhere, a distinctive script may be associated with more overtly nationalist goals: the gothic (*Fraktur*) script used in Germany acquired some symbolic status for nationalists in the 1930s, just as supporters of smaller Indian languages sought to defend them by creating distinct scripts for them. By contrast, introduction of the Roman alphabet can be presented as symbolizing progress, as in the case of Turkey (though here it was Arabic script rather than an indigenous script that was being discarded). Earlier, in 1908–09, Albanian nationalist leaders had decided on the Latin rather than the Arabic script, marking their own western orientation (Babuna, 2004: 296). In China, too, script reform was strongly associated with modernization and the need to promote literacy. In addition to the simplification of the Chinese alphabet, the Communist Party promoted a variant of the Roman alphabet, *pinyin*, after its accession to power in 1949 (see Seybolt and Chiang, 1979).

The state may also play a big role in determining the route followed by dialects or vernaculars in becoming standard languages. Europe offers many examples of this process, beginning with a major change in official language use in the aftermath of the Reformation (Baggioni, 1997). Between about 1550 and 1650 there took place in Europe what has been described as the 'first ecolinguistic revolution': the major states completed the process of shifting for official purposes from Latin to the 'national' language, a language that had been developed (in respect of standardization and lexical development) at varying paces. Thus the English, French, Dutch, Spanish, Portuguese, Danish and Swedish languages became the major media of official communication, commerce, education and cultural life in the countries with which they were associated. Italian and German enjoyed similar development, though their territories lacked political unity; Florentine Italian was, for example, standardized in Tuscany in the sixteenth and seventeenth centuries (Stergios, 2006). By the eighteenth century, Russian had followed; and Turkish had a special position within the Ottoman empire.

These languages were still, of course, the languages of the elites, but when in the nineteenth century the mass populations of Europe came into contact with the states in which they found themselves a 'second ecolinguistic revolution' took place. By the middle of the nineteenth century a number of new languages (including Hungarian, Czech, Serbo-Croatian, Finnish, Bulgarian and Romanian) were being developed and were on the path towards official status; others (including Albanian, Estonian, Latvian, Lithuanian, Slovak and Slovene) followed the same path at a later stage (see Baggioni, 1997: 41–221). Other languages followed more exceptional paths. Thus Polish had enjoyed official status in Poland before the partitions (1772–95); Greek had been used for purposes of religion and commerce within the Ottoman empire even before the establishment of the independent Greek state in 1830; and the linguistic evolution of Norway defies brief description. The old 'official' language, essentially Danish in its written form, had been re-baptized 'Norwegian' in 1814 after Norway was detached from Denmark and, as a consequence of systematic, state-sponsored planning, it has been pushed in a 'more Norwegian' direction, especially in spelling and vocabulary; it is now known as *Bokmål*. From the nineteenth century this has been challenged by a 'more authentic' Norwegian standard, *Landsmaal*, based on the western dialects; now known as *Nynorsk*, this is also an official language (see Haugen, 1966b; Oftedal, 1981).

The process of what Einar Haugen (1966a) described as 'language development' tended to proceed through four stages:

1 *Selection of norm*: choice of a dialect, speech form or existing writing convention that will become the standard for the new language (a decision that may be taken on political, social or other grounds).
2 *Codification of form*: standardization of major aspects of the selected norm, including (1) orthography (implying agreement on a writing and spelling system, manifested

in the preparation of alphabets and spelling books), (2) syntax (implying adoption of agreed rules of linguistic behaviour, manifested in the preparation of grammars) and (3) vocabulary (implying the emergence of a common lexicon, manifested in the preparation of dictionaries).

3 *Elaboration of function*: development of the language, especially by extending its vocabulary to suit all the needs of the society it is intended to serve.

4 *Acceptance by community*: adoption of the new standard by elites and people for official and unofficial purposes; this and stage 3 are obviously interdependent, since there will be no need to elaborate function unless a minimum degree of acceptance of the newly standardized language is forthcoming (based on Haugen, 1966a; 1966b: 16–26; see also Haugen, 1983; Edwards, 2009: 226–9; for a different set of developmental stages, see Hroch, 2000: 70–84).

Obviously, only a few dialects out of many thousands have made this progression (some examples have been mentioned above). Political factors played a big role, with the banning or suppression of such established literary traditions as Arabic and Ladino in Spain, Ruthenian in Poland-Lithuania, Welsh in Britain, and Occitan in France (Kamusella, 2011: 770). In many other cases, efforts to develop a separate standard language faltered. Latgalian and Flemish, for example, never managed to assert their linguistic independence respectively of Latvian and Dutch. In China, major dialects of Chinese spoken by many millions of people, such as Cantonese, continue to be recognized only as dialects, and thus have lower status than regional minority standard languages, such as Uyghur (Dwyer, 1998). The history of language also suggests that the process described above is not irreversible: Latin fell victim in the past, and such languages as Irish may well do so in the future, with a retraction to stages 1 and 2. Some languages, such as Frisian, continue to weaken as a consequence of language shift (to Dutch) and language change (with importations from Dutch; Feitsma, 1981).

LANGUAGE AND POLITICS

It will be clear from the discussion above that politics affects language: the status of many languages has been based on essentially political choices. But our central concern in this book is with influence in the opposite direction: with the impact of language on politics. Before doing this, however, we need to look at the broader social implications of language.

Language and social power

The interdisciplinary field of sociolinguistics sheds a great deal of light on the social significance of language.[1] One area of particular interest is the relationship between language

---

1 For general introductions to sociolinguistics, see Trudgill (1974); Holmes (1992); and Montgomery (1995). For useful readers, see Giglioli (1972), and Pugh, Lee and Swann (1980); and for discussion of more specialized topics with political implications, see Fishman (1971–72, 1978); Edwards, (1994, 2009). On the more specific topic of language planning, see Rubin, et al. (1977).

use and various forms of social identity. It is clear that in many languages there is a strong connection between speech form and social class. This is the case in England, for example, where particular speech modes are seen as indicating a lower social status. The position has been summarized as follows:

> Culminating in notions of 'received pronunciation', the period from the late eighteenth century onwards was to see the creation, and consolidation, of a number of national stereotypes to this end in terms of speech: the 'educated accent', the 'public school' accent, the 'Oxford' accent, 'talking without an accent', 'talking proper', and eventually 'BBC English' too. … Like class itself, accent was, in effect, to become a major national obsession over this time (Mugglestone, 1995: 6).

There is nothing objective about this connection: linguistic conventions seen as associated with high status in one society (such as England) may have quite the opposite connotations in another (such as the USA) (Edwards, 2009: 65–72). But if accent reflects social class, it can also powerfully condition one's status in everyday life. In countries such as England, where the coincidence between class and accent is extremely high, one's accent immediately influences relationships with others with whom one is engaging in a transaction. By allowing speaker A to self-define socially in relation to speaker B, it increases the chances of a deferential or a resentful response (if speaker B is lower), or of a condescending or impatient response (if speaker B is higher), other things being equal.

If subtle differences within a language can be responsible for social consequences on this scale, what are the implications of the coexistence of entirely different languages – especially if one has not been 'modernized' to the same extent as the other? In most such situations of language contact, members of the various language communities occupy different but frequently mutually dependent positions in the social structure. This has two consequences for relations between the communities in question. First, a common medium of communication will need to be arrived at. This will typically be the language of the dominant group, and the cost of acquiring bilingual skills – and the concomitant disadvantages – will be borne by the subordinate groups. There are, however, historical exceptions to this. In some societies, landlords were familiar with the language of their peasants. The Norman-French rulers of medieval England eventually capitulated to the language of those whom they had conquered. Later, the Scottish Stuart dynasty took over the throne of England, but this represented a victory for English culture throughout Britain, since English became the language of the court. Similarly, the accession of the Manchu dynasty to the imperial throne spelled the beginning of the end for the Manchu language in China, since the Manchu elite began to switch to the language of Beijing.

The second consequence is that subordinate languages may be stigmatized. It is salutary to recall that only a century ago being a French speaker in Quebec was associated with menial status in the eyes of the Anglophone minority, an educated Finnish speaker was considered an anomaly by the Swedish-speaking minority, and the phrase 'French in the parlour, Flemish in the kitchen' provided a reasonably accurate summary of the relationship between the two language communities in Belgium. As will be seen in Chapter 7, the status of Czech in relation to German in Bohemia was similarly low, and this is also the fate of speech forms that are dialects of major languages, such as that known as 'Black English Vernacular' in the United States (Edwards, 2009: 75–82).

It should also be stressed that it is political privilege and socioeconomic advantage that endow certain languages (and, more rarely, dialects) with a higher status than others; there is nothing intrinsically 'superior' linguistically in one language as opposed to another (Edwards, 2009: 53–72). English may possess a more extensive vocabulary and a bigger literature than Zulu, for example, but neither language is more or less adequate for dealing with the social contexts in which it is used. The 'higher' status of the former derives from the privileged social status of the population with which it is associated. But this objective reality will never silence those who (whether outsiders or those brought up in a particular marginalized language) criticize such languages for their 'inferior' status. Thus Alexander Lukashenko, President of Belarus but himself a poor speaker of Belarusian, described the official language of his country as 'a poor language, in which one cannot express great thoughts' (Leshchenko, 2004: 338). Lowland Scots has been described as 'a wonderful gibberish' and as 'in the main mis-spelt and mispronounced English', having in Glasgow, 'a debased industrial variety' (Aitken, 1981: 85). But in reality such descriptions amount to implicit judgements about the *speakers* of these languages, which intrinisically are neither deficient nor lacking status.

Three useful terms are commonly applied when describing circumstances of language contact. The first, 'bilingualism', needs to be divided into two categories, and it needs to be distinguished from a less familiar term, 'diglossia'.

- **Personal bilingualism**. This refers to circumstances where a single individual is fluent in two languages (fluency, of course, is a matter of degree, so the question of whether a particular individual is 'bilingual' may be a matter of judgement). A very extensive literature addresses the linguistic, psychological, social, political and policy features of personal bilingualism (see Mackey, 1970 [1962]; Hoffmann, 1991; Romaine, 1995).
- **Societal bilingualism**. Regardless of the extent to which individuals are bilingual, whole societies may be linguistically divided, posing a set of challenging issues for policymakers. Again, this matter is addressed by a large literature (see Laponce, 1987, for a useful overview).
- **Diglossia**. This term was coined to describe a special form of personal bilingualism, where people use two varieties of the same language under different conditions. The 'high' variety is typically used for formal religious, political and educational purposes; the 'low' variety for domestic and other colloquial purposes (Ferguson, 1972 [1959]). The concept was later generalized to refer to the use of any two languages (and not necessarily related ones, or dialectal variants) in these kinds of relatively discrete domains (Fishman, 1980).

These terms have obvious implications for a large number of contexts of language contact. Social relations will necessarily be influenced by configurations of bilingualism, and patterns of diglossic language use are particularly revealing of the relationship between language and society. But these considerations have particular implications for the relationship between language and the state, the topic to which we now turn.

Language and political power

The concept of diglossia is of central importance in illuminating the process by which modern language regimes have emerged, and in defining the relationship between language and politics. When politics was the preserve of the few, issues of language appeared to matter little; but the link between language and politics is much more significant in the modern state, which appears to encounter singular problems when society is not unilingual. Sometimes, the diglossic pattern is a straightforward one: in Sardinia, for instance, Italian functions as the high-status language, with Sardinian as the domestic one (Schjerve, 1981). Luxembourg offers a more complex example: Luxemburgish is the overwhelmingly dominant home language, but two others, French and German, are used for formal matters (Hoffmann, 1981). Pakistan is yet more complex, with English functioning as the official language, and Urdu (spoken by about 8% of the population) as the national language, with other languages confined to regional status or the home (Hussain, 2000: 140–5).

In order to simplify further discussion, let us focus on the issue of the relationship between language and the state (rather than on that between language and politics more generally). One point emerges immediately. Since the number of spoken languages (numbering several thousand, by any count) is much greater than the number of states (less than two hundred), clearly some states will be bi- or multilingual in respect of number of speakers. But even if the number of languages in the world were the same (or less than) the total number of states, it is likely that multilingual states would still exist, since so many languages straddle state boundaries. As the bureaucracy and political leadership of a state must – however rudimentary the state may be – have an agreed language for purposes of administration and communication, we can examine schematically the status of this language in relation to other languages spoken in the society in question, as in Table 3.2.

Here, we begin with the case where the official language is not spoken by anyone as a first language. This is a reference to the kind of classical diglossic situation already discussed: the use of Latin as a language of state throughout medieval Europe, for example; of classical Chinese in China until after the Communist revolution; of Katharevusa in Greece until 1976 (Frangoudaki, 1992); and of English in India. In the second category, an extremely important one, a local minority language is used for official purposes, as in the case of Spanish in Paraguay. There, Guarani, an indigenous Tupian language spoken by most of the population, survives as the common language of domestic intercourse (see Rubin, 1985), but there are many other cases. In Europe's African and Asian colonies, the metropolitan language, spoken originally only by a small settler community, was the high-status language, and in their early stages of national development many – or perhaps even most – European countries fell into the same category. The third category may represent a development of the second, or it may have arisen for other reasons. Here, the official language is that of a majority of the population, but minority languages survive, and their speakers are constrained

Table 3.2 Relation of official language to linguistic composition of society

Speakers of official language	Speakers of unofficial languages	Type of language regime	Examples
None	All	Traditional diglossic society	Medieval France; pre-20th century China; Arab states
Few	Many	Emergent multilingual society with diglossia	France to 19th century; African and Asian colonies of European empires
Many	Few	Society with dominant official language	France in 20th century; most European states; USA
All	None	Unilingual society	Iceland; Portugal

to interact with the state through the medium of the majority language. Most of the contemporary states of Europe, and many outside Europe, fall into this category. Finally, we have the unilingual state, where the spoken language is also the official one. Entirely pure examples are not easy to find, but we might consider Iceland, Denmark and Portugal (but in the case of Denmark the position of the Faroes and of Greenland needs to be taken into account; and in the case of Portugal, some would argue for the cultural distinctiveness of the Azores and Madeira).

We can also find countries that may have progressed through all four categories. Medieval France, with Latin as its official language, certainly fell into the first category; the switch to French as the official language caused it to move into the second category, where it remained until the late nineteenth century; the gradual collapse of minority languages before the cultural power of French caused the country to move into the third category at that point; and it is possible that linguistic minorities are so insignificant today that France may well be located in the fourth category (leaving aside the implications of recent immigration).

A number of points of qualification need to be made about this categorization. First, it ignores the linguistic complexity of the societies in question; the number of coexisting languages ranges from one to many, and their relative demographic and social significance may vary enormously. Second, it ignores the relationships between these languages: some may be extremely closely related to the official language, while others are remote from it, a feature of very considerable practical significance. Third, it ignores the degree of personal bi- or multilingualism, another factor with a bearing on relations between language groups. Fourth, it ignores the possibility of polyglossia: in addition to the language of the state (such as English in India or Tanzania) on the one hand, and the local languages on the other, there may be yet other languages that have an intermediate status (such as Swahili in Tanzania) or an otherwise separate standing (such as the use of Sanskrit for religious purposes in India, or Latin in western Europe). Finally, this categorization ignores the fact that, as in Canada and Finland, there may be *two* official languages rather than just one (in an additional unusual case, discussed below, one effectively *unilingual* country, Ireland, has designated *two* official languages).

It should be pointed out in conclusion that the placing of a society in one of these categories rather than another, and an individual's location within a particular group in any of these societies, is not of merely academic or symbolic interest. Being a native speaker of a language that is not the official language of the state in which one lives places one at an immediate disadvantage: the dominant language will be an acquired one, and those who have learned it as a second language will be able to rival native speakers in competence only with the greatest difficulty. Speakers of non-official languages, in other words, have to undertake the costs (educational, psychological and perhaps financial) of acquiring competence in another language. In the emerging European Union, for instance, those who are native speakers of the effective working languages of the bureaucracy, English, French and German, enjoy a considerable advantage over those who are not. On the other hand, if societal bilingualism is reflected in a bilingual state structure, it may be the formerly dominant group that is placed at a disadvantage: its members are much less likely to have command of the formerly unofficial language than native speakers of the latter are of the official language. For this reason, many English speakers in Wales feared the advent of autonomy: any bilingual requirement that might accompany devolution would be likely to place them at a disadvantage in relation to the Welsh-speaking population (which is effectively bilingual).

LANGUAGE AND NATION

We turn, finally, to a matter of central importance for this book: the link between language and identity (or, more specifically, national identity).[2] Language is of the greatest practical significance: as the modern state has developed, it has become increasingly difficult for any group or individual to avoid confronting the issue of language – typically, by learning the rudiments of reading and writing the official language in school. But language is also of great cultural significance: it is not just a medium of communication, but also the bearer of a literary heritage, even if this is overshadowed by oral lore. It also forms a vital link with the past.

What gives language its particular salience in the modern state is the frequency with which, as we will see in Chapter 8, membership of a linguistic community appears to be translated into membership of an ethnic or national community. But the correspondence between linguistic and national or ethnic frontiers need not be precise. Indeed, we may identify four rather distinctive variants on this relationship. These are described graphically in Figure 3.2, which uses circles to represent linguistic communities and squares to represent nations or ethnic groups. Thus, the first category, (a), is that in which a number of linguistic communities exist within the boundaries of a single nation: the question that arises is whether a nation can exist in the absence of a *common language*. In the second, (b), this is reversed: a number of nations exist within a single linguistic community, with implications for the question of whether a *distinct language* is a prerequisite to nationhood. Category (c) represents

---

2 For further discussion of the points made in this section, see Coakley (2008); for excellent overviews of Switzerland, Belgium and Finland, respectively, see McRae (1983, 1986, 1997).

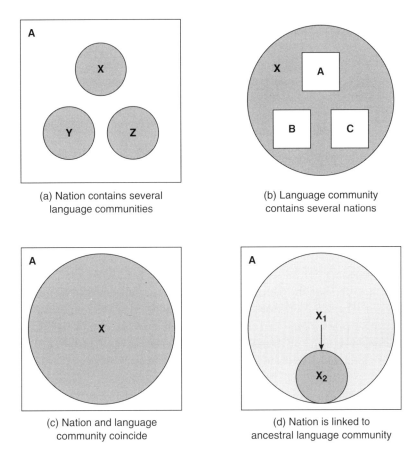

(a) Nation contains several
language communities

(b) Language community
contains several nations

(c) Nation and language
community coincide

(d) Nation is linked to
ancestral language community

Figure 3.2 Four types of relationship between language communities and nations

Note: Nations are represented by squares and language communities by circles.

the pattern regarded as 'natural' by early cultural nationalists: the boundaries of nation and language community coincide, and the nation has a *common, distinct language*. Finally, there is the unusual category (d), where the ancestral language may once have extended as far as the current frontiers of the nation, but where it no longer does so. Instead, most members of the nation speak a metropolitan language, though valuing the ancestral language for symbolic reasons. This is a special case where the nation does not have a common language, and its main language is not distinct. The next subsections consider the four types in turn.

Multilingual nations

The first and most challenging category is that in which the nation is composed of two or more distinct linguistic communities. Clearly a state may be multilingual, but this characteristic is much less frequently attributed to the nation (as that term has been defined in Chapter 1).

Table 3.3   Language and identity, Switzerland, 2003

	Identity pattern (%)					
Language	*Linguistic group only*	*More linguistic group than Swiss*	*Equally linguistic group and Swiss*	*More Swiss than linguistic group*	*Swiss only*	**No. of cases**
German	6	12	20	13	49	672
French	5	22	29	10	34	210
Italian	15	15	36	0	34	69
Other	3	3	17	8	69	72
All	6	14	22	11	46	1,023

Note: the question was 'Some people think of themselves first as Swiss. Others may think of themselves first as [linguistic group]. Which, if any, of the following best describes how you see yourself?', with options *Deutschschweitzer*, *Suisse romande* and *Svizzero-italiano*: for linguistic groups. Percentages total 100 horizontally.

Source: Computed from International Social Survey Programme, 2003 (National Identity II, ZA no. 3910); www.gesis.org

There are good reasons for this. The set of deeply ingrained values and perspectives that are shared by members of the nation typically require the support of a common language to sustain them. The sense of shared history and culture that is so vital an ingredient in national identity expresses itself uncomfortably across language boundaries, if it can do so at all. For this reason, many of those who write about nationalism argue that sharing a *common language* is a prerequisite to being a nation.

Can we find any exceptions? Are there cases where nations (in the sociocultural sense defined in Chapter 1) exist despite internal linguistic divisions? In much of Asia, and also in Africa, the boundaries of states have commonly been inherited from territorial carve-ups by colonial European powers, and linguistic diversity is more common than linguistic uniformity. It is likely that the anti-colonial struggle, or at least opposition to foreign intervention, may have facilitated the work of nationalist elites bent on building alliances across linguistic frontiers in each of these cases. In China, the dominant position of Mandarin Chinese and the role of the Communist party no doubt helped; and in such African cases as Angola, Senegal and Nigeria, the adoption of the language of the former colonial power as the language of the political class helped to provide a single language of wider communication.

What about linguistically divided societies in Europe? Table 3.3 presents some data dealing with language and identity in Switzerland, a case where some experts take the view that the nation is imperfectly formed (Chollet, 2011), though others have argued persuasively that large-scale associational mobilization can successfully overcome problems of linguistic diversity in forging a strong sense of Swiss identity (Wimmer, 2011). Data of the kind presented in Table 3.3 need to be interpreted carefully. When survey respondents are asked which of several geographical levels they primarily identify with, there appears to be a surprising intensity of local and regional attachment – regardless of qualitative assessments of intensity of national identity. In the question whose results are reported here, respondents were invited to rank themselves on a scale ranging from exclusive regional identification (in this case, with one of Switzerland's three main language communities) to exclusive national identification (with Switzerland). The data do show strong levels of identification with

Switzerland, regardless of the language spoken; and German speakers, historically the most numerous group by far, tend to show the strongest levels of Swiss identification (perhaps surprisingly, given the additional challenge from powerful cantonal identity in German-speaking Switzerland). But we need to be aware that when similar questions are asked in other countries the answers are very hard to interpret: in such reputedly state-nationalist countries as France and Poland, for instance, the same survey data show *lower* levels of national identification than in Switzerland.

Multinational linguistic communities

Language frontiers, like other frontiers, have the effect not only of dividing larger populations; they may also serve to unify the populations that they enclose. For this reason, possession of a *distinct language* has often been described as a factor conducive to the construction of national identity. But it will take relatively little reflection to come to the conclusion that this cannot be a necessary condition for the existence of a nation. Serbs, Croats and Muslims have fought each other in the name of their separate nationhood, though speaking the same language; the English-speaking Irish rebelled against the British in the early twentieth century, as the English-speaking Americans had done in the late eighteenth century; and there is no obvious perception among French-speaking Swiss or Belgians that they belong to a broader French nation. Four western languages that had become powerful vehicles of colonialism – English, French, Portuguese and (Castilian) Spanish – were sufficiently strongly associated with external settler communities for the language to acquire a permanent foothold in remote continents; but the colonial communities eventually developed a national identity separate from that of the homeland. Indeed, there is some evidence that elements of dialectal variation developed in varying degrees, and these are likely to have helped reinforce separate patterns of national identity.

Although it is difficult to identify national communities precisely within these large language communities, an effort to do so is made in Table 3.4. This also adds a fifth interesting case, the broad Arabic language community. In each case, the 'national groups' (a term used to avoid the more demanding 'nations') are listed in approximate order of size. It is striking that the home of the English language, England, is overshadowed by the United States, where the English-speaking population is almost five times greater; that the home of Portuguese is similarly overshadowed by Brazil, which has 16 times the number of Portuguese speakers; and that the number of Spanish speakers in Mexico is three times that of Spain (whose Spanish-speaking population is, indeed, surpassed also by those of Colombia and Argentina).

The lists of 'national groups' within the language communities in Table 3.4 illustrate the great difficulty of defining the boundaries of nations precisely. Within the English-speaking group, for instance, there are problems in equating American identity with the English-speaking population of the United States (quite apart from the distinct variants of English spoken by many blacks, a growing proportion of the population is Spanish-speaking). In the United Kingdom, similarly, there is an interesting interplay between 'British' and lower levels of identity, with Welsh, English and in particular Scottish offering a vigorous challenge to

Table 3.4   Potential national groups by major linguistic community

Linguistic community				
English	*Spanish*	*Portuguese*	*French*	*Arabic*
American	Mexican	Brazilian	French	Egyptian
British-English	Colombian	Portuguese	French Canadian	Algerian
Scottish	Argentinian	(Others)	Belgian-Walloon	Moroccan
Irish	Spanish		French Swiss	Sudanese
Welsh	Venezuelan			Iraqi
Canadian	Peruvian			Syrian
Australian	Chilean			Tunisian
New Zealand	Cuban			Palestinian
(Others)	Ecuadorean			Libyan
	Salvadoran			Jordanian
	(Others)			Lebanese
				(Others)

the 'British' label. Canadian identity is similarly problematical, even from the perspective of English speakers: does the typical anglophone image of 'Canada' include the province of Quebec? There are other difficult cases, such as the large English-speaking population of South Africa; it might be suggested that its members do not constitute a distinct nation but form part of a larger group within South Africa.

Similar difficulties could be cited in the case of the Spanish-, Portuguese- and French-speaking groups, and among Arabs the difficulties are even greater. Though bound together by a standard written language, the spoken language is highly differentiated, not just between different countries, but also frequently within them (this is particularly the case, for instance, in Egypt and Iraq). But quite apart from differences between Arabic speakers themselves, and other forms of clashing identity, many of the populations mentioned in Table 3.4 live in countries that contain sizeable populations that speak other languages, or at least identify with them: a large Kurdish minority in Iraq, a Coptic minority in Egypt (though its language has now disappeared except for ritual purposes), and Berber minorities in Algeria and Morocco. The position in Sudan before its breakup in 2011 was most challenging of all: the Arab population was confined to the North, while a majority of the population spoke other languages, including African languages in the South and Nubian in the North.

In the case of the languages listed in Table 3.4, then, there appears to have been a strong degree of internal fragmentation along national lines. There may still exist certain emotional bonds between those who speak a common language, and loose anglophone, francophone, hispanic or lusophone identities may exist, but it seems that more profound loyalties lie at a lower level. The German-speaking community is also problematic. It is no doubt the case today that this is divided into three groups (German proper, Austrian and Swiss German), but only a few decades ago the notion of a common Austrian–German identity found powerful support in both countries. In the case of Arabic, though, notwithstanding greater internal linguistic differentiation, it would appear that in addition to national identities there remains a strong pan-Arab identity, assisted perhaps by geographical proximity, common problems and shared enemies – though challenged more recently by the rise of Islamic sentiment. We nevertheless find interesting variations on this, such as efforts in the United Arab Emirates to promote an Emirati identity that would serve to distinguish the population more clearly from that of Saudi Arabia. The complexities of the Lebanese case also merit comment. Notwithstanding the dominance of the Arabic language, the population tends to look in two directions: Muslims towards their Arab neighbours, Christians towards Europe. Thus, the role of French as a *second* language can play a role in differentiating Maronites from Muslims (Joseph, 2004: 194–8).

Nations with a common, distinct language

In discussing the link between language and identity in the case of the Germans, we are already approaching the third category: that where language community and nation coincide. This is the case where sense of being a nation is buttressed by possession of a *common, distinct language*: internal solidarity is enhanced alike by shared speech and by the boundary that separates the speech community from others. This tendency for linguistic and national boundaries to coincide is obvious among such peoples as the Japanese and the Koreans. However, it is Europe that provides the most numerous examples. The multilingual Habsburg, Ottoman and Romanov empires of the early twentieth century dissolved into a patchwork of new states whose boundaries largely coincided with linguistic ones – based on the claim that these language communities were in fact nations. This was entirely compatible with the views of intellectuals such as Johann Gottfried Herder, as discussed in Chapter 1: language was seen as the key to national identity, with the implication that each language community constituted a nation. The evidence of contemporary observers in the late nineteenth and early twentieth centuries indeed confirmed this: membership of the nation was seen as implying use of the national language; and exiting from the linguistic community was associated with abandonment of the nation. By the interwar period, it had become possible to measure this association more precisely, as state censuses in central and eastern (but not western) Europe began to provide information on both language and national identity.

The outcome of cross-tabulation of census questions on ethnic nationality and language in selected cases at different points in time is presented in Tables 3.5 and 3.6. These data depend in many ways on cross-tabulations offered by the national statistical offices that were responsible for analyzing the census; in many cases, even when separate questions on language and ethnic identity were asked we do not have the material to compare answers to these two questions, largely because the association between the two was so strong that such comparison was not considered necessary. Table 3.5 explores the association between language and ethnic nationality in the three Baltic republics just before the collapse of the Soviet Union. In the case of the three titular nationalities the relationship was extremely strong, with almost all members of these groups speaking their titular languages (Estonian, Latvian and Lithuanian). Among the larger minority nationalities (the Russians in all three cases, and the Poles in Lithuania), there was a similarly strong relationship; it was among the smaller, more territorially dispersed minorities that this relationship

Table 3.5 Ethnic nationality and language, Baltic Republics, 1989

Ethnic Nationality	Language (%)				Population
	Republican	*Russian*	*Own*	*Other*	
Estonia					
Estonian	98.9	1.0	–	0.0	963,281
Russian	1.3	98.6	–	0.1	474,834
Ukrainian	1.2	54.5	44.2	0.1	48,271
Belarusian	0.7	67.1	31.9	0.3	27,711
Polish	8.3	63.4	20.0	8.3	3,008
Other	23.4	39.7	36.6	0.3	34,462
Total	62.4	34.7	2.8	0.1	1,551,567
Latvia					
Latvian	97.4	2.6	–	0.1	1,387,757
Russian	1.1	98.8	–	0.1	905,515
Belarusian	2.5	64.8	32.2	0.5	119,702
Ukrainian	0.9	49.4	49.5	0.2	92,101
Polish	14.7	54.2	27.3	3.8	60,416
Other	11.2	35.9	51.3	1.6	101,076
Total	52.0	42.1	5.7	0.2	2,666,567
Lithuania					
Lithuanian	99.6	0.3	–	0.1	2,924,251
Russian	4.1	95.6	–	0.3	344,455
Polish	5.0	9.2	85.0	0.7	257,994
Belarusian	2.5	53.3	40.5	3.7	63,169
Ukrainian	3.0	45.3	51.1	0.6	44,789
Other	10.3	36.1	51.9	1.8	40,144
Total	80.2	11.7	7.9	0.3	3,674,802

Note: 'Republican' nationality refers to the titular nationality, i.e. respectively Estonian, Latvian and Lithuanian; 'own' refers to the titular language of the nationality. Percentages total 100 horizontally.

Source: Calculated from CIS Stat (1996)

Table 3.6 Ethnic nationality and language, Romania, 2002

Ethnic community (group)	Mother tongue (%)						Total population (000s)
	Romanian	*Magyar*	*Romanes*	*Ukrainian*	*German*	*Other*	
Romanian	99.9	0.1	0.0	0.0	0.0	0.0	19,400
Magyar	2.2	97.6	0.1	0.0	0.0	0.0	1,432
Roma	51.5	4.5	44.0	0.0	0.0	0.0	535
Ukrainian	7.4	0.2	0.0	91.8	0.0	0.4	61
German	18.6	10.7	0.1	0.0	70.3	0.2	60
Other	17.5	0.9	0.0	0.0	0.3	81.3	194
Total	91.0	6.7	1.1	0.3	0.2	0.7	21,681

Note: percentages total 100 horizontally.

Source: Calculated from Romania (2002: Table 3)

was weaker. Table 3.6 shows a similar pattern of relationships in Romania in 2002, with ethnic Romanians, Magyars and Ukrainians speaking their respective languages; but the relationship becomes weaker in the case of the small German minority, and especially among the territorially dispersed Roma.

Nations linked to an ancestral language

Finally, we need to consider a residual category. There are circumstances where the nation is identified with a community whose main language is shared with an adjacent community but which nevertheless has a strong sense of its own identity, typically linked to an ancestral language (in some cases, this may be directed at a classical language that has long since disappeared from everyday use). Ireland represents a good example. Up to the early seventeenth century the Irish (Gaelic) language was the dominant one in almost all regions and among almost all classes. But vigorous policies of anglicization, through colonization of the northern part of the country by settlers from Scotland and England and substantial transfer of the ownership of much of the rest of the country into English-speaking, Protestant hands, produced a predominantly English-speaking landed class and English speaking towns. In the nineteenth century the culture of the towns began to pervade the countryside, so that, by the middle of the century – the first point for which we have reasonably accurate evidence – a majority of the population was English speaking (see Chapter 8). Yet, ironically, as Karl Deutsch (1957: 36) remarked, Irish nationalism took off in the late nineteenth century precisely at a time when the process of anglicization was reaching its culmination. The new Irish nationalist elite was overwhelmingly English-speaking in background and used English as their medium of communication, but increasingly paid deference to the decaying ancestral language. This deference was clearly symbolic only: consciousness of the country's linguistic heritage could help to reinforce the nationalist movement, but attempting to reverse the process of language decline seems to have been too costly in a number of respects.

In Scotland, separate patterns of language shift (from Gaelic to English) and of language change (with the gradual erosion of the distinctiveness of the Lowland Scots speech form) were similarly, ironically, compatible with a steady rise in Scottish nationalism. In Wales and the Basque Country, but especially in Brittany, we find a pattern of development similar to the Irish one: the shift to the respective metropolitan languages (English, Castilian Spanish and French, respectively) did not fatally undermine nationalism.

Indeed, in Wales and the Basque Country the electoral expression of nationalism has been growing precisely as the position of the indigenous language has weakened (though the heartlands of support for the Welsh nationalist party, Plaid Cymru, remain in the Welsh-speaking districts). In the Basque Country, identity tends to be based more on descent and local roots than on language (Beck, 1991). The continuing – but not exclusive – link between language and national identity in these cases is illustrated in Table 3.7, which breaks Welsh and Basque survey respondents into three categories: those who are native speakers of the language or in any case fluent in it, those with some knowledge of it, and monoglot speakers of the metropolitan language. If these three groups are then broken down according

Table 3.7   Language and identity, Wales and Basque Country, 2001–05

	Identity pattern (%)					
Language	*Region only (Welsh, Basque)*	*More region than state*	*Equally region and state*	*More state than region*	*State only (British, Spanish)*	**No. of cases**
Fluent Welsh	46	32	20	2	0	266
Some Welsh	27	35	27	6	5	335
English	19	22	32	13	14	1,372
All	24	26	30	10	11	1,973
Basque	74	16	9	0	0	350
Some Basque	20	34	42	2	2	408
Spanish	11	20	48	10	12	619
All	29	23	37	5	6	1,377

Note: The question was as reported in Table 3.3. The surveys date from 2001 and 2003 (Wales, pooled data) and from 2005 (Basque Country). Percentages total 100 horizontally.

Source: Computed from Wales Life and Times Surveys (2001–03), UK Data Archive study no. 5249; Social and political situation in the Basque Country (2005), CIS study no. 2593.

to their ranking on the same scale as that used in Table 3.3 (a five-point scale ranging from 'Basque only' to 'Spanish only', and from 'Welsh only' to 'British only'), the gap between the two most different language groups is extremely striking: monoglot speakers of the metropolitan languages tend to opt much more strongly for 'British' and 'Spanish' identities than fluent speakers of the peripheral languages, who identify themselves as predominantly Welsh (78%) or Basque (90%) respectively. It should, of course, be noted that monoglot speakers of the metropolitan language are more likely to be associated with recent immigrant origin – a feature that is likely to influence responses to this question.

CONCLUSION

What, then, are we to conclude from this preliminary examination of the interplay between language and nationalism, and of the effect of the former on the latter? Our conclusions might be summarized under three headings: linguistic, sociolinguistic and social psychological.

First, it is necessary to stress the complexity of the issue of language. The key point here is not the large number of languages, or the many unrelated language families into which these may be grouped. Most of these (both languages and language families), however interesting they may be to linguists, are socially and politically insignificant because of their lack of demographic weight – they simply have too few speakers to matter politically. One language family, the Indo-European one, is of overwhelming importance, and within this only a limited number of languages carry actual or potential political weight. But despite the small numbers, the issue of complexity remains. Genealogical trees of languages offer a useful metaphor for the evolution of languages, but they are not designed to imply specific patterns of relationship as in the case of human family trees. Especially when languages are closely related, there may be no precise physical boundary between their spoken variants; instead, they are separated by nothing more than a fuzzy gradient or dialectal continuum.

Second, the huge social and political importance of language can scarcely be understated. Language is much more than a communication system that may (or may not) be aesthetically pleasing to listeners, and that is the bearer of a rich (or limited) corpus of literature. Subtleties of expression – so powerful in impact that we take them for granted and scarcely notice them – may be used to define relationships between individual speakers and groups. Given the centrality of language to the life of the state, being a speaker of the official language places one in a position of distinct advantage over those who are not. In multilingual societies, the potential for conflict over language is thus immediate. But since, in addition to its practical significance, language tends to be bound up with sense of personal and group identity and to be associated with powerful group symbols, its potential to give rise to deep, emotion-based loyalties is also very great.

Third, then, the very powerful link between language and sense of community has a strong bearing on national identity. Long-standing generalizations that equate nations with language communities cannot stand up to empirical testing. It is true that there are many societies – in central and eastern Europe, but also in many other regions – where the boundaries of language communities and of nations are almost coterminous. But many major language communities, such as the English- or Spanish-speaking worlds, are clearly divided into a number of nations. Similarly, some nations are clearly multilingual; in Africa and Asia we frequently find relatively successful efforts at nation building across language frontiers. Societies where the indigenous language is yielding to a metropolitan one, as in Europe's Celtic fringe, offer examples of a different path towards nationhood. Notwithstanding these exceptions, though, it is vital to recognize the profound impact that language has had on national identity.

It is appropriate to conclude with a warning about another feature of the language–nation relationship that we cannot afford to forget. This chapter has focused on the effect that language may have on national identity, but we should recall that influence may also be exercised in the opposite direction. The very fact that a community sees itself as a nation may encourage it to see its language as more distinct from other languages than it is in reality; but it may also actually promote language change and, as in the case of the Norwegian–Danish relationship, cause a steady differentiation between the 'national' language and linguistically adjacent ones. As in the case of other correlates of national identity, then, we need to be aware of the bidirectional nature of causation: language may well encourage a particular pattern of national identity, but national identity may have its own impact on language patterns.

4

NATIONALISM AND RELIGION

INTRODUCTION

In an increasingly secular world, the continuing impact of religious values is often over-looked. This may be attributable to the fact that in many societies the religious presence is so commonplace that it is not even noticed, except, perhaps, by the outsider. It may be strikingly public, as when the *muzim* calls Muslims to prayer from the public address system of the mosque five times a day, or the bells of the Catholic church toll at midday and at 6 pm to remind the faithful to say the Angelus, a prayer commemorating the incarnation of Jesus. It may take the form of religious ceremonies with a social dimension, as in the case of baptisms, weddings, funerals and other rites of passage, such as the Catholic confirma-tion (accepting the pre-teen as a full church member) and the Jewish bar-mitzvah (marking a coming of age). Among many other areas, it may affect dietary habits: rejection of pork and other non-kosher foods by many Jews, for instance; insistence on halal products by Muslims; avoidance of beef (meat of the 'sacred cow') by Hindus; and the tradition of fasting and abstinence from meat on Fridays and other penitential seasons on the part of Catholics, especially in the past.

Religion is much more than a set of prescriptions relating to private life, though. It is deeply embedded in social life (for excellent overviews of the sociology of religion, see Kurtz, 2007; Lundskow, 2008). The belief system associated with it may also have signifi-cant political implications, and it may have an impact on the process of social and political identity formation. These issues are discussed in the rest of this chapter, which begins in the next section by exploring the nature of religion. We continue in the following section by looking at the political implications of religion and of religious belief, and conclude in the last section by narrowing the focus to a particular aspect of politics – the question of national identity.[1]

---

1 This chapter develops themes outlined in Coakley (2002).

RELIGION AND ITS NATURE

How can we account for the pervasiveness of religion in so many contemporary societies? In the early twentieth century, the Polish anthropologist Bronislaw Malinowski identified forebodings about death and desire for immortality as central features of human psychology. He saw religion as a powerful response to these forebodings: it offered a compelling alternative to fear of annihilation, with its 'supreme gift', the promise of continued life (Malinowski, 1954 [1925]: 47–51). While it is tempting to regard religion as pertaining only to people's relations with the afterlife and the non-material world, one early classic definition drew the term's boundaries more broadly. According to Émile Durkheim (1915: 47), religion is 'a unified system of beliefs and practices relative to sacred things, that is to say, things set apart and forbidden – beliefs and practices which unite into one single moral community called a Church, all those who adhere to them' (for a critical discussion of Durkheim's definition, see Pickering, 1984: 177–87; and for a more general discussion of the definition of religion, see Aldridge, 2000: 13–32). As well as broadening the defining criteria (most strikingly, by omitting reference to the question of God and the afterlife), this draws attention to the combination of belief and ritual that lies at the centre of the concept of religion. In discussing the nature of language in Chapter 3, we looked at three major features: its functional role, the manner in which it divides humanity, and the pattern of competition between languages. We may ask similar questions about religion: about the nature of ritual and belief, about the classification of religions, and about their boundary defining role.

Religious belief and practice

Different religions share many common features. As well as the 'beliefs and practices relative to sacred things' that Durkheim saw as being at their core, we need to consider the corpus of sacred texts that inspired these, and the religious rituals, organizations and structures to which they have given rise (see Park, 1994: 38–9).

First, at the level of doctrine and core belief, religions try to offer an account of where human beings stand within a broader cosmos – within the universe as it exists in time and space. Religions such as Hinduism and Buddhism rest on an assumption that humans are reborn in another form after they die, and direct themselves towards ways of overcoming the cycle of birth, death and rebirth by a process of self-liberation. They may, as in the case of Hinduism, recognize the role of gods such as Vishnu and Shiva in this process. By contrast, religions such as Christianity rest on the assumption that a single God (who descended to earth as Jesus Christ) oversees the cosmos, and is the ultimate arbiter of what happens to human souls in the afterlife (for overviews of the beliefs of the major religions, see Smith, H., 1991; Burke, 1996). From these starting points emerge the various ethical systems that we associate with particular religions—ethical systems which, for all their variety both between religions, and within particular religions such as Christianity, tend to share certain overlapping principles, such as worship of the divine and respect for other humans.

Second, in elaborating their doctrines, religions typically draw inspiration from clearly identifiable sacred texts: the Vedas for Hindus, the Torah for Jews, and the Qur'an for

Muslims, for instance. These may differ in their centrality to the religion in question and for different groups within that religion, and there may exist a set of complex relations between such texts. Thus, for Christians, the Bible is the central source of authority, but particular groups may defer to an additional source: the *Book of Mormon* for Latter-Day Saints (Mormons), for instance, or Mary Baker Eddy's *Science and health* for Christian Scientists. There are usually revered founders of these religions: for example, Siddhārtha Gautama (the Buddha), Moses, Jesus and Mohammed for Buddhists, Jews, Christians and Muslims, respectively.

Third, religious rituals tend to take similar forms. Aside from personal prayer and private worship, their most public aspects are expressed through collective ceremonies, entailing gatherings in temples, churches, synagogues or mosques to mark sacred occasions in the calendar, or events in the lives of individuals or communities. To varying degrees, religious buildings constitute important symbols of collective religious commitment, with doctrine shaping their physical design (Park, 1994: 199–207). But simple geography may supplement elaborate architecture: in many religions, pilgrimage to sacred places is an important additional element of ritual, whether this is directed to holy cities such as Rome, Jerusalem or Mecca, or to physical features such as sacred rivers, wells, mountains or trees. Aside from pilgrimages, other sacred locations may be identified, as in the case of native American attachment to particular landscapes, or Marian shrines among Catholics (Super and Turley, 2006: 49–65).

For practical reasons, religion in general requires organization. Religions commonly attribute special status to a cadre of clergy, with priests, rabbis, mullahs and monks undergoing rigorous training and being endowed with a special status as interpreters of the faith and as teachers. In many religions (though by no means all), this requires the creation of training centres and seminaries, which in turn normally require financial support, implying the need for fund-generating activities, with the level of supplementary organization which that may entail. Some religions (such as Anglicanism and certain other mainstream Protestant churches) may be governed also by a higher, episcopal tier; and some (such as Catholicism) may be organized along strict hierarchical lines, running from the Pope, claiming universal jurisdiction, through bishops at diocesan level, and then through parochial clergy, down to the laity.

Classification of religions

Unlike the classification of languages, where the genealogical typology makes sense as an interpretative device, and overshadows all others, classification of religions may take place along a number of dimensions. The first and most obvious has to do with the core question of religious belief, distinguishing between religions which are agnostic about the existence of a supreme being or god, such as Theravada Buddhism, and those for which divine existence is central, with the latter group further divided into monotheistic religions such as Christianity, Islam and Judaism, and polytheistic ones, such as Hinduism (Park, 1994: 36–7). Second, and of particular importance for this book, a long-standing distinction has been made between 'universalizing' religions (such as Christianity and Islam), which claim that

Table 4.1 Population by major religion, 2005

Religion	Adherents (millions)	%	Comment
Semitic origin			
Christians	2,134	33.1	Approx. 52% RC, 21% Protestant, 10% Orthodox
Muslims	1,309	20.3	Approx. 84% Sunni, 15% Shia
Jews	15	0.2	
Indian origin			
Hindus	860	13.3	
Buddhists	379	5.9	Approx. 56% Mahayana, 38% Theravada
Sikhs	25	0.4	
Jains	5	0.1	
Other			
Chinese folk religion	405	6.3	
Tribal religions, shamanism	256	4.0	
New religions	108	1.7	
Other religions	37	0.6	Includes Taoists, Confucians, Shintos and Bahais
None			
Non-religious	769	11.9	
Atheistic	152	2.3	
Total	6,454	100.0	

Source: *Encyclopaedia Britannica*; Barrett (1982: 6)

their message is for all humanity and actively pursue converts, and 'ethnic' religions (such as Judaism and Shintoism), which identify themselves with a particular population group to which membership is substantially confined (Sopher, 1967: 4–13). Third, we may distinguish between religions on the basis of zone of birth, with those of Semitic origin and those of Indian origin dominating the globe, and a third residual category covering the remaining smaller religious systems. The first group includes Judaism as well as two other religions with Semitic roots, Christianity and Islam; the second includes Hinduism and Buddhism. There would be an argument for also identifying another category, religions of Chinese origin (including Confucianism and Taoism), but their classification as religions rather than as non-religious ethical systems is unclear.

An effort is made in Table 4.1 to summarize the manner in which the global population is broken down by religion (and by denomination within the major religions) around the year 2005. In the case of religions of Semitic origin, formal membership criteria are relatively clearly defined, though this will not necessarily tell us very much about levels of practice and belief. Within these religious groups, there is a strong tendency towards geographic clustering, with Protestantism strong in northwest Europe and North America, Catholicism in southwest Europe and Latin America (but strongly represented also in North America), and Orthodoxy based in Eastern Europe. Islam is strongest in North Africa and Southern Asia, with its Shia variant particularly strong in Iran. By contrast, the major religions of Indian origin are much less clearly defined both in doctrine and membership. The visibility of the Hindu

Table 4.2 Reported religious composition of Northern Ireland, Netherlands and Japan, 1961–66

Northern Ireland, 1961	(%)	Netherlands, 1960	(%)	Japan, 1966	(%)
Catholic	35	Catholic	40	Shinto	81
Presbyterian	29	Dutch Reformed	28	Buddhist	80
Church of Ireland	24	Orthodox Reformed	9	Christian	1
Other	12	Other	4	Other	.
Total	100	Total	81	Total	162

Source: Computed from *Statesman's yearbook* (1969–70)

cultural system is obviously strongest in India, with Buddhism prominent in much of the rest of East Asia. It is more difficult to generalize about the remaining categories in Table 4.1; some, such as the Bahais, may be relatively clearly defined; in the case of others, such as Shintos and Confucians, classification as religion may be problematic, and the boundaries of the cultural system may be quite imprecise (for further details on geographical distribution, see Al Faruqi and Sopher, 1974; Smart, 1999).

Religion and social boundaries

There are at least two major areas in which religion has significant implications for social boundaries, and in each there is a striking contrast with the role of language: the nature of religious differentiation, and the spatial distribution of religious groupings.

Varying levels of belief. Religious belief varies qualitatively and in intensity within the individual, and may be dispensed with altogether (unlike language – in the contemporary world mastery of the locally dominant language is essential). The position of religion in this respect may be seen from Table 4.2, which illustrates the formal religious composition of three societies in the 1960s (chosen to illustrate the stark picture presented at that time). In Northern Ireland, the exclusive character of religions affiliation is clear: the population can be divided between a small number of denominational boxes. The Netherlands illustrates the extent to which people may opt entirely out of denominational categories: 24% of the population is missing – it had no religion. In Japan, by contrast, the reported proportions exceeded 100%: clearly, Shintoism and Buddhism are not mutually incompatible. Of course, these differences are an artefact of crude measurement techniques that attribute a degree of objectivity to religious affiliation that in reality it does not possess – precisely because of the qualitative nature of religious belief.

This porousness of religious boundaries is illustrated by the great difficulty of even establishing the size of such belief systems as Taoism and Confucianism. But it is also shown in the remarkable capacity of world religions to accommodate local religions and belief systems. This was a feature of Islam in the Balkans, which adapted itself to traditional folk religions (Bieber, 2000: 21–4); of the Orthodox church among the Chuvash, in compromising with traditional pre-Christian beliefs and practices (Vovina, 2000); of Catholicism in Latin

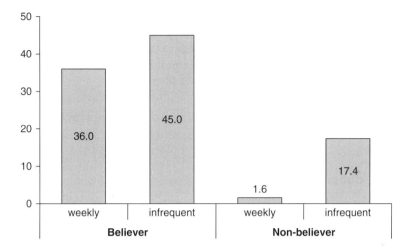

Figure 4.1   Levels of belief and practice of US Catholics, 2008

Note: 'Believers' are those subscribing to core Catholic doctrine; 'weekly' and 'infrequent' refer to levels of attendance at worship, with non-attenders grouped with the latter; N=384 (311 weighted)

Source: American National Election Study, 2008 (ICPSR study no. 25383)

America, in adapting to pre-colonial religions to produce new, syncretic belief systems; and of both Christianity and Islam in absorbing certain features of African religions (Tshibangu, Ajayi and Sanneh, 1993). Such compromises extended to the phenomenon of 'Crypto-christianity' in the Balkans, with Christians professing Islam while secretly practising their own religion (Babuna, 2004: 290).

Even when formal membership is clearly defined, through such rituals as baptism or confirmation, the commitment to doctrine and compliance with ritual may be incomplete. This is clearly the case with the Protestant population of Europe (Coakley, 2009); and the position within the Catholic population of the USA is illustrated in Figure 4.1. Here, survey respondents who identify themselves as Catholics are divided into four groups. Those who comply with certain minimum formal requirements of practice (church attendance on Sundays) and belief (acceptance of the doctrine of transubstantiation) account for only 36% of the sample. A large group (45%) are non-practising believers; and a sizeable group who describe themselves as Catholics neither practise nor believe (17%). Not surprisingly, the proportion of non-believing practicers is negligible at 2%. Similar patterns can be identified in the case of other religions: in reality, religious belief and practice constitute a gradient, and there is no clear dividing line that differentiates practising believers from the indifferent.

Furthermore, at least in Europe, there has been an historical trend towards secularization, defined as 'the process by which sectors of society and culture are removed from the domination of religious institutions and symbols' (Berger, 1967: 107). But secularization is a multidimensional phenomenon, and the pattern of change that has been taking place in western societies has proceeded at varying rates along different dimensions, characterized more by growing indifference to religion than by adoption of counter-religious principles (Bruce, 2002). Neither should it be assumed that secularization implies a transition to rationalism; the end-state is rather one where 'instead of religiosity expressing itself in new sects with enthusiastic believers, it is expressed through piecemeal and consumerist involvement in elements of a cultic world' (Bruce, 1996: 234). This world includes very demanding sects, such as the Unification Church (of Sun Myung Moon) and Scientology, as well as less demanding and mutually compatible 'new age' beliefs (such as astrology, occultism and Feng Shui on the more 'spiritual' end of the spectrum, and aromatherapy, yoga and transcendental meditation on the other).

The spatial dimension.   The centrality of religion in the public sphere has been diminishing over time, with implications for the logic of spatial concentration (the profile of language has been quite the opposite, a trend reinforced by the growth of the modern state and the requirement that each language possess a substantial body of speakers). If we use as a benchmark of the changing status of religion the provisions of the peace of Augsburg (1555), which endorsed the principle *cuius regio, eius religio*, implying that subjects should follow the religion of their prince, we may see the extent of change. This principle ultimately left a lasting imprint on northern and southern Europe, with homogeneously Lutheran states in such areas as Scandinavia, and homogenously Catholic ones in France, Italy and Iberia; but even then more complex patterns of religious adherence appeared elsewhere (Wallace, 2004: 191–4).

Related to this is an intrinsic tendency for religions not to require the kinds of spatial boundaries that are so characteristic of language: adherents of different religious denominations may intermingle freely in a world where religious belief and practice are private matters, but language requires critical mass, and intermingling does not remove the need for a language of wider communication (Laponce, 1987). The position in Switzerland over the period 1850–2000 is shown in Figure 4.2, which contrasts the position in the country's two main linguistic regions with that in its two major religious zones. Although the unilingual character of the former has been eroded, especially in recent decades, this nevertheless remains strong; by contrast, the once-impressive unidenominational character of the cantons has broken down much more thoroughly, with the emergence of a new pluralism and deconfessionalization. This is illustrated by the experience of the two small, traditional, rural Appenzell half-cantons, created in 1597 to reflect a religious division. Each continues to be overwhelmingly German if measured by mother tongue, with a drop from 99% to 93% in Appenzell Innerrhoden and from 99% to 91% in Appenzell Ausserrhoden; but over the same period the proportion of Catholics in the former dropped from 94% to 81%, and of Protestants in the latter from 90% to 51%.

Even those who have warned against reading too much into apparently declining patterns of religious practice have acknowledged that the increasing differentiation of religion from the public sphere has been an undeniable feature of the contemporary world (Casanova, 1994: 211–14). This of course facilitates religious pluralism, with members of diverse religious communities coexisting peacefully. But the decline in religious belief has also had more fundamental implications for social and scientific advancement. As Berger

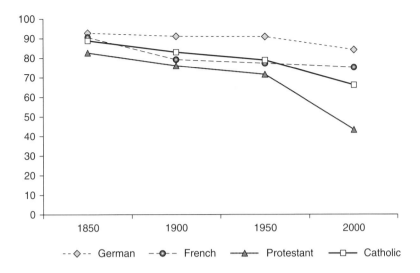

Figure 4.2 Coherence of linguistic and religious territories, Switzerland, 1850–2000

Note: The dashed lines refer to the percentage of German speakers in 19 predominantly German-speaking cantons and of French speakers in five predominantly French-speaking cantons; the unbroken lines refer to the percentage of Protestants in 13 traditionally Protestant cantons and of Catholics in 12 traditionally Catholic cantons

Source: Derived from Switzerland (1851, 1904, 1956); and from Statistik Schweiz, www.bfs.admin.ch/bfs/portal/de/index.html

(1967: 112–13) put it vividly, 'a sky empty of angels becomes open to the intervention of the astronomer and, eventually, of the astronaut'. One outcome of this process was that space was created for the appearance of new, secular belief systems, such as nationalism.

RELIGION AND POLITICS

It will be clear from this discussion that religion is potentially of great political significance, and that it may have important implications for the process of identity formation; indeed, in many of the most prominent conflicts in the contemporary world, religion seems to play a critical role (Ruane and Todd, 2010: 67). Before looking at the relationship between religion and national identity, however, we need to examine its more general social and political implications. We may divide these into two broad categories. The first is the set of indirect consequences of religious organization and belief: the manner in which religion may have an unintended effect on social and political behaviour. The second is the much more obvious dimension of direct political consequences: the impact of specific forms of religious doctrine on political life.

The political implications of religious organization

Quite apart from their explicit teachings, religions may have significant implications for social organization that in turn have political consequences. First, their ritual and ceremonial aspects may play an important role in community building: in erecting social boundaries between those who believe and practise in accordance with the norms of a particular religion and those who do not. Second, to varying degrees religions require professional personnel in the form of clergy, and these may be available to play an important secular leadership function as well. Third, transmitting the principles of the faith calls for some form of teaching, requiring the establishment of at least rudimentary educational networks, which in turn may have implications for political development. Fourth, certain religions extend the educational function well beyond mere teaching of literacy: they may make a substantial contribution to language development, a process whose implications for nationalism have been discussed in Chapter 3.

Religious ritual and ceremonial may play an important role in community building – in showing people from otherwise diverse cultures what they have in common and what differentiates them from others. The pilgrimage in Catholic, Hindu, Buddhist and especially Islamic traditions is an example of this (Barber, 1991). When Muslims participate in the *Hajj* (the annual pilgrimage to Mecca), for instance, the experience brings members of the faithful from a wide range of cultures together in a shared, intense ritual. When Hindus bathe in the Ganges on the occasion of great festivals, they similarly express their shared religious heritage, regardless of the linguistic frontiers that may divide them. Shared ritual and geographically transposable religious practice have a similar impact. Before the reforms of the Second Vatican Council (1962–65) came into effect, for example, Catholics from all over the world could share in celebration of the Latin mass, with priests using identical sequences of words and actions from Vienna to Valparaiso.

Religion also provides the conditions for the emergence of an educated clerical leadership whose role may extend well outside the other-worldly. A network of clergy imbued with a commitment to the central values of the faith is generally capable of acting as an effective medium for communication with the masses. Of course, oral lore and family socialization also have a role to play, especially in local religions. But more commonly, passing on the principles of religion requires a significant educational effort, and perhaps the establishment of a network of schools, staffed either by clergy, by para-clerical workers or by lay teachers, but in any case promoting the emergence of an educated class which can provide leadership not just in the religious but also in the secular domain.

The appearance of a system of schools may have another impact. These may be primarily religious, as in the case of the Muslim *madrassa*, but they may also have a strong secular component, as in the Protestant parochial schools, in which training in literacy has been a central concern. Indeed, especially among the more evangelical Protestant denominations, the cultivation of literacy has been a foremost objective, since this, by opening the door to Bible reading, is seen as the key to salvation. This contrasts with the position in the Catholic church, with its commitment to a moral code which is interpreted by a hierarchically organized clergy. Profound consequences flow from this: for political cultural values, and even for educational priorities. Some of these values have been explored in the sociological literature since the time of Max Weber (who identified the 'Protestant ethic', with its emphasis on individual responsibility, as an important driver of economic change). It is by no means accidental that the creation of mass education systems in Catholic southern Europe lagged significantly behind the pace of development in Protestant northern Europe, and wide gaps in literacy levels arose between these two types of society (and, indeed, between Catholics and Protestants within denominationally mixed societies). Lawrence Stone (1969: 77) summarized the difference between the two main religions in a memorable sentence: 'The Catholics were fearful of heresy because of Bible study, whereas the Reformers were fearful of superstition because of lack of Bible study.' But this difference was not universally expressed, with more complex patterns and less stark differences between Protestants and Catholics in literacy levels in such cases as Germany (Strauss, 1984).

The impact of religion on social development may extend further. For some religions, an ancient sacred language was used as the language of wider communication at an elite level, and as a language of worship: Latin for Catholics, Old Church Slavonic for most Orthodox Christians, Hebrew for Jews, Classical Arabic for Muslims, and Sanskrit for Hindus, for instance. For the more evangelical, however, the emphasis is on the vernacular. Among Protestants, the centrality of the Bible as the instrument of salvation leads to a perception that it should be read as directly as possible, in the vernacular. In many instances, this led not just to intensive efforts to promote literacy, but to even more demanding programmes of language development in the case of communities whose languages were not standardized. For example, the origins of the Ethnologue language database referred to in Chapter 3 (www.ethnologue.com) lie not in an abstract interest in language, but in missionary commitment; it is produced by the Summer Institute of Linguistics, which describes itself as 'a faith-based nonprofit organization', which is 'motivated by the belief that all people are created in the image of God', with an implicit Christian message (see Edwards, 2009: 123–5). Translation of the Bible into the languages of the people was a major project of the post-reformation period, resulting not just in the provision of an extensive devotional literature, but also in crucial steps in the modernization and development of marginal languages.

The political message of religion

Aside from its indirect political impact, religion may have a quite explicit message for the political order. First, it may act as a powerful ideological support, reinforcing the status quo and the legitimacy of current rulers. This role is sometimes played indirectly: religion occupies a space that would otherwise be filled by alternative and potentially subversive views of the world. Second, it may have a more aggressive function, seeking not so much to support the state as to shape its character. This may have implications for political mobilization: religion may contribute to conflict between different policy priorities, given the thrust of different religious ethical codes.

Religion and the state.   For some religions, access to state power is of central importance. One attempt to categorize religions in this respect concluded that Judaism and Christianity, which originated as minority religions, lacked this drive, but that Islam, Hinduism and Confucianism saw access to power as essential, with Buddhism lying somewhere in between (Green, 2003: 4–8). This may understate the political ambition of the Christian churches; perhaps Christianity is happy to stand aside from involvement in the political world where it is a minority religion, but the Protestant state churches of Britain and Scandinavia suggest that it may also be more politically assertive, and the Catholic church made efforts to promote its position as state church in the Catholic monarchies of southern Europe, though commonly having to settle for a kind of 'caesaro-papist' compromise (where the monarch ruled not just the state but also, in temporal affairs, the church).

When church and state are closely linked, religion may play an important function in legitimizing the existing social and political order. At its most solemn, this takes the form of the inclusion of religious-type statements in the constitution, as in the case of Muslim Indonesia, Catholic Ireland, Orthodox Greece and Protestant Norway (Markoff and Regan, 1987: 167–71). A more vivid example of the conservative potential of religion emerges from its use to persuade American slaves that compliance with the principles of social organization in the American South was ordained by God. Methodist missionaries in Alabama in 1843, introducing the catechism to the local Black population, discovered that an earlier set of catechetical responses was more familiar, with even the sin of adultery redefined to bolster the position of slave owners:

> On one occasion, after reading the Decalogue to a large class, the Missionary asked: 'What is the meaning of thou shalt not commit adultery?' The answer was: 'To serve our heavenly Father, and our earthly master, obey our overseer, and not steal anything'. On another occasion the question was propounded: 'What did God make you for?' It was promptly answered: 'To make a crop' (West, 1893: 605).

Certain of the other major religions are at least implicitly supportive of the political status quo. Thus, Hinduism rests on the principle of a cosmic order, justifying the Indian caste system and sacred kingship as part of this, implying near-dictatorial powers for the monarch, and extending to a perception of kingship as divine (Smith, B., 2003). Along similar lines, Buddhism endorses the notion of kingship and of the harmonious society (Lewis, 2003). Official Buddhism reinforced the monarchy in Burma and Siam, allowing kings to identify with great religious figures (Ileto, 1999: 195–6). Confucianism, similarly, for all its variety, rests on an emphasis on proper behaviour of ruler and ruled, stressing merit and virtue as central principles (Csikszentmihalyi, 2003). Religious principles were once invoked in traditional Catholic states, sometimes extending to the 'divine right' of the monarch to rule. The Russian constitution of 1906 proclaimed that 'The supreme autocratic power is vested in the Emperor of all the Russias. It is God's command that his authority should be obeyed not only through fear but for conscience's sake.' Even with the overthrow of traditional rulers, it was possible to repackage this ideology into support for a secular republic, as in France (Rémond, 1999: 121), or for similar revolutionary regimes elsewhere.

Religion may also function as an instrument of empire: the imperial mission may be justified by the need to 'save' populations by converting them to the 'true faith'. Thus, European colonial rule in Africa was assisted by the advance of Islam and Christianity and the decline of traditional religion (Opoku, 1985). In Indo-China, conversion to French Christianity in the mid-nineteenth century was an important agency of colonialism (Ileto, 1999: 198–201). The Spanish conquest of the Philippines in the sixteenth century was facilitated by the fact that most of the population followed animist religions, which had limited capacity to resist the Christian message; significantly, Mindanao, where Islam had already established itself, resisted this process, with implications for developments at a much later date (Anderson, 1998: 194–5). Indeed, the conversion of the *mestizo* (mixed Chinese and Filipino) group was driven by the prospect that this might lead to a further major victory: the conversion of China to Christianity (Wickberg, 1964).

Religion and public policy.   It is true that religion may also justify rebellion in certain circumstances – especially where revolutionary political elites are animated by religious values and are linked to the clergy in opposition to the dominant ruling group (Robinson, 1987). But where it receives militant expression, it typically fills an assertive, state-shaping role. Such attitudes have emerged in predominantly Muslim societies, with a claim that Islam is the 'final and complete revelation of God' (Esposito, 1998: 328–9). They have also been obvious where Catholics have constituted a majority of the population, as the following much-cited quotation illustrates (taken from the organ of the Jesuit order in Rome, *Civilta Cattolica*, in April 1945):

> The Roman Catholic Church, convinced through its divine prerogatives of being the only true Church, must demand the right of freedom for herself alone, because such a right can only be possessed by truth, never by error. As to other religions, the Church will certainly never draw the sword, but she will require that by legitimate means they shall not be allowed to propagate false doctrine. Consequently, in a state where the majority of people are Catholic, the Church will require that legal existence be denied to error, and that if religious minorities actually exist, they shall have only a *de facto* existence, without opportunity to spread their beliefs (cited in Pfeffer, 1958: 37).

In such cases, religion may endow not just domestic policy but also foreign policy with a militant, crusading zeal. It has been pointed out that most religions are characterized by a dual motif, with prophets commending peace and love of one's enemy, but with warriors proclaiming a vigorous defence of religious principle. The latter preoccupation has been particularly pronounced in the Judeo-Christian tradition, with the image of God as a god of war, destroying his enemies (Kurtz, 2007: 247–54). For example, during the presidency of George W. Bush (2001–09) religious values seem to have reinforced the US administration in its goal of winning a self-proclaimed 'war on terror', and overthrowing an 'axis of evil' (Iran, Iraq and North Korea). But a variant of Protestant fundamentalism with strong support in the USA and some followers elsewhere has a much more specific political message: according to 'Christian Zionism', the establishment of the state of Israel represents a crucial fulfilment of biblical prophecy, and is to be followed by the 'second coming' of Jesus Christ and the establishment of the kingdom of God on earth – a belief with obvious implications for policy in the Middle East.

The more specific public policy implications of religious belief may also promote political conflict. The clear-cut belief structures and detailed ethical systems of the main monotheistic religions originating in the Middle East set them apart from the principal Eastern religions, with their emphasis on societal harmony (Stackhouse, 1987: 415). Since, however, these religions vary in their interpretation of God's will, different, competing policy prescriptions may be the outcome. Thus, in predominantly Protestant states with large Catholic minorities (such as Germany, Switzerland and the Netherlands in Europe, and the United States, Canada, Australia and New Zealand in other continents), Catholic elites engaged in a long struggle for the preservation of what they identified as core Catholic values. This normally extended to efforts to carve out a distinct Catholic segment of the public sector (including the health and welfare systems but, in particular, the schools) which would be informed by distinctively Catholic values -- a near-universal recipe for political conflict, with Protestants arguing that services provided and paid for by the state should be subject to state regulation alone, and rejecting demands for Catholic control.

There have also been significant differences of emphasis between religions on more specific public policy matters. Thus, Catholics have been traditionally concerned with ensuring that the legal system supports a conservative position in areas of sexual morality, including contraception, divorce and homosexuality; for fundamentalist Protestants, the corresponding preoccupations were in the area of the sale and use of alcoholic drink, restrictions on gambling, and the need to ensure observance of the Sabbath (Sunday) as a day of rest. These were highly visible differences, with each side placing a different emphasis on the balance to be aimed at between personal morality and state enforcement in the respective cases; but they rested on a shared value system, which caused both denominations to converge in the late twentieth century in the face of what each saw as the more terrible menace of the secular state.

There may also be profound differences within formally unidenominational societies. In certain Islamic societies, such as Turkey and Egypt, secular elites have struggled to retain control of the state structure in the face of strong challenges from Muslims advocating a closer link between public legislation and *Sharia* (Islamic) law. Elsewhere, as in Iran, the influence of religious leaders has been much greater, and there has been evidence of the growing political appeal of fundamentalism, resulting in new links between the political and religious domains (Piscatori, 1986). The visibility of such conflicts in the contemporary world may cause us to forget that similar divisions were characteristic of most of Catholic Europe, where the French revolution led to the crystallization of deep political conflict between clerical and 'liberal' (that is, anticlerical or secular) tendencies, as in France, Belgium, Austria and Italy (Whyte, 1981). In these cases, the role of the Catholic church as a state church was ultimately overthrown, secular education, health and welfare systems were introduced, and social legislation increasingly ignored the views of religious elites. Parallel tensions within Protestant societies received only limited political expression (Coakley, 2009), though conservative Protestantism was a powerful political force in Northern Ireland and in South Africa's old regime (see Wallis and Bruce, 1986: 227–359), as well as in the southern United States. Outside the world of the great monotheistic religions, political activism on the part of Buddhists in Sri Lanka and of Hindus in India is a reminder of the significance of religious values and identities for political mobilization.

RELIGION AND NATION

As we have seen in Chapter 1, religion has frequently been identified as an important ingredient (though not an essential one) in nationalism, but the relationship between the two is complex and multi-faceted: religion may constitute an analogy, an explanatory factor, an ingredient, and/or a form of nationalism (Brubaker, 2012). In many cases, it has been argued, early forms of ethnoreligious identity were later transformed into political nationalism, as in the impact of Judaism on Israeli identity, the Tudor reformation on English nationalism, and Orthodoxy in the Balkans and the Caucasus (Armstrong, 1995: 36–8). Some observers have even argued that nationalism is itself a form of religion. Carlton Hayes (1926: 93–125), for example, highlighted what he saw as similarities: nationalism was a new creed, with its own gods, rituals, theological system, holy days, and other classical accoutrements of conventional religion; and he entitled his summary of his lifetime's reflection on the subject *Nationalism: a religion* (Hayes, 1960). Other influential early scholars came to similar conclusions (Hertz, 1944: 121; Kohn, 1944: 23–4). More recently, nationalism has been dubbed a 'civic religion' (Llobera, 1994: 134–7), and a 'political religion' (Smith, A., 2000b: 792).

This analogy will not, however, help us much in analyzing the nature of the relationship between religion and nationalism. To start with, the concept of a 'secular religion' is self-contradictory, at least if we are to accept a conventional definition of religion. Furthermore, as John Hutchinson (1994: 66–77) has pointed out, notwithstanding the extent to which nationalism depends on religion, certain intrinsic characteristics of the latter push in quite a different direction. Unlike nationalism, the great religions are universalistic and transethnic; their orientation is towards the spiritual world rather than towards the material world; and their written languages have historically been 'dead' ones. How, then, can religion feed in to nationalism?

Steve Bruce (2003: 78–83) has suggested that religion is frequently to be found at the heart of nationalism for two reasons. First, there is a compelling historical argument: as he puts it, 'religion was there first' (2003: 78), winning people's loyalties in a pre-national period, and therefore defining a context for the appearance of nationalism. Second, it fulfils key social functions, including provision of a sense of community and an organizational infrastructure with the capacity to service not just religious but also many secular needs. We may add another consideration here: it commonly represents a reminder of the origins of those who practise it – origins which sometimes lay outside the current political jurisdiction, whether as a consequence of migration or of boundary change. Two other perceptive assessments of the significance of religion for nationalism reinforce these points. Anthony Smith (1986: 34–7) identifies three important elements: a close relationship, in many cases, between ethnic origin myths and religious belief; religious sectarianism as a potential support for nationalist separatism; and the contribution of a particular religion's organizational base in supplying educated personnel and developed channels of communication to the nationalist project. Pedro Ramet (1989: 299) examines five areas where religion may play a constitutive role in group identity and nationalism: its capacity to provide cultural links to the historical past of the community; its boundary-reinforcing character; the leadership role commonly played by the clergy; its function as a badge of group identity; and its contribution to the development of the national language. We may group these overlapping dimensions to give us a four-part framework for examining the significance of religion for nationalism: its indirect social role through such areas as education and language development; its direct ideological role in elevating the status of a particular people; its contribution through its organizational structure; and its function as a boundary-defining and boundary-maintaining mechanism. This framework is used in the rest of this section.

The indirect social contribution of religion

As the last section has shown, the impact of religion on society is to be felt not merely in the areas of values and rituals; the dissemination of ideas and, in most cases, the management of ceremonies depend on the existence of a relatively sophisticated organization. We have also seen that religions imply an effective communication system, one capable of disseminating a complex religious message, with a mixture of narrative and normative content, to all potential adherents of the faith. The resulting institutional framework, religious in its original source of inspiration, may be diverted to serve more secular gods. This potential contribution of religion to the temporal world applies with particular force to nationalist movements: religious institutions help to provide an organizational infrastructure and a potential cadre of leaders who are open to mobilization by nationalists.

To the degree that religion concerns itself with attempts to spread its message to existing or potential believers through the vernacular language, furthermore, it proceeds down a path that is particularly attractive to certain types of nationalists. It was as a consequence of such efforts that by the nineteenth century small Protestant communities, such as the Estonians and the Latvians, found themselves with relatively well-developed school systems and extensive vernacular literatures (though their Catholic Lithuanian neighbours fared less well). In Europe's Celtic fringe, the Welsh language, though existing in the shadow of one of the world's most vigorous cultures, has been relatively successfully maintained, with the democratic tradition of Protestant non-conformism offering significant assistance (by contrast, extensive state support failed to prevent the near-extinction of the Irish language in Catholic Ireland, and Catholic Brittany has experienced an even more dramatic process of assimilation of Breton speakers to the French language).

The contribution of religion in this respect plays a central role in preparing the path for nationalism: it has the capacity to provide essential organizational resources, ones whose penetrative power is a central ingredient in the formation of ethnic identity (Enloe, 1980: 360–6; Armstrong, 1982: 201–6). But it must be emphasized strongly that there is nothing deterministic about this. In serving as a facilitator of at least symbolic communication and as a provider of a vital social infrastructure, religion may pave the way for nationalism; but it may also prepare the way for movements or ideologies that are *incompatible* with nationalism – ones that, for example, are international in character. This aspect of religion prepares the ground, then, for nationalist mobilization, but this ground may be occupied by competing political forces.

The ideological contribution of religion

In assessing the ideological contribution of religion to nationalism, it is necessary to revert to Sopher's (1967) distinction between two types of religion: the *universalizing* (henceforth, 'universalist') religion – whose message, it is claimed, is valid for all humankind and for whose more committed members proselytist or missionary activity is seen as normal – and the *ethnic* religion, whose message relates to a specific people. Minor ethnic religions may, of course, be perceived as obstacles rather than as contributors to the nation formation enterprise: tribal or folk religion may have a focus that is purely local or regional, leading to charges that it is parochial and divisive, and that it impedes larger-scale national integration. In this respect, it resembles local languages or patois, which may either themselves become the basis for the creation of a new nation, or perish through absorption in a wider cultural experiment.

The main contribution of ethnic religions to the nationalist project arises from their role as bearers of historical memory – their sacred texts are simultaneously documents of religious inspiration and records of the historic antecedents of the people (Safran, 2008a). Thus, for example, the Old Testament of the Bible is seen as describing not just the relationship between God and humanity, but also the history of the Jewish people, thereby endowing religion with a particular place in the evolution of Israeli nationalism (see Cohen, 1987: 42–63; Wald, 2002). There are other well-known examples of this relationship, such as the contribution of Hinduism to the growth and development of Indian nationalism (van der Veer, 1994) and of Shinto in promoting Japanese nationalism (Brown, 1955: 114–17; Fridell, 1983; Toyoda and Tanaka, 2002).

Almost by definition, universalist religions cannot have the same effect. To the extent that their goal is the conversion of all of humankind to the 'true faith', and given the relative success of this effort over a wide geographical area, such religions undermine their own capacity to contribute to processes of nation formation. Consistent with this perspective, the Indian Muslim leader Muhammad Iqbal criticized nationalism as a tool of colonialism, calculated 'to shatter the religious unity of Islam in pieces' (Esposito, 1998: 339). Nevertheless, these religions may be associated with processes that depart from the universalistic logic implicit in their global vision. Internal divisions, including doctrinal revolt, may compromise the unity of the religious community, providing justification not just for religious sectarianism but also for political secession.

Thus, for example, though less traumatic than the divisions that were to emerge within Christianity, Tibetan and Theravada Buddhism were regional variants of one of the great religions of Asia, and were associated with national distinctiveness in their territorial domains. Already in the seventeenth century, the predominance of Shia Islam had set Persia apart from the rest of the Muslim world, and especially from the Ottoman empire, with its

Sunni tradition (Armstrong, 1982: 236–7). A clearer example of the implications of religious division is offered by the emergence of Sikhism out of Hinduism in the fifteenth century – a development that amounted, in effect, to the creation of a new ethnic religion (see Ahmed, 1996). Within the Christian world, the division between the eastern (Orthodox) and western churches in 1054 left a legacy whose political significance became clear only in later centuries, though the differences between the two sides were more obvious in the area of ritual than in that of belief.

Further doctrinal revolts, especially in the West, had an important effect later on the nation formation process. Thus, the Hussite secession in the early fifteenth century, though ultimately crushed by the military and political resources of the Habsburgs, left a lasting imprint on religion in the Czech lands, and provided Czech nationalism with an evocative historical myth that was waiting to be rediscovered in the nineteenth century. The Protestant Reformation provides the most effective example of the political implications of doctrinal revolt. The reformers were in general geographically distant from Rome, and there was an important political dimension to their protest (Rémond, 1999: 111–13). This had a double significance. First, the clash with Rome took several different ideological forms, with Lutheranism dominant in Germany and Scandinavia, Calvinism in the Netherlands, Scotland and parts of Hungary, and a distinctive variant, Anglicanism, in England. Second, the organization of the new denominations took on a distinctively 'national' form, with new independent churches appearing in areas that coincided with existing monarchies.

While helping in such cases to delimit a boundary with outside groups, religion may also help to unify the community and strengthen its political leadership. Nation formation in the major states of western Europe (England, France and Spain) can be traced back to early, pre-modern religious roots, as rulers used an easily available and emotive force to build national unity, although later on these founding ideologies had to be discarded in building up a broader, modern community (Marx, 2003). In southeast Asia, Theravada Buddhism was the official religion in Burma, Siam, Laos and Cambodia, helping to preserve these 'ethnic empires'; and the Chinese religions of Vietnam performed a similar function there (Christie, 1996: 6–8). While religion assisted the colonial enterprise, it was also available to anti-colonial movements. Thus, nation building in the Philippines was facilitated by the fact that the population was overwhelmingly Christian (Anderson, 1998: 328), and Buddhism was important in mobilizing nationalism in Burma, as was Islam in Indonesia and Pakistan (Pluvier, 1974: 75; Hussain, 2000: 145–50).

Of course, religion was a potential resource for separatist movements at a lower level as well. The struggle of the Moros ('Moors', or islamicized population) in Mindanao against the Philippine state is one example of this. But religion also plays a role in the case of the Arakan (Muslims in Buddhist Burma) and Patani Malays in Thailand – and even in the case of the Aceh movement, based on a powerful Islamic ideology and memory of separate statehood, but within the Islamic state of Indonesia (Christie, 1996: 129–90). In the former Yugoslavia, Bosnian Muslims in general refused to declare themselves Serbs or Croats; once their identity as 'Muslims in a national sense' was recognized in the 1960s there was an upsurge in identification with this category (Babuna, 2004: 304).

The organizational contribution of religion

While doctrinal revolt did not always lead to secession, this was commonly the outcome; and there were also cases of organizational secession in the absence of any significant doctrinal differences. As we have seen, the reformation in Europe was associated not just with the rise of Protestantism but also with the creation of national churches. The new Protestant monarchies were entirely independent of each other, constituting separate churches and sharing doctrinal perspectives and ritual practices to varying degrees, and playing a vital role in the development of state-centred nationalism. Similar developments took place in Catholic countries such as Spain and France, with monarchs seeking to build loyalty based on shared religion, which emerged as 'a crutch for building or broadening community and national unity' (Marx, 2003: 26).

The relationship between the growth of nationalism and the establishment of autonomous churches took a different form in Orthodox Europe. In the Balkans, the consolidation of Ottoman rule resulted in an end to the autonomy of the Serbian Orthodox church centred on the patriarchate of Ipek (Peć) in 1766, and of the Bulgarian one centred on the bishopric of Ohrid in 1767. Organizational control was instead vested in the Greek patriarchate of Constantinople, whose 'phanariot' officials (so called because of the district in Constantinople, Phanar, with which they were identified) were responsible for the cultural affairs of the Orthodox population of the empire. Thus, from the point of view of Serbian and Bulgarian nationalist leaders, the Islamic Turkish political rulers posed little threat at the cultural level; the real threat came from the Greek phanariot religious elites. As Ottoman control receded, a struggle for autonomy and for the establishment of 'autocephalous' (in effect, independent) Orthodox churches was an important concomitant of political nationalism, and the two processes reinforced each other. Autocephalous status was established in Greece (1850), in Serbia (partly in 1832, fully in 1879), in Bulgaria (1872) and in Romania (1885) (see Attwater, 1961: 81–115; Petrovich, 1980; Ramet, 1989: 303–4).

An even more vivid illustration of the importance of religion for nationalism is provided by the case of Montenegro. This isolated, Serbian-inhabited territory had resisted the full establishment of Ottoman power, and constituted an interesting example of theocratic rule after 1516, with its bishops serving also as temporal rulers (indeed, from 1737 to 1852 the succession was handed on from uncle to nephew, an interesting mechanism for circumventing the implications of celibacy). With the ending of the autonomy of the patriarchate of Peć in 1766, however, Montenegro's independence of Constantinople was expressed through its transfer to the jurisdiction of the Russian Holy Synod (Attwater, 1961: 83). In 1920 it became part of the Serbian church. Reflecting the link between nationalism and religious organization, however, there were movements for the independence of the Montenegrin Orthodox church in the 1990s, as there had been in the 1960s in the case of the Macedonian Orthodox church (Bruce, 1996: 97). The Macedonian Orthodox Church proclaimed its independence in 1967, though this was not recognized by the main Orthodox churches; its Montenegrin counterpart followed suit in 1993.

Sometimes, the level of reorganization extended further than establishment of autonomy. In response to changed political circumstances, most of the Orthodox leaders of Polish western Ukraine recognized the pope as their head in 1596 (becoming 'Greek Catholics' or Uniates), a change whose consequences are still to be felt in Ukraine (Johnston, 1992). The Orthodox Romanians of Transylvania followed the same path in 1697 (Oldson, 1992). Incidentally, while this switch may have brought these peoples into conformity, as Uniates, with the religion of their ruler, the Emperor, it was to have the opposite effect after 1918: now part of Ukraine and Romania, the Uniates no longer shared the predominant Orthodox affiliation of the majority in the new states (Hann, 1993).

The boundary-defining role of religion

Geographical boundaries between religions are far from permanent, as we have seen, and the boundaries of states, though typically stable, are not permanent either. Consequently, political and religious borders which once coincided may, as a result of political change, come instead to cut across each other, leaving minorities on the 'wrong' side. In these circumstances, and where the state has never managed to ensure religious uniformity in the first place, religion may play a key role in enhancing group consciousness and national identity. Where such religious frontier issues appear, the role of religion has been described as substantially a boundary-defining one: it helps to link members of the group, and to distinguish them from non-members, by identifying an external threat to communal identity (Barker, 2009: 29–38). We may first consider a set of examples where religion seems to play such a role, and then assess the durability of such borders in the context of declining religious commitment.

Religion and boundaries. The instrumental character of religion in encouraging communal identity is obvious from a number of cases. The leaders of the Orthodox minorities in the Balkans, already mentioned in connection with their struggle for autocephalous status, also had an interest in encouraging political nationalism, and the two movements tended to reinforce each other (Jelavich and Jelavich, 1977: 14–16). From the point of view of the Orthodox church, the preservation of the spirit of Christian unity against Islam was a priority, and 'the faithful were taught that they had lost their freedom because of their sins, but that the day would come when their church would emerge triumphant' (Jelavich and Jelavich, 1977: 4). In eighteenth-century Poland, with its unstable political leadership leading to frequent interregnums, the Catholic primate, the Bishop of Poznan, commonly filled the gap as *interrex*, a role which observers have seen as in effect continuing under Cardinal Wyszynski in the years around the fall of communism (Rémond, 1999: 117). This no doubt also drew on the role that the Polish Catholic church had played before 1918 in providing a link between Poles in Protestant Germany and Orthodox Russia during the years when Poland was partitioned.

Catholicism played a similar role in Ireland, as 'the economically and politically dispossessed Irish appropriated Catholicism as the marker of their resistance against English colonisation', with religion thus playing an empowering role in distinguishing the Irish both from Britain and from the Anglo-Irish Protestant landowners (Dillon, 2002: 48). Other examples of similar status, with the church leadership defending a Catholic minority which at times felt beleaguered, include Quebec, where it helped to reinforce the identity of the francophone community against anglophone, Protestant Canada (Grand'maison, 1970; Guindon, 1988), and possibly Belgium, during its period of incorporation into the Protestant Netherlands in 1815–30.

Particularly strong links between religion and national identity may be seen when the religious border coincides with an ethnolinguistic one. In Malaysia, for instance, the three major groups, the Malays, Chinese and Indians, are distinguished also by religion (Islam, Buddhism and Chinese religions, and Hinduism, respectively). The Greek and Turkish Cypriots are similarly divided along religious lines, between Orthodoxy and Islam, respectively. In Sri Lanka, where the dominant Sinhalese population is overwhelmingly Buddhist, the Tamils are mainly Hindu (but a section of the Tamil-speaking population, known as Moors, is of Islamic background). There is a similar relationship between language and religion as markers of identity in the case of the (Muslim) Uyghurs in Xinjiang, China, and of Sikhs in Punjab, India, but evidence from recent decades suggests that religion became the more important marker, since language was relatively comfortably accommodated by the state (Reny, 2009).

Elsewhere, though, religion may cut across linguistic boundaries rather than reinforcing them, and it may serve as a source of ethnic differentiation. Thus, as Figure 4.3 shows, there is a strong relationship between religion and national identity in English-speaking Northern Ireland, with Catholics predominantly classing themselves as Irish and Protestants as British (but with a large minority of each opting for a new category, 'Northern Irish'). Figure 4.4 presents even starker data in respect of Serbo-Croatian-speaking Bosnia-Herzegovina. Those identified with a particular religion described themselves as associated almost exclusively with a predictable national group: Catholic Croats, Orthodox Serbs, and Islamic Bosniaks or Muslims. Here, as in Northern Ireland, those not belonging to the major religions are

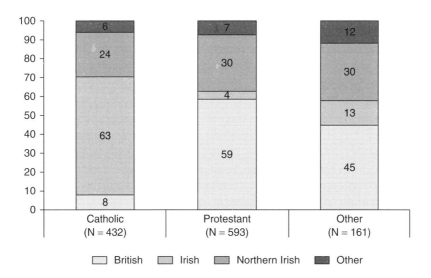

Figure 4.3 National identity by religion, Northern Ireland, 2008

Source: Northern Ireland Life and Times Survey, 2008 (www.ark.ac.uk/nilt)

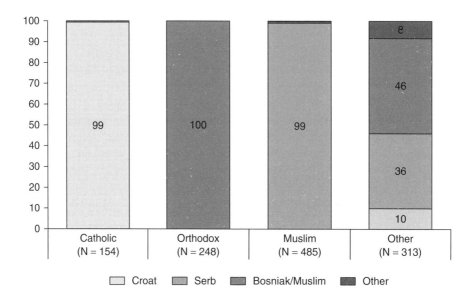

Figure 4.4 National identity by religion, Bosnia, 2001

Source: World Values Survey, 2001 (www.worldvaluessurvey.org)

more divided in their allegiance, but it is likely that their sense of national identity matches their ancestral religious affiliation. Of course, religion need not have this effect. Religious divisions within Germany, Switzerland and the Netherlands posed a significant challenge to nation builders, but this was ultimately overcome.

In a number of societies, these minorities have been seen as distinctive primarily on religious rather than linguistic grounds. Further examples, drawn from evidence from early twentieth-century Europe, are described in Table 4.3. Certain of these groups (the Masurians and the Memellanders) seem to have disappeared; others (the Setuds, the Latgalians and the Pomaks) continue to exist, though in depleted numbers. They resemble minorities elsewhere (like the Sri Lanka Moors, mentioned above, or the East Timorese) who share a language with an adjacent group but are distinguished from them most obviously by religious affiliation. Elsewhere, though, language managed to transcend religious differences in unifying peoples, as in the case of the Albanians, who were divided along religious lines. The population was traditionally predominantly Muslim, but internally divided, and with Catholic and Orthodox minorities (Babuna, 2000: 79, 2004: 311–12).

Implications of secularization. The question of secularization and of the status of 'lapsed' adherents of the 'national' religion poses particular difficulties for the notion of national identity based on religion. Does exiting from religious belief imply opting out of national identification? The answer, of course, is 'no'; national identification is much more emotionally profound and more complex in its origins than routine subscription

Table 4.3 Examples of distinctive religious minorities in interwar Europe

The minorities listed here were unusual in that they shared a language with an adjacent or surrounding population (though sometimes speaking a distinct dialect of this), but were differentiated from it in religion, and tended to label themselves differently from that population.

Masurians. Polish-speaking inhabitants of Masuria in northeastern Poland, traditionally Protestant in religion, many of whom identified as 'Masurian' rather than Polish (Blanke, 1999). No such group was identified in the Polish census of 2002 (which, however, recorded other regional national groups, including 173,000 Silesians and 5,000 Kashubians).

Memellanders. Lithuanian-speaking inhabitants of the Klaipeda or Memel district of northern Lithuania, traditionally Protestant in religion, many of whom identified as 'Memellander' rather than Lithuanian (Misiunas, 1968). No such group was reported in the Lithuanian census of 2001.

Setuds. Estonian-speaking inhabitants of the southeastern border region between Estonia and Russia, traditionally Orthodox in religion, many of whom identifed themselves as Setud rather than Estonian (Hurt, 1904; Jääts, 2000). None was reported in the Estonian census of 2000, but the Russian census of 2002 reported 197 Setuds.

Latgalians. Latvian-speaking inhabitants of the southeastern Latvian province of Latgale, traditionally Catholic in religion, many of whom identified as 'Latgalian' rather than Latvian (Plakans, 2011). None was reported in the Latvian census of 2000, but the Russian census of 2002 reported 1,622 Latgalians.

Pomaks. Bulgarian-speaking inhabitants of the Rhodope mountains in southern Bulgaria, traditionally Muslim in religion, many of whom identified as 'Pomak' rather than Bulgarian (Apostolov, 1996, 2001: 104–19; Konstantinov, 1997). The 'Pomak' label was not used in the Bulgarian census of 2001, but at that time there were 131,531 Muslims of Bulgarian ethnic background.

to confessional principles. Atheistic Muslims in Bosnia and non-believing Protestants in Northern Ireland seem capable of the most intense forms of ethnic attachment. But in such cases there is typically a perception of loose affiliation – genealogical rather than ideological in character – to a denominationally defined community, to the ancestral faith, though consciousness of this may be other-imposed, or it may itself be a consequence and not merely a cause of conflict (Lynch, 2000). Efforts to monitor ethnicity in Northern Ireland have thus moved away from religious adherence to identification with a culturally defined religious community as the only feasible way of taking account of the large numbers who now claim to have no religious belief (Fair Employment Commission for Northern Ireland, 1998: 5).

Many of these dilemmas are illustrated vividly by the special (and challenging) case of national identity within the United Kingdom (see Colley, 1992). As is well known, Anglicanism played a particular role in shaping English national identity, helping to define it in contradistinction to Catholic France. But it served poorly as the 'national' religion of Great Britain, or of the United Kingdom: Scotland was wedded to Presbyterianism, Protestant dissent (including, eventually, Methodism) overshadowed Anglicanism in Wales, and most of the Irish were Catholics. The wider label 'Protestant' could, however, act as a marker of British identity, and seems to have been so adopted. But this link was substantially undermined by the decline in religious commitment and demographic transformation, especially after the Second World War. It seems then to have been replaced by a more generalized form of Christianity, embracing also Catholicism, which still served to distinguish Britain from irreligious France (though this association too has weakened; McLeod, 1999). Thus, English Catholics were once a suspect minority (Clayton and McBride, 1998); now their ethnonational loyalty is generally accepted.

There are also circumstances where nationalism may have been assisted in the past by variations in intensity of belief in unidenominational societies. The image of the Catholic Bretons remaining true to the faith of their fathers in secular France survived until the twentieth century, notwithstanding an ambiguous relationship between the Catholic church and the Breton language (Boomgaard, 2008). The religious zeal of the Catholic Flemish within secular Belgium similarly reinforced Flemish nationalism (Edwards, 2009: 100–1). The traditional Catholicism of the Slovaks within secular Czechoslovakia reflected a sharply different relationship with nationalism in the two parts of that state, with a close link in Slovakia and a more negative image of Catholicism in the Czech lands (Froese, 2005). There was a similarly strong relationship between Catholicism and Basque nationalism in its early phases (Payne, 1971). In each of these cases, it should be emphasized, this relationship had faded by the late twentieth century, with nationalism now resting on a more secular basis.

Religion may, then, be a surrogate for some other characteristic, such as ethnic or at least regional origin. Thus, in Northern Ireland, being a Protestant is not simply a matter of religious belief: it evokes memories of the British heritage among those who see themselves as descendants of seventeenth-century Scottish or English colonists, and acts as a badge of differentiation in respect of the 'native Irish' Catholic population with its indigenous Gaelic roots. It also coincides with important cultural differences (Mitchell, 2006: 59–68). In the Balkans, the gap between Croats and Serbs, which divides a single linguistic community, coincided with the long-established frontier between the Habsburg and Ottoman empires, whose Christian populations became divided in loyalty between Rome and Constantinople (with an ethnic Muslim group also emerging on the Ottoman side of the border). Before the establishment of an independent Poland and Lithuania, the Masurians and Memellanders had been separated for centuries from the main areas of Polish and Lithuanian settlement through their political and administrative inclusion in Lutheran East Prussia. The Setud, though speaking Estonian, had lived for centuries in Russia proper, just outside the boundary of the Baltic provinces. The Latgalians in Latvia had belonged to the pre-partition Catholic Polish-Lithuanian Commonwealth, not to the Protestant Baltic provinces. Outside Europe, East Timorese nationalism set a predominantly Christian population against its Islamic Indonesian rulers, but the legacy there of long-established Portuguese rule that helped solidify the frontier between East Timor and the west of the island (and, indeed, the rest of Indonesia), with its Dutch heritage, was, perhaps, the critical factor. In each of these cases, then, religion pointed to a long history of separate paths of geopolitical orientation: it was seen as a marker of the ethnic community to which one belonged.

CONCLUSION

As we have seen, therefore, notwithstanding the extent of apparent secularization in the contemporary world, religion continues to constitute a powerful social and political force. It performs a vital psychological function in offering human beings the prospect of eternity – of life after death. To varying degrees, it also offers a path towards supernatural assistance in times of trouble in this world, through intercession with the other world. But at the social level it has a pervasive if not always visible influence in contemporary societies: again, varying from religion to religion, it has had an impact on the emergence of the modern state, with its educational and other public institutions.

The impact of religion on politics has also been profound. Especially in the past, churches commonly supplied political leaders, and church and state were intimately linked. This gave religion vital access to state resources, and it also gave the world of politics a weighty instrument for political mobilization, especially where it promoted values of self-sacrifice and group solidarity in respect of other religious groups (Hasenclever and Rittberger, 2000). Its impact may help to endow the state with crusading zeal in its dealings with other states, but it may also, in the case of denominationally divided societies, threaten the integrity of the state. Nevertheless, it seems clear that whether the national struggle ends in victory or defeat, having God on one's side is an important moral boost – victories are then divinely ordained, just as defeats are 'God's will', in either case legitimating the collective struggle.

As regards its impact on national identity, religion plays an uneven role. There are societies, such as China, where its significance is now slight. Elsewhere, even if society has become substantially deconfessionalized, the imprint of religion continues to be visible. This is particularly the case where, for historical reasons, religion has become embedded in the national myth, and membership of the nation is seen as implying affiliation to a particular religion. Since conversion between religions is exceptional rather than the norm, religion's stability gives it an important role in the long term in acting as a pointer to ethnic origin, and a mechanism for sustaining a sense of national identity.

Religion, then, may offer not just the promise of a better life to come but also a guide to action in one's current life. Its potential impact on nationalism ranges from overt ideological sustenance to indirect organizational support. But we need to be careful to distinguish cause and effect. The discussion above has focused on the impact of religion on nationalism, but the symbiotic nature of this relationship should be borne in mind. Ethnic religion may well promote nationalism, but nationalism is also likely to encourage ethnic religion. Similarly, although the pursuit of autocephalous status may encourage political nationalism, it is also in part a consequence of the latter (just as linguistic differentiation may be a consequence rather than a cause of political separatism). The processes just discussed *may* encourage nationalism, but they cannot fully define its contours: they may help to separate members of the nation from persons of other denominations, but they also link them with the rest of what is claimed to be a universal church except in the case of ethnic religions. We need, therefore, to look further in accounting for the more intense patterns of nationalism with which even universalistic religions are sometimes associated.

5

NATIONALISM AND HISTORY

INTRODUCTION

In the course of the 1990s, as Australians debated their past – and in particular the legacy of the dispossession and marginalization of the aboriginal population – tempestuous 'history wars' broke out, dividing both professional historians and political leaders. On one side were advocates of what has been described as the 'three cheers' version of Australian history, celebrating the country's achievements; on the other was the 'black armband' approach, sympathetic to the plight of the aborigines. Prime Minister John Howard sided strongly with the former:

> This black armband view of our past reflects a belief that most Australian history since 1788 has been little more than a disgraceful story of imperialism, exploitation, racism, sexism and other forms of discrimination. I take a very different view. I believe that the balance sheet of our history is one of heroic achievement and that we have achieved much more as a nation of which we can be proud than of which we should be ashamed (McKenna, 1997).

In this, Prime Minister Howard was articulating a very characteristic view of nationalist leaders, to the effect that the presentation of history should reinforce a positive self-image of the nation. Public ritual commonly incorporates direct or implicit references to the past, and to historical continuity with the nation's ancestors. In the USA, for instance, Congress approved *The American's Creed* in 1918 – a statement of commitment to 'those principles of freedom, equality, justice, and humanity for which American patriots sacrificed their lives and fortunes'. But such examples of official thinking could be multiplied. In 1922, for instance, the aim of history teaching in newly independent Ireland was defined as being 'to develop the best traits of the national character and to inculcate national pride and self-respect ... by showing that the Irish race has fulfilled a great mission in the advancement of civilisation' (cited in Coakley, 1994b: 124). Similarly, a Syrian government decree in 1947 defined the role of history as being 'to strengthen the nationalist and patriotic sentiments in the hearts of the people … because the knowledge of the nation's past is one of the most important incentives to patriotic behaviour' (cited in Lewis, 1975: 65).

Recourse may be had to history and even to archaeology in justifying contemporary claims to disputed territory, as is clear from the very extensive historical section in the Israeli Foreign Ministry website and such official publications as *The land of promise* (Israel, 2003), or from the use in Palestinian schools of textbooks that state a prior Palestinian claim to the same land (Manor, 2003: 26–31). The value of archaeology to nationalists resides in its openness to a wide variety of interpretations, its potential to prove early occupation of particular territories and its capacity to identify sites that may become important national monuments (Díaz-Andreu and Champion, 1996:19–20). In settler societies, of course, its role is quite different, as in North America, where archaeology is seen as a matter for the indigenous population rather than for the 'nation' (Díaz-Andreu, 2001). Even a passing familiarity with the political uses of history will give meaning to the slogan in George Orwell's novel *1984*: 'who controls the past controls the future: who controls the present controls the past'.

Scholars have for long acknowledged the importance of historical memory (Smith, A., 1999). French philosopher Ernest Renan (1823–92) famously described 'the common possession of a rich heritage of memories' as a key ingredient in nationhood (Renan, 1896: 80). As one early observer put it:

> It is probable that the most potent of all nation-moulding factors, the one indispensable factor which must be present whatever else be lacking, is the possession of a common tradition, a memory of sufferings endured or victories won in common, expressed in song and legend, in the dear names of great personalities that seem to embody in themselves the character and ideals of the nation, in the names also of sacred places wherein the national memory is enshrined. … Heroic achievements, agonies heroically endured, these are the sublime food by which the spirit of nationhood is nourished: from these are born the sacred and imperishable traditions that make the soul of nations (Muir, 1917: 48–9).

Not surprisingly, then, new nationalist projects are associated with new approaches to the past. Thus, the study of the Italian language and history was given central status in Piedmontese schools after the 1848 revolution, with popular history books reflecting a new 'Italian' identity (Chilosi, 2007). Post-Ottoman Turkey was faced with a similar challenge of rewriting its history, much of it now centred on a celebration of the leader of the revolution and founder of the Turkish Republic in 1923, Mustafa Kemal Atatürk (1881–1938) (Wilson, 2007). Following the collapse of the Soviet Union, Belarus faced the challenge of creating a new national identity, based on a re-interpretation of the past (Leshchenko, 2004: 334–7). Ukraine faced a similar challenge, but was able to build on and broaden an existing tradition of nationalist history, though not without resistance in the more russified parts of its northeastern districts (Popson, 2001: 327; Kuzio, 2005; Rodgers, 2006). In Tajikstan, new school textbooks reflected a shift from the Soviet-era interpretation of the republic as home to many peoples to an emphasis on its status as home of the Tajiks, with their thousand-year history (Blakkisrud and Nozimova, 2010). In Montenegro, too, two versions of Montenegrin identity emerged, with competition between Serb identity and a more inclusive form of Montenegrin identity resting on different interpretations of the past (Malešević and Uzelac, 2007).

We need to look at three dimensions to the relationship of history and nationalism. The first is the nature of the process by which 'official' or 'national' history is produced. Second, it is worth exploring whether common features are to be found across the historical myths of various peoples. Third, the contribution of historical consciousness to national identity formation needs to be examined more directly.[1]

THE WRITING OF HISTORY

Normally, popular writing on history depends on the work of professional historians. But academic historians themselves do not necessarily agree on the nature of their enterprise. Some accept the famous but minimalist dictum of the nineteenth-century German historian Leopold von Ranke that history seeks to provide an account of 'how it really was' – to describe the past accurately. For others, history is an unfolding tale, where particular events can be linked to a broader theme, as in the 'Whig interpretation of history', an approach characterized by an apparent commitment to a view of history as a matter of inexorable progress, and its study as correspondingly value-laden (Butterfield, 1931; see also Collingwood, 1946; Carr, 1986; Day, 2008). It is, of course, a short step from detecting general themes in history to identifying specific historical trends, such as struggles for freedom, independence and unity of a kind that are close to the nationalist project.

It is not surprising, then, that historians provide ample material for political publicists and propagandists. Historians may be engaged in a quasi-scientific exercise, but many of them are also prepared to lend their pens to the nationalist agenda. It has been observed that South Slav (Serb, Croat and Slovene) historical textbook authors 'in their specialised monographs … produced works that met the criteria of impartiality expected of scholars, but in their school textbooks, their writings followed the national flag' (Jelavich, 1990: 176). In this, South Slav historians were not alone. Elsewhere, too, professional historians simplified the conclusions of their research, and textbook authors borrowed selectively in producing narrative national tales. This could result in the creation of versions of history that were replete with misrepresentations of the past, as in the case of many US high school textbooks (Loewen, 1996). There is nothing particularly surprising in this development. Indeed, to quote once again one of the more celebrated authors on the subject, Renan, 'forgetfulness, and I shall even say historical error, form an essential feature in the creation of a nation; and thus it is that the progress of historical studies may often be dangerous to the nationality' (Renan, 1896: 66).

Myths about the past thus have a particular importance for national identity, a point profoundly appreciated by the state (Berger, 2009). For this reason, the question of who controls

---

1 This chapter develops themes outlined in Coakley (2004).

their creation and dissemination is especially significant. Broadly speaking, there are two possibilities. First, and most obviously, the state authorities possess exhaustive resources in this respect, including control of the educational system (Breuilly, 2009: 16–17). The state can also influence or even control the public communications system, including the mass media. On the other hand, there are circumstances where regional counter-elites make a vigorous effort to challenge the dominant state perspective, perhaps using regional institutions or relying on independent political organizations. This distinction corresponds with one we have already seen in other areas, such as language and religion, and is discussed further in later chapters: all aspects of the nationalist project are strongly influenced by the extent to which nationalist elites already control state resources, or are forced to confront these. The versions of national history that are now dominant in western Europe were by and large created and propagated over a lengthy time-frame by the ruling political elites there, whereas in central and eastern Europe these were commonly created by counter-elites who had limited influence over state resources (though they often had considerable influence at a substate level).

State institutions and historical myth

In the typical established modern state, the creation of historical myth was a routine and uncontested matter – something so taken for granted that it formed part of a kind of 'banal nationalism', a set of values that forms an unquestioned backdrop to everyday life (see Billig, 1995). The history of the ruling dynasty provided the core of the story: its achievements were glorified and its shortcomings, if acknowledged at all, were explained away. Royal institutions symbolized long historical continuity, and this was documented in genealogical accounts of the evolution of the dynasty and of its role in parenting much of the political establishment. State ritual reinforced this, providing a continual reminder of the antiquity of the ruling institutions. Thus, in Britain, coronation ceremonies, state funerals, royal marriages, the trooping of the colour on the Queen's birthday and Remembrance Day all serve to bolster the image of a nation deeply rooted in history. Veneration of the monarchy became possible in the late nineteenth century precisely because the monarch's real powers had been lost; as in other monarchies, such occasions were ones of 'invented ceremonial splendour', though still incorporating some venerable traditions (Cannadine, 1983: 120–1, 161). While the intentions of those behind such ceremonies are clear, though, we cannot always be sure of their actual impact on spectators and participants (Uzelac, 2010).

Useful though monarchical traditions may have been, in cases where the monarchy collapsed or was altogether sidelined it proved possible to transfer the mantle of legitimacy seamlessly to the new order: it was easy for republican regimes to replace the crown with 'the people'. Thus, the post-revolutionary French state was able to redefine much of the heritage of the monarchy and eventually create new commemorative occasions, such as Bastille Day. New states could also follow this path: in the United States, Independence Day, Memorial Day and the anniversaries of Washington's and Lincoln's birthdays serve a similar function (Lane, 1981: 252–84). Such national days seem to act as 'powerful tools that bind past, present and future generations together' (Elgenius, 2007: 88), a central function of the nationalist mission.

The public narrative of the life of the state was also reported in state almanacs and private serial publications reporting on and highlighting the antiquity of the dynasty. Here, but also in states where there is no royal family, accounts of the history of the state appeared in the writings of professional historians linked to different types of learned institution. The universities of course played a central role in this process, but national science academies supplemented this (their sphere extended over humanities disciplines such as history in varying degrees). Early examples of scientific bodies whose sponsorship of learning covered the whole spectrum of disciplines include the Académie française (1635), the Leopoldine-Caroline Academy of the (German) Holy Roman Empire (1652), the Royal Society (1660) in London, and the Academies of Science in Berlin (1711), Saint Petersburg (1725), Stockholm (1739) and Copenhagen (1742). Quite apart from the volume of literature deriving from these sources, various private individuals wrote about aspects of their country's history, whether for specialist readerships or for the general public; and, especially as literacy levels increased, popular accounts of vivid episodes in the past and other forms of related popular literature were produced on a large scale.

The historical narrative emanating from the state was not always particularly successful in securing widespread acceptance, especially when its efforts were half-hearted. This was clearly the case in the Russian, Austro-Hungarian and Ottoman empires, but even in western Europe the project of creating a state history that would embrace all of the people proved too great a challenge in certain cases. Thus, one study of Spain has concluded that separatist tendencies in Catalonia and the Basque Country may be traced back to a failure to invent 'a national history that is more than the sum of the separate histories of its component nationalities' (Boyd, 1997: 307). Even more dramatically, the United Kingdom altogether failed to create a 'national' history. There were, of course, many histories of England, and quite a few of Scotland, of Wales and of Ireland, but histories of Great Britain were rare, and histories of the United Kingdom virtually non-existent – a reality that no doubt reflected big regional differences, but also contributed to them (see Kearney, 1989: 1–9). Instead, absence of territorial integration was reflected in the existence of separate academies in Scotland (the Royal Society of Edinburgh, 1783) and Ireland (the Royal Irish Academy, 1785), and mass education systems entirely independent of the English one developed in these countries in the nineteenth century.

Outside Europe, there were similar issues. In Latin America, no single pattern for the construction of a myth of the past has emerged. In some cases, such as Mexico, Creole elites (descendants of European settlers) appealed to pre-hispanic culture, and in particular to the architectural and artistic legacy of the Aztecs. In others, such as Peru, perhaps for fear of promoting an indigenous revival, their counterparts rejected this past and stressed the creation of a new national culture, notwithstanding the rich heritage of the Inca empire. Further south, in Argentina, Chile and Uruguay, the indigenous past was dismissed as uncivilized and barbaric (Gutiérrez, 2007). The African experience was similarly varied. In Zimbabwe, efforts to create a 'national' history enjoyed uneven success, with a particular version lending support to the Mugabe regime, but in Kenya the state 'lost control of the past' (Ranger, 2009). In Australia, similarly, as we have seen, disputes over the status of the aboriginal population extended from academic and public debate to the presentation of material in the National Museum of Australia (Wellings, 2009). One distinctive view was expressed by a nationalist commentator in the 1930s: Australia was 'a country without any castles or ruins … not staled by history and tradition' (Moran, 2002: 1019). This was a country in which land could be freely occupied by settlers in accordance with the doctrine of *terra nullius* (the notion that the land belonged to no-one and was therefore available for settlement). Such dismissal of pre-colonial history extended elsewhere. British historian Hugh Trevor-Roper dismissed the prospects for African history: 'at present there is none, or very little: there is only the history of the Europeans in Africa. The rest is largely darkness, like the history of pre-European, pre-Columbian America. And darkness is not a subject for history' (Trevor-Roper, 1965: 9). Such a narrow interpretation of 'history' itself serves political ends, and it has in any case been refuted by the work of African historians (Falola, 2001: 223–60).

Non-state institutions and historical myth

The difficulty of the state in controlling ideological production in certain of the cases discussed above was complemented by the relative success of regional interests in presenting an alternative ideological structure. In certain Latin American countries, such as Ecuador and Bolivia, it was the indigenous population that exploited the pre-hispanic past (Gutiérrez, 2007). In many parts of Europe, the absence of a state presented a formidable challenge to would-be nation builders. The problem was especially acute in cases where (as for the Estonians, Latvians, Slovenes and especially the Slovaks) the home territory did not enjoy any reasonable degree of administrative autonomy, and might not even have had a name. By contrast, where some kind of autonomous institutions existed (as in Finland, Ireland or Bohemia), these provided a potential focal point for the production of 'national' history. This potentially subversive process typically took place under royal patronage, and with the active encouragement of members of the loyal local nobility, who were thus – usually unwittingly – sowing the seeds of future separatist nationalism (Coakley, 1980; see also Hroch, 2000: 11–12).

Some of the bodies that played a leading role in this process, such as the Royal Irish Academy mentioned above, the Finnish Society of Science (1838) and the Royal Bohemian Society of the Sciences (dating in its original form from 1775), resembled the broad national science academies discussed earlier. But others had a more specifically cultural or historical mandate, and were vital in promoting research into the largely forgotten or ignored cultures of their countries, and thus in providing material for nationalist myth makers. Examples include the Finnish Literary Society (1831), the Society of the Museum of the Homeland in Prague (1822), and the Irish Archaeological Society (1840) and its successors. Organizations of this kind also appeared in other countries which had a less developed infrastructure of learned societies. Examples include the Latvian Literary Society (1824) and the Estonian Learned Society (1838), crucial organizations in giving members of the local intelligentsia a mechanism where the people's past could be explored.

It is not surprising, in these circumstances, that a particular role in the process of nation formation has been attributed to individual historians. For the Czechs, the *History of Bohemia*

(1836–76) by František Palacký (1798–1876) played such a role (Zacek, 1964). Among the Bulgarians, the *Slavonic-Bulgarian history of the peoples, tsars and saints* produced in the eighteenth century by an Orthodox monk, Father Paisii (1722–73), had a comparable influence in the longer term (Crampton, 1997: 46–52). A work by Simonas Daukantas (1793–1864), *The character of the ancient Lithuanians and Samogitians* (1845), laid the groundwork for Lithuanian nationalist ideology (Trumpa, 1965). But the list of influential nationalist historians could be extended greatly – to include also the Transylvanian historians and Uniate priests Petru Maior (1756–1821), Samuil Micu-Klein (1745–1806) and Gheorghe Şincai (1754–1816) for the Romanians, Mykhailo Hrushevsky (1866–1934) and others for the Ukrainians, and Antonio de Bofarull (1821–92) for the Catalans.

Aside from output formally described as 'history' (which varied greatly in scholarly quality), popular quasi-historical writing about the past and works of historical fiction were also produced on a considerable scale. This form of nationalist writing was frequently more accessible to the public than straightforward historical works: the popular literary output of Zacharias Topelius (1818–98) in Finland, for instance, or the historical novels of Sir Walter Scott (1771–1832) in Scotland. Indeed, literary-historical works (including novels, stories and poetry that presented idealized images of the past) played a considerable role in the growth of nationalism among the Ukrainians, Czechs, Poles and Danes (Brunn, 1992b: 331).

NATIONALIST HISTORY

Whatever the mechanisms by which 'national' history came into existence, it is reasonable to expect certain common themes to emerge (for example, we would expect it to celebrate the past greatness of the nation). It is indeed likely that the instrumental considerations that lie behind the nationalist version of history will result in the highlighting of certain episodes in the past, and the downplaying of others. There is much to be said for the judgement of an acute Romanian observer that 'history always justifies everything' (Boia, 2001: 46). As a leading political scientist put it some decades ago:

> The early nationalist, like the religious reformer … professes to be rediscovering when indeed he is innovating. History serves him as a grab-bag from which he instinctively selects past themes that suit his present purpose … the historical themes he invokes are significant not as hypotheses of historic causation but as part of a psychological search for symbols of confidence in the present (Rustow, 1967: 40–2).

Common themes running through nationalist history are by no means confined to the glorification of a nation's past and the demonization of its enemies, as may be seen from an examination of the many case studies of nationalism in particular countries, and useful comparative analyses and overviews (for example, Znaniecki, 1952: 35–45, 83–100; Smith, A., 1984, 2000a; Brunn, 1992b; Schöpflin, 1997; Wilson, 1997; Thiesse, 1999). These themes are typically combined to form a nationalist myth of history. 'Myth' here is not intended to imply historical inaccuracy; the term is used to describe 'an imaginary construction …

which serves to highlight the essence of cosmic and social phenomena, in close relation to the fundamental values of the community, and with the aim of ensuring that community's cohesion' (Boia, 2001: 29). In principle, we find three types of historical myth in nationalist historiography: myths of origin (which relate to two rather distinct issues, the remote ancestry of the nation and its moment of 'birth'); myths of development (dealing with such characteristic topics as the golden age, the dark age and the age of struggle); and myths of destiny (with two common themes, the notion of the national mission and, in some cases, an aspiration for the restoration of the national territory).

The importance of these themes tends to vary from one nationalist movement to another. But it is striking that elements of each of these types of myth are potentially present in all nationalist movements. These may be difficult to detect, especially if the raw materials for particular types of claim are inadequate. For example, it is not easy for Slovene nationalists to point to a medieval 'golden age', nor for their English counterparts to identify an 'age of oppression'; and defining a 'national mission' may not be easy in all cases. Nevertheless, if standards of historical evidence are relaxed sufficiently (as they commonly are), it is likely that versions of history of a most improbable kind will appear, though not necessarily themselves the work of mainstream historians. Imaginative embellishments of this kind are not always incorporated in the most generally accepted version of the national historical myth, though they may have some influence over its content.

Myths of origin

Of all components of the nationalist myth, the most ubiquitous is the effort to account for the origins of the nation; such an account seems to be an essential ingredient in any nation's self-conception. Chapter 9 discusses (and dismisses) primordialist interpretations of nationalism, which see it as a long process extending over centuries rather than a phenomenon of relatively recent history, associated with large-scale social and economic change over the past two centuries. But the primordialist interpretation of the nation is central to nationalist self-understanding: normally, a single group or a single people is identified as the prime ancestor (Connor, 1992). This may also be further elaborated, through the identification of a specific moment that marked the birth of the nation.

The genealogy of the nation.   The capacity to trace a people's roots to an ancient and noble heritage has obvious implications for national solidarity. Sometimes, it is apparently easy to establish such a connection, perhaps because the contemporary nation still resides in the land of its claimed ancestors. Thus the Greeks of today identify with the glories of ancient Greece; Scandinavians trace their origins to the bellicose but adventurous seafaring Vikings; and Germans can look back to the sturdy Teutonic tribes.

In other circumstances, the draw of ancient ancestry is even stronger. The more miserable a people's standing in the present, arguably, the greater the attraction that is offered by any apparently convincing argument that those same people are descended from noble forebears (Glatz, 1983). Thus, it must have been gratifying for peasants in the Highlands of Scotland to learn that their ancestors came from an ancient, great Celtic realm in Asia, and that their Gaelic language was 'the language of Japhet, spoken before the deluge, and probably the speech of Paradise' (Shaw, 1780: preface). This formed part of a pattern by which similar biblical origins were claimed for Flemish, Welsh, Danish and several other languages (Edwards, 2009: 103–10). One enthusiastic Magyar scholar claimed that Adam was a Magyar, and similarly extravagant claims were made regarding the ancient roots of the Serbs (Jászi, 1961 [1929]: 264). More recently, similar claims have been made for the Maronites of Lebanon, one of whose interpreters asserted in 1984 that they were descended from the Phoenicians and that they had been located in the same area for three million years (Joseph, 2004: 198–200).

Links to biblical personages are a recurring theme in myths of descent. For Christians, the Old Testament possesses a particularly elevated standing, and claims have been made on behalf of some of the smaller peoples of western Europe to their having descended from one of the tribes of Israel. Examples include 'British Israelites' in Northern Ireland, claiming descent from Abraham and Jacob, and some Welsh voices in the past, claiming descent from one of the grandsons of Noah (Williams, 1988; Buckley, 1989: 183; Morgan, 1983: 67). The fabled warrior peoples of the east provided further impressive potential as ancestors: early Polish historians could claim a Sarmatian origin for their people, and their Hungarian counterparts could stress their Scythian ancestry (Hensel, 2002). The Roman empire also provided an attractive model, and we find claims among Lithuanian nationalists that their people were of Roman descent (Puzinas, 1935: 3–10). Romanians, similarly, argued that they were descended from Roman colonists in Dacia (Buse, 2002). Albanians claimed to represent the ancient Illyrians, renowned already in the age of Homer – and thus predating Slav presence in this part of the Balkans.

In other cases, emphasis on biological ancestry is replaced by the notion of cultural affinity with a presumed ancestral group: the national historical myth acknowledges multiple origins in respect of descent, but asserts the primacy of just one (see Smith, A., 1984). Thus, Irish history tells of the settlement of the island by four groups of people before the Celts, and by others, such as the Vikings and Normans, at a later stage; but, in this view, the Celts emerged victorious against both their predecessors and later invaders, and constitute the true stem of the Irish people. Indeed, eighteenth-century historians traced these early settlers back to the Phoenicians and thus to the cradle of civilization in the Middle East (Hutchinson, 1987: 55). English history allows a romantic place to the ancient (Celtic) Britons, around whom the tales of Arthur and the Knights of the Round Table are woven, but stresses their defeat by the invading Germanic tribes (Jutes, Angles and Saxons); and it was the culture of the Saxon and the name of the Angle that was eventually to triumph – not only over the Vikings, but also over their Norman relatives whose dynasty eventually asserted its political dominance. For the French, the story was more complex: the heritage of the continental Celts, the heroic Gauls, was romanticized, as was their leader, Vercingetorix, but the political role of the Franks as romanized Teutons who created the French state was also acknowledged.

The birth of the nation. In many cases, national history incorporates a particular episode in which the 'nation' was crystallized into its 'modern' form. Quite apart from the issue of descent, it was important to establish a link between the nation and its territory.

This was relatively unproblematic where a claim could be made that the nation had existed in the same territory 'from time immemorial'. The Greeks, for example, claimed to have been located on the same soil since before the beginning of recorded history, giving them a particular entitlement to their land. The Basques, similarly, were claimed to be a pure-blooded race, descended from Noah, and located in their homeland since the Deluge (Greenwood, 1985). In Iran after the revolution of 1979, the new regime continued an earlier emphasis on the antiquity of the nation, which, once again, was said to be in its current location 'from time immemorial' (Ram, 2000).

However, in many cases the nationalist myth acknowledged a migration of the ancestors, even if at a particular point in time they settled permanently in their current location, thus establishing a decisive presence. The Irish and the Welsh, for example, acknowledged that their Celtic ancestors had moved across Europe, to settle eventually in Ireland and Wales. The Huns and Finns came from the east, to make their own of Hungary and Finland respectively. The Turkic Bulgars had also migrated from the East, but adopted a Slavic language and culture. In these cases, later nationalists identified with these particular population groups, relegating to a subordinate position the claims both of those who had been there earlier and those who were to arrive later. In many cases, they were happy to popularize medieval legends that associated the 'nation' with a particular incident, such as decisions made by the brothers Lekh and Czech, claimed ancestors respectively of the Poles and Czechs, to settle in their countries on first encountering them (a third brother, Rus, made his appearance later, and filled a similar role for the Ukrainians; see Nowicka-Jeżova, 2002). A similar tale about the settlement of the Hungarians on the basis of a decision by their ancestor, Arpad, was also popularized.

Not surprisingly, given the complexity of the early history of the nation, especially if it was associated with substantial population movement and settlement, nationalist histories often point to crucial dates in the establishment of the nation. For the English, the Battle of Hastings in 1066 (which marked the decisive establishment of Norman rule) was of particular significance; it led to the creation of the 'modern' English state in which the numerically dominant (Germanic) inhabitants were eventually to triumph (Melman, 1992). For the Irish, the Battle of Clontarf in 1014 (when Viking intrusions were brought under control) was of comparable, if admittedly less durable, importance.

Commonly, a strong link between a critical moment in the life of the nation and adoption of a new religion was identified. In the case of Norway, Denmark, Poland and Hungary, conversion from paganism to Christianity was seen as 'the nation's birth certificate'; similarly, the baptism of Clovis was interpreted as an important event in French history, even though at the time of his baptism Gaul was already Christian (Rémond, 1999: 109–10). For the Ukrainians, the adoption of Christianity and the baptism of Prince Volodymyr in 988 were later interpreted as a formative moment in the emergence of the nation (Berkoff, 2002).

Myths of development

Nationalist versions of history continue the story of the nation's past by recounting its struggle for independence and unity over the centuries. A relentless theme of national progress commonly runs through this, though the many setbacks on this path are noted. Three types of distinctive theme recur in these accounts: the primitive golden age, when national development flowered dramatically; the dark age, when the nation's path of development was cut short, typically by the intervention of foreigners (who either swept in an era of oppression or encouraged national disunity); and the national struggle to restore the golden age, by re-establishing the unity and independence of the nation.

The golden age.   One of the most characteristic – but not always obvious – episodes in nationalist historiography is the notion of the 'golden age', a distant period when the nation enjoyed its greatest achievements. Usually, three themes run through the notion of the golden age, and nationalist elites vary in the emphasis that they place on one or another of these. They refer to the politico-military world, the sociocultural dimension and the domain of literary achievement.

The vision of a glorious political and military past is exceptionally attractive to the politically marginal. Thus, Lithuanian peasants could be told that they were heirs to the vast Grand Duchy of Lithuania, which at its greatest extent in the sixteenth century stretched from the Baltic to the Black Sea. For the Czechs, the golden age was the reign of Charles IV, King of Bohemia in 1357–78 and Holy Roman Emperor, under whose rule Prague became one of the most important cities in Europe. For the Serbs, the golden age arrived in the reign of Stefan Dušan (1331–55), whose kingdom covered a large swathe of the Balkans, much more extensive than contemporary Serbia. For the Bulgarians, the corresponding period was that of the second Bulgarian Empire in the early thirteenth century. As Fr Paisii put it to his fellow-Bulgarians, 'In the entire Slavic race the Bulgarians have had the greatest glory, they first called themselves tsars, they first had a patriarch, they first became Christians, and they ruled over the largest territory' (cited in Todorova, 1995: 75). This was, of course, a singular piece of oversimplification, since the Bulgarians were of substantially non-Slavic origin, notwithstanding their embrace of Slavic language and culture.

Yet military prowess was not the only source of ancient greatness. For the Irish, more accustomed to losing battles than to winning them, the path of military distinction was unpromising. In an era when religion was important, though, greatness could lie in the area of spiritual achievement. The Irish golden age lay in the second half of the first millennium, when Ireland, the 'island of saints of scholars', was presented as shining like a bright torch in spiritually benighted Europe and sending missionaries forth to convert the European heathen. Holiness and fidelity to the truth in a world that was full of corruption was central to the self-image of many other peoples, including, most notably, the Jews. The golden age could be characterized also by significant social accomplishments. Marginal communities commonly claimed native adhesion to forms of primitive but impressive democracy, set against the authoritarianism of their oppressors – thus Ukrainian nationalists looked back to the era of the free community of Cossacks, while Poles, not always consistently, stressed their link to Slav democracy. Literary attainments were yet another pointer to a great past, as discussed in Chapter 6: many nationalist entrepreneurs tried to find a national epic that would emulate the importance of Homer's *Iliad* for the Greeks, and some succeeded.

The dark age.   For many nationalist movements, the 'dark age' was brief, or almost non-existent. For others, it was a dominant theme. It tended to take two forms – again, ones that were not mutually exclusive. The two had in common the notion of intervention by alien forces – either directly, by the assertion of explicit political and military control, or indirectly, through the fomenting of dissent and encouragement of political disunity. These resulted respectively in an era of national oppression and an era of national fragmentation. In this context, nationalist historiography served the useful function of identifying and, where appropriate, demonizing the external enemy, in some cases generating a catalogue of brutality and treachery on the part of this group and its agents.

The era of oppression is a very distinctive theme in nationalist historiography. It was, the argument runs, external intervention that brought the golden age to an end and ushered in a new period where the people were ruled, often with great brutality, by foreign masters. An example of a traditional nationalist interpretation of Irish history is presented in Figure 5.1. In this perspective, the Norman invasions of Ireland that began in 1169 initiated the process by which the country became subordinated to the neighbouring island, and marked the beginning of 750 years of 'English' oppression, characterized by unending conflict. Parallel to this, the independence of the Czech lands was gradually undermined, and the Battle of the White Mountain in 1620 marked the decisive subordination of the Czechs to the Habsburg monarchy and the beginning of the 'dark age' (*temno*). Further south, Bulgarian defeat in 1396 ushered in almost five centuries of oppression under the 'Turkish yoke'.

These examples could be multiplied, but in yet other cases it was unity rather than independence that was seen to be lacking. This was allegedly the case among the Germans, divided between many small states; and France, Denmark and to some extent Austria could be blamed, at least in part, for this state of affairs. In Italy, too, absence of unity was seen as deriving not just from internal divisions; the malign influence of foreign powers such as Austria was given some of the blame.

The age of struggle.   Myths of national oppression tend to be closely related to myths of struggle. If the ills of the nation were attributable to external oppression, then the struggle for freedom became an important theme. If the problem lay in disunity, then the solution was to be found in a rather different direction – in a struggle for unity.

The freedom struggle is one of the more powerful components in the nationalist historiographical myth. Over the centuries, the argument runs, the fight against oppression was unceasing – suspended, perhaps, for years or even for decades, but never abandoned. Four distinctive phenomena recur in nationalist tales of the freedom struggle.

First, there are many *brave heroes* whose military attainments helped to make the nation great or, at least, helped to sustain national pride. Some of these were presented as great military leaders, such as William Wallace (1272–1305) and Robert the Bruce (1274–1329) for the Scots, Frederick the Great (1740–86) for the Germans, and Michael the Brave (1558–1601) for the Romanians. Much more recently, the Inkatha Freedom Party in South Africa was able to build on certain aspects of the Zulu past – such as elevating the leadership role

Figure 5.1   A nationalist interpretation of Irish history

Source: Republican (Irish nationalist) wall poster (1993)

of King Shaka (1787–1828) in cultivating Zulu nationalism (Golan, 1994). Lesotho, simi-larly, sought to create an identity for itself that was separate from that of South Africa by stressing the legacy of King Moshoeshoe in creating the Basotho people, and highlighting the British decision in 1868 to exclude it from the Union of South Africa (Rosenberg, 1999). Other heroes were noble martyrs – for the Irish, Robert Emmet (1778–1803), who died to preserve the spirit of freedom (national martyrdom is, indeed, a common theme in this con-nection). Yet others were Messiah-type figures, who rose up to inspire their people and lead them to a new life, such as Joan of Arc (1412–31) for the French. This category forms an abundant store for the creation of national statues and monuments, and can form the basis for a powerful nationalist hagiography.

Second, there are *dishonourable traitors* who, by siding with the enemy, undermined the national struggle. Many of these are reported as having died gruesome deaths, and suffered dishonour both before and after leaving this life. This was the alleged fate of Dermot MacMurrough (1110–71), responsible for the Norman invasion of Ireland. In England, Guy Fawkes (1570–1606), noted for his unsuccessful attempt to blow up the Houses of Parliament in 1605, played a similar role in the catalogue of national traitors.

Third, there are *glorious victories*, when the armed forces of the nation managed to defeat a powerful enemy (though typically winning only the battle, not the war). Again, these are sometimes the subject of physical monuments or later rituals (for example, the lifting of the siege of Derry in 1689 and the Battle of the Boyne in 1690 are still vividly remembered by Ulster Protestants, and commemorated by marches each August and July respectively).

Finally, there are *honourable defeats*, where the national forces fought bravely but were overcome by superior numbers and, perhaps, by treachery. There is less cause to remember these, but they nevertheless occupy a distinctive place in nationalist memory, since they show that even in its darkest hour the nobility of the nationalist cause can survive (examples are the Battle of Kinsale in 1601 for the Irish and the Battle of the White Mountain in 1620 for the Czechs; see Petráň and Petráňová, 1998).

In the case of movements for unity, the national struggle is seen as pitting the nation-building elite against retrogressive, parochial forces that stand as obstacles to unity. But an external dimension may also be present, as is illustrated by the story of William Tell, the legendary Swiss hero of the fourteenth century who fought against the Austrians.

Myths of destiny

What does the future hold for the nation? Nationalist historiography offers two types of answer, one general and vague, the other specific and politically loaded. The first is the identification of some kind of 'national mission'. The second is the identification of the ancestral 'national territory', the target territory of the nationalist movement.

The national mission. The idea that a particular people may have a distinctive mission within humanity is a recurring one in nationalist ideology. Not only may there be individual Messiah-type figures who participate in the national movement, the nation itself may have a messianic function to perform. First, it may be endowed with an important political function – to demonstrate to others how they should govern themselves, if not to do it for them, and to uphold the rule of law. Second, it may have crucial functions to perform in the socioeconomic domain – to promote notions of material innovation and progress. Third, and quite differently, it may have a spiritual or intellectual mission to uphold.

The notion of a national political mission will necessarily be confined to those countries which themselves possess a distinguished record of contemporary achievement (for smaller nations, any political mission must be sought in other directions – in the promotion of ideals of internationalism, for instance). Thus, as Europe's powers began to flex their muscles in the late nineteenth and early twentieth centuries, the judgement that their way of life was superior to that of the developing world (with the British shouldering the 'white man's burden' and the French undertaking a *mission civilatrice*) gained increasing currency (see Chapter 2). Imperial intervention in Africa and Asia could thus be justified in part on the grounds that it was bringing the benefits of civilization to the native populations. This was carried a step further by the Nazi state, and those peoples who found themselves under communist rule were similarly assured by their elites that their 'more advanced' system of political and economic organization should be exported to other parts of the world. Nor have these images perished with the end of the Cold War: American nationalism continues to rest heavily on a profound belief in the superiority of the 'American way of life', and in the appropriateness of its adoption in other parts of the world (a belief that is not incompatible with periods of isolationism and withdrawal from international involvement).

But if the American national historical myth rests substantially on an image of political harmony and military power, it also has a second, more technocratic strand: the 'American way of life' implies not merely a particular form of democracy but also a free market economy and a compelling commitment to socioeconomic 'progress' (Loewen, 1996: 254–70). For other nations, too, the national self-image may be strongly linked to notions of economic and technological advance (this was the case with the English after the Industrial Revolution, for example, and for the Japanese in the latter part of the twentieth century). On a smaller scale, adjacent populations could seek to project contrasting images of each other. Thus, Catalans were claimed to be 'practical, economical, realistic people possessing a work ethic', a distinctive form of civilization setting them apart from the more backward Castilians (Brunn, 1992a: 149), and the Ulster Protestant self-image as a progressive, entrepreneurial people set that community apart from the image of economically regressive Irish Catholics.

For smaller, poorer countries, or for more marginal ones, neither political nor economic models are likely to be sufficiently impressive to constitute an example to the world. Small peoples may nevertheless be able to find solace in their own exceptional virtues. For the Czechs, the values of rationalism and humanism could be advanced against the romanticism and militarism of the Germans, at least in the ideals of such leaders as Tomáš Masaryk (1850–1937). The Swiss could see themselves as 'an ideal paradigm of direct democracy and the sturdy defence of liberty' (Roshwald, 2006: 184). Elsewhere, a more profoundly spiritual mission might well have been defined. Religion often exercised a powerful force in this: the nation would 'play a part in the accomplishment of God's plans'. Poland, like Spain, Croatia, Hungary and the Romanian principalities, could present itself as a bastion of Christianity (Tazbir, 2002). It was similarly argued that Spain had a mission to spread the Catholic faith, and Russia a role as guardian of Orthodoxy, as heir to Byzantium and home to the 'third Rome'. For the Irish, the value of spirituality could be exalted to contrast with the materialism of the English (indeed, we find references to 'Ireland's spiritual empire', created by a worldwide network of Catholic missionaries capable of exerting a subtle religious influence, to rival the political empire of the British). The Indian mission was to save humanity from western materialism, through 'religious spiritualism and metaphysical profundity' (Kohn, 1946: 6).

Some national elites were able to present their nations as having a special role as a 'chosen people'. Leaders within certain national communities (such as Israelis, Ulster Protestants, Armenians and Afrikaners) indeed saw national existence as part of a covenant with God – one which might not just bless the 'chosen people', but also confer on them a mission to the rest of humanity (Akenson, 1992; Smith, A., 1992, 1996, 2003; Roshwald, 2006: 174–212). For a time this was also a component in France's self-image – as 'the chosen nation, called upon, after Christ's coming, to be the one to carry on the Israel of the Old Testament' (Rémond, 1999: 110–11). Similar elements are to be seen in Serb nationalism (Hastings, 1999).

The national territory.   If the concept of a national mission is lacking in precision, another component that is commonly to be found in nationalist historiography is more specific. This is the notion of the national territory. In Europe, this generally derives from the image of the golden age: the nation is entitled to re-establish its greatness by reconquering the territory that once belonged to it – even if much of this is now occupied by other peoples (see Coakley, 1983, 2004). But such views are to be found elsewhere. Chinese communist leader Mao Tze-Dong (1893–1976) expressed the view in 1936 that 'Burma, Indo-China, Korea and Mongolia are illegally annexed parts of China which must be restored to it' (Yahuda, 2000: 28). The concept of national territory thus acquires particular political significance because the territory in question is contested, part of it being occupied by members of other groups. But this need not at all deter the nationalist historical cartographer; as it has been put, 'a good propagandist knows how to shape opinion by manipulating maps' (Monmonier, 1991: 87).

Figure 5.2 illustrates the political impact of the image of the national territory. Where this becomes a politically salient matter, this is usually because this territory is much more extensive than the territory predominantly occupied by the community for which it is a target. The examples on the left of the figure represent three cases whose political significance is now less immediate. These include the Hungarians, whose 'Lands of the Crown of St Stephen' extended, *inter alia*, over Slovakia and Transylvania, and the Czechs, whose 'Lands of the Czech Crown' included the almost exclusively German Sudetenland (it is interesting that in the latter case the image of the 'national territory' did not extend to Slovakia, a factor that no doubt facilitated the break-up of Czechoslovakia in 1993). For the Lithuanians, the 'historic national territory' could be seen as extending over vast areas of Belarus and Ukraine; even the 'historic capital', Vilnius, was traditionally non-Lithuanian in its ethnic composition. The fact that Lithuanians would have been a minority in the most extensive definition of this territory, together with geopolitical realities after 1918, left the Lithuanians with only their ethnic territory; but following annexation to the USSR in 1940, Vilnius was 'restored' to Lithuania. One of the most striking examples is the case of the Israelis, with their powerful image of the biblical lands, which until the mid-twentieth century were overwhelmingly Palestinian Arab in composition; but this ethnogeographical fact has done little to weaken the appeal of the image of 'the land of Israel' (*Eretz Israel*).

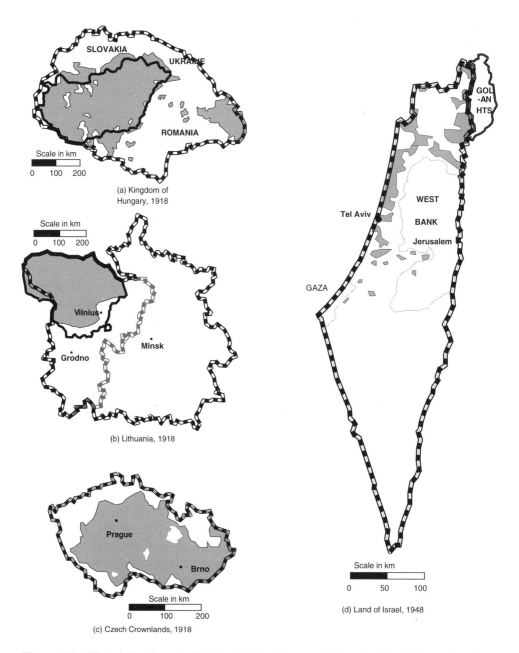

Figure 5.2 'Historic' lands and ethnic territories: Hungary, Lithuania, Czech Lands, Israel

Note: Dotted double lines refer to the claimed 'national territory' (in Lithuania, the thicker line indicates the maximum and the thinner line the minimum claimed territory); continuous lines indicate current international borders; shaded areas are those occupied predominantly by members of the titular nationality in 1897 (Lithuania), 1910 (Czech Lands, Hungary), or Jewish-owned land in 1948 (Israel).

These examples could be multiplied. Bulgaria, Romania, Greece and Turkey have all had conflicting visions as to how far their 'national territories' extend. The disputed status of Macedonia is a further example – a territory claimed at various times, using 'historical' criteria, by Bulgarians, Greeks and Serbs. Serbia has had its own difficulties, since its historical 'cradle', Kosovo, is now overwhelmingly Albanian, and the image of its national territory is an extensive one. Much of the conflict in the former Yugoslavia arose not simply from Serbian attempts to control areas in which they were ethnically dominant, but rather from vigorous efforts to translate this historical-geographical blueprint into reality. Finally, the Irish constitution until 1999 defined the 'national territory' as 'the whole island of Ireland, its islands, and the territorial seas', even though its northeastern corner, the British province of Northern Ireland, was predominantly populated by Protestants, who rejected the claims of Irish nationalism.

HISTORY AND THE NATION

The links between national identity and the nationalist version of history, with its overtly emotional content, seem obvious; they seek 'to justify the present with reference to origins and to link the two ends of history by means of intermediary markers' (Boia, 2001: 84). But it is appropriate to look in greater detail at the manner in which different components of the historical package respond to particular challenges in the nationalist mission – to explore the functions that nationalist history may fill in the nationalist project. This matter is addressed in the first part of this section. The second part examines variations in the impact of nationalist history.

Functions of nationalist history

There can be little doubt as to the overwhelming influence of nationalist historical myth. It has been argued that 'grounding national history on essentialised historical narratives contributed in significant ways to a politics of radical othering which justified diverse forms of exclusion and mass murder' (Berger, 2007: 24). Where the 'national mission' is seen as having biblical roots, for instance, it may provide compelling justification for the use of ruthless methods to advance the interests of the nation. Thus, the image of the Israelites slaughtering the Canaanites has been interpreted as offering a powerful role model for North Americans expanding into their own 'promised land' in the nineteenth century, and for Afrikaners on their 'great trek'; and the sense of being a 'chosen people' in the case of the British, French, Dutch and even Japanese 'aggravated the self-righteous zeal and casual cruelty with which members of those nations carried out their colonial conquests' (Roshwald, 2006: 182).

But it may well be the case that the components in the nationalist myth correspond to a range of more specific political functions. Having analyzed a large number of cases, John Breuilly (1993: 381–90) identified nationalist ideology as responding to three functions: *coordination* of heterogeneous groups behind a common set of demands, *mobilization* through appropriate political channels, and justification of the *legitimacy* of the national struggle in the wider world. This overlaps with a more detailed specification of the functions of nationalist history, as codified in a 'politics of remembrance':

- *definition* of the conceptual boundaries of the nation
- *reinforcement* of a sense of pride in national achievements
- *promotion of commiseration* over unjust suffering that justifies compensation
- *legitimisation* of the current national struggle by reference to its roots in the past
- *inspiration* regarding the bright future of the nation (Stevenson, 2004: 906–7).

This five-element classification forms a useful basis for helping to explain the significance of the various components that are to be found in nationalist historiography. It dovetails neatly with the set of themes identified above as recurring ones in nationalist history. The function of *definition* is filled by myths of origin, which can be used to persuade people as to their distinguished and exclusive ancestry, a consideration whose importance increases with deterioration in contemporary life conditions, as reflected in social status and material well-being. The myth of the golden age fills an obvious *reinforcement* function, demonstrating the capacity of the nation, when free, to express itself in ways of which all can feel proud, and offering the promise of potential regeneration (see Smith, A., 1996). The dark age, similarly, provides a reassuring explanation as to why the performance of the nation in more recent centuries has been less than impressive; to the extent that a single explanation may be forthcoming, this will be found in the phenomenon of alien intervention and oppression – a myth clearly calculated to *promote commiseration*. This, in turn, provides an important *legitimization* of the national struggle to re-create a free, united, independent state through which the nation can express its individuality – from 'golden age' through 'degraded present' to utopian future (Levinger and Lytle, 2001). The people can once again be made aware of the reason that this form of national self-expression is so crucial: the nation has a distinctive mission to humanity, one that should further enhance the sense of pride of its members. This tendentious version of 'national history', with its important *inspiration* function, can point also to more specific objectives; it can target a particular 'national territory' that ought to constitute the national home, and over which the nation should be able to exert full control.

Some elements in the nationalist mythology may be multifunctional. Thus the myth of origin not only serves to enhance the definition of the nation; it may also legitimize the national struggle, demonstrating that the nation's claim to a particular territory is strongest because it 'got there first', as in the case of arguments between Germans and Danes in respect of Southern Jutland, and between Austrians and Slovenes over their shared borderlands (Thaler, 2012). Disputes of this kind will also be found in Finland (Swedish versus Finnish), Sri Lanka (Tamils versus Sinhalese), the Czech lands (Germans versus Czechs) and even Northern Ireland (where some Protestants claim that the seventeenth-century 'plantations' that brought them from Scotland represented in reality a *return* to Northern Ireland, from where they had migrated centuries earlier). Similarly, the myth of the golden age fills a double function. On the one hand, it provides a people that may be suffering from socioeconomic and cultural deprivation with a self-validating image of former greatness, one that allows members of the nation to hold their heads high in a context where other nations enjoy much greater power and prestige in the present. But it also implies a political project for the future that is entirely compatible with the nationalist agenda: the reassertion of national freedom and unity are commonly presented as prerequisites to the re-establishment of the golden age.

Impact of nationalist history

Compiling an ideological package is, of course, only one step in the creation of an effective nationalist myth; ensuring its widespread acceptance throughout the community is another. Here, again, the outcome will depend overwhelmingly on one central issue: whether nationalist elites control power in their own state, or whether they are at the head of a movement whose objective is, by one means or another, to seize state power. In the latter case, the elites sometimes enjoy a good deal of formal power at the level of the region, but ultimately they are subject to the control of the authorities of the central state.

There can be no doubt about the range of resources that the modern state possesses when it comes to shaping the values of its citizens. Mass communications media are in varying degrees subject to governmental influence and control, and public education has normally been rigidly supervized. Since the nineteenth century, states have typically engaged in a process of civic education designed to turn all citizens into loyal subjects, either explicitly by the direct cultivation of loyalty to the symbols of the state, or implicitly through control of the curriculum in such sensitive subjects as history, or by both mechanisms. In addition to helping to disseminate an 'official' version of history, the state can also influence values through its capacity to control symbols and rituals. It is, after all, the state that determines regulations about display of the national flag, performance of the national anthem, design of coinage and postage stamps, construction of monuments, the holding of processions and parades, and all other aspects of public ritual, as discussed in Chapter 6.

Substate elites face a much greater challenge. Under liberal regimes they may have free access to the state media, and they may also operate an independent communications media system of their own; and at least under federal regimes they are likely to be able to exert a considerable degree of control over the educational system. Public monuments and statues may be independently funded, and parades and processions may be largely a matter of private initiative, and thus available as an instrument to nationalist counter-elites; but the state does, at least in theory, typically exercise the ultimate right of control over these symbols and rituals. States may, indeed, be extraordinarily tolerant of expressions of peripheral national autonomy. In such cases, the position of the state can sometimes appear incompatible with predictable criteria of rationality. In nineteenth-century Ireland, for example, British educational policy used the school system to promote values of tolerance (which required the exclusion of history from the curriculum, since Protestant and Catholic versions were in sharp conflict) rather than seeking to use the teaching of history to inculcate a sense of emotional affiliation with the state. Indeed, it eventually permitted the teaching in

Ireland of a nationalist version of history that was implicitly – but strongly – dysfunctional for the state itself (see Coakley, 1982, 1994b).

If, however, all else fails, and nationalist elites are unable to colonize or otherwise influence the curriculum in the state educational system in their own region, other options are open. Private schools may be established and, although these may be required to conform to certain conditions imposed by the state, they may be able to exercise a degree of curricular autonomy. Newspapers and public reading rooms, similarly, may be used to propagate nationalist forms of history (subject, of course, to whatever regime of control the state may wish to apply). But there are other agencies over which the state has no control: discourse in the family, informal story telling among local groups, and the intellectual endeavours of secret societies or openly organized independent clubs, for instance (Rerup, 1992). A powerful role may thus be played by forces far removed from state control – by 'the interaction of generations, the collective, unreflective memory of individuals and groups' (Brunn, 1992b: 330). By these and other means, particular images of the past may be preserved and disseminated autonomously.

CONCLUSION

Notwithstanding the idealistic targets professional historians may set for themselves, then, the 'historical' works that come to the fore as part of the process of nationalist mobilization owe little to the quest for truth and much to the pursuit of political goals. This is reflected both in the themes that are identified as central to the nation's story and by the manner in which these are interpreted. The significance of the different components in the set of themes discussed above obviously varies from one society to another. In some smaller 'nations' without even the elements of the history of a state structure in the past, the national myth may stress popular culture and folklore rather than political history, and some of the seven key elements may be skipped over. At the other extreme, in many countries with a long-established territorial identity and history of statehood, national identity may be so secure that there is little need to dwell on developments in earlier centuries. In some cases, indeed, regimes make a deliberate attempt to break with the past. The French revolutionaries sought to do so, declaring 1792 to be Year I and sweeping aside, with uneven success, much of the baggage of the past; and their American counterparts were similarly future-oriented, with Thomas Jefferson declaring that 'the dead have no rights ... Our Creator made the world for the use of the living and not of the dead' (cited in Gillis, 1994: 7).

The great value of nationalist historiography to nationalist political elites is, however, clear: it can be used to justify not only past actions but also current or planned political programmes. In many respects, its importance increases in proportion to the shaky nature of its empirical foundations; the nations which most need a myth of their 'great past' are those which do not have one. Historical memory may, then, play a major role in compensating for other 'shortcomings' in the process of nation formation. It has been argued that it has served to overcome differences of time and place among the Jewish people (Paine, 1989). We may, no doubt, expect a similar exercise in the creation of a common history to accompany the European integration project; and growing cultural diversity and disposition to acknowledge the role of indigenous peoples in other continents poses a significant challenge that may stimulate further revision of national historical stereotypes.

From the perspective of the elites who shape ideological messages, the creation, development and dissemination of historical myth are of central importance (though they are by no means the only instruments available in the battle for the minds of the masses). It helps politically excluded groups in their pursuit of power; and it helps those who already have power to continue to hold it. This is illustrated in particular by the manner in which historical messages are shaped to serve new political and social realities. Interpretations of the past have a necessarily fluid character, and we will find major projects in historical revision accompanying changes of direction in the nationalist project, as in contemporary Ireland, Quebec and central Europe (Brady, 1994; Cardinal, Couture and Denis, 1999; Auer, 2004: 16–18). Changes have been detected also in American school history texts, with idealization of Washington and diminishing emphasis on Lincoln reflecting the growing influence of conservatism (Hutchins, 2011). These processes pose particular problems to elites: as past events are reinterpreted, the clash between old and new becomes obvious, with potentially disruptive consequences.

Of course, it needs to be emphasized that stereotyped versions of 'national history' are but one aspect – albeit a central one – of nationalist ideology. They are embedded in a wider, more general myth of the national culture, one that extends to other areas such as literature, theatre, music, folklore and sport. We consider these more systematically in Chapter 6.

6

NATIONALISM AND PUBLIC CULTURE

INTRODUCTION

On 26 June 1969, the El Salvador soccer team defeated Honduras in Mexico City in a playoff to qualify for the World Cup, and the already tense relationship between the two countries spilled over into mutual hostility at popular and governmental level. A week later, following a break in diplomatic relations, open warfare broke out between the two countries and, though it finished within a few days following intervention by the Organization of American States, several thousand people had been killed and several hundred thousand had been displaced. The origins of the 'football war' were much more profound than the outcome of the match that sparked it: economic tensions associated with Salvadoran migration to Honduras were a major underlying cause (Cable, 1969). But the episode illustrates the extent to which a sporting event can apparently be associated with intense levels of nationalism and can have far-reaching political consequences.

Where do sport and other apparently non-political phenomena fit in the study of nationalism? A celebrated contribution by the psychologist Abraham Maslow several decades ago identified a 'hierarchy of needs'. Humans, he argued, respond to five needs that might be ranked upwards from the most basic, and only when needs at one level are satisfied do people move on to the next level: physical survival, safety (protection from danger), love (friendship and sense of belonging), esteem (desire for achievement and reputation), and self-actualization (self-fulfilment, or attainment of that of which one is capable) (Maslow, 1943). This provides a useful starting point for this chapter, where we begin with the implications of the pursuit of the most fundamental needs, such as shelter, food and clothing and their resulting material culture. We then move to two areas that – like nationalist values themselves – clearly respond to higher categories in Maslow's need hierarchy. The first is culture in a broad sense (including literature, music and the visual arts). The second is the topic discussed above: sport. Like the implications of 'history' for nationalism discussed in Chapter 5, those aspects of public culture which are associated with national achievement not only strengthen national solidarity, but also feed on it – they are both causes and consequences.

Table 6.1 Cultural dimensions of nationalist activity

Field	Type of cultivation		
	Salvage	*Production*	*Propagation*
Language	Research into grammar, vocabulary	Dictionaries, grammars, basic literature	Books; use of language in schools, newspapers
History	Preservation of historical material, archival work	Writing, publication of basic historical texts	Teaching of history in schools; museums
Material culture	Recording of artefacts, preservation of monuments	Promotion of 'national' buildings, dress, food	'National' architecture, costumes, cuisine
Intellectual culture	Collection of folklore, popular songs, folk art	Production of poetry, songs, ballads, art	Books; song and literary festivals; galleries
Sport	Compilation of data on folk games; preservation	Codification of rules of 'national' games	Promotion of competitive sports; stadia

Source: Based on Leerssen (2006)

Rather than continuing with a check-list of social characteristics associated with nationalism, though, it is appropriate at this point to take stock more systematically. Joep Leerssen (2006) has produced an intriguing three-dimensional model that runs the gamut of relevant cultural activities. First, borrowing loosely from Hroch (1985), he suggests a three-stage sequence that will commonly be encountered: *types* of cultural cultivation ranging from inventorization, through elementary production, to involvement of the masses. Second, he distinguishes four *fields* within which these types of cultivation may operate: language, discourse (including literature and history), material culture (including painting, sculpture and architecture), and 'immaterial culture' (including music, folkdance, pastimes and sports). Third, he effectively (but not explicitly) introduces a third dimension: the nature of the *agencies* responsible for this process of cultivation, whether 'bottom-up' (such as associations, reading rooms, clubs and newspapers) or 'top-down' (state agencies, including universities, academies and other official institutions).

The first two of these dimensions are cross-classified in Table 6.1. Leerssen's own table has been amended here by reorganizing the fields: literature has been grouped with the fourth category, here labelled 'intellectual culture', and sport has been extracted to form a fifth category. A further potential candidate that features in this book, religion, is not included: its distinctive organizational forms and universalist priorities place it in a different category from the fields listed here. The contents of the resulting cells illustrate the kinds of activity involved in each case. It is not possible to incorporate the third dimension in a table of this kind, but if the table is seen as a floor-plan, we may imagine a two-storey house where the first floor corresponds to unofficial agencies and the second floor to official ones. In each case, there is a corresponding cell structure. This model offers a useful framework for exploring change in three of the fields not so far examined: material culture, intellectual culture and sport (the other two, language and history, are the subject of earlier chapters).

117

MATERIAL CULTURE AND THE NATION

When peoples from remote parts of the world first came into contact, differences in material culture and lifestyle were usually the most obvious features that set them apart: housing, dress and culinary habits at first sight stood out even more than language and religion. Such differences were noted in many travellers' tales from the seventeenth century onwards. In the early nineteenth century, for example, the English travel writer Henry Holland described his encounter with a group of shepherds (who may be identified as Vlachs, a dispersed minority in the Balkans whose members speak a Romance language). They were making their annual journey from the mountains to the coast in what is now the Greek–Albanian border area. The procession, including about a thousand horses and flocks of sheep, with two Orthodox priests bringing up the rear, formed an astonishing two-mile-long entourage of a kind that was utterly unfamiliar to Holland:

> The greater part of the men were clad in coarse, white woollen garments; the females in the same material, but more variously coloured, and generally with some ornamented lacing about the breast. Their petticoats scarcely reached below the knee, shewing nearly the whole length of the stockings, which were made of woollen threads of different colours, red, orange, white, and yellow. Almost all the young women and children wore upon the head a sort of chaplet, composed of piastres, paras and other silver coins, strung together, and often suspended in successive rows, so as to form something like a cap (Holland, 1815: 92).

Differences in dress and lifestyle are just one aspect of material culture; they are considered here alongside two other components, housing and culinary traditions. In each case, it will be possible to detect elements of the kind of progression from 'salvage' to 'propagation' that Leerssen describes. It will also be clear that there is a tension between the ethnic and the universal. To the extent that the global population is divided in respect of housing, dress or cuisine, this tends to follow regional (rather than ethnic or national) lines. This refers both to 'supranational' and 'subnational' regions. There are, for example, recognizable similarities in East Mediterranean cuisine, so that the difference between a Greek coffee and a Turkish coffee may be down to whether one orders it in Athens or Istanbul. By contrast, big regional differences within Norway mean that folk costumes will distinguish people from, say, Gudbrandsdal from those from Hardangerfjord.

Settlement and housing

The history of housing reflects the story of human responses to physical geography, with, in one account, a progression through six stages, from the transient dwellings of nomadic societies, such as the Bedouin tent or the Plains Indian tepee, to the permanent buildings of sedentary agricultural societies, such as the Hungarian farmstead or the New England homestead (Schoenauer, 2000: 11–13). Urbanization promoted further evolution in housing styles, with the emergence of distinctive eastern and western cityscapes.

Many settlement types and housing styles eventually became associated with the ethnic communities that had developed them, and ethnographers have collected abundant material relating to the physical culture of the peoples of the world (see for example, Bromley, 1988). Notwithstanding its potential to reinforce national distinctiveness, however, ethnic entrepreneurs have made little use of the defence of traditional housing as an element in their programmes, perhaps because this would entail a hopeless battle against global forces.

The impact of globalization on vernacular dwelling styles has been profound, with a steady erosion of distinctive ethnic house styles in the face of plans and layouts imported from elsewhere, required by expectations of greater physical comfort, facilitated by technological developments, or imposed by the needs of modern city dwelling. New-style bungalows dot the Irish countryside where once there stood thatched cottages, apartment blocks have replaced the distinctive wooden dwellings of Finnish villages, and modern houses have supplanted the igloos of the Inuit. Commonly, these changes have formed part of a state modernization programme designed to enhance the living standards of the population. The policy of 'systematization' followed by the Romanian communist regime in the late 1980s is an example: designed to create a network of 'agrarian industrial centres' to replace what were seen as unviable villages, it was likely to have the effect (so calculated, western critics mistakenly asserted) of obliterating many of the distinctive Hungarian and German villages of Transylvania (Brubaker et al., 2006: 83–4; Turnock, 1991: 259). It is, indeed, likely that more homogeneous housing patterns will substantially confine those anxious to express their identity through their homes to reliance on such non-essential ornamental flourishes as coats of arms, religious symbols or flags.

When we move from the domestic to the public domains, however, we commonly find nationalists making use of public architecture. Ancient architectural monuments may be presented as physical evidence of the antiquity and artistic achievements of the claimed forebears of the nation (as in the case of the Giza pyramids for Egypt, the ruins of Machu Picchu for Peru, and the Forbidden City in Beijing for China). Many public buildings were consciously constructed to stimulate national pride (see Andrieux, 2006), and striking architectural works, such as the Sydney opera house and the Eiffel Tower, may become much-loved national symbols. Official reaction to such monuments (as represented, for example, by the destruction of statues in the aftermath of regime change) is an interesting barometer of the state's self-image (Pohlsander, 2008: 13–22). Recent examples include the removal of statues of Lenin following the collapse of communism in central and eastern Europe after 1989, the destruction of the statue of Saddam Hussein after the fall of his Baathist regime in Iraq in 2003, and attacks on representations of the Gaddafi regime in Libya following its overthrow in 2011.

Dress and costume

Like other aspects of material culture, the evolution of clothing reflected both matters of climate and availability of resources and technologies; and it responded in varying degrees to pressure for protection, for adornment, and for modesty (Rubinstein, 1995: 16–27). The notion of clothing as protection helps to explain much of the variation in styles over the long term, with climate playing a major role (Tortora, 2005). But historians generally take the view that clothing, far from simply providing warmth and comfort, was designed also to respond to other traditional or even irrational needs (Ribeira, 1986: 12). Dress type (including colour and quality of cloth, design and ornamentation) symbolizes the status of the wearer, sending an indirect but powerful message (Joseph, 1986; Roces and Edwards, 2007). The state commonly sought to regulate forms of dress through sumptuary codes, which determined what was appropriate for each social group. In Tudor England, for example, the use of crimson or blue velvet was confined to the nobility, gold and silver cloth to the higher nobility, and purple silk to the royal family (Hunt, 1996: 411). Female modesty was a priority in the Christian tradition, which attached particular attention to the dress of women, who were expected to bear the burden of maintaining chastity in a world of excitable men. The covering of women's hair among Christians was surpassed in certain Islamic societies by an injunction also to cover the face, and there were parallel restrictions in other cultures (Ribeira, 1986: 13).

Dress thus came eventually to be seen as a marker of several aspects of identity: ethnic background, class, age and, most obviously of all, sex. It may allow us to distinguish clearly between people who belong to certain occupational groups (such as soldiers or clergy) and those who do not, and to identify accurately the internal classifications within these – sometimes very fine ones, such as military rank and regiment. The association of clothing (and related aspects of appearance, such as hairstyle and, for men, types of beard) with particular ethnic groups is especially striking. In the Philippines, for example, *mestizos* wore a distinctive dress – a blend of Spanish, Indio and Chinese styles (Wickberg, 2000 [1965]: 33). In Greece in the past, traditional dress differentiated the Albanian, Sarakatsani (migrant shepherds speaking a Greek dialect) and Vlach minorities from the rest of the population, but already in the nineteenth century the characteristic *foustanella* (a piece of clothing resembling a kilt) worn by Albanian males had been adopted by Greeks as their national costume (Welters, 1995).

As in the case of language shift, a move from minority ethnic or regional clothing to that of the dominant group was often promoted by the state, which almost everywhere seems to have seen a potential threat in cultural distinctiveness, and even in clothing styles. Table 6.2 reproduces extracts from three documents, spread over four centuries, that illustrate this process in the case of the English state. The medieval statutes of Kilkenny (1366) represented an attempt to assert cultural control over English colonists in Ireland, seeking to prevent them from using the Irish language, but also from adopting Irish customs or modes of dress, or even from riding horses in the Irish manner (without a saddle). The Laws of Wales Act (1535) was directed against similar distinctiveness on the part of the Welsh, not just marginalizing the Welsh language but also seeking to eliminate the 'sinister usages and customs' associated with it. In Scotland, similar legislation in 1746, after the Jacobite rebellion of 1745, sought not just to disarm the Highlands (many of whose clans had mobilized behind the Stuart pretender to the throne) but also to ban Highland dress, including the kilt. On the other hand, a dress code is sometimes imposed on marginalized groups with a view to maintaining an ethnic boundary. In India and Sudan, for instance, many educated locals who wished to wear European clothes were discouraged by the British, as this 'implicitly

Table 6.2   England confronts the Celtic threat: selected legal texts

Statutes of Kilkenny [Ireland], 1366

Whereas at the conquest of the land of Ireland and for a long time after, the English of the said land used the English language, mode of riding and apparel, and were governed and ruled ... by the English law ... but now many English of the said land ... live and govern themselves according to the manners, fashion, and language of the Irish enemies ... whereby ... the allegiance due to our lord the King, and the English laws there are put in subjection and decayed, and the Irish enemies exalted and raised up contrary to right; ...

It is ordained ... that no alliance by marriage, gossipred, fostering of children, concubinage or amour or in any other manner be henceforth made between the English and Irish ... that every Englishman shall use the English language and be named by an English name, leaving off entirely the manner of naming used by the Irish; and that every Englishman use the English custom, fashion, mode of riding and apparel, according to his estate; ... that the commons ... use not henceforth the games which men call 'hurlings' with great clubs at ball upon the ground ... but that they apply and accustom themselves to use and draw bows and throw lances and other gentle games which appertain to arms; ... it is forbidden that any ... tympanours, poets, story-tellers, babblers, rymours, harpers or any other Irish minstrels shall come amongst the English.

Laws of Wales Act, 1535

Albeit the dominion, principality and country of Wales justly and righteously is and ever hath been incorporated annexed united and subject to and under the imperial crown of this realm ... yet notwithstanding, because that in the same country principality and dominion divers rights usages laws and customs be far discrepant from the laws and customs of this realm, and also because that the people of the same dominion have and do daily use a speech nothing like nor consonant to the natural mother tongue used within this realm ...

His Highness therefore ... minding and intending to reduce them to the perfect order, notice and knowledge of his laws of this realm, and utterly to extirp all and singular the sinister usages and customs differing from the same, and to bring the said subjects of this his realm and of his said dominion of Wales to an amicable concord and unity, hath ... ordained, enacted and established, that ... all [properties shall be inherited] after the English tenure, without division or partition, and after the form of the laws of this realm of England, and not after any Welsh tenure, nor after the form of any Welsh laws or customs; and that the laws ordinances and statutes of this realm of England ... shall be used practiced and executed in the said country or dominion of Wales ... all [law officers] shall proclaim and keep [all courts] in the English tongue; ... no person or persons that use the Welsh speech or language shall [hold office] unless he or they use and exercise the English speech or language.

Act of Proscription [Scotland], 1746

Whereas ... many persons within [named Highland shires] still continue possessed of great quantities of arms, and there, with a great number of such persons, have lately raised and carried on a most audacious and wicked rebellion against his Majesty, in favour of a popish pretender ...

Be it enacted ... that from and after the first day of August 1746, it shall be lawful for the respective lords lieutenants of the several shires above recited ... to issue, or cause to be issued out, letters of summons ... to bring in and deliver up ... his and their arms and warlike weapons; ... no man or boy, within that part of Great Britain called Scotland, other than shall be employed as officers and soldiers in his Majesty's forces, shall on any pretence whatsoever, wear or put on the clothes commonly called *Highland Clothes* (that is to say) the plaid, philebeg or little kilt, trowse, shoulder belts, or any part whatsoever of what peculiarly belongs to the highland garb; and that no tartan or party-coloured plaid or stuff shall be used for great coats, or for upper coats.

Source: Curtis and McDowell (1943: 52–9); Horn and Ransome (1957: 656–61); Williams (1967: 556–60)

shook the foundations of imperial dominion, which were based on notions of difference' (Sharkey, 2003: 47).

Use of dress as a conscious expression of ethnic distinctiveness has been limited. The wearing of the kilt in Scotland was revived in a more elaborate form as part of 'the romantic rehabilitation of Highland dress' in the late eighteenth century, following the repeal of the Act of Proscription in 1782 – significantly, at a time when this had ceased to be the characteristic dress of the Highlands (Chapman, 1995: 8). The revivalists went further, attributing distinctive tartan patterns to different 'clans', entities which no longer had any kind of widespread reality (Trevor-Roper, 1983: 23–31). The African-American head-wrap, imported from West Africa and used by female slaves, was discarded as a symbol of servitude, but revived by a younger generation of African American women as a gesture of ethnic protest and solidarity (Griebel, 1995). The revival of the Palestinian wedding dress provided a similar symbolic link between a dispossessed people and their traditional villages (Seng and Wass, 1995). Such protests may also carry economic clout. In India, for example, Gandhi's *khadi* campaign was directed at promoting the use of Indian homespun cloth against imports from Britain as part of a nationalist campaign (Eicher and Erekosima, 1995: 160). Sometimes, a more restrained but expressive item is used. In the Philippines during the revolution of 1986, wearing yellow implied being pro-Aquino, while red and blue implied support for the Marcos dictatorship (Roces, 2007: 19) – a practice with many counterparts elsewhere.

In general, the effect of global social forces has been to marginalize ethnic costumes in favour of cosmopolitan wear. With its emphasis on difference, tradition and stability, ethnic dress contrasts strongly with world fashion (which stresses global uniformity, modernity and change), not just in its *haute couture* expression, but also in its mass forms, which include jeans, t-shirts, baseball caps, business suits and various types of footwear (Eicher and Sumberg, 1995: 299–301; Lentz, 1995: 283). There remain societies where local dress is worn on major festive occasions, such as weddings or national days. But, except where they are sustained by strong local cultures, ethnic costumes tend to disappear as items of everyday dress, as clothing associated with poverty is cast aside for modern, international dress. A quotation from one young indigenous woman from near the central city of Riobamba in Ecuador illustrates the attitude of those anxious to shed traditional clothing also in other parts of the world – and, indeed, of those keen to shed their traditional but peripheral languages, as described in Chapter 3:

> Now there are more and more Indian girls from other villages who go to high school in Riobamba who no longer wear the Indian dress. They are ashamed of their heritage and don't want to be treated like Indians anymore. They think they can better themselves socially by wearing other clothes and rejecting their parents, but they're fooling themselves. Classmates and others notice right away that they're Indians. They aren't accepted as real *mestizos*, but they do think that they're better than their parents. When relatives from the village visit them, they act as though they don't know them. They don't say hello, or they even claim to their *mestizo* schoolmates that they're their servants from the country! (Lentz, 1995: 287–8).

Cuisine and food

The aphorisms of the French epicurean Brillat-Savarin (2007 [1825]) draw attention to the link between food and politics: 'the destiny of nations depends on the manner in which they are fed', he observed, before raising the question of identity: 'tell me what kind of food you eat, and I will tell you what kind of man you are'. Of course, food provision is itself a political question, with big differences between states, and between social groups within states, as regards access to appropriate diet and general food security – an issue with clear political implications. Attitudes towards food are embedded in a wider world of eating rituals, and, indeed, of a broader etiquette governing social contact outside meal-times. Norbert Elias (2012 [1939]: 107–28, 472–8) has described how the west European aristocracies used elaborate codes of table manners as an instrument of power, useful not just in a domestic context but also in establishing colonial hegemony.

The relationship between food and national identity is reflected in the uncomplimentary terms by which members of one nation often describe another, as when native Indians of Canada refer to Inuit as 'Eskimos' (eaters of raw meat), English speakers refer to French, Germans and Italians respectively as 'Frogs', 'Krauts' and 'Macaronis', and the French retaliate by calling the English 'Rosbif', a corruption of 'roast beef' (Murcott, 1996). Some groups' aversion to particular foods may become a marker of identity, as in the refusal of religious Jews to eat the flesh of the pig in a pork-eating Europe – though this taboo was shared with other ancient peoples of the Middle East (Phoenicians, Egyptians and Babylonians) as well as with Muslims later (Harris, 1997 [1985]). For Hindus, it is beef, the meat of the 'sacred cow', that is avoided. In many cases, too, a 'national drink' is identified – Scotch (Scottish) whisky, Russian vodka or Czech beer, for example. By contrast, in certain societies it is abstinence from alcohol that constitutes a marker of identity.

The term 'gastronationalism' has been coined to describe a particular attachment to food as a symbol of the nation (there may be a covert economic dimension to this, as in policies of national food labelling within the EU) (DeSoucey, 2010: 448–9). Commonly, cookbooks play a role in producing a 'national' cuisine, as in France (Ferguson, 1998: 601), Iran/Persia (Harbottle, 1997: 106), India (Appadurai, 1988) and parts of Africa (Cusack, 2003). In its later years, the communist regime in Romania went a step further: it was planned that, as part of a programme of homogenization, the Romanian diet would be standardized – planned meals prepared according to scientific principles would be served in communal eating halls (Kligman, 1998: 35).

As objective differences disappear in the face of global economic and cultural integration, identities may, paradoxically, be reinforced, with competing communities highlighting marginal differences between them – what Freud (1963 [1930]: 51) described as 'the narcissism of minor differences', and Ignatieff (1999: 95–6) developed further in relation to rivalries between nations. An example is the phenomenon of the 'English breakfast', whose popularity expanded well outside its original upper-class base in the nineteenth century (O'Connor, 2009). Comprising a substantial meal whose classical centrepiece is a plate of fried egg, bacon, sausage and other ingredients, subtle differences converted the 'English' breakfast into 'national' variants elsewhere. Thus, in Ireland the addition of some fried black pudding converts this meal into an 'Irish breakfast'; and in Northern Ireland this is in turn converted into an 'Ulster fry' by the inclusion of potato cake. But ethnic narcissism can operate through more deadly agents than cholesterol: as Conversi (1994) observes, cultural similarity can be a factor in promoting intergroup violence, as in the case of Croats, Basques and Kurds, who have been substantially assimilated into an adjacent culture.

In a world of international trade, ethnic food, as van den Berghe (1984: 394–5) has perceptively pointed out, may fall victim to its own success. Thus the Italian pizza and German *Wurst mit Brötchen* became quintessential elements of American cuisine, thereby losing their distinctiveness; ironically, they were subsequently re-exported as pizzas and 'hot dogs' with a distinctively American flavour. Indeed, the forces of globalization had a big impact on national culinary traditions. French food itself is an example: it became an early international model, the cuisine of choice for many wealthy Europeans and Americans (Mennell 1985: 134–5; James, 1997: 75–7). Similar social processes were at work at other levels, as American food (such as burgers, Coca-Cola, and Kentucky Fried Chicken) became available throughout the world (Watson, 2005 [2000]). But the culinary traffic was not all in one direction: Asian dishes (from China, India, Japan and elsewhere) penetrated the West (Bestor, 2005 [2000]). As an indicator of this process, by 1992 Indian takeaways already outnumbered traditional fish and chip shops in Britain (James, 1997: 81–4). This culinary globalization has old roots; dating from the time of Columbus, it was stimulated by the Industrial Revolution and massive population movement in the late twentieth century, and facilitated by technological change (Goody, 1982: 154–5; Mennell, Murcott and Otterloo, 1992: 75). This process has not continued without resistance: McDonald's, Kentucky Fried Chicken and Coca-Cola have sometimes attracted the ire of anti-globalization protestors and other opponents of what they see as American imperialism, often expressed in boycotts and demonstrations (Watson and Caldwell, 2005: 2).

THE ARTS AND THE NATION

As Eric Hobsbawm (1995: 11) observed, 'art has been used to reinforce the power of political rulers and states since the ancient Egyptians'. The capacity of the arts to be mobilized behind the goals of nationalism became clear in early nineteenth-century Europe, with the emergence of the romantic movement (Artz, 1962: 224). Usually parallel to the efforts of linguistic revivalists, folk songs and tales were collected, patriotic songs and anthems were composed, historical novels and patriotic poems were produced, and the visual arts commemorated national landscapes and events (Thomson, 2004). Once again, the transition from 'salvage' to 'propagation' described by Leerssen (2006) is obvious. So too is the tension between the ethnic and the universal. David Aberbach (2003: 269) suggested that 'national poetry' is a contradiction in terms, since nationalism is public and poetry is private. But the arts pose a more fundamental dilemma: in their most developed forms, they are of universal, not just national, appeal. It is true that in their folk forms they may be presented as expressions of national distinctiveness, but in their 'high' art forms their appeal is potentially universal; they can be mobilized in support of the nationalist project only if they are presented as expressions of national greatness. Thus, Picasso, Dvořák and Hemingway may be projected as adding lustre to the national tradition of the Spanish, the Czechs and the Americans, respectively.

Literature

Given the emotive capacity of words, it is not surprising that literary output has been a formidable ally of nationalism (Sharkey, 2003: 127–33). As we have seen in Chapter 5, a 'rediscovery' of the past was a central component in most nationalist movements. But rather than simply dealing with facts about the past as historians did, it was possible for folklorists to seek to retrieve and popularize the wisdom and traditions of the people, and to celebrate the nation's literary heritage. An early generation of researchers sought to salvage folk tales, songs and poetry from the mouths of peasants and from the obscurity of libraries and other repositories. The work of Jacob Grimm in the early nineteenth century is an example: in addition to groundbreaking work in German philology, he collected old German folk songs, stories and poems, and with his brother Wilhelm published a collection of fairy tales, the popular abridged version of which would delight generations of children across the world.

Commonly, the material being unearthed was open to political interpretation, offering a perspective on the 'great past' of the nation. In Scotland, James Macpherson published his own version of the Gaelic epic, *Fingal*, in 1761–62, seen by English readers as refer-ring to a past that was sufficiently distant to be politically unmenacing (Pittock, 1991: 73). This had a major impact on nineteenth-century romantic nationalism in Europe, as others tried to follow his lead. For the Germans, the early medieval *Nibelungenlied* displayed the impressive extent of national cultural history. In Finland, the *Kalevala*, based on old folk songs, was published in 1835 by Elias Lönnrot, and had a major impact on Finnish nation-alism (Hautala, 1969; Wilson, 1978; Battarbee, 2007: 83–7). There followed its Estonian equivalent, *Kalevipoeg*, published by Friedrich Kreutzwald in 1857, with a comparable popu-lar influence (Raun, 1985). Similar Irish collections appeared, celebrating the Red Branch Knights and other mythical heroes (Hutchinson, 1987: 114). Sometimes, heroic tales were frankly composed with only a passing basis in folklore – the Latvian epic *Lāčplēsis* ('Bear slayer'), published by Andrejs Pumpurs in 1888, is an example (Viķe-Freiberga, 1985). But unacknowledged invention carries its own price. Macpherson's work was exposed in the nineteenth century as largely the creation of his own pen rather than that of its putative author, the mythical warrior bard Ossian. The Dvur Králové and Zelená Hora manuscripts 'discovered' by Václav Hanka in 1816–17 and apparently constituting a Czech rival to the *Nibelungenlied* were later exposed as forgeries (Mann, 1958). Likewise the *Chronicle of Huru* (1856), a literary historical work which purported to show continuity between medieval Romania and the Roman past, was also eventually proven to be a forgery (Boia, 2001: 47–8).

Outside the domains of the major languages of western Europe, a separate publica-tion infrastructure normally had to be established, and doing this was often an important contribution to the nationalist movement. In Hungary, the elites had been struggling since the 1790s to advance the position of the Magyar language in a two-sided battle against

Latin, the traditional official language, and German, the emerging language of the Habsburg dominions; and they won a signal victory in 1825 with the establishment of the Hungarian Academy of Sciences, designed to cultivate and publish in Magyar (Barany, 1968: 117–20). This encouraged leaders of the Serbs of Hungary to establish a similar body in 1826, the *Matica srbska* (Serbian foundation), to promote the Serbian language (which received little support either in its heartland, the autonomous Principality of Serbia, part of the Ottoman empire, or in independent Montenegro). The *Matica* became not just an important instrument for the promotion of Serbian literature in Vojvodina, but also the model for similar societies elsewhere in the Slavic world (Kimball, 1969). Thus, a key Czech counterpart, the *Matice česká*, was established in Prague in 1831, and maintained a very active publishing role for the rest of the century (Nolte, 2007: 86–8). Similar bodies were established to promote the language and literature of the Croats in 1842, the Slovaks in 1863, the Slovenes in 1864 and the Poles of Galicia in 1882 (Kimball, 1969; Herrity, 1973).

The contribution of literature to nationalism was not confined to the publication of the poetry and prose of struggling languages that were being revived. There was also a more established side to this among cultures with a longer publishing tradition, where literary figures were prepared to play their role in creating a 'national' literature and in inspiring their readers with patriotic values. Thus, Goethe and Schiller in Germany, Coleridge and Byron in England, Lamartine and Hugo in France, and their many colleagues and counterparts in other countries, helped to remould the character of literature along national, romantic lines (Artz, 1962: 240–66). Even where this tradition was weaker, significant literary figures emerged – for example, Petöfi, Mickiewicz and Pushkin in Hungary, Poland and Russia respectively, and a range of writers among the South Slavs and elsewhere.

Such literary movements were not always confined to the ancestral language. The Irish cultural revival of the late nineteenth century had an important linguistic dimension, but its literary expression was mainly in English, as figures such as Yeats, Synge and Lady Gregory sought to produce a new, hybrid literature that would be English in form (if making liberal use of Irish modes of speech) but largely Gaelic in inspiration; they sought, with limited success, to bridge the gap between the Gaelic and English traditions (Watson, 1994: 13–34). Later, in the newly independent states of francophone Africa, post-colonial elites sought to engage in nation building through the dissemination of officially approved literature from the centre. In the Congo, this process has been described as almost a manufacturing one, with top-down engineering by ideologues and state-sponsored official literature (Thomas, 2002: 2). In Asia and the Middle East, nationalist forms of literature also emerged, largely in reaction to European imperial intervention, as in the case of Tagore in India, Shawqi in Egypt, Rusafi in Iraq and Iqbal in Pakistan (Aberbach, 2010). The 'national novel' also played a role; it helped to shape patterns of national identity both in Latin America (Anderson, 1998: 338–59) and elsewhere.

One institutional consequence of the flowering of national literature was the establishment of national libraries to collect and house it. Alongside these went national theatres, important organs in national movements: it has been observed that 'words spoken from the stage made a deeper impression than primitive poems and popular novels' (cited in Kimball,

1964: vii). In the established states of western Europe, such as France and Britain, there were long literary traditions and well-established theatres. But political decentralization had prevented a similar evolution in central and eastern Europe. Among the Germans, despite Schiller's complaint that 'we will never become a great nation without a national theatre', theatres were tentatively born in the late eighteenth century, but initially performed relatively few German works (Kimball, 1964: 11). Such developments were slow elsewhere too. The Czech National Theatre, described as 'a monument and symbol of the Czech rebirth', was opened only in 1883, after a long struggle (Kimball, 1964: ix, 79). In Ireland, similarly, the movement to establish a national theatre was a vital component in the literary revival, culminating in the establishment in 1904 of the Abbey Theatre, conceived by Yeats as a 'national shrine' (Hutchinson, 1987: 134). Later, with the emergence of film, it became possible for nationalist views to be disseminated to much wider audiences through this dramatic and gripping medium.

Music

At first sight, music might appear to have less obvious significance for nationalism than literature: melody and harmony are politically neutral. But songs have words, and operas have plots, and these may either subtly or obliquely convey nationalist messages. A folk song rescued from disappearance in rural Ireland in the mid-nineteenth century achieved international fame for the beauty of its melody, but the addition of words and a title immediately raised political questions. Known to Irish nationalists as the 'Derry air' and to Ulster unionists as the 'Londonderry air', it symbolizes the ease with which music may serve a nationalist cause (O'Shea, 2009).

As we have seen, the collection of folk tales and poetry normally extended also to folk song, and the singing of tunes that reflected national history in many cases became a key component in the national revival. This could apply even in the case of religious or love songs – the theme might be universal, but the mode of expression was presented as 'national'. Epics and ballads were of particular interest to the apostles of national revival. The collection of Irish folk music, and its popularization by Thomas Moore in the early nineteenth century, played a crucial role in the national revival. Vuk Karadžić, a pioneering explorer of the Serb language, collected and published two influential volumes of what he described as 'Serbian' folk songs in 1814–15 (Wachtel, 1998: 32–3). In the late nineteenth century, the production and publication of anthologies of Yiddish songs in Central Europe strengthened the cultural basis of Jewish nationalism. There were parallel developments in Denmark. Sometimes, the state was involved – even in the case of Austria, where a major project, *Das Volkslied in Österreich*, that began in 1902 and aimed to publish the folk songs of the Austrian provinces in their entirety, was potentially subversive of the unity of that multinational empire (Bohlman, 2004: 56–7, 92–5).

Sometimes, musical activities assumed more organized forms – especially in the mid-nineteenth century, when choral singing spread across Europe, often inspired by religious values (Bohlman, 2004: 49–50). An example is the Welsh *eisteddfod*, a cultural festival with medieval roots that acquired a more continuous form in the early nineteenth century, culti-vating Welsh folk music and helping to promote the self-image of Wales as a 'land of song' (Morgan, 1983: 56–62, 74–9). From the mid-1820s there was a growing movement for the establishment of choral societies in the German states; these were able to escape pro-scription because their superficial objectives were artistic and non-political – 'the study of four-part male voice harmonies' (Düding, 1987: 36). By 1848, there were more than 1,100 of these, with at least 100,000 members, organizing festivals, developing a repertoire of patriotic songs, and adopting a national organization in 1862 (Düding, 1987: 36–45). This stimulated similar activity elsewhere, as among the Latvians (Karnes, 2005: 230). From 1869 onwards, great Estonian song festivals played a similar role. Initially organized precisely with the intention of stimulating a sense of national identity among the people, they later became a superficially non-political mechanism behind which a powerful but implicit political mes-sage could hide (Tall, 1985). From the 1860s, similar choral societies were established among the Serbs, Croats and Slovenes (Milojkovic-Djuric, 1985). These traditions have sometimes had relatively recent political relevance, as in the case of public song meetings in Denmark during the Second World War as a form of resistance to the Germans (Brincker, 2008) and the use of song festivals during the final days of Soviet rule in Estonia at the end of the 1980s – in each case, powerful but oblique forms of nationalist protest.

National anthems play a particular role in symbolizing the nation. The national anthems of European states are anything but 'national' as regards melodic structure; there is exten-sive cross-national borrowing. For example, the present German national anthem began its life as a Croatian folk song in what is now Burgenland in Austria, was converted into what later became the 'Emperor's hymn' by Franz Joseph Haydn in one of his quartets, was dis-carded by Austria in 1918, but then taken up by Germany, where it has managed to survive even its use as a 'battle hymn of German chauvinists' during the Nazi period (Eyck, 1995: 163–79; Bohlman, 2004: 51–5). The melody of the British national anthem, *God save the queen*, was also used in several other European states, and in the USA (as *My country, 'tis of thee*). The words of national anthems may cover common themes, including 'independence, liberty, unity, praise of country and countrymen, and hopes for future blessings' (Eyck, 1995: xiv–xvi). But the fervour with which the American national anthem is sung (with everyone facing the national flag and holding their right hands over their hearts) can leave little doubt about the emotional significance of *The star-spangled banner*, and this collective emotion is reproduced elsewhere, if in less demonstrative form.

With its dramatic content and capacity for metaphorical representation, opera has some-times been seen as a particularly potent instrument of nationalism. Italian opera has often been held up as an example, with Rossini's *William Tell* (1829) and Bellini's *Norma* (1831) depicting rebellion against a foreign empire (even if located in the Middle Ages or ear-lier). While it has been argued that the operas of Verdi did not represent nationalist intent (Rosselli, 2001), there can be little doubt as to their appeal to nationalist sentiment, notably in the case of such works as *Nabucco* (1841). But even non-political themes can serve the national cause if the music is sufficiently beautiful, as in the case of Smetana's *Bartered bride* (1866), an important cultural landmark for the Czechs (Bohlman, 2004: 83).

The development of 'national' music did not necessarily begin and end with the collection and popularization of folksongs. These were frequently later transformed into 'high cultural music', and used by established composers (Schöpflin, 2001: 194–5). The best-known examples of composers whose work was embraced as 'national' include Dvořák and Smetana for the Czechs, Bartók and Kodály for the Hungarians, Borodin, Rimsky-Korsakoff and Moussorgsky for the Russians, Sibelius for the Finns, Vaughan-Williams for the English, Grieg for the Norwegians, and Schumann and Wagner for the Germans. There were parallel developments in the Balkans, among Romanians, Bulgarians, Serbs and Greeks, and the music of Chopin was celebrated by Polish nationalists (Samson, 2007).

Quite apart from musical content, instruments themselves may have associations with particular peoples. Thus, Russian music is commonly associated with the balalaika, Spanish flamenco music with the nylon-stringed guitar and Indian music with the sitar. In Hungary, a status of national authenticity was attributed to the *tarogato* (a double-reed wind instrument), which was adopted as a national symbol (Schöpflin, 2001: 196–7). In Wales, the triple harp (a version of the Italian baroque harp) began to be seen in the early nineteenth century as 'the ancient national instrument' (Morgan, 1983: 77), while in Scotland it was the bagpipes that came to be seen as distinctively linked to the national tradition. Such priorities are often recorded in musical museums, which reflect perceptions of the role of music and of musical instruments in the national story, whether these express national distinctiveness, as in Hungary and Slovakia, or imperial achievement, as in France (Bohlman, 2004: 25–7).

Visual arts

As in the case of music and literature, an early generation of national revivalists saw the collection of objects of folk art as a significant activity. Like them, too, art has a global character that cuts across national boundaries. Nevertheless, efforts to cultivate a distinctive 'national style' in such areas as painting have been common. In the nineteenth century, the rise of nationalist ideology provoked a shift in emphasis away from a shared European past, as painters and sculptors began to abandon biblical and classical themes, taking on instead themes from 'national history' (Storm, 2009: 557). A new genre of 'historical' painting began to show the influence of vernacular styles, artists addressing a much wider audience than the aristocracy and the upper bourgeoisie, and pursuing original and distinctive approaches (Facos and Hirsh, 2003: 5–9). 'National' art helped to idealize the nation, highlighting its symbols, history, heroes and folk, as well as its landscapes (Leoussi, 2004).

The new emphasis on national history was largely focused on rural folk and scenery, with a tendency towards strong regional imagery. This was reflected, for example, in sculpture and painting in nineteenth-century France, with its glorification of Vercingetorix and the ancient Gauls – an ambiguous cult of the Celtic past that could serve the ideological interests not just of the nation-state, but also those of regional resistance, and even of pan-European integration (Dietler, 1994). Often, contemporary themes reflected current ethnonational tensions, as in Picasso's *Guernica* (depicting the bombing of the Basque town of that name in 1937).

129

The state was also prepared to mobilize the arts. In the early nineteenth century such established states as Britain, France and Spain sought to establish new links between national identity and public art. The royal collections of France and Spain formed the core of new national galleries, the Louvre (1793) and the Prado (1819); in England, by contrast, the royal collections remained precisely that, resulting in the foundation of a separate, autonomous National Gallery supported by parliament in 1824 (Tomlinson, 2003). As in the case of other great 'national' institutions like theatres, museums and libraries, the possession of a 'national' gallery became an important target for nationalist efforts in smaller countries as well.

SPORT AND THE NATION

The evolution of sports is a story of the transformation of often violent and anarchic pursuits into forms of mock violence with formally codified rules – rules designed to ensure fairness and to reduce the prospect of personal injury (Elias, 2008a [1971]). As in other areas of intercultural contact, here, too, a familiar pattern of reduction in the distinctiveness of national sports and a dissemination of international varieties emerged. This is considered in the first half of this section. We then turn to one of the consequences of that standardization that is less obvious in material culture and the arts: the many forms of international competition for which it was a precondition.

Games, athletics and identity

Many peoples celebrate the antiquity of their 'national' sports. Thus, the mythical Irish warrior Cúchullain was famous not just for his exploits in battle but also for his prowess in the sport of hurling, a game played with stick and ball that continues to be seen as one of the 'national games' of the Irish. In Scotland, a similar sport, shinty, together with the Highland games (featuring such unusual competitions as sheaf tossing and caber throwing), has been seen as a marker of traditional Scottish distinctiveness (Bairner, 2001: 60–2). Likewise, lacrosse is seen as a native Canadian invention.

Sport can play a significant role in enhancing the national self-image and in the nation-building process more generally. Thus, rugby has played a role as a major unifying force in Wales, and soccer has fulfilled a similar role in Latin American countries (Allison, 2000). It seems likely that elsewhere, too (as in England and France) prowess on the sporting field playing for the national team helps to enhance the public image of immigrant groups and to help the process of minority integration. There are times when the organization of sports is deliberately intended to reinforce national morale. This was the case with the *Turngesellschaft* (gymnastic society) founded by Friedrich Jahn in Berlin in 1811 as part of an explicitly nationalist project. It expanded into a national movement with a central organization in 1861, and was intended to promote feelings of German national solidarity through joint physical exercises (Düding, 1987: 24–7, 45). This was the model for a similar Czech initiative, launched as the Prague Gymnastic Club in 1862. Known as the *Sokol* movement (*sokol* means 'falcon', a symbol of heroism in Slav folklore), this became a central component in Czech nationalism

(Nolte, 2007: 88–94). Similar organizations were established in Slovenia, Croatia, Serbia and Bulgaria (Lipoński, 1999: 219–20). The cultivation of 'Gaelic' games (football and hurling) in Ireland formed an important, self-conscious part of nationalist mobilization in the late nineteenth century, with substantial overlap between membership of Gaelic sports clubs and militant nationalist organizations, and the *camán* or hurling stick acquiring some status as a national symbol. The movement was characterized by vehement opposition to 'foreign' games, such as soccer, rugby and cricket (Cronin, 1999: 83–91). In this, it echoed the opposition within the *Turngesellschaft* to the spread of soccer in Germany (Dunning, 1999: 75).

In divided societies, not surprisingly, sport may accentuate divisions. Thus, in South Africa, cricket was traditionally seen as the game of the English, and rugby of the Afrikaners (Allison, 2000: 348). In Northern Ireland, rugby and cricket are almost exclusively Protestant, and Gaelic football almost exclusively Catholic; soccer is predominantly Protestant, with Catholic participation substantially confined to three clubs. The sectarian division extends to Scotland, where it is reflected in the two leading Glasgow soccer clubs, Celtic (Catholic) and Rangers (Protestant) (Bairner, 2001: 31–58).

Like the other cultural features discussed in this chapter, however, sport easily crosses national frontiers: it is freely exportable, and is often carried to remote countries by emigrants, military forces or sociocultural influence. Thus, the quintessential American sport, baseball, evolved from an old English game, rounders (Allison, 2000: 345). In Canada, it was not lacrosse that ultimately became the 'national' game, but (ice) hockey, a sport believed to have been invented there and then exported to other countries (Bairner, 2001: 123–4). But it was England, with its vast overseas possessions and imperial reach, that had the biggest global impact on sport, with three English games eventually achieving the status of truly international ones, marked by the creation of a world cup in soccer in 1930, cricket in 1975 and rugby in 1987 (Allison, 2000: 345). Other sports, such as horse racing, wrestling, boxing, tennis, fox hunting, rowing, croquet and athletics, also conformed to codes originally determined in England (Elias, 2008b [1971]: 107).

The process by which these games achieved international status was linked to imperial expansion. The ideological justification for their dissemination was articulated explicitly in the *Toronto Patriot* in the 1830s: 'British feelings cannot flow into the breasts of our Canadian boys through a more delightful challenge than that of British sports' (Holt, 1989: 223). Not surprisingly, then, sport has been described as 'a most pervasive and enduring theme in the history of British imperialism', all the more powerful because its influence is unconscious and superficially non-political (Stoddart, 1988: 673). Cricket was seen as an ideal mechanism for conveying the values of the English gentleman and for the cultural assimilation of alien elites; and efforts to export it, though mixed in outcome, enjoyed spectacular success in such large countries as India and such small ones as Barbados (Holt, 1989: 212–23). Indeed, so enthusiastically were some English sports taken up abroad that they eventually overshadowed those sports in the country that invented them: for many decades, English teams have been able to take nothing for granted when competing against Pakistan and the West Indies in cricket, against South Africa and New Zealand in rugby, and even against such non-'British' countries as Brazil or Argentina in soccer.

If we consider the impact of globalization on sport, then, we can see the international advance of such sports as soccer as dominating the globe in much the same way as the English language. Parallel to the process by which languages were standardized through the selection of a central dialect, its codification, its elaboration, and its dissemination through-out the community (see Chapter 3), what might be described as 'folk sports' were subjected to a similar process of standardization, with soccer formalized in 1863 under the Football Association and rugby in 1871 under the Rugby Football Union (Dunning, 1999: 62–4, 80–105). As with weaker dialects, local sporting codes were in general unable to resist the centralizing influence of English football, and in particular that of soccer. Italian and Latin American football variants may have survived as local curiosities, but such sports are in general unable to compete against the dominant code. There are a few exceptions however. In the mother country of soccer itself, rugby of course continues to pose a serious challenge, offering a vibrant alternative model that has international appeal. 'Gaelic football' in Ireland was standardized separately, with the establishment of the Gaelic Athletic Association in 1884, and currently overshadows both soccer and rugby as a popular game in Ireland (Cronin, 1999: 70–116). Australian rules football has also played a significant role in the formation of Australian national identity (Cronin, 1999: 67–8), while in the USA American football continues (alongside baseball and basketball) to be a symbol of national sport.

Competition and conflict

This chapter began by drawing attention to a conflict – a soccer match between El Salvador and Honduras – that seemed to highlight the potential significance of sport for nationalism. It may indeed be the case that, just as politics is said to be war by another means, so too may sport be seen as conflict through another medium. The passions aroused by competitive sports commonly spill over into spectator violence but it would be a mistake to see national or other such loyalties as necessarily lying behind this. A study of English soccer support-ers in 2000–02 concluded that support for the team had only an indirect relationship with English nationalism (Abell et al., 2007). Research into 'football hooliganism' suggests that rioting between supporters of rival teams is a form of non-specific aggression that may (but need not) be presented as an expression of nationalism (Dunning, 1999: 142–58). In any event, the strongest passions are sometimes evoked by leading soccer clubs which no longer represent their titular base – few players and only a minority of supporters of Manchester United, for example, come from (or have any connection with) that city. This can extend even to national level, where flexible rules allow 'national' teams to recruit widely for players. Thus, when Ireland's soccer reputation was at its height in the 1990s, its management and most of its players were English, though with sufficient Irish blood to qualify for the team – one Irish grandparent was enough (Holmes and Storey, 2011: 260).

Nevertheless, it is clear that in many circumstances international sports may reinforce national identity, or even provide a safety valve. In 1956 Hungary played a particularly com-bative match against the Soviet Union in the semi-finals of the Olympic water polo tourna-ment, shortly after the crushing of the Hungarian anti-communist uprising by Soviet troops.

In 1972, Czechoslovakia defeated the Soviet Union in a famous ice hockey match, hailed as a symbolic reversal of the 1968 Soviet invasion of Czechoslovakia. In 1990, when tensions between Serbs and Croats were high, a soccer match between Zagreb and Belgrade degenerated into violence (Nielsen, 2010: 89–90), and some years later, after the war between Croatia and what remained of Yugoslavia, a soccer match between the two countries moved one Croatian player to express the view that 'this is not to be regarded as just another football match … there are too many women in Zagreb crying over lost husbands and sons for that' (Holmes and Storey, 2011: 255). In the 1970s, the captain of the Welsh rugby team is said to have stirred up his players as follows before an encounter with their traditional rivals: 'For 1500 years the English have polluted our land … exploited our resources … raped our women … Gentlemen, this afternoon we are playing the English' (Allison, 2000: 351). Alan Bairner recalled his own experience as a Scottish supporter at the annual match against England at Wembley stadium:

> We were the underdogs, the plucky fighters, one of whose national heroes, Robert Bruce, had derived inspiration from a spider and had taught us all that we should try, try, and try again. The English on the other hand were arrogant. Their country was larger and more powerful than ours and they deserved to be taken down a peg or two. … Victory allowed Scots to feel good about themselves. Defeat meant a period of introspection and low self-esteem as the nation wallowed in collective despair. … As junior partners in the United Kingdom, Scots needed the sporting contest with England as an element in a constant struggle to maintain a separate identity (Bairner, 2001: xiv).

While victory in particular sports may be important for national solidarity, gaining admission to the universal sporting body, and performing well in its games, is seen as a key endorsement of nationhood. As it has been put, 'to be considered a nation is to possess the symbolism of national flag, membership of the UN, a national airline and an Olympic gold' (Cronin, 1999: 62). The Olympic Games can thus become a major forum for nationalist expression. For the host nation, the event becomes a showcase through which the outstanding features of the nation may be exhibited; and for all nations it is a mechanism for displaying national athletic prowess. While the Olympic movement itself has consistently stressed its non-political character, politics has always been an integral and pervasive presence (Hill, 1993: 84; Senn, 1999: x). Indeed, it seems clear that in a context where teams are organized through national committees and symbolized by national flags and anthems, the transnational ideal of the Olympic Games is 'doomed to fail' (Wright, 1977: 30).

CONCLUSION

The very diverse cultural characteristics discussed in this chapter have in common the fact that none has an immediately obvious bearing on nationalism. The three clusters fit in very different ways into Leerssen's (2006) framework: salvage is particularly relevant in respect of material culture, given the levelling impact of globalization; propagation and popularization rather than preservation of the past are the main focus of competitive sports; and all three types of 'cultivation' are important for the arts and intellectual culture. These fields vary greatly in their centrality to human life. Some, such as housing, food and clothing, are basic and inescapable; others, such as literature, music and art, are seen by many as luxuries; yet others, such as sport, are clearly options in which many engage either actively or passively. Three aspects of the relationship between these features and nationalism need to be explored in conclusion, each of them marked by a strong tension: between 'banal' and what we may describe as 'bizarre' nationalism; between universal and local expressions of identity; and between the pursuit of superiority rather than just distinctiveness in public culture.

Michael Billig has argued that the 'flagging' of nationhood, by which people are subtly reminded of their identity, is constant and omnipresent: especially in large, long-established nations, flags and other symbols of national identity are not noticed because of their very ubiquity, and national identity is so secure that it is taken for granted. By contrast, smaller, more peripheral nations often have to articulate their identity more explicitly, wrongly attracting the judgement that they are more nationalist (Billig, 1995: 5). As Hobsbawm (1983) has pointed out, in the period 1874–1914 a whole set of new 'traditions' was invented by European ruling elites: public rituals, monuments, national days, sports, even military uniforms and postage stamps – all designed to establish bonds of loyalty, unobtrusively binding citizens to the state. Study of these everyday phenomena has shown their subtle capacity to reinforce national identity. Postage stamps may depict, in miniature, historic triumphs, myths and landscapes (Cusack, 2005); coins may offer permanent reminders of the symbols of the nation, as in Malta (Baldacchino, 2009); television weather maps recall its frontiers, as in Belarus (Leshchenko, 2004: 342); and natural features symbolise its landscapes, as in the Cliffs of Dover for the English, Mount Fuji for the Japanese, or the Alps for North Italian (Padanian) nationalists, for instance (Marsland, 2001; Huysseune, 2010). But the role of the national flag is particularly important – it is an object of veneration in China, and especially in the USA, where schoolchildren pledge allegiance to it daily (Kolstø, 2006). The pledge itself is a solemn statement of identity: 'I pledge allegiance to the flag of the United States of America, and for the Republic for which it stands, one nation under God, indivisible, with liberty and justice for all.'

But the kind of 'banal nationalism' discussed by Billig and associated with these routine dimensions of culture may be replaced by other more assertive forms of nationalism in certain circumstances. Flying the national flag may have 'banal' status in London, Beijing or Canberra, but not in Belfast, Skopje and Jerusalem. Instead, we often find more overt articulations of nationalism – not banal, but representing what may be labelled 'bizarre' beliefs about the nation and its character. What is notable about the features discussed here, then, is not their normally banal character, but rather the ease with which they may be captured by nationalist elites for inclusion in a myth of the nation – they may move from being passive objects that are barely noticed to become subjects of concern to the population at large, in the manner projected in Leerssen's model. Distinctive features of 'national' housing, dress or cuisine may be stressed as having a particular importance for the nation, or, more commonly, 'alien' forms in these areas may be resisted. The same applies to literature, music and the arts, and even to sport: 'national' markers are to be defended, and 'alien' ones to be resisted. Even in circumstances where the levelling effects of globalization are leading to world-scale cultural assimilation, or perhaps even precisely because of this process, minor markers of difference may be attributed a particular role in defining the nation.

Second, the boundaries associated with the features discussed here are normally highly diffuse. Literature, music and the visual arts are of universal appeal, and in principle we might expect them to be more effective in bridging than in creating boundaries between nations. Material culture varies, but it does so from one global region to another, and differences tend to be gradients rather than sharp frontiers – traditional houses, folk costumes and culinary traditions may indeed be geographically differentiated, and they may sometimes have a strong ethnic component, but they commonly group people in global regions, or differentiate them by subnational regions. Writing that is hailed as 'national' may draw attention to regional themes; thus Mickiewicz's famous epic poem, *Pan Tadeusz* begins 'Lithuania, my fatherland', reflecting the background of Mickiewicz outside ethnic Poland (Eile, 2000: 8–9), and Chopin's *mazurkas* (by contrast to his *polonaises*) celebrate Masuria, a region, not Poland, the country. Even sport tends to follow frontiers that are more strongly defined by geography than by ethnicity. However, when the state enters the equation these generalizations need to be modified, as new 'national' modes of expression, and of sport, are articulated.

The third point concerns the ease with which the cultural features discussed here may be seen as indicators not just of the distinctiveness of particular nations, but also of their superiority. Popular belief in the superior suitability of national housing arrangements, in the beauty of national costume and in the gastronomic qualities of national food may be widely shared, and the food, at least, of certain other nations may be considered suspect. In the areas of literature, music and the arts, international competitions are seen as providing 'objective' evidence of national superiority when writers, musicians or artists receive international acclaim. This is outstandingly true of sport, where international competitions may show not merely a capacity to defeat traditional enemies on the sports field, but also, sometimes, the achievement of global pre-eminence. But it may apply even to music. Quite apart from reputational matters (relating to the alleged superiority of Italian opera, for example, or of German symphonic music in the nineteenth century), formally organized events offer an opportunity to record feats of musical achievement. These may refer to festivals of classical song or instrumental performance, or to record sales in the area of popular music. However, such events as the annual Eurovision song contest offer an extraordinary opportunity for countries – especially for those which get few opportunities to excel in other areas – to demonstrate their prowess by winning a widely viewed international event, and hosting the same event the following year (Bohlman, 2004: 1–11). The achievement of distinction and attainment of distinctiveness in the fields discussed in this and previous chapters are interesting features of modern nations; but simply describing these will tell us little about why they are important, or how the nationalist programme to which they are related has emerged. This big question is addressed in Part Two of this book.

PART II
NATIONALIST MOBILIZATION

7

NATIONALISM AND SOCIAL STRUCTURE

INTRODUCTION

When airline passengers are stopped for further investigation by airport security staff, by immigration police or by customs officers, there is commonly an underlying pattern: their identity documents, physical appearance, body language or mode of dress draw attention to them as standing out in some manner – as being 'different' in a way that might reward further investigation. The officials in question are unlikely to be operating at random: they have formed a hunch that certain characteristics offer a clue to an individual's worldview and behaviour.

This may extend to the political world. It has commonly been suggested that nationalism is linked to the social background of those involved: that Kurdish nationalism in Turkey is a distinctive concern of alienated young people (Alkan, 2008), for example, or that Flemish nationalism in Belgium is particularly attractive to blue-collar workers (Billiet and Witte, 2008: 261–2). Indeed, social scientists have for long sought to explain why particular social groups seem to be disposed to accept specific ideologies. When such approaches were in their heyday, two specialists in social analysis put the question as follows: 'Why does Monsieur Rouget, age 24, blond hair, brown eyes, a worker in a large factory, vote Communist?' (Przeworski and Teune, 1970: 19). The answer, the authors argued, lay in the demonstrated probability that particular social characteristics (such as age and occupation) dispose people to support distinctive ideologies – though they stressed the unlikelihood that such an approach would provide a complete explanation for political preference.

Przeworski and Teune made no further reference to apparently redundant information that they supplied about Monsieur Rouget: that he had blond hair and brown eyes. The literature on voting behaviour indeed ignores phenotypical characteristics such as facial features, but in the process of nationalist mobilization these may be endowed with a particular significance. As we have seen, national identity is strongly but unevenly influenced by other human characteristics, such as language and religion (Chapters 3 and 4), it is closely linked to historical consciousness and to public culture, which not only help to shape nationalist values but are also themselves products of these values (Chapters 5 and 6), and it may in certain circumstances be associated with race, as well as being invariably linked to gender (Chapter 2). But it may also be associated with other social characteristics that have been shown to be politically important.

What social factors seem to be associated with nationalist values? Electoral studies seek to explain voter support for political parties or party types (or 'families') by exploring the impact of a range of background variables: social class (to use a broad term that brings together occupation, income and level of education), gender, region of residence, religion, marital status and age, for example. Some of these variables (such as marital status and age) may indeed have implications for support for particular types of movement, including nationalism, but their impact is life cycle-dependent. All old people have once been young, and all married people have once been single, so if age and marital status matter, we would expect people's views to evolve as these characteristics change, and we would not expect to find in these variables a robust explanation of national loyalty.[1]

By contrast, while an individual's social class may change, it tends to be more stable. With increased geographical mobility, region of residence, too, is no longer unvarying (though the region within which people spent their formative years may leave a deep impact). The present chapter thus focuses on three characteristics that take us closer to an examination of nationalism as a dynamic process: the significance of the relationship between language and class, the impact of socioeconomic change, and the role of region.

CLASS AND NATION

When languages coexist, as we have seen, their speakers are commonly differentiated not just by speech and writing norms, but also in social standing. Thus, speakers of peripheral languages (such as Galician, Breton or Irish), especially in the past, found themselves in an unequal relationship with the locally dominant metropolitan language (Castilian Spanish, French and English). Speakers of these languages tended not only to reside in geographically peripheral areas, but also to live on the socioeconomic margins, filling humbler positions in the labour market. But social marginalization may also be the fate of more established languages, depending on context. Thus, the status of Flemish (Dutch) in Belgium was clearly inferior to that of French, and that continues to be the case in respect of Alsatian (German) in the hinterland of Strasbourg, on the Franco–German border. By contrast, in Canada it was French speakers in Quebec who were seen in the past as representing a community that was inferior to the dominant anglophone one.

---

1 Study of a large volume of survey data dealing with support for four nationalist parties in western Europe suggests the following relationships: *Vlaams Blok/Vlaams Belang* support in Flanders is strongly associated with low levels of church-going and low occupational status, and fairly strongly associated with lower educational levels and younger voters; Sinn Féin support among Northern Ireland Catholics is strongly associated with lower occupational status and younger voters, and fairly strongly associated with lower educational levels; Scottish National Party support is strongly associated with low church attendance and less strongly with lower educational levels; and in the first two cases there is also a weak association with men rather than women. Support for Plaid Cymru in Wales, however, shows no significant association with any of these characteristics, but a very strong association with knowledge of Welsh. Based on logistic regression analysis of European Social Survey cumulative data file, rounds 1–3, 2002–06 (Flemish data, N = 2,066); Northern Ireland Life and Times Surveys, 1998–2004 (Catholics only, N = 4,087); Scottish Social Attitudes Surveys, 2001–03 (Scotland, N = 2,136) and Wales Life and Times Surveys, 2001–03 (Wales, N = 1,392), both from ESRC Devolution and Constitutional Change Programme combined dataset.

If we look at societies where intercommunal differences have been politically mobilized, then, disparities between the life conditions of the various groups seem to be a recurring factor. We may identify two critical features: labour force differentiation, with the clustering of members of particular groups in specific occupations or industries, and a more systematic process of status stratification, with some groups experiencing lifestyle patterns that are significantly more or less privileged than others. A third should also be noted: the tendency of particular groups to monopolize elite positions.

Labour force differentiation

Coincidence between language and occupation was a well-known characteristic of the nineteenth and earlier centuries. As Friedrich Engels observed in the mid-nineteenth century in respect of Russia, Hungary, Romania and Turkey:

> The handicraftsman, the small shopkeeper, the petty manufacturer is a German up to this day in Petersburg, Pesht, Jassy and even Constantinople; while the money-lender, the publican, the hawker – a very important man in these thinly populated countries – is very generally a Jew, whose native tongue is a horribly corrupted German (Engels, 1979 [1852]: 44).

Engels's observation is supported by a great deal of statistical evidence, and much of this is illustrated below. It is important to stress, though, that the argument here is that the relationship between national divisions and socioeconomic ones is often very strong – but rarely, if ever, perfect. In other words, it would be difficult to identify a country where all members of one national group enjoy a superior social position to all members of a second group. On the other hand, we will rarely encounter circumstances where the relationship between the communities is entirely devoid of socioeconomic content. As it has been put, 'observable economic discrepancies are near universal concomitants of ethnic strife', though these generally result from the fact that population groups tend to inhabit distinctive territories, and interregional economic differences alone will often account for differences between national groups (Connor, 1984a: 343–4).

There are many examples of the process of ethnic clustering in the labour force, and the relationship between communal or linguistic groups and social structure may contain elements of a cultural division of labour, with the earmarking of particular occupations for specific groups. Some smaller ethnic communities may, for example, be defined in relation to their occupation: this was once the case among a branch of the Saami in Scandinavia, whose identity was linked to their role as reindeer herders, or 'tinkers' in Ireland (a small group now more generally known as 'Irish travellers'), who traditionally worked as itinerant makers of tin products. Specific historical processes may also have produced such relationships. The settlement of African slaves in the Americas as farm labourers and domestic servants left a permanent mark on the ethnic composition of the USA and other countries. Nineteenth-century settlement of Indian indentured labourers as sugar plantation workers in the West Indies, Mauritius and Fiji gave these colonies a characteristic ethnic structure. The role of Jewish communities in central and eastern Europe was also distinctive, as Engels pointed out, with concentration in particular occupations (as tailors, traders, goldsmiths and moneylenders, for instance). Chinese minorities in much of southeast Asia, Indians in West Africa and Armenians in the Ottoman empire are further examples; they have been collectively labelled 'middleman minorities', reflecting their concentration in trade and commerce, commonly acting as brokers between dominant and subordinate groups (Bonacich, 1973).

The strong association between occupational categories and ethnic divisions has weakened over time, with the abolition of slavery, the regulation of indentured labour arrangements, and relaxation of restrictions on labour mobility, including especially that of the Jews – and eventually the elimination of Jewish minorities in central and eastern Europe. But there are still distinctive niches in many societies which continue to be dominated by particular groups. For example, in Malaysia in 2006, when the Chinese accounted for just 23% of the total population, they made up 48% of the major professional groups (including 72% of accountants, 53% of architects and 47% of engineers); the Malays, 61% of the population, made up only 40% of the professions (Malaysia, 2008: 37, 235). In Fiji in 1976, when native Fijians made up 46% of the population and Indians 47%, there was a similar imbalance in the professions, with Fijians accounting for 17% and Indians for 60% (Fiji, 1977: 354–99). These examples could be multiplied: the disproportionate representation of African Americans in the domestic service sector, for instance, or of immigrant minorities in the hospitality sector in Europe.

Social stratification

The occupational categories just discussed are not merely different; they also coincide with a distinctive pattern of status differentiation, especially in traditional or transitional societies. These circumstances present fertile terrain for the growth of strong patterns of national sentiment. As a leading analyst of the nationalities question in the Habsburg monarchy, the prominent Social Democratic theorist Otto Bauer, put it:

> The nationalism of the minority develops yet more strongly where a social, a class conflict is linked to the national conflict. Thus for the Germans in Livland, for the Poles in Ukraine, who as landlords hold sway over a peasant population of another nationality; thus for the Jews, Greeks and Armenians in the East, who live as traders and usurers in between peasants and craftsmen of another nationality, and thus for the Germans in the Czech parts of Bohemia and Moravia, for the Walloons in the Flemish region of Belgium, who comprise the bourgeoisie in regions whose workers, petty bourgeoisie and peasants belong to another nation. But nationalism must naturally receive its strongest stimulus where the minority does not exercise the role of the privileged and exploiting classes but holds a servile and exploited position. Here, nationalism draws nourishment from the hatred of the exploited for the exploiter (Bauer, 1980 [1911]: 477–8).

European society in the nineteenth century indeed offers many examples of this relationship. It was not just socially stratified; this stratification was in varying degrees legally recognized. The division of French political society into three 'estates' (the nobility, the clergy and the bourgeois 'third estate') up to 1789 is a well known example, but this form of organization survived in other societies until the early twentieth century (the survival of the British House of Lords until 1999 as representative of the British hereditary nobility is a less obvious example). The logic of interdependence between the major estates was summarized in Russia in the 1850s in the same manner as it might have been in western Europe: 'every estate has its own role in the state: the clergy pray, the nobles serve in war and peace, the peasants plough and feed the people, and the merchants are the means that provide each with what it needs' (cited in Freeze, 1986: 11).

But being a peasant or a landed noble does not just mean that two people spend their working days in different ways; the peasant has a low income, a poor standard of education, limited mobility prospects, little political influence and low social standing by comparison with the nobleman. If whole cultural communities are tied in to differentiation of this kind, the implications for politicization of the cultural division obviously increase: the difference may be presented not as a coincidental set of contrasts in the labour market, but as systematic disadvantage, with members of one community much more likely to be unemployed, to be disproportionately represented in less prestigious occupations, and to enjoy a generally lower standard of living. Thus, in Finland, where a four-estate system survived until 1906, the nobles were Swedish-speaking and the peasants overwhelmingly Finnish-speaking; the clergy were mixed; and the towns, initially mainly Swedish-speaking, became arenas for small-scale linguistic competition as the proportion of Finnish speakers increased.

Figure 7.1 shows the position in four societies where there were deep social divisions between emerging national communities. In the Baltic and Lithuanian districts of Russia which match the present territories of the three Baltic republics, the measures used are mother tongue and legal social class (*soslovie* – a yardstick that needs to be used with caution, since in many cases it fails to coincide with actual socioeconomic class divisions). The Estonian case illustrates the steady rise in the proportion of Estonian speakers and the corresponding decline in the position of the German-speaking population (which constituted the traditional economic, cultural and political elite in Estonia and Latvia) as one moves down the social scale from hereditary nobility to peasants. A similar pattern may be seen in Latvia and Lithuania, though with some variation. In Lithuania (traditionally ruled at local level by the Polish gentry) we find, as expected, that the hereditary nobility is dominated by this group; but there is a surprising number of Lithuanian 'nobles'. This may easily be explained: in the areas of the former Polish–Lithuanian Commonwealth, the legally defined hereditary nobility or *szlachta* was extremely large, extending to about 8–10% of the population, though many of its members lived in a state of impoverishment worse than that of better-off peasants (Wandycz, 1974: 4–5). This also helps to explain the large number of Polish 'nobles' in Latvia: these lived overwhelmingly in the southeastern province of Latgale, part of Poland–Lithuania until the eighteenth-century partitions. The important position of the Yiddish-speaking (Jewish) population in the two main urban groups in Lithuania should also be noted. In each of these societies, the

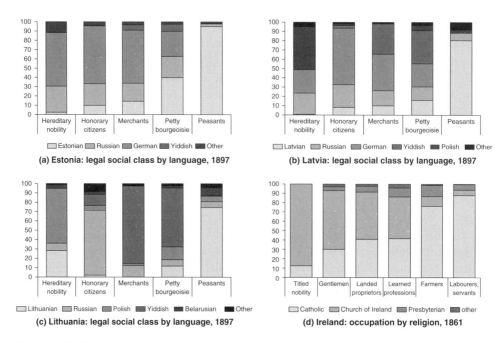

Figure 7.1 Relationship between class and national background, Estonia, Latvia, Lithuania and Ireland, nineteenth century

Note: Territories approximate the present territories of Estonia, Latvia and Lithuania (based on groups of provinces (*gubernii*) and districts (*uezdi*). Irish data refer to the island of Ireland. Classes and occupations are selected.

Source: Computed from Russia (1899–1905); Ireland (1863)

same kind of trend in linguistic relations was observable as that described in respect of Bohemia:

> Czech became the language of the despised and exploited classes. ... The upper classes scorned the Slavic language 'as if the same befits only the common rabble'. Little wonder that each who rose to a place in the upper social strata, who acquired wealth, higher education, or an elevated position in the administrative apparatus or the army, was ashamed to speak the language of peasants and servants (Bauer, 2000 [1924]: 172).

This relationship was true of the Irish case, too, with the Irish language consigned to marginal status, but Figure 7.1 uses different criteria to assess crucial relationships here: religion rather than language, and occupational group rather than legal class. The pattern is similar to that in Estonia, with the proportion of Protestants falling and Catholics rising as one moves from higher- to lower-status groups. Many other examples could be cited. In Bosnia in 1910, the proportion of Muslims fell as socioeconomic status declined: they made up 91% of landowners with tenants, 71% of landowners without tenants, 57% of free peasants and 5% of tenants (Babuna, 2004: 292). Colonial society in southeast Asia was characterized by a division between three communities, each 'defective in its social composition': the European elite, the Asian middle sector, and indigenous society making up the bulk of the population (Pluvier, 1974: 72).

In the contemporary world, it is typically the minority that will experience lower social status, as in the case of many immigrant groups in western Europe, and many indigenous groups such as the Bretons in France or the Welsh in the UK; but some minorities are characterized by relatively high social status. This was the position, for example, among southern Irish Protestants, Swedish speakers in Finland, Poles in Lithuania and the German minorities in Estonia and Latvia in the interwar period (Coakley, 1990). Whites in South Africa constitute a similar example, as did Tamils in Sri Lanka and French speakers in Belgium in the past. In Malaysia in 2004, similarly, if we use mean monthly gross household income as an indicator, Malays fell 17% below the national average while Chinese were 37% above it (computed from Malaysia, 2008: 246).

There is a final set of distinctive examples to which attention should be drawn. In settler societies with a sizeable indigenous population, there tend to be large differences between the two communities, with the indigenous one residing in rural areas (often very poor and remote ones), occupying the most menial occupations, and characterized by a relatively low standard of living (with high unemployment and infant mortality levels, and low literacy and life expectancy rates). Figure 7.2 uses a very simple indicator to illustrate the gap between the communities in four countries: relative income levels. The tallest bar in each country represents the position of the dominant group (non-hispanic whites in the USA, English speakers in Canada, the non-aboriginal population in Australia, and the European-origin population of New Zealand). Except in the USA, the shortest bar shows the position of the indigenous population, with its income level in all cases well below that of the dominant group; for example, in Canada it is 60% of the level of the main English-speaking community. The USA is an exception; African-American households have an even lower level of income than native American ones.[2]

Political control

Another feature of the ethnic division of labour that is characteristic of divided societies is particularly significant politically. The dominant group typically tries to retain control of the public service, and in particular of the civil service and the security forces, and long-term structural relations between such groups and segments of the administrative system may evolve. In particular, positions at the apex of political power tend to be confined to one group. In Malaysia, for example, the position of head of state is confined to the nine hereditary Malay sultans, and the army and security forces are disproportionately Malay in

---

2 Because the indicators are defined differently in the four cases, it is not possible to use them to make cross-case comparisons; it can *not* be concluded from this figure that aboriginal Australians are much better off than their Canadian counterparts.

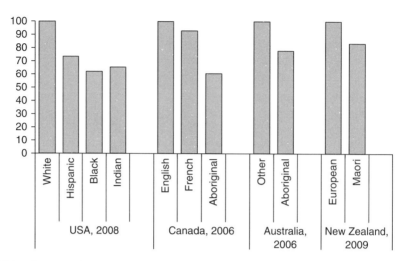

Figure 7.2 Comparative median income levels of selected groups, USA, Canada, Australia and New Zealand, 2006–09

Note: Data refer to median household income (US), median income of those earning income (CA), gross household income of at least AUD10,000 (AU), and median weekly income of those aged at least 15 (NZ), with the position of each group expressed as a proportion of the dominant group (100). Some individuals may belong to more than one group.

Source: US Bureau of the Census, US Community Survey, 2006–09 (www.census.gov); Statistics Canada, Census of 2006, selected demographic characteristics (www.statcan.gc.ca); Australian Bureau of Statistics, 2006 census of population and housing (www.abs.gov.au); Statistics New Zealand, New Zealand income survey June 2009 quarter (www.stats.govt.nz)

composition (Enloe, 1978). In Fiji, similarly, the native hereditary chiefs continue to enjoy substantial political influence through the Council of Chiefs, and the armed forces are almost entirely ethnic Fijian. Such relationships commonly survive political settlements, and may continue to give rise to resentment. In South Africa in 1974 the armed services were not only almost exclusively white, but overwhelmingly Afrikaner (accounting for an estimated 85% in the army, 75% in the air force and 50% in the navy); a year earlier, while the police service was 40% African, Africans were overwhelmingly concentrated in the lower ranks, with the upper ranks 98% white (calculated form Enloe, 1975: 23, 26). It took some time after the end of the *apartheid* regime for this pattern to change. In 2001, whites, though accounting for only 19% of all those employed (and 12% of the population), made up 54% of those in the powerful 'legislators, senior officials and managers' category (computed from South Africa, 2001: 63). In Northern Ireland, the security services were traditionally overwhelmingly Protestant; as recently as 1992, only 8% of police officers were Catholics. Notwithstanding a sharp increase in Catholic recruitment, by 2008, when Catholics accounted for 45% of the monitored labour force, they comprised only 20% of full-time security sector employees (overwhelmingly police) (computed from Northern Ireland, 2008: 3, 119).

The role of the military is particularly important. It is true that the army can play an integrative role, reflecting the ethnic structure of the population and contributing to national cohesion. But in many societies ethnic divisions are simply reflected within military structures. Thus, the British had maintained separate communal regiments in India on the grounds that the various groups had 'different customs, traditions and eating habits' that could not easily be integrated (itself possibly a 'divide and rule' strategy). This structure continued in independent India, though in a context of 'indianizing' the officer corps, requiring cadets to acquire knowledge of Indian culture, music, dance and food (Thomas and Karnad, 1991: 129–30, 134–5). In Nigeria, similarly, the Africanization of the military entailed the replacement of its overwhelmingly expatriate officer corps on the basis of what was in effect an ethnic quota system (Wright, 1991: 183–4). This resulted in a 'capping' of the traditionally powerful but numerically modest Ibo group. By contrast, in Ethiopia the Amhara group continued to hold a dominant position – in 1970, though only about 19% of the population, they comprised an estimated 70% of the officer corps (Welch, 1991).

SOCIOECONOMIC CHANGE AND NATIONALISM

So far, the focus has been mainly on relatively static relationships – a set of sample images has been presented of the interaction between social position and ethnic structure in selected societies at particular points, with only incidental reference to change over time. But relationships of this kind are of course dynamic, and changes in the relative standing of the coexisting groups may be potentially destabilizing. If the socioeconomic gap between the groups increases, the underprivileged group will resent the relative deterioration in its standard of living; but if the socioeconomic gap narrows, the privileged group may see a threat to its position of dominance. This was the dilemma faced by Northern Ireland, where Catholics were traditionally more likely to be unemployed and to fill lower-status positions than Protestants, and Belgium, where the Flemish population occupied a similar role. In each case, as the gap narrowed, the resources available to the subordinate group increased. In the Belgian case, the relative position of the two communities was eventually reversed.

Aside from changing socioeconomic status, though, the cultural boundary between coexisting groups may also change as a result of contact in the labour market. There are, as we have seen, circumstances where whole communities are collectively tainted with the label of inferiority in relation to the dominant culture. This relationship may lead to two types of outcome. First, the dominant culture may spread outside its traditional core areas (in the ruling class and the privileged groups in the towns), penetrating other social classes and extending over the countryside. Second, the peripheral culture may establish a bridgehead in the towns, later expand its zone of influence, and ultimately conquer the territory in which it is concentrated.

Figure 7.3 seeks to represent these processes schematically as they played out in much of late nineteenth-century Europe. The triangles symbolize the power pyramid of traditional society: dominated by the aristocracy and landed gentry at the apex, the middle group is the burgher class in the towns, with the peasants accounting for the great mass of the

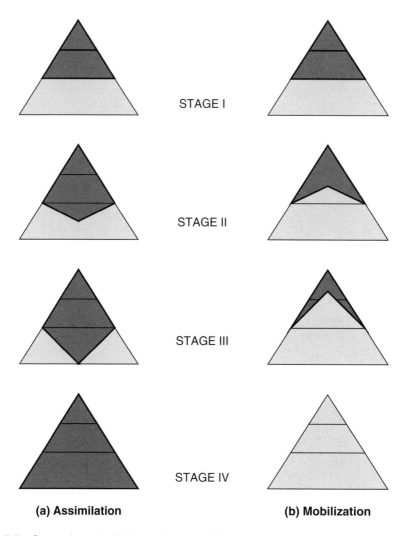

Figure 7.3 Stages in assimilation and mobilization of peripheral cultures

Note: The three layers within each triangle represent the three main traditional social groups (from the top, nobility, burghers, peasants). Dark shading refers to the metropolitan culture, light shading to peripheral culture.

population. In the first stage, the urban middle class shares the culture of the aristocracy, with the countryside dominated by peasants speaking a peripheral language; in the following stage two different patterns emerge, those of assimilation and mobilization.

Cultural assimilation

In variant (a) of stage II (assimilation, on the left), the outcome is victory for the dominant culture: peasants migrating to cities are assimilated to the urban language, which itself begins to spread to the countryside. In stage III of this variant, the former language of the peasants has been reduced to marginal status, confined to isolated pockets rather than holding its own in a coherent territory. Finally, it disappears altogether. Examples abound: the Irish, Scots Gaelic and Breton languages have already advanced far down this path, Welsh and Basque may follow, and Cornish and Manx have already reached the end of the road. The process was described in 1861 by John Stuart Mill by reference to the pattern then already underway in France, which he saw as unproblematic:

> Experience proves that it is possible for one nationality to merge and be absorbed in another; and when it was originally an inferior and more backward portion of the human race the absorption is greatly to its advantage. Nobody can suppose that it is not more beneficial to a Breton, or a Basque of French Navarre, to be brought into the current of the ideas and feelings of a highly civilised and cultivated people – to be a member of the French nationality, admitted on equal terms to all the privileges of French citizenship, sharing the advantages of French protection and the dignity and prestige of French power – than to sulk on his own rocks, the half-savage relic of past times, revolving in his own little mental orbit, without participation or interest in the general movement of the world (Mill, 1861: 29).

For good measure, Mill added that 'the same remark applies to the Welshman or the Scottish Highlander as members of the British nation'. In much of central and eastern Europe, observers identified model (a) as the inevitable one. This was in particular the view of Marxists, who, anticipating the extreme language of the 1930s, predicted the disappearance of *Völkerabfälle* (ethnic trash) as the progressive cultures of the towns advanced. As Engels described it:

> The importance of the German element in the Slavonic frontier localities, thus rising with the growth of towns, trade and manufactures, was still increased when it was found necessary to import almost every element of mental culture from Germany; after the German merchant and handicraftsman, the German clergyman, the German schoolmaster, the German *savant* came to establish himself upon Slavonic soil. And lastly, the iron tread of conquering armies, or the cautious, well-premeditated grasp of diplomacy not only followed, but many times went ahead of the slow but sure advance of denationalisation by social developments (Engels, 1979 [1852]: 44).

Of course, the process of assimilation in many cases arose from less belligerent forces. Later Marxists, such as Otto Bauer, described the process in less stark terms, seeing assimilation as occurring only in particular circumstances. The process was illustrated in the pattern of migration from the Czech lands to Vienna. Just as Germans emigrating to the big industrial centres of the USA inevitably took up the English language and customs, losing their German identity, so too were Czech workers who migrated to Vienna absorbed without trace in the dominant German culture. Thus, Czech apprentices from peasant or skilled manual backgrounds were quickly assimilated, though the process was more difficult with more mature migrant workers, who themselves remained Czech, but whose children were assimilated (Bauer, 1979 [1912]: 1004). The process has been vividly described in the rather different context of late nineteenth-century France, where knowledge of French was limited, but 'the peasant was ashamed to be a peasant; he was ashamed to be uncivilised; he agreed with his judges that there was something valuable and vastly superior that he lacked, that French civilisation and notably anything from Paris were clearly superior and clearly desirable' (Weber, 1976: 7). The critical period here seems to have been the decades spanning the nineteenth and twentieth centuries, when French culture won a decisive victory: 'Roads and railroads brought hitherto remote and inaccessible regions into easy contact with the markets and lifeways of the modern world. Schooling taught hitherto indifferent millions the language of the dominant culture, and its values as well, among them patriotism. And military service drove these lessons home' (Weber, 1976: 493–4).

Similar processes of course took place outside Europe. In those parts of the world in which political nationalism emerged as the ultimate victor in the struggle against European powers, the latter commonly left their language and much of their culture as part of the colonial heritage. In the Philippines, the attraction of *mestizo* culture (perceived as high status) helped assimilate the Filipinos to it (Wickberg, 2000 [1965]: 137). This process advanced most rapidly in the Americas where, even when indigenous communities have remained strong or *mestizo* communities have emerged, indigenous languages have largely yielded to the pressure of metropolitan European ones (the position of Guarani in Paraguay, spoken by most of the population, is one of the important exceptions). In sub-Saharan Africa the process of assimilation of elites to European languages of wider communication is far advanced, but this has extended only in part to the rest of the population. In Asia, the major indigenous languages have survived, even though in many societies, such as India, English continues to play a role of considerable political significance.

Many illustrations of this pattern could be given. It is reflected, for instance, in the process of intergenerational language shift. Four examples are used in Figure 7.4. The most dramatic pattern is illustrated in the top part of the figure, showing the rapid decline of Breton as one moves from older to younger age cohorts, and the more gradual replacement of Frisian by Dutch. In each of these cases, expressions of indigenous nationalism have been weak. The bottom part of the figure illustrates the position in respect of two groups, the Irish and the New Zealand Maori, where the process of assimilation to the dominant language (English in each case) is far advanced. These two cases are, however, particular interesting as instances of linguistic assimilation which has coexisted with strong expressions of nationalist mobilization.

The progress of such patterns of linguistic assimilation is illustrated in Figure 7.5 in the case of France. The initial pattern (Figure 7.5a) shows the French language largely confined in the early nineteenth century to the Île-de-France and *départements* adjacent to this. Already by 1863, though, the penetration of French into the South is clear, with this process continuing up to the end of the century, as Figures 7.5b and 7.5c show. Recent survey data allow us to project the trends in the twentieth century, and to plot the decline of regional languages.

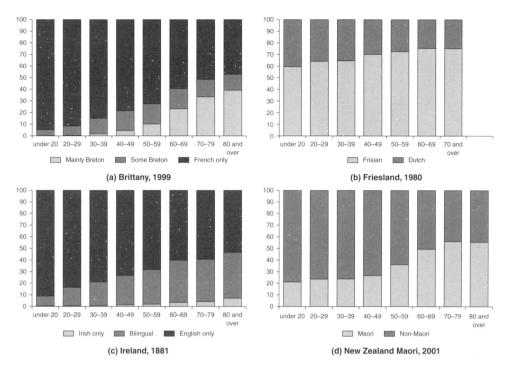

(a) Brittany, 1999

(b) Friesland, 1980

(c) Ireland, 1881

(d) New Zealand Maori, 2001

Figure 7.4 Declining languages by age group, Brittany, Friesland, Ireland and New Zealand Maori, 1881–2001

Note: Data refer to language in which brought up as a child (Brittany, Friesland) and knowledge of languages (Ireland and New Zealand); bilinguals are grouped with other Maori speakers in New Zealand. Speakers of foreign languages are grouped with French and Dutch respectively in Brittany and Friesland.

Source: Computed from survey *Étude de l'histoire familiale* (1999, INSEE), Réseau Quetelet, no. lil-0173; survey *Taal yn Fryslan-1* (1980, DANS); Ireland (1882); New Zealand census 2001, available www.stats.govt.nz/census/2001-census-data

Data on childhood language broken down by age cohort from a major survey linked to the 1999 census, used in Figure 7.5d to illustrate the further retreat of regional languages in France by about 1950, show that by the end of the century regional languages had virtually disappeared. In only two *départements* was there a majority of those born in 1970 or later who had been exposed to a regional language in childhood (one in Corsica, the other in Alsace); and in only two more *départements* (the other *département* in each of the same two regions) did this proportion exceed 20%.[3]

---

3 Computed from *Étude de l'histoire familiale* (1999, INSEE) survey conducted as part of the French census, March 1999; data supplied by Réseau Quetelet, no. lil-0173 (N=380,481). The question of particular interest here was: 'in which language, dialect or *patois* did your parents usually speak to you when you were a child, about five years old?' with separate answers in respect of father and mother, and in relation to intensity of use. For general description and analysis, see Héran, Filhon and Deprez (2002) and Clanché (2002).

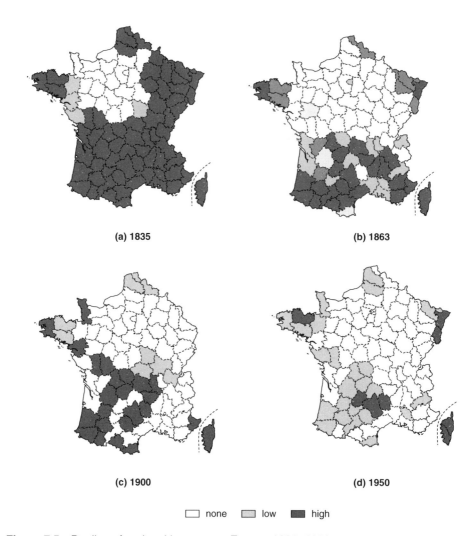

(a) 1835   **(b) 1863**

(c) 1900   **(d) 1950**

☐ none   ▨ low   ■ high

Figure 7.5   Decline of regional languages, France, 1835–1950

Note: Maps refer to contemporary ethnographic estimates of language use (1835), data on non-French speaking communes and schoolchildren, 1863; Eugen Weber's estimates for the turn of the century using a wide variety of sources, 1875–1908; and to reported childhood language of those living in 1999 who were born before 1955.

Source: Derived from Weber (1976: 68, 75); data from the French Ministry of Public Instruction reported in Weber (1976: 498–501); computed from survey *Étude de l'histoire familiale* (1999, INSEE), Réseau Quetelet, no. lil-0173

Elsewhere, regional elites acted as a barrier to political centralization and linguistic assimilation. Where they were not simply elites, but leaders of a locally dominant 'high' culture, they constituted a more formidable obstacle to cultural uniformity. Thus, for example, the spread of Russian culture in the Baltic and Lithuanian provinces was impeded by the existence there of an entrenched local aristocracy (the Baltic German barons and the Polish *szlachta* respectively). By contrast, the absence of any such group (or, rather, the presence of an anglophone

one) hastened the spread of English at the expense of Cornish in Cornwall (Payton, 2004: 122–79). The English were dramatically successful in Ireland too. Figure 7.6 illustrates the steady expansion of the English language there. Predominantly Irish-speaking in the early nineteenth century, most of the island was English-speaking by 1851, and this process continued until the twentieth century. However, this example is one of several salutary ones which show that linguistic assimilation can proceed *alongside* nationalist mobilization.

Bauer (1980 [1912]) used his observation of such processes in the Habsburg monarchy to devise a set of 'laws' of national assimilation (see Table 7.1). Six of the eight 'laws' are simple and plausible. It is obvious, for example, that minorities are more likely to be assimilated if they fall below a certain crucial level in absolute size, in relative size, and in degree of territorial concentration. In these circumstances, critical mass is compromised: the requirements for a viable language community are undermined, and intermarriage with the locally dominant group is likely to result in children brought up in the locally dominant language. Assimilation is also facilitated if the minority is close culturally and in other respects to the dominant group; if it has not been mobilized politically behind a nationalist movement; and if the power resources of the dominant group are overwhelming.

One of the two remaining 'laws' is rather more complex. Bauer proposed that a particular social group is more or less likely to assimilate depending on its relationship with corresponding social groups in the dominant community, and he offered a detailed description of the likelihood with which the main social groups would integrate. In general, he argued, the more proletarian elements are the more assimilable, but their extremes (the most oppressed social elements and the most advanced) tend to resist assimilation. For other classes, the probability of assimilation is contingent: peasants tend to assimilate to the locally dominant peasant culture, and the petty bourgeoisie to the culture of its clients: 'The Czech shopkeeper remains Czech in the German city where he finds his customers among Czech workers; he becomes a German where he depends on German customers. The Romansch petty bourgeoisie of eastern Switzerland are germanized through tourism: the *lingua del pane* (language of bread) overcomes the *lingua del cuore* (the language of the heart)' (Bauer, 1980 [1912]: 613). A particular importance attaches to the status of the locally dominant classes (the landed class and the bourgeoisie): these will tend to assimilate to the ruling nation where they already enjoy close political and economic links with it, drawing the rest of the population in their wake. They will resist this process only if the peripheral population possesses elements of a similar class structure (for overviews of the complexity of the assimilation process in western societies, see Lucassen, Feldman and Oltmer (2006: 286–9) and Vermeulen (2010)).

The final 'law' is particularly interesting. It has been further developed by Karl Deutsch (1966 [1953]): the probability of assimilation will depend on the pace of social 'mobilization', or entry to modern society (the term 'mobilization' is used in a different, political sense in other chapters of this book). As Deutsch put it, if this rate is low, the minority will tend to be assimilated; but if it exceeds a certain critical threshold, the minority will launch into the kind of process described in variant (b) of Figure 7.3 ('mobilization', on the right). If a marginal rural culture is mobilized rapidly (through being brought into intense contact with the metropolitan culture, through settling in the towns or entering the integrated labour

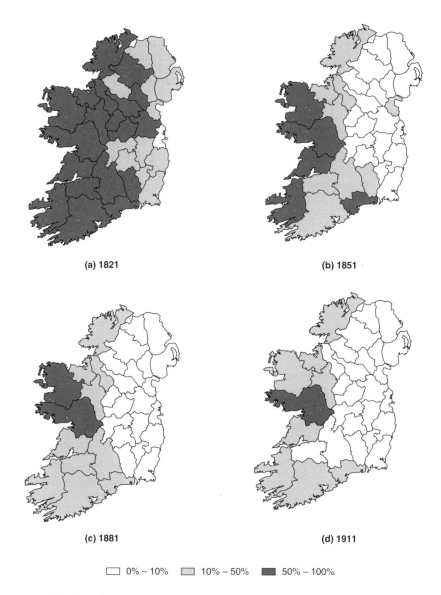

(a) 1821   (b) 1851

(c) 1881   (d) 1911

☐ 0% – 10%   ▨ 10% – 50%   ■ 50% – 100%

Figure 7.6   Decline of the Irish language, 1821–1911

Note: Maps refer to estimates of language use (1821) and to official census data reporting knowledge of Irish (including Irish–English bilinguals).

Source: Derived from Anderson (1828); Ireland (1856, 1882, 1912)

market), the pace at which it is assimilated to the dominant culture may simply be too slow: a critical mass of speakers of the peripheral language develops in the towns, becoming the embryo of an emerging middle class. If, however, this process is slower, the metropolitan

Table 7.1   Bauer's 'laws of national assimilation'

1. The larger the minority, the less the pull of the majority, and vice versa.
2. The smaller the minority as a proportion of the total population, the easier the process of assimilation.
3. Assimilation is easiest where the minority is dispersed and settled among the majority; it is more difficult when the minority is separated from the majority and lives together in its own neighbourhoods; and it is completely impeded when it occupies an entirely separate linguistic enclave.
4. Assimilation is easier when minority and majority are similar in race, culture, religion and language.
5. Minorities assimilate only when they find within the majority a class that resembles them in respect of class position, occupation, qualification and culture.*
6. Assimilation is made easier by economic, social, political and religious struggles, but is made more difficult by national struggles.
7. The larger a nation in population, wealth, power and culture, the greater its attraction for foreign minorities in its area, and the greater the resistance of its own emigrants to assimilation.
8. The weaker and less continuous the immigration of the minority and the stronger and more continuous the immigration of the majority, the easier the process of assimilation.

*A more detailed elaboration of the position of various classes is offered.
Source: Bauer, 1980 [1912]

---

culture manages to absorb the new migrant waves, and ultimately to disseminate itself in the countryside (see Chapter 9).

Cultural mobilization

The outcome described in the left-hand side of Figure 7.3 is, then, far from inevitable. The alternative pattern (illustrated on the right-hand side of Figure 7.3) is one in which, in stage II, following the emergence of an embryonic middle class based on the peripheral language, the traditionally dominant group is overwhelmed by the more numerous speakers of this language (reinforced by a steady flow from the countryside). Ultimately, the peripheral group becomes dominant, perhaps assisted by a political victory that offers it powerful administrative support. Again, there are many examples, including Finnish (whose struggle was against the traditionally dominant Swedish culture), Estonian and Latvian (against German), Lithuanian (against Polish), Czech (against German) and Slovak (against Magyar) (see Krueger, 2009).

A characteristic feature of these developments is illustrated in Figure 7.7: the steady movement of the rural population into the cities (in this case, into what would become the capital city). The taking over of Finnish towns by Finnish speakers is represented in part (a) of the figure, which shows how the Swedish-speaking city of Helsingfors became the Finnish-speaking city of Helsinki in the late nineteenth century, and the steady continuation of this process into the twentieth century. The movement of Czechs into Prague followed a parallel pattern. Similarly, German-speaking Reval became Estonian-speaking Tallinn, while German-speaking Pressburg became Magyar-speaking Pozsony, and then Slovak-speaking Bratislava. It is noteworthy that in these two cases two powerful 'external' groups were in contention: Russians and Germans in Tallinn, and Germans and Hungarians in Bratislava.

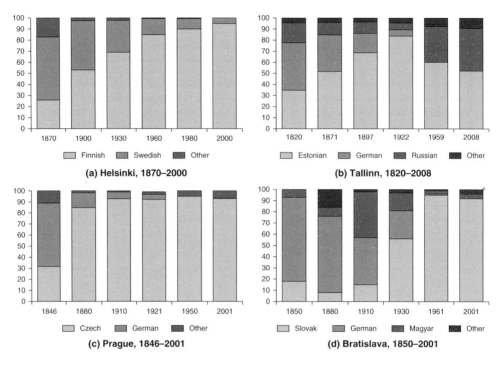

Figure 7.7 Linguistic competition in Helsinki, Tallinn, Prague and Bratislava, nineteenth and twentieth centuries

Source: Derived from Loit, 1994, and a wide range of official and unofficial sources

REGION AND NATION

The discussion so far has focused on circumstances of contact between communities separated by class divisions regardless of their place of residence. Introducing a regional dimension – where the tension is between relatively privileged and underprivileged geographical parts of a state – draws attention to further differences, ones which are of particular political significance, since a region, unlike a social group, is a potential state. In this section we consider three aspects of the regional dimension: the extent to which regional divisions coincide with the kinds of cultural division that may be open to nationalist mobilization, the issue of structural differences between regions that might be exploited by nationalist elites, and, briefly since it overlaps with nationalist mobilization more generally, the process of regional political mobilization.

Lest there be any doubt about the difficulties associated with the concept of 'region', we may consider the several conflicting uses of the term that have been identified by, say, Keating (1998a, 1998b: 9–10) or Smouts (1998). Even in the case of the European Union, whose public policy process relies so heavily on regional policy, empirical identification of regions is problematic (Smouts, 1998: 31–3). The associated nouns, 'regionalism' and 'regionaliza-tion', pose similar challenges (Paasi, 2009: 122). Here, by 'region' we mean a reasonably large substate territory whose identity is defined by an administrative or a perceived cultural or geographical border.

Region and culture

Cultural groups vary greatly in the extent to which they are linked to a specific territory. We may consider three patterns, each of which is illustrated in Figure 7.8. The first pattern is *intermingling*. As Figure 7.8a shows, each of Northern Ireland's 26 local government districts is mixed; in only one does the minority fall below 10%. As in the case of Lebanon, pennin-sular Malaysia and Fiji, for instance, the communities do have particular geographical zones of concentration, but by and large they are widely dispersed throughout the whole territory of the state.

Figure 7.8b illustrates the position in Belgium according to the 1947 census: this showed a very high level of polarization, with French speakers accounting for only 4.9% of the population in Flanders and Dutch speakers for only 2.0% in Wallonia. Indeed, it is pos-sible to draw a straight line through Belgium from west to east that will coincide almost perfectly with the linguistic boundary. This pattern of clear-cut polarization is disrupted by the position of Brussels – a mainly French-speaking island in a Dutch-speaking sea. Cyprus joined this category following Turkish military intervention in 1974: a new 'green line' now separates the area of Turkish control from that administered by the government of the Republic of Cyprus. After a massive exodus of Turks to the North and of Greeks to the South, a pattern of stark spatial polarization emerged; by 2002, the proportion of Turks in the (southern) Republic of Cyprus was 0.1%, and of Greeks in the North 0.2% (Coakley, 2003b: 296). The former Czechoslovakia constituted a similar example, with overwhelming concentrations of Czechs and Slovaks in their respective republics before the partition of the state in 1993.

Use of relatively large administrative districts may give an exaggerated impression of the extent of intermingling. Thus, Figure 7.8 shows the city of Belfast as being impres-sively mixed; but this overstates the extent of overlap on the ground. In many middle-class districts, it is true, the population is genuinely mixed, but, especially in working-class hous-ing estates, there tends to be a very high degree of segregation, commonly marked by the construction of 'peace walls' to separate Catholic and Protestant neighbourhoods. A more thoroughgoing example of this form of ghettoization is presented by the case of Cyprus, as illustrated in part (c) of Figure 7.8. Here, prior to the 1974 war, the Turkish population was not concentrated in any one district. However, the island's villages tended to be entirely mono-ethnic, namely Greek or Turkish.

The significance of this discussion has to do with the key link between nations and their territories. For the Flemish, the Slovaks and the Turkish Cypriots of today, there is a clearly defined territory which they can claim as their own (though this claim may be contested). Their identity can rest on territorial roots, and not just on cultural factors such

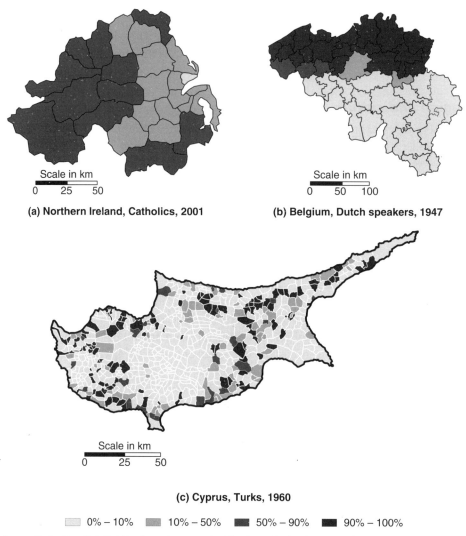

(a) **Northern Ireland, Catholics, 2001**

(b) **Belgium, Dutch speakers, 1947**

(c) **Cyprus, Turks, 1960**

0% – 10%   10% – 50%   50% – 90%   90% – 100%

Figure 7.8   Spatial distribution of groups in Northern Ireland, 1991, Belgium, 1947, and Cyprus, 1960

Source: Derived from Northern Ireland census, 1991 (www.nisra.gov.uk); Belgium (1949–54); Cyprus (1962)

as language. But for the Turkish Cypriots of the 1960s, for Northern Irish Catholics and for the Chinese in Malaysia, there is no such link to territory: identity must be defined in some other way (perhaps not just culturally, but also through a claimed relationship with a 'mother country'). This is critical not just for the formation of national identity, but also for the construction of a nationalist ideology and, in particular, for devising a political programme: the option of secession or assertion of territorial autonomy is effectively foreclosed for groups which do not have a territory of their own. The case of the Jews is an example. By the late nineteenth century, the Jewish population was scattered widely over the world (of the estimated 10 million in all, about 52% lived in the Russian Empire, 25% elsewhere in central and eastern Europe, and 10% in the United States; computed from *American Jewish yearbook*, vol. 1, 1899–1900: 285). It was also scattered widely within Russia, and the effort by the Soviet authorities to establish a Jewish 'homeland' in Birobidzhan in the Russian Far East, in 1934, never flourished. A 'Zionist' movement, focusing on the demand for a Jewish state in Palestine, thus developed as a significant strand in Jewish nationalism.

Region and economy

Interregional differences obviously acquire a particular significance when they coincide with cultural differences, but the regional variable is itself of independent importance. Geography may reinforce economics in setting particular regions apart from each other. The most obvious gaps between rulers and ruled occur in the context of colonial empires, where outlying territories (for example, in Asia or Africa) are politically subject to imperial cores (typically in Europe). But similar relationships have been identified within European and other states. Each state typically has a 'focal area' which normally contains the capital and dominates the political, economic and cultural life of the state; this commonly (but by no means universally) coincides with an historical 'core area' out of which the state originally emerged, such as the Île-de-France in France, the Southeast in England and Piedmont in Italy (Mellor, 1989: 60–5).

The process of early state building often left a legacy that endured into the nineteenth and twentieth centuries, as tensions between the focal area and peripheral areas persisted. Lafont (1967: 143–70) described the relationship between France's nation-building core and culturally distinct provinces such as Languedoc and Brittany as a form of 'internal colonialism', with the centre dominant in regional industry and investment, and in control of agriculture, distribution networks and even tourist resources, even while agricultural activities and extractive industries were being conducted by the population of the region. Arnaud (1980) made a similar argument in respect of the incorporation of the Occitan region in France. As Weber (1976: 485) put it more explicitly in relation to metropolitan France: 'the famous hexagon can itself be seen as a colonial empire shaped over the centuries: a complex of territories conquered, annexed, and integrated in a political and administrative whole, many of them with strongly developed national or regional personalities, some of them with traditions that were specifically un- or anti-French'. The process by which the Southeast of England asserted its political control over the British Isles, similarly, has been described as 'the making of an English empire' (Kearney, 1989: 157–88). But the internal colonial model has also been applied more explicitly in respect of the relationship between England and its Celtic peripheries, based on the argument that peripheral nationalism there was a function of resistance to exploitation by and exclusion from the political centre (Hechter, 1975: 30–4, 341–51). While this account offers useful insights into the English–Irish relationship, its adequacy especially in respect of Scotland has been strongly criticized (see Page, 1978; Keating, 1988: 13–14).

However useful the 'internal colonial' approach may be, there are cases where its applicability is not obvious. Figure 7.9 illustrates the relative position of outlying regions in four countries. In each case, the comparison is with the 'national average' of the measure in question, using an indicator of economic development for a date around the middle of the twentieth century, a time before the nationalist mobilization that was to begin in the 1960s or 1970s, but close enough to it to have been a significant background factor. The United Kingdom illustrates a common pattern: Scotland and Wales, and particularly Northern Ireland, fell well below the average in per capita wage and salary levels, and far below the level in Southeast England; and the pre-independence relationship between Ireland and England would have shown similar disparities. In Canada, similarly, the province of Quebec fell below the national average in income (excluding government transfers), and well below the core area of Ontario. In Spain, a different measure, the coefficient of industrial production, indeed shows Galicia falling below the national average, but Catalonia and the Basque Country fall well above this. In Yugoslavia, measures of tangible wealth per capita show a similar trend, with the most separatist regions, Croatia and Slovenia, emerging as clearly the wealthiest (but with the poorest ethnically delimited region, Kosovo, also showing strong separatist tendencies).

These examples suggest, then, that while relatively underprivileged regions may sometimes be home to forms of regional nationalism, this is by no means always the case: in the mid-twentieth century the Maritime provinces of Canada were less well-off than Quebec, but it was in the latter that nationalism was to develop. In Spain and Yugoslavia, it was in the wealthiest and most developed regions that nationalist mobilization was strongest. Indeed, this phenomenon – countries where the focal area is less developed in socioeconomic terms than the outlying regions – recurs widely. This was the case, for example, in the Ottoman empire as regards its European possessions, and in the Russian empire as regards the Baltic provinces. Thus, while economic deprivation and relative underdevelopment provide ammunition to regional nationalist elites (who can ascribe their backwardness to exploitation by the centre), their counterparts in economically advanced regions may raise similar arguments (to the effect that their wealth is being siphoned off by an avaricious centre, possibly to subsidize poorer regions).

Two final points need to be made about the character of interregional differences. The first is that they are not static. The gap between rich and poor regions may increase, but more commonly governments seek to bridge this gap by using regional development policies and other such instruments. For example, data from 1948 show the index of average wages and salaries per capita in the UK ranging from 121 in London and the Southeast to 66 in Northern Ireland (Deane, 1953: 133); but similar data for 1959–60 that include all income sources (including transfers) show the range now reduced – from 111 in London and the Southeast to 82 in Northern Ireland (Holmans, 1965: 17). Quite apart from the efforts of governments, regional economies may wax and wane. Thus in Belgium, where the French-speaking southern region of Wallonia was for a long time the power house of economic growth, a sharp shift in regional fortunes has been taking place – as traditional heavy industries have fallen into decline, investment has shifted northwards to the new, high-technology

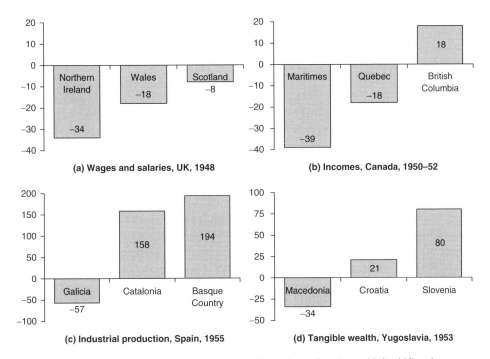

Figure 7.9 Indicators of economic development in selected regions, United Kingdom, Canada, Spain and Yugoslavia, *c.* 1950

Note: The bars represent deviations from the overall index for the country in question (100). The indicators are indices of (a) average wages and salaries per head of total population, 1948; (b) relative levels of per capita personal income exclusive of government transfers, 1950–52; (c) coefficients of industrial production excluding energy, 1955; (d) reproducible tangible wealth per head, end 1953.

Source: Computed from Deane (1953: 33); McInnes (1968: 445); Germán (2006: 881); Vinski (1961: 20)

industries of Dutch-speaking Flanders, resulting in a reversal of the traditional economic relationship between the two parts of the country. In a rather different context, the relationship between Northern Ireland and the Republic of Ireland was shaped by similar changes in the late twentieth century, with the North's traditional economic lead (due to its predominance in such areas as textile manufacturing and heavy engineering) giving way to the South (where high-technology industry and financial services were growing precisely as traditional industries were in decline).

Second, regions are not monoliths, but are themselves internally divided along geographical or other lines – sometimes deeply so. Quite apart from possibly having a complex ethnic composition, significant regional fault-lines may be present: in Scotland between the industrialized, urbanized, more anglicized Lowlands and the more agrarian, rural, residually Gaelic Highlands, or in the Basque Country between the strongholds of Basque culture in the industrial North and the more agrarian southern province of Álava, where the Basque language is much weaker. Such differences, too, can have significant political implications.

Regional mobilization

Land or territory has long been seen (alongside *people*) as a major stimulus of identity (Doob, 1964). But human attachment to territory and the drive to control it by military might or legal title is not merely a matter of sentiment: land has itself been a key resource from agrarian times onwards (Mellor, 1989: 53–4). Not surprisingly, then, mobilization based on regionalist demands has been a common phenomenon. One late twentieth-century study of 'global mini-nationalisms' (a term the author equates with regionalist movements) listed 66 such movements worldwide – 29 in Europe, 12 in the Middle East, 12 in Africa, nine in Asia and four in North America – without exhausting the universe of cases (Snyder, 1982: 22–4). A more specialized study of Africa identified a much larger, less definite number of cases of 'subnationalism', referring to 'movements by regional actors to pursue greater autonomy within the nation-state, a relatively loose degree of political separatism, or out-right secession' (Forrest, 2004: 5). This definition is strikingly similar to the understanding of nationalism that underlies this book. But it also overlaps with the concept of 'tribalism', a term which, alongside its associated term 'tribe', lost favour as an analytical tool in the study of African societies, largely because of the extent to which it was seen as politically loaded (Ekeh, 1990: 662–5).

Anssi Paasi (2009: 134–6) distinguishes four stages – which may coincide rather than being consecutive – in the institutionalization of regions: *territorial shaping* and boundary definition over a long period of time; *symbolic shaping* through the endowment of the region with an identity, and especially with a name; *institutional shaping*, such as the emergence of regional cultural features, formal or informal, including dialect; and *establishment* of the region through its recognition as part of the territorial structure. If we interpret this loosely, and combine the second and third of these stages, we may devise a useful framework for considering three aspects of the regional phenomenon: the processes of territorial definition, identity formation and political articulation.

Territorial definition. The territorial definition of a region may depend on several factors. One is geography: a region may be defined simply because it is an island, as in the case of Iceland, Ireland, Cyprus or Taiwan, or because it possesses 'natural frontiers' of another kind, such as French claims to the left bank of the Rhine. But geography alone will rarely if ever determine the boundaries of a region. Why is it, for example, that Ireland and Britain are seen as separate, but the North and South Islands of New Zealand are seen as part of the same country? Why are the Channel Islands linked to the United Kingdom rather than France, and the Faroe Islands to Denmark rather than the United Kingdom? The answer presumably lies in long-term processes of politically driven territorial formation. In addition to the creation of larger states, local political circumstances may have resulted in the appearance of territorial entities whose persistence over centuries gave them the appearance of being natural – the German, Austrian and Italian states, for instance. Shifting international frontiers may have a similar effect, sometimes even counteracting powerful linguistic or cultural factors.

Identity formation.   Perhaps the most basic step in identity formation has to do with acquisition of a name – a process in the course of which self-designation and designation by outsiders commonly compete (Safran, 2008b). Regions described solely by reference to points of the compass (for example, the 'Northeast') are being defined implicitly by reference to a larger territory of which they are a part, and this may also be explicit if the compass point is combined with a geographical name (as in the case of 'Northern Ireland'). For this reason, regional activists commonly seek to devise or appropriate a more exclusive name (such as 'Ulster' in the case of Northern Irish Protestants), though these may be contested. For example, when Macedonia's independence was recognized in 1993, due to objections from Greece (which reserves the word 'Macedonia' for its own northern province) it was forced to use the name 'Former Yugoslav Republic of Macedonia', or FYROM.

In its early stages, the name may be a group name rather than a territorial one. The authority of ancient tribal chiefs was commonly based on the group rather than on the territory, as in the designations *Rex Visigothorum* and *Rex Vandalorum* (Tägil, 1999: 37); even today, one ruler is designated 'King of the Belgians' rather than 'King of Belgium'. Elsewhere, the shift from very local self-designations to broader descriptions was an important stage in the development of regional and later national consciousness. In the nineteenth century many residents of the Baltic provinces of Estland and Livland referred to themselves as *maarahvas*, or 'country people' (Raun, 2003: 132), and in the early twentieth century many residents of districts in Polesia in what was then Eastern Poland described themselves as *tutejszy*, or 'local people' (Fleming, 2006: 13). The shift to self-designation as 'Estonian' and 'Belarusian', and of the territory in which they lived as 'Estonia' and 'Belarus' respectively, was a critical stage in regional and national evolution. There were fewer problems with regional identity when this was reinforced by a tradition of statehood, as in the German regions (Keating, 1998b: 85–94; Lindeborg, 1999). In Africa and Asia, many names (like borders) were arbitrarily imposed by European imperialists, but were nevertheless accepted by the first generation of nationalists (Sharkey, 2003: 16); at a later stage, many were changed to indigenous forms (so Ceylon became Sri Lanka and Northern Rhodesia became Zambia).

Where boundary changes were responsible for the appearance of a new region, the process of identity formation has been complex, as in the case of Schleswig on the German–Danish border and Alsace on the German–French border. In the case of Polesia (part of Russia to 1918, then Poland to 1945, then the Soviet Union), efforts were made by Polish gentry to persuade *tutejszy* that they were not Russian, and by Russian officials to convince them that they were not Polish, with Belarusian a not unacceptable compromise on the part of both (Tomaszewski, 1985: 110–11). There were similar patterns in other borderlands of the Soviet Union: long-term inclusion in Russia has been responsible for the appearance of separate Karelian and Moldavian regions and identities, even though local residents speak what may be regarded as variants of Finnish and Romanian respectively (see Schrad, 2004). The drawing of a border between the Karachai-Balkars and

Chechen-Ingush made a similar contribution to their becoming separate peoples (Rakic, 1998: 604). Upper Silesia is another important illustrative case. This region has had a particular history on the frontiers of Poland and Germany, and it continues to contain elements of a regional identity (Bialasiewicz, 2002: 119–24; Kamusella, 2011). The multi-cultural character of border regions is also illustrated by Scania in southern Sweden, for-merly part of Denmark (Johansson, 1999: 26), Carinthia and Burgenland in Austria, on the borders respectively with Slovenia and Hungary (Gullberg, 1999), the Banat region of southwest Romania near the Hungarian border (Batt, 2002a), and the Ukrainian–Slovak and Turkish–Georgian border areas (Hann, 1995). The complexity of the interaction between identity patterns and shifting frontiers is well illustrated by a story that is no doubt apocryphal but that points to a certain geopolitical reality. In the Transcarpathian region of Ukraine, a tale was told of an old man who was born in Austria-Hungary, went to school in Czechoslovakia, did his army service in Hungary, was imprisoned in the Soviet Union, and spent his old age in Ukraine – all without ever leaving his village (Batt, 2002b: 155).

Political articulation.   Regionalist demands were expressed with particular vigour in Europe from the late 1960s onwards, and have tended to take a variety of forms: left- or right-leaning, based on the notion of modernity and progress or of conservative rural defence, and with varying cultural bases and political demands (Keating, 1998b: 52–5; Cole, 2007). Observers have been particularly struck by the success of a new Italian party, the *Lega Nord*, in promoting 'Padanian nationalism' in Italy (Keating, 1998b: 87–8; Paasi, 2009: 130). It has been argued that this even resembles the well-established nationalist movement in Catalonia, with its emphasis on protection of regional privileges, its opposition to the centralizing tendencies of the state, and its support for European integration as a counterweight to this (Giordano and Roller, 2001). By contrast, the position in six interface regions in the East European post-communist world is mixed, with sharply varying levels of regional consciousness (Gerner, 1999: 207–10). Regional mobilization is at its most characteristic when it enjoys a reasonably strong cultural base, as in Bavaria and certain other German *Länder*. But this appears not to be a necessary condition: such mobilization may take place even where there are few, if any, expressions of a separate regional culture, as in certain US states, such as Texas. In such cases, we may encounter use of symbols (such as flags, anthems and regional insignia) that bear some resemblance to those of fully-fledged nations.

Finally, we need to distinguish between regional mobilization and nationalist mobiliza-tion. The latter may be seen as one of the most distinctive forms of regional mobiliza-tion, and as such will be discussed in the next chapter. There are indeed close structural similarities between the two processes: between 'nation building' in larger territorial entities and regional resistance to this process, resistance that may amount to a 'nation building' enterprise at a lower level (Keating, 1998b: 19–35). The boundary between the expectations of the region and those of the nation-state lies in the area of exclusivity in its fullest form: nationalism lays claim to absolute sovereignty and to the unqualified allegiance of citizens, though the reality of such sovereignty is rare even in the context of the Westphalian treaties (1648), which are seen as having given rise to the modern sovereign state (Keating, 1998b: 16–17). Regionalism, by contrast, allows for multiple tiers of authority and identification: the population of the region shares a wider 'national' affiliation, as in the case of the various protest movements in France, at least in the past, that could better be described as 'regionalist' than 'nationalist' (Zimmer, 2003b: 52–3). Outside Europe, too, regionalism may challenge state-centred nationalism, as in peninsular Malaysia, where Malays traditionally had a strong attachment to the regional state and its ruler (Pluvier, 1974: 89–90).

CONCLUSION

One critic of naïve economic explanations carefully acknowledged the significance of socioeconomic divisions for nationalism: economic discrepancies may be experienced particularly vividly when they coincide with an ethnonational dimension (Connor, 1984a: 350). As we have seen, such coincidence was common in traditional and transitional societies, and it continues to be a feature of the contemporary world. Sense of economic grievance has the capacity to envigour feelings of cultural marginalization, and to promote forms of nationalist mobilization in which social and cultural demands feed off each other. Such mobilization is even more likely in the context of changing relationships between groups – whether a function of individual mobility in the labour marker or change in the relative collective fortunes of whole regions.

Indeed, we may often see regional mobilization as a kind of truncated nationalism: sharing the main features of nationalist movements, but falling short in critical ways of classical nationalism, typically by advancing less ambitious goals. Identifying regionalism is normally easy if the region in question has a distinctive culture, and especially language. Thus, as well as forms of mobilization in Scotland, Flanders and Catalonia that may be described as nationalism, we find forms of mobilization in Cornwall, Brittany and Sardinia that are often described as 'regionalism' (though the distinction between the two types is far from clear-cut). There is a demand for recognition of a separate regional identity, but this either fails to strike a chord with most of the population of the region, or its political demands are confined to the area of cultural or administrative autonomy. Interestingly, the same predictions that have been made about the dire fate that awaits nationalism in a global world have also been made about regionalism. However, the regional level increasingly attracts admirers for reasons of scale: states may be too small as units for global economic competition, but they are commonly too large to provide a focal point for cultural identification and active citizenship (Paasi, 2009: 123).

Once we move outside the familiar old characteristics, such as language and religion, whose impact on national identity has for long been acknowledged, we encounter great difficulties in identifying social features that have an impact on nationalism. Occupational and social class differences may be important, and region of residence may have a major effect. But when this is the case, these variables seem to play the role of reinforcing some other difference, such as language or religion, rather than being important simply in their own right. Class or regional differences, in other words, however great, do not of themselves translate into forms of national conflict; they function as a lubricant for the nationalist motor rather than as a supply of fuel. This leaves us, then, with the question of accounting for the connection between the factors already considered (including, in Part One, race, language, religion and public culture, with gender playing a special role) and the evolution of nationalism – the subject of the rest of this book.

8

TYPES OF NATIONALIST MOBILIZATION

INTRODUCTION

In popular culture, nationalist activism is typically presented in clear-cut, binary fashion. We may see this in the area of film: *Braveheart* (1995), for example, pits a courageous Scottish rebel against the English throne, and *The patriot* (2000) depicts a struggle between resourceful American revolutionaries and their powerful British opponents. But nationalism is rarely so straightforward – not only is it not a battle between good and evil, it is typically not even a contest between two sides. We need to turn, then, to the various forms that nationalism may take – a vast field, especially if we extend the time dimension backwards to the late eighteenth century, and the space dimension outwards to cover the globe.

We have already looked in earlier chapters at the interplay between patterns of national identity and cultural and social factors. What are the implications of this relationship for nationalism at different historical periods in different parts of the world? Looking for common features across such movements presents a formidable challenge, but we nevertheless try to meet this in the first section of the chapter, by focusing in particular on the most prominent actors in the nationalist process and by trying to identify a core nationalist ideology. This is followed by an examination of three geopolitically distinct forms of nationalist movement, each of which may be further subdivided: we may label them integrationist nationalism, colonial nationalism and separatist nationalism.

COMMON FEATURES

Perhaps surprisingly given the diversity of nationalist movements, it is possible to identify certain common features in their life cycles. Two areas of similarity stand out. The first has to do with the agents of nationalism: who are the crucial actors who seek to shape the future of their nations? The second has to do with the programme followed by these actors: are there distinctive themes across movements?

Nationalist actors

In classical nationalist rhetoric, there are only two sides to the story, and only two crucial sets of actors: the nation and its leaders in one corner, and the nation's enemies in the other. The latter are normally identified with hostile external forces, though domestic allies or fifth columnists are frequently identified. For purposes of the rest of this chapter, however, we distinguish not two but three crucial sets of actors which, it can be argued, are always present in principle but not necessarily in practice.

Centre and periphery. The complex set of relations that underlies nationalist mobilization may usefully be set in the context of the concepts of 'centre' and 'periphery' discussed in Chapter 7. By the former we mean not the geographical central point of a politically organized territory but rather the location in which political resources are concentrated. By 'periphery' is meant an outlying area which is subject to the political control of the centre. But relations between centre and periphery commonly follow a rather more complex path. The literature on imperialism, focusing on relations between European powers and their colonies in Africa, Asia and elsewhere, has for long stressed the complex and often subtle ways in which effective power may be exercised over great distances. For example, Johan Galtung (1971: 83–5) used insights from Lenin's theory of imperialism to identify four groups: a centre and a periphery *within each* of a 'centre nation' and a 'periphery nation'. If, to avoid terminological confusion, we call the centre and periphery nations respectively 'metropolitan' territory and 'region' (which may be a distant colony), we may relabel these actors as the metropolitan centre, the metropolitan periphery, the regional centre and the regional periphery.

Galtung's central argument was that there is harmony of interest between the two centres; conflict of interest between the two peripheries (and between the metropolitan and regional territories in general); and a particular conflict of interest between the regional centre and the regional periphery. These conflicts extend over several domains. The metropolitan centre is dominant economically, with industrial production concentrated in its territory; culturally, it controls the supply of ideas and education; and politically, it makes long-term decisions, offers institutional models and provides military protection. The regional periphery, by contrast, lacks economic vigour, being primarily a supplier of raw materials such as agricultural produce; culturally, it is a consumer of ideas and educational resources provided by the centre; and politically it complies with decisions of the centre, accepts its institutional models and provides low-ranking military personnel rather than commanders (Galtung, 1971: 91–4). The relationship between the two is often summarized in a distinctive geopolitical feature: the capital of the region is chosen to suit the interests of the metropolitan area rather than those of the region itself. It is commonly located at the geographical point that is physically most accessible to the metropolitan territory (from which, indeed, transport links to all regions tend to radiate outwards as spokes, with few intersecting lines of communication). It is thus no surprise that Dublin, close to the British coast, has for centuries been the Irish capital, or that Åbo (Turku, close to Sweden), lost this position to Helsinki (close to Russia) shortly after Russia acquired Finland from Sweden in 1809.

Given the prominence of their political roles, the concepts of 'metropolitan centre' and 'regional periphery' are relatively familiar (even if the terms themselves are not particularly evocative). The 'regional centre' requires further discussion. In the most typical cases, the regional centre originated in colonization from the metropolitan centre. But the metropolitan centre was sometimes able to co-opt a section of the regional periphery, a group which was derided by nationalist elites as collaborators; Slovaks sympathetic to the Hungarians in the nineteenth century, described by their critics as 'Magyarones', are one of many examples (Maxwell, 2005: 386). One very common pattern was, however, an alliance between the metropolitan centre and another locally important group. Thus tsarist Russia relied on the Germans in the Baltic provinces, the British on the Straits Chinese in Malaya and the Karens in Burma, the Dutch on the Ambonese in what was then the East Indies, and the French on the Montagnards in Indo-China (Christie, 1996; Kratoska and Batson, 1999: 312–13), to cite but a few. These alliances were, in many cases, to come back later to haunt those who were party to them.

Although Galtung had in mind relationships between European metropolitan areas (such as France and Britain) and geographically remote 'regions' (such as Algeria and India), it is possible to adapt his perspective for much broader purposes. As discussed in Chapter 7, Robert Lafont (1967: 140–83) saw state consolidation processes in France as a form of 'internal colonialism', and Michael Hechter (1975: 30–4) applied a similar framework to the geopolitical development of the United Kingdom. In each case, it was argued, an imperialist-colonial-type relationship characterized the impact of the metropolitan centre on such peripheral regions as Languedoc and Ireland, and the reaction of these regions to the centre. Stein Rokkan and Derek Urwin, after directing a major comparative review of centre–periphery relations within European states (Rokkan and Urwin, 1982), identified the critical dimensions of conflict between metropolitan and peripheral areas in a way that can be seen as overlapping with those described by Galtung: economic, military-administrative and cultural (Rokkan and Urwin, 1983: 14–18). The outcome of the struggle in these areas, they suggested, would determine whether peripheral areas were detached as independent states or were fully integrated within the metropolitan territory.

This identification of dimensions of conflict gives us an indication of the types of agent that we may expect to be involved. We have already considered the reference by Engels to the role of merchants, handicraftsmen, clergy, schoolmasters, *savants* and 'the iron tread of conquering armies' in the nation-building process (Engels, 1979 [1852]: 44; see Chapter 7). This was put more vividly by the Kenyan writer, Ngŭgĭ wa Thiong'o (1977: 88): 'The missionary had traversed the seas, the forests, armed with the desire for profit that was his faith and light and the gun that was his protection. He carried the Bible; the soldier carried the gun; the administrator and the settler carried the coin. Christianity, Commerce, Civilisation: the Bible, the Coin, the Gun: Holy Trinity'. In similar mode, if from a very different starting point, Rokkan (1969, 1970) highlighted the role played in the nation-building process in Europe by three groups: the church, the landed aristocracy and the urban interest. Other well-known analyses rest on a perception of the centrality of similar groups. Gellner (1983: 9–11), as well as identifying these three groups, adds a fourth: the administrative class. It is striking that Paul Brass (1985: 33–49), basing his argument mainly on Asian examples, sees the local aristocracy and local religious elites as playing a critical role in shaping the outcome of the tension between integrationist and separatist forces. Much of the literature on nation building shares with the literature on imperial expansion a tendency, then, to ascribe a leading role to three sets of actors: politico-military-administrative, economic-mercantile, and cultural.

We need to distinguish here between two levels of analysis that cut across each other. The first is a geopolitical distinction between the metropolitan territory and the region, with the latter divided into a regional centre (normally with close political, economic, and cultural links to the metropolitan centre) and a regional periphery (more detached from the metropolitan centre in each of these areas). The regional centre is not necessarily just an elite group: it is potentially a sizeable population, though disproportionately privileged. The second level of analysis cuts across this: within the metropolitan centre there are well resourced and powerful political-bureaucratic-military, economic and cultural elites; these have their counterparts in the regional centre; and such elites are to varying degrees present in the regional periphery, where they tend to be weak, if they exist at all. The nature of the support base of these elites is of considerable importance, though its character varies greatly from one context to another (Breuilly, 1982: 300–33; Coakley, 1992b).

A model of nationalism. It is possible to devise ideal-type descriptions of the evolution of the relationship between metropolitan centre, regional centre and regional periphery, and three of these are summarized in Figure 8.1. The first representation (Figure 8.1a, top left) illustrates the initial position: three notional entities, the metropolitan centre, the regional centre and the regional periphery, coexist within the same geopolitical context – typically as members of the same state or 'governance unit' (to use a broader term coined by Hechter, 2000: 9). Their interrelations evolve in the three zones already discussed, centring on three crucial groups of actors: military and administrators, merchants and economic entrepreneurs, and religious workers and educationalists. In its struggle for military-political, economic and cultural control, the metropolitan centre enters into particular relationships (whether of alliance or of antagonism) with the regional centre; but this becomes a triangular relationship, as the regional periphery resists or complies with these pressures, typically reacting in a differentiated way to the regional centre and the metropolitan centre. The outcome of the struggle between these forces determines the ultimate relationship between the region and the metropolitan centre – whether it will be absorbed and become part of a larger nation, or whether it will itself form the basis for a new nation (which may be controlled either by the regional centre or the regional periphery).

The relationship between these forces may depart from the predictable pattern of an alliance between the metropolitan centre and the regional centre against the regional periphery. Sometimes the regional periphery seeks the support of the metropolitan centre against the regional centre (as in the case of Estonian and Latvian peasants in the nineteenth century looking to the Russian tsar to protect them against their Baltic German masters, or the Maori seeking to enlist British backing for their struggle against European New Zealanders). Reciprocally, the metropolitan centre may attempt to undermine the regional centre by supporting the divergent interests of the regional periphery (as in the case of the Habsburg disposition to use the Ruthenians (Ukrainians) against the Poles, or the Slovaks and Romanians against the Hungarians).

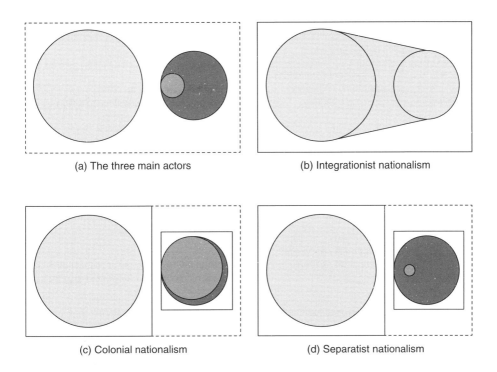

(a) The three main actors   (b) Integrationist nationalism

(c) Colonial nationalism   (d) Separatist nationalism

Figure 8.1   Nationalism and metropolitan–regional relations

Note: Rectangles refer to states or governance units, with dotted lines indicating former or potential states; the large circle on the left represents the metropolitan territory, the smaller one on the right the peripheral region; the smallest circle represents the regional centre.

Figure 8.1 suggests three types of outcome to competition between the three interests. In the first (Figure 8.1b), the metropolitan centre emerges victorious: it decisively extends its military and political reach and integrates the region economically and culturally. In the second (Figure 8.1c), the regional centre possesses sufficient resources to assert its independence of the metropolitan centre while simultaneously vanquishing the regional periphery, which is marginalized politically, economically and culturally. In the last pattern (Figure 8.1d), it is the regional periphery which emerges victorious, shaking off the dominance of the regional centre in these domains and winning political independence.

Indeed, in the rest of this chapter, we will consider precisely these three outcomes, looked at from the standpoint of the respective groups. To make a rather complex and dense discussion a little easier, Table 8.1 gives examples of the types of process we propose to explore. First, the nationalism of the metropolitan centre is a form of *integrationist nationalism*: it seeks to integrate the outlying territories, thus coming into conflict with the regional centre. But its efforts to advance the process of national homogenization may force it into confrontation with the regional periphery too. It may also come into conflict with other metropolitan centres over borderlands claimed by both, in a form of irredentist nationalism (though irredendism may also be associated with separatist nationalism).

Table 8.1 Examples of types of nationalism

Key group/example	Dominant feature	Comment
Metropolitan centre	*Integrationist nationalism*	
Prussia	Territorial unification	Creation of wider German state
Île-de-France	Cultural integration	Centralization of state and dissemination of French culture
Pakistan	Irredentism	Claim over Jammu and Kashmir, regarded as external portion of 'national territory' occupied by an adjacent power
Regional centre	*Colonial nationalism*	
Argentina	Creole nationalism	Establishment of independence from Spain and of dominance over indigenous population. Issues: (1) relative power of indigenous population; (2) homogeneity of Creoles
Regional periphery	*Separatist nationalism*	
Estonia	Peripheral nationalism	Establishment of autonomy in respect of Russia and assertion of rights of Estonian as opposed to German culture
Algeria	Anti-colonial nationalism	Establishment of independence from France, in opposition also to *pieds noirs* (*colons*). Issues: (1) relative power of *colons*; (2) status of indigenous culture

Second, the rather less common nationalism of the regional centre is a form of *colonial nationalism*: it involves a struggle for independence directed against the metropolitan centre, while possibly contending also with a challenge from the regional periphery. The programme of pursuing independence is viable for the regional centre only if the regional periphery is prepared to accept its lead, or is too weak to do anything about it. But the regional centre may itself be divided, and various forms of settler or 'Creole' nationalism may be generated by internal rivalries within it.

Third, one of the most common of all kinds of nationalism is the *separatist nationalism* of the regional periphery. This may be directed first and foremost against the regional centre, perceived as the real enemy of the regional periphery and as the primary and self-seeking agent of malign external rule. It may also be directed against the metropolitan centre, in circumstances where the position of the provincial centre has been neutralized, especially in the form of anti-colonial nationalism. But it may also find expression in a struggle for authenticity between competing groups within the regional periphery.

The nationalist programme

Given the extraordinary diversity of nationalist processes, a diversity that will emerge clearly in the rest of this chapter, it is surprising to find widely shared features in the nationalist programme. It is true that European nationalist ideologists were in many cases able to borrow from the writings of influential early figures, such as Herder and Fichte, either directly, if they were able to read German, or indirectly, where these ideas were disseminated at second hand. But it is likely that many nationalist apologists never came across these even indirectly. Furthermore, unlike other ideologies such as socialism, such theoretical writing as exists has tended to be case- and context-specific, never reaching the level of a defensible general theory, as we have seen in Chapter 1. The similarities in nationalist thought are therefore all the more striking. Equally impressive is the manner in which this ideological package was popularized through processes of simplification (and in particular the creation of stereotypes), repetition (though speeches, newspapers, rallies and songs) and concreteness (through symbolism and ceremonial) (Breuilly, 1982: 344).

At the core of the nationalist package lie concerns with culture and national sovereignty (Benner, 2001), but there are more specific recurring themes. John Breuilly (1982: 342), for instance, identified three central ideas that are not necessarily mutually consistent: the notion of the national community as a unique, historically evolved collectivity; the view that this community is entitled to have its own state; and a political conception of the nation as a body of citizens. At a more concrete level, Florian Znaniecki (1952: 8–100) saw four components as having a particularly effective role (they overlap with the discussion of historical myth in Chapter 5): the cult of heroes, a myth of common descent and racial unity, attachment to a particular national land as a common and exclusive group possession, and the notion of defence against common enemies. Frederick Hertz (1944: 21–4) identified four 'national aspirations': *unity* of the nation in the political, economic, social and cultural domains; *freedom* of the nation from external powers; *distinctiveness* in relation to other peoples; and *distinction* among nations by promoting national prestige. These perspectives overlap, but collectively suggest that we may summarize the core nationalist ideology under three headings:

- An historical conception of the nation as a community with a shared past, perhaps with a common descent and racial background, and with a homeland of its own (see Chapters 2 and 5).
- A cultural understanding of the nation as an entity whose unity and distinctiveness (in such areas as language) is to be preserved, and whose prestige and mission to humanity is to be promoted (see Chapters 3, 5 and 6).
- A political ambition to secure the unity of the nation in relation to potentially disruptive forces within its own borders, and to establish its autonomy in relation to external rivals (discussed further in this chapter).

This may seem like an unusually specific list of core features, but the frequency with which we find them in individual nationalist movements is striking. There are forms of nationalism where some of these considerations appear not to apply. The myth of common descent is by no means always present, for instance: American nationalism, though once associated with the idea of a 'WASP' (White Anglo-Saxon Protestant) heritage, now rests on the notion of a 'melting pot' within which peoples from different ethnic backgrounds (or, at least, 'white' ones) are blended, and Mexican nationalism defines the nation as a mixture of indigenous and settler peoples. But the broad historical, cultural and political components appear to be universally present: although the emphasis varies from case to case, all nationalist movements rest on an understanding of the nation as a community with a shared past, seek to defend its cultural distinctiveness and to assert its prestige in relation to other nations, and strive to advance its unity and independence (or at least autonomy). Self-determination may be more modestly defined: in pre-1918 Europe, for example, it usually referred to autonomy rather than independence (Hroch, 2000: 116–21), and this was true also of later movements, such as the Puerto Rican and Catalan ones (Lluch, 2011). Small, dispersed groups such as the James Bay Cree in Canada may set their sights even lower, pursuing only recognition – not even autonomy (Ramos, 2000).

As well as the core described above, many nationalist movements offer a social programme. Hroch (2000: 12) sees promotion of the socioeconomic development of the nation as one of the three key features of the national programme of subordinate European peoples, alongside political and cultural demands. Such a programme is important in enlisting mass support, especially if, as in much of Asia, foreign colonialism can be blamed for social and economic ills, and it rests on demands for economic emancipation, social justice, combating poverty and wiping out backwardness, possibly with elements of religious revivalism (Pluvier, 1974: 74). This programme has more profound roots where it implies a confrontation between advanced western colonial powers and the 'backward' peoples they governed, with a tension between the incorporation of 'progressive' western components while retaining 'civilizing' eastern ones, a dilemma faced by Indian nationalists (Chatterjee, 1986: 36–53). Chinese nationalism faced a comparable choice: whether to westernize to defend itself against the west, or retain Chinese principles (Yahuda, 2000: 25–6). Subordinate peoples elsewhere faced a similar dilemma; but this does not mean that they were invariably left-leaning since substate nationalism is neither intrinsically left- or right-wing in orientation, as Flemish, Walloon and Quebec evidence shows (Erk, 2005, 2010).

INTEGRATIONIST NATIONALISM

In the first of the three patterns of nationalist mobilization that we consider, the tripartite network of relationships outlined above is least useful as an interpretative tool. The metropolitan centre is relatively clearly defined; the distinction between the regional centre and the regional periphery is less so. Nevertheless, we should take note of the capacity of regional elites to resist the centralizing programme of the metropolitan centre, even if in this they were ultimately unsuccessful. As regards the nationalist programme and ideology, the emphasis is on political unity, though all of the other classical ingredients are present. We may consider three variants. First, in some cases the challenge perceived by the nation-building elite is the imperative of political unification. Second, following the achievement of political unity, there may be a drive to complete this process at the sociocultural level by striving for a high level of cultural uniformity or homogeneity. Third, even after the completion of one or both of these processes, 'unfinished business' may remain: a fragment of the 'national territory' may lie under occupation by a foreign power, or otherwise be separated from its self-proclaimed kin state, resulting in an irredentist claim.

Territorial unification

From the point of view of the metropolitan centre, whether driven by considerations of state or by nationalist ambition, political and cultural integration of its territory is commonly a prime objective. There are three main patterns at the political level. In the first, a territory has been assembled early through gradual territorial expansion. In the second, disunity is the major challenge. The third pattern is one where nationalism has a dual political objective: there is an interplay between the pursuit of independence and of unity.

In the first pattern, political integration forms part of the nationalist agenda, but political unification begins early. Switzerland claims a foundation date of 1291, when the three 'forest cantons' of Schwyz, Unterwalden and Uri committed themselves to an 'eternal alliance', but in reality its contemporary territorial identity was defined by the gradual accretion of new territories – it acquired a new reality as a federation in 1848, following a civil conflict, the '*Sonderbund* war', between the state-building Protestant cantons and independent-minded Catholic cantons in 1847. The formation of France, Russia, China, the United Kingdom and other states followed a similar pattern, with the steady but by no means irreversible expansion of an original core territory and the incorporation of outlying areas. In some cases, the transition to modern statehood was marked by a cataclysmic event. The French revolution that began in 1789 created a new centralized state out of the loosely organized lands which the French monarchy had governed, completing the integration of the directly ruled *pays d'élection* and bringing the more autonomous *pays d'état* under central control. This was hailed as both 'the first modern nationalist revolution' and 'the model for modern nationalism in other European countries' (Llobera, 1994: 179). In such cases, territories that now seem 'natural' were in fact the result of historical accident, and the ultimate physical shape of the state would have been hard to predict.

In the second pattern, the attainment of territorial unification is proclaimed by nationalists as the fulfilment of their dream, as in the case of Germany and Italy (Seton-Watson, 1977: 91–8, 102–7). Thus, for Giuseppe Mazzini (1805–72), the creation of a united Italian republic was the ultimate goal, echoing the call of Johann Gottlieb Fichte (1762–1814) for a unified Germany. In both cases, the process of unification was, however, driven less by popular nationalism than by the expansion of a core territory. Italy, consisting in the early nineteenth century of a handful of independent states and subject territories, was unified in a number of stages under the leadership of the Kingdom of Piedmont. Piedmontese control was extended over most of northern Italy between 1859 and 1870, leaving only parts of the northeast to be included in 1918. Germany had possessed a level of notional unity since the middle ages through the Holy Roman Empire (a strangely labelled entity that had once indeed included Rome, but which later acquired a 'German' tag). But the nominal overlordship of the 'Holy Roman Empire of the German Nation' (headed in its later years by the Austrian Habsburg dynasty) allowed for the emergence of hundreds of effectively independent states; in the year of the outbreak of the French revolution, 1789, there were said to be 1,789 such states (Geiss, 1997: 27), ranging in size from Prussia and Bavaria to tiny entities such as the city of Speyer and the abbey of Berchtesgaden. The Empire finally ceased to exist in 1806 and its complex maze of territories was reconstituted in 1815 as the German Confederation, the northern part of which came under Prussian control in 1866. Finally, the unified German Empire was proclaimed in 1871, significantly excluding Austria and the Habsburg dominions; the King of Prussia became Emperor of Germany.

As already indicated, these unification processes were elite driven, with a central role being played by the Piedmontese prime minister Count Cavour (1820–61) and his Prussian counterpart Count Bismarck (1815–98). In the German case, it is true, they were also assisted by a process of economic unification through the *Zollverein* or customs union that linked many German states to Prussia, the powerful economic driver of the process (Schulze, 1987: 15–16). Although popular nationalism did not make a significant contribution to these processes, it was not altogether absent, through such organizations as the *Deutscher Nationalverein* (1859) (Düding, 1987: 44–9) and the *Società nazionale italiana* (1857) (Riall, 1994: 70–4) in Germany and Italy respectively – each with a limited membership basis.

We need to consider also a 'hybrid' pattern, where the pursuit of independence challenges the goal of unification in its centrality to the nationalist programme. The first and most complex variety of this links political unification with colonial nationalism. Thus, while the formation of the United States of America was mainly a process of territorial unification and expansion, it was kicked off by an independence struggle on the part of the original 13 colonies, which declared their independence of Great Britain in 1776. As in several other cases of territorial unification, it took a civil war in 1861–65 to decide whether the United States was indeed a 'state' (as the Northern victory in the civil war showed it was). The process by which six other British colonies formed the Commonwealth of Australia in 1901 was similarly complex, with the extension of independence from the United Kingdom and the creation of an Australian identity as very gradual later processes. With important differences to be noted later, the process of 'confederation' that began in Canada in 1867 followed a similar path. The creation of the Union of South Africa was yet more complex, given the non-British background and history of separatism in two of its component units, the Transvaal and the Orange Free State.

In the second variety of the hybrid pattern, there is a more obvious link between the unification process and separatist nationalism. Romanian nationalism was concerned not just with liberation of the core provinces of Moldavia and Wallachia from the Turks (achieved by 1878), but also with establishing unity with the Hungarian province of Transylvania (achieved in 1918) and with the Russian region of Bessarabia (achieved temporarily, 1918–40). For Serbian nationalists, similarly, the Serbian kingdom that achieved international recognition in 1878 was just the core of a state made up of the South Slavs, which itself was created in 1918 on unification with Montenegro, Austrian-administered Bosnia-Hercegovina, Slovenia (part of Austria), Croatia (part of Hungary), and other territories of Hungary and Turkey. The creation of a Polish Republic in 1918 also reflected a combined drive for independence (from Russia, Germany and Austria-Hungary) with a movement for unification (of the formerly Russian 'Congress Poland' core with other territories from the three powers between which Poland had been partitioned in the eighteenth century).

Cultural integration

Mere political and institutional unification is rarely sufficient to produce political stability; unless the state is to rely on coercion, a minimum level of identification with it is essential. When Austrian foreign minister Metternich famously described Italy in 1847 as merely 'a geographical expression', he was not exaggerating: there was little identification with the concept of Italy, and less than 3% of the population actually spoke Italian (Clark, 1998: 2). This position changed only slowly: notwithstanding the institutionalization of a centralized state in 1861, big divisions continued, with most of the population continuing to speak local dialects (Clark, 1998: 98–9). As the nationalist writer and former Piedmontese prime minister, Massimo d'Azeglio, put it: 'Italy is made; now we must make Italians' (Seton-Watson, 1967: 13). While analysts of German nationalism commonly take linguistic homogeneity for granted, this did not describe reality in the nineteenth century (nor does it do so in the twenty-first century). Standard German has always coexisted with entrenched regional dialects. So powerful were the latter that some dialects broke away as alternative standards: Dutch already in the seventeenth century, and Luxembourgish in the twentieth. The dialects of Switzerland and Austria of course survive on the other side of a long-established border, but those of Bavaria and other regions continue even within the structures of the German state. Other states faced similar challenges. The Swedish government succeeded over time in transforming the language of Scania, previously part of Denmark, with the population becoming Swedish identifiers (Østergård, 1996 [1992]).

Elites within the modern state generally see themselves as imperilled if their cultural base is that of a minority (Kaufmann and Haklai, 2008). Securing the dissemination of a language of wider communication and moulding citizens' values to match those of the state thus constitutes an important challenge. The agencies principally responsible for the process of cultural integration were predictable: the school system (especially where, as became increasingly the case, school attendance was mandatory for all children) and the military (especially where, as was generally the case, conscription was the norm). But these routine, implicit sources of cultural assimilation and political socialization could be reinforced by other, more direct ones: by a communications system (including newspapers, radio and television) that was to varying degrees open to elite control, and by other overt messages from the nation-building elites. There are many tales of the measures used by teachers to promote a shift from the marginal language to the one of prestige, including symbols of humiliation and pain, such as the punishment stick: the Welsh 'Not', the *bata scoir* (Ireland), the *maide-crochaidh* (Scottish Highlands) and the *symbole* (Brittany and elsewhere in France) are examples. As folklore had it, any child using the local language was given a stick to hang around the neck, and had to wear this until another child offended; at the end of the day the child wearing the stick was punished.

Elite-driven integration was to be seen at its most assertive in the early part of the twentieth century in Europe, when nationalist leaders elevated the nation to a special status within the state. But it has continued to the present, with many examples from such contexts as the Soviet successor states, where, from the perspective of the new ruling elites, the national project was incomplete. As Rogers Brubaker (2011: 1786) put it, 'the new states were national in form, but not in substance'; in nationalist eyes, they were 'organizational shells that had to be filled with national content, bringing population, territory, culture and polity into the close congruence that defines a fully realized nation-state'. Elsewhere, as in Sub-Saharan Africa, the expansion of the reach of the state itself constituted a mechanism for transcending linguistic diversity and overcoming the consequences of arbitary borders: health, housing, and education programmes became instruments in fostering a broad sense of national unity (Kpessa, Béland and Lecours, 2011).

Europe also contributed a notable authoritarian framework for nation consolidating efforts of this kind, especially with the rise of fascist and quasi-fascist governments in the 1920s and 1930s. Although its European expressions have been addressed in greatest detail, Michael Mann (2004: 31–43) offers a valuable corrective to the view that this was a discrete, largely European phenomenon. In fact, it straddled the globe. In addition to the replacement of formally democratic regimes by authoritarian ones in China, Japan, and most of Latin America, the 'impeccable parliamentary institutions' of the USA, Canada, Australia, New Zealand (with some qualifications), South Africa and Rhodesia were for a long time racially exclusive – namely, intended for whites only (Mann, 2004: 38-9). Even within Europe, while it is possible to distinguish between 15 former parliamentary regimes that had become rightist dictatorships by 1938 and 12 which had not, there is a case for seeing the gap between the two as a gradient rather than a rigid line (Mann, 2004: 43–8).

Whether or not it succeeded in taking state power, fascism, with its emphasis on political unity and cultural putity had a particularly close relationship to nationalism, as we have seen in Chapter 2 (Nolte, 1965: 21; Hayes, 1973: 51–62; Payne, 1980: 7). This was particularly true of its Nazi variant in Germany (Blinkhorn, 2000: 41), though less so of the Vargas regime in Brazil (1937–45) or of the Perón regime in Argentina (1946–55) (Paxton, 2004: 192–200). Many right-wing nationalist regimes continued until the late twentieth century: Salazar's *Estado Novo* in Portugal up to 1974, Spain under Franco's *Falange* up to 1975, and Taiwan under Chiang Kai-Shek's *Kuomintang* until about 1991. Radical nationalism of this kind may be found also within democratic party systems, such as the Progress parties in Denmark and Norway, the British National Party, the *Front National* in France and the then *Vlaams Blok* in Belgium (Ignazi, 1997: 48).

Irredendist nationalism

Sometimes, nationalist leaders push the demand for national unification outside the borders of their states. The phrase *Italia irredenta* ('unredeemed Italy'), a reference in particular to territories of northern Italy remaining under Austrian control after the establishment of the Italian state, provided a root for a new expression, 'irredentism', referring to a form of nationalism comprising territorial claims on one or more adjacent states on the ground that they rightly belong to the 'national territory' (see also Chazan, 1991: 2). If Italy provided the term, Germany offered the most impressive list of examples. Like other national unification movements, the German unification project entailed not just the creation of new links between German states, but also conflicts with neighbouring states – notably with Denmark over South Schleswig and with France over Alsace and Lorraine. But where was the process of unification to stop? It has been suggested that there were at least four conceptions of the territory of Germany, with varying territorial implications. The most ambitious formed the basis of Nazi policy, and was achieved in the run-up to the Second World War, with the annexation of Austria and the Sudetenland in 1938, and further territorial expansion and 'repatriation' of certain outlying German minorities after 1939. Indeed, some pan-Germans included other established states (Switzerland and the Netherlands) within their list of 'lost territories'.

There are many other examples of irredentism. Hungarian nationalists were embittered by the partition of the old Kingdom of Hungary in 1918, when regions with large Magyar populations were separated from the truncated Hungarian state and allocated to Czechoslovakia and Romania. The Irish complained volubly at the partition of their island in 1921, with the United Kingdom retaining six Ulster counties, and, as we have seen in Chapter 5, made a constitutional claim to jurisdiction over the whole island of Ireland. Other well-known examples include the Argentinian claim to the Malvinas/Falklands Islands, the Chinese claim to Taiwan, the Serbian claim to Kosovo, the Spanish claim to Gibraltar, and the competing claims of Afghanistan and Pakistan over the Pashtun tribal areas, of Armenia and Azerbaidzhan over Nagorno-Karabakh, and of India and Pakistan over Kashmir.

The potential for irredentism is particularly great in Africa, where colonial boundaries commonly cut through the territories of local peoples. This resulted in some striking claims for external territories, as in the overlapping claims of Somalia and Ethiopia, of Mauritania and Morocco, and of parts of southern and western Africa (Neuberger, 1991). On the other hand, the colonial experience itself tended to promote a steady differentiation of those living on either side of the new borders, as they operated within contrasting social and political systems (Forrest, 2004: 18–19), assisting a longer-term resolution.

COLONIAL NATIONALISM

The second pattern of nationalist mobilization illustrates the tripartite network of relationships much more effectively: this is, indeed, central to the dynamics of this form of nationalism. Here it is the regional centre that is the assertive actor, fighting a determined battle against a former external ally in the metropolitan centre; but the viability of this challenge depends on the capacity of the regional centre to hold off any threat from the regional periphery. The emphasis is not so much on unity as on independence. We may detect three distinctive themes. The first is the battle against the metropolitan centre, with colonists challenging the former motherland – classical colonial nationalism, which we may also label 'Creole nationalism' after the *criollos* (American-born descendants of European settlers in

Spanish America). Second, to varying degrees the regional centre needs also to take on and marginalize the indigenous population, which typically lacks the resources to fight back in an effective way. Third, the superior position of the regional centre may permit it the luxury of internal division, with two or more communities of settler origin engaged in a struggle for dominance.

Creole independence

We have already referred to American nationalism in the context of the original union of the 13 colonies, but that union could only take place if the colonies were independent in the first place. The history of the American revolt against British rule is well known. The descendants of the original settlers (whom we may identify as a regional centre) were able to contemplate this because of their strength in relation to the metropolitan centre, but also their overwhelming dominance in relation to the indigenous population (the regional periphery). It has been estimated that at the beginning of the nineteenth century the Native American population had fallen to about 600,000 (Thornton, 2000: 23). But the white population of the 13 colonies, overwhelmingly of British origin, amounted to 3.2 million already in 1790, rising to 4.3 million in 1800 (derived from US Bureau of the Census, 1975: 8). This decisive demographic supremacy underscored the clear dominance of the white population in all other major respects, allowing the luxury of revolt.

The independence movements in Latin America in the early nineteenth century contrasted with the position in the United States in a number of respects: in the different dynamics of the relationship with the regional periphery, in the relative ease with which independence was achieved, and in the subsequent tendency towards fragmentation rather than unification. To start with, the indigenous population was much more significant than in North America, though declining as one moves southwards; thus, in 1810 Indians made up 60% of the population of New Spain (Mexico and its northern territories, and central America), and *mestizos* a further 22%; but they amounted to less than 25% of the population of Chile at the same time (Domínguez, 1980: 29–32). Second, although the enthusiasm of the Creoles for independence varied, the collapse of Spain in 1808 following invasion by Napoleon removed a vital link to the mother country, rendering rule from Spain impossible for the moment. The occupation of Portugal by the French in 1807 had rather different consequences: the royal family fled to Brazil, which they continued to govern until 1822, when the king's son declared Brazilian independence. Third, although Brazil remained intact, the territories of the four Spanish viceroyalties – New Spain, New Granada (the northern part of South America), Peru and Rio de la Plata – fragmented further following independence. To take one example: although Argentina, the core territory of Rio de la Plata, dates its independence from 1816, it had in reality been independent since 1808, and three of the outlying territories of the viceroyalty eventually established their independence: the territories that were to become Uruguay, Paraguay and Bolivia (Lynch, 1973: 37–126).

One of the factors seen as explaining the rise of independence movements in the Spanish colonies was a fracturing of internal territorial-administrative organization along local lines

(Barton, 1997: 48–9). This kind of administrative-military breakdown on the part of an imperial state is the starting point for Theda Skocpol's comparative analysis of the French, Russian and Chinese revolutions: the breakdown lifts the lid on underlying class tensions, ushering in a period of conflict that is resolved only when a new, more stable administrative-military structure is set in place (Skocpol, 1979: 285–7). Andrews (1985) uses this model to analyze the role of domestic power relations in the pre-independence period. There was a tension between the local Creole elites and the European administrative class, with its policies of economic and political centralization, modified by fear of an underclass increasingly pushed towards rebellion by economic factors. The collapse of the Spanish state in 1808 left the Creoles with few options. Where the dangers of mass rebellion were great, as in Cuba, Mexico and Peru, they stood by Spain; where there were few Indians, as in Argentina, they did not; and in Venezuela, with a large and restive slave and free black population, the Creole declaration of independence was followed by a predictable domestic revolt. Developments in Saint-Dominigue (Haiti) were a salutary lesson: the drive for independence by the colonial class was followed by a successful slave revolt and the transfer of power to this formerly subordinate group – a menacing example to Creoles elsewhere in Latin America (Graham, 1994: 29–36).

While the driving force behind Creole nationalism was political, the cultural dimension (in the broadest sense) was not absent. A comparative study of the nation formation process in the 'new world' (the settler collectivities in the Americas and Oceania) highlights the extent to which the image of pioneering settlers in a virgin land lay at its core; but at a particular point this collectivity began to see itself as distinct from the metropolitan motherland, and to devise an alternative collective imagination with its own utopian vision (Bouchard, 2000). Australia, like Canada and New Zealand, at first defined itself as a 'British nation'; in pursuing a new identity to reinforce social cohesion, 'the test of the bush' was attractive, with its image of 'dynamic and enterprising' pioneers (Darwin, 2010: 396–7). The pattern varied greatly from one society to another, with the image of the indigenous population incorporated at least in part in Canada, Australia and New Zealand, but remaining almost entirely excluded from the American historical myth (Moran, 2002; Hoxie, 2008).

In many other cases, Creole nationalism had a more precarious lifespan. Colonial nationalism among the leaders of Irish Protestants (about a quarter of the total population) flowered in response to the American revolution, resulting in the assertion of Irish legislative independence in 1782, but melted away in the early nineteenth century, which turned out instead to be an era of Catholic nationalist mobilization (Garvin, 1981: 14–20; English, 2006: 115–71). The political leadership of the white population of the British colony of Southern Rhodesia (about 5% of the total) resisted British disengagement and ultimately declared independence in 1965, creating a white-ruled state that lasted until 1980, when it was replaced by the Republic of Zimbabwe headed by the indigenous nationalist ruler Robert Mugabe. In Algeria, the position of the Creole population, the *pieds-noirs* (11% of the total in 1954), was too insecure to allow anything more than passing contemplation of revolt against France, and this group had to acquiesce in the eventual French decision to withdraw in 1962. A contemporary description of these French *colons* in Algeria sums up the position of many other Creole communities:

> The *colon*, like man as a whole, is the child of his environment – an environment numerically hostile to him and to his culture as long as the Algerian Muslim is not permitted to share it. Such an environment takes from the *colon* the 'luxury' of democratic solutions in his ever-present conflict with the Algerians. For such solutions would undermine the very basis of the status quo from which the *colon* so richly profits. Assimilation of the minority-majority is not a real alternative in the mind of the *colon*, for it would both change the nature of the dominant French culture and provide unwelcome competition. This in turn would remove the attraction which first brought many of the *colons* to Algeria. This political and economic necessity is often translated by the *colon* into a sense of racialist superiority, thus making impossible a challenge to his privileged status (Gillespie, 1960: 14).

The indigenous issue

In those cases where colonial nationalists succeeded in establishing a regime sustained by the regional centre, there remained to varying degrees a challenge from the regional periphery. In Latin America, apart from its southern tip (including Argentina, Chile and Uruguay) and Brazil, the indigenous population has remained relatively large and politically significant. In most cases, it now takes the form of a *mestizo* population with small purely European and indigenous minorities, but in two notable cases, Bolivia and Peru, indigenous peoples make up about half of the population. Although in Peru there is a long history of the marginalization of indigenous peoples, in Bolivia the election of an indigenous political leader, Evo Morales, as President in 2005 was a significant symbol of the potential power of indigenous politics.

In other cases, the indigenous population is now so small as a proportion of the total population (2% or less) that it carries little political clout; this is the position in the United States, Canada and Australia, for instance. Sometimes, governments may choose to make a gesture to the indigenous peoples, but such gestures are made from a position of complete demographic security. Thus, Australian prime minister Kevin Rudd apologized in February 2008 for the 'profound grief, suffering and loss' that had been inflicted on Aborigines, and four months later Canadian prime minister Stephen Harper apologized for the 'profoundly negative' consequences of Canada's assimilationist policy through a residential school system.

The position of the Maori in New Zealand stands out from the pattern in these three countries. To start with, Maori constitute a much larger share of the population (15% in 2001). Second, they are much less culturally divided, with traditional links to a single language – unlike the several hundred languages (and many unconnected language families) associated with the indigenous populations of Australia, Canada and the United States. Third, they have a more securely embedded constitutonal and legal position, with the Treaty of Waitangi (1840) between the Maori chiefs and the British crown, however contested its political basis, offering minimum formal guarantees to the indigenous population (Orange, 1997). This contrasts with the unequal treaties imposed on the North American Indians, and the relatively defenceless position of the Australian Aborigines.

Settler divisions

In imperialist-type relations, the regional centre usually has close cultural and historical ties with the metropolitan territory. But this is not always the case, as we will see in the next section. Accidents of settlement or colonial history sometimes produce complex alliance patterns. It is worth considering two such cases, where the path of settler nationalism was clouded by competition between an old regional centre and an emerging new one: Canada and South Africa.

The French involvement in North America that culminated in the creation of the vast colony of New France left a lasting francophone heritage in the northern part of the continent. But after this area came under British rule in the eighteenth century, its linguistic character inevitably changed, with English-speaking settlers from Europe and fleeing loyalists from the USA spearheading the creation of a large anglophone community. Tension between linguistically defined groups predated the formal creation of the contemporary federal Dominion of Canada in 1867, and was reinforced by religion, with a strong association of Protestantism with the English language and of Catholicism with French.[1] The regional centre was thus itself divided, between a dominant English-speaking population and a subordinate French-speaking one. This left a deep mark on ethnic consciousness, with the gradual emergence of a strong national identity among French speakers, especially in Quebec (Meadwell, 1993). The pattern in anglophone Canada was different: there is evidence of a shift from an earlier type of ethnic nationalism (emphasizing the British heritage) to a more inclusive form of 'civic' nationalism (Igartua, 2006: 12–15).

The main respect in which the South African case deviated from the Canadian one was the size of the regional periphery – an indigenous population that constituted an overwhelming majority of the population rather than succumbing to catastrophic population decline. As in Canada, the original regional centre was made up of non-British settlers: Dutch colonists who began settling in the cape area in the late seventeenth century. Following the introduction of British rule in 1795, a wave of British settlement began, with the descendants of the original settlers (eventually known as 'Boers', and whose Afrikaans language began to diverge from Dutch) moving further inland. The Boers fought unsuccessfully to preserve the independence of the republics they established in Transvaal and the Orange Free State during two bitter wars against the British in 1880–81 and 1899–1902. The creation of the Union of South Africa in 1909 thus sought to bring together two rival groups of European origin in a state with a predominantly African population. Unlike Canada,

---

1 By 2001, 90% of French speakers were Catholics, as opposed to only 30% of English speakers; computed from Statistics Canada, Census 2001, using religion and language used most often at work for the population aged over 15 at work: www12.statcan.ca/english/census01/products/standard/themes/

where English speakers outnumbered French speakers by about two to one already in 1871, in South Africa Afrikaners have always outnumbered English-speaking South Africans (in 2001, the white population was approximately 40% English- and 60% Afrikaans-speaking). There thus developed separate and distinctive patterns of nationalism among Afrikaners (Dubow, 1992), English-speaking South Africans (Lambert, 2005) and the African population (Lodge, 1983).

SEPARATIST NATIONALISM

In the last of the three patterns of nationalist mobilization, the tripartite network of relationships is again central, even though it is unevenly present. The main battle here is commonly not between the regional periphery and the metropolitan centre, but rather between the regional periphery and the regional centre, with the latter regarded as an ally of the metropolitan centre. Once again, the nationalist programme is dominated not only by the idea of independence (with respect to the metropolitan centre), but also with the preservation or assertion of distinctiveness (in relation to both the metropolitan centre and the regional centre). We may identify two variants. The first is classic peripheral nationalism, where the regional periphery forms part of the domestic territory of the metropolitan centre; it struggles against both the metropolitan centre (especially in the political domain) and the regional centre (especially in the cultural domain). In the second, the structure of the conflict is similar, but the regional periphery is geographically remote from the metropolitan centre. While fighting against the metropolitan centre, it is often prepared to accept its language and culture, which is typically shared with the regional centre, as in anti-colonial nationalism. We need also to consider two other issues: the implications of the survival of the regional centre after independence, and potential conflict about authenticity within the regional periphery.

Peripheral nationalism

There are innumerable case studies of peripheral nationalism, and a few comparative studies. Some of these have generated persuasive models of phases through which nationalist movements have progressed. Partha Chatterjee (1986: 49–51) proposed a three-stage model of anti-colonial nationalism (a phenomenon rather distinct from peripheral nationalism as discussed here). A four-stage model incorporating cultural, political and economic components has been proposed for post-communist eastern Europe (Dostál, 1991: 106–8) and another has been suggested for Bangladesh (Jha, 1980). But one specifically European model has been especially influential. This derives its value from the manner in which it narrows the focus to a distinct kind of nationalism, and confines its analysis to a number of European cases. The work of the Czech comparative historian Miroslav Hroch (1968), influenced by Marxist social theory, shares with Karl Deutsch, Benedict Anderson, Ernest Gellner and others a reliance on the centrality of social change (though Hroch parts company with Gellner in significant respects). Hroch sees the evolution from feudal society to capitalist society as crucial, with the advent of modern capitalist society characterized by three major landmarks: the bourgeois revolution, the Industrial Revolution and the emergence of the organized working class. Parallel to this, a national movement passes potentially through three phases, marked by a progressive enlargement of the range and ambition of those involved (it should be stressed that Hroch consciously refers to this phenomenon as a 'national' movement, not a 'nationalist' one):

- In phase A, sections of the established classes develop an interest in the language and culture of the periphery for antiquarian or cultural reasons.
- In phase B, this interest begins to acquire distinct political overtones and the process of nationality formation starts, with emerging leaders from the peripheral population promoting cultural revival and articulating distinctive demands for civil and political rights.
- In phase C, a mass movement with definite political objectives develops and nation building proper begins.

The model was not designed to include 'larger' nations (such as the Poles and the Hungarians), which tended to follow a different course. This is not a reference to size or scale. Hroch uses the terms 'smaller' or 'non-dominant' to describe nations with an incomplete social structure. This category corresponds with the so-called *geschichtslos* or 'historyless' nations dismissed by Engels (see Chapter 7) – nations not so much lacking a history (it is hard to imagine such an entity), or even lacking a history as an autonomous political entity, but lacking a complete social structure. The landed aristocracy, the group which provided political leadership in traditional societies, was missing; it belonged to another national group. Hroch illustrated this model by reference to the Czech, Lithuanian, Estonian, Finnish, Norwegian, Flemish and Slovak national movements, differentiating between them on the basis of the relationship between the phasing of economic and cultural change. A later English edition added the case of the Danish minority in Schleswig (Hroch, 1985), while later still a parallel Czech volume included also Ireland, Croatia, Slovenia, Latvia, Catalonia and the special cases of Wales, Brittany and Belarus (Hroch, 1986).

Hroch's model is remarkable in its capacity to account for the evolution of national movements not just in the central and east European cases on which he relied initially, but also in western Europe. It provided a useful structure on which Leerssen (2006) based his stages of 'cultural cultivation', as discussed in Chapter 6, and it may also be accommodated neatly to embrace the tripartite structure discussed in this chapter. In phase A (which we may label 'cultural exploration'), the regional centre played a leading role: it was such groups as the Irish Protestant landed gentry, the Baltic German pastors, the Polish *szlachta* in Lithuania, the German-speaking aristocracy in Bohemia and these groups' counterparts elsewhere that first encouraged research into the language, history and antiquities of their regions, and scholars from outside played a similar role (Hutchinson, 1987: 36–7). In phase B (we may call it 'elite organization'), while isolated members of the regional centre continued their involvement, the principal activists were increasingly drawn from the regional periphery, with school teachers, journalists and other members of the emerging middle class playing a central role. In phase C (which may be labelled 'mass mobilization'), popular politics is born, and peasants and rural and urban workers are mobilized, typically under the leadership of the middle class, behind a national movement that may be united behind a single party (as in Ireland) or divided along ideological lines (as in the Czech lands).

There is nothing surprising about the evolution described by Hroch in respect of its internal dynamics. In phase A, leadership could only have come from the regional centre since it alone possessed the resources to support the kind of scholarly work that was needed to help salvage the decaying culture. The withdrawal of the regional centre from this project in phases B and C was predictable since its interests were threatened by the rising tide of peripheral nationalism. The transition to the later phases was associated not just with profound socioeconomic change, but also with radical institutional reform, with the advent of freedom of expression and political organization, suffrage extension, and other aspects of parliamentary and institutional reform of a kind that shaped the evolution of political organization in western Europe too (see Lipset and Rokkan, 1967; Rokkan, 1970). The programme of the national movements also tended to share common features: promotion of the peripheral language, a struggle for civil rights and autonomy, and the development of a complete social structure, including the creation of an educated class in the areas of administration, culture and commerce.

But there is nothing inevitable about this evolution either. For all of the movements that made the transition to phase C, there were many which stopped short at phase B, or even phase A; and there have been many cases of potential cultures that never even got as far as phase A. Hroch in fact identified four patterns, which he related to the timing of the process of political modernization. In the first 'integrated' type, phase B occurred under the old, pre-democratic regime, and the transition to phase C coincided with the revolution that ushered in modern political life (as in the case of the Czechs in the mid-nineteenth century). In the second (labelled 'delayed'), the transition was slower: phase C was reached only after the installation of modern political conditions (as in the case of the Lithuanians). In the third 'insurgent' type, the transition was more rapid, with phase C being reached already under the old regime (resulting in reliance on armed insurrection, as in the case of the Serbs, Greeks and Bulgarians). In the 'fragmented' type, political modernization was kicked off at an early stage, and it was possible for phase C also to be reached early (as among the Basques and Catalans) (Hroch, 2000: 55–8).

Hroch suggested that the timing of these developments was a function of three features. The first was the extent to which the political regime was modernized or still operated under autocratic norms. The second was the structure of the non-dominant ethnic group – in the most characteristic cases, it was 'incomplete', but among the Poles and Magyars the indigenous nobility survived, while among the Greeks and Norwegians there were substantial entrepreneurial and high bureaucratic classes. The third was the availability of raw historical materials that could reinforce collective identity and strengthen the case for autonomy, such as a legacy of a separate political identity in past centuries. These two latter conditions – possession of a complete social structure and a heritage of medieval statehood – facilitated the early adoption of a programme of self-determination (Hroch, 1995).

Hroch's model has been tested against a wide range of other cases, including the Basques (Puhle, 1982), Macedonians (de Jong, 1982), Ukrainians (Magocsi, 2002: 38–54), Belarusians (Bekus, 2010) and other nations within Russia (Appleby, 2010). It has also been used in relation to more established national movements, such as those in the Netherlands, Germany and Russia (Maxwell, 2010: 874). Notwithstanding its European focus, efforts have been made to explore its applicability elsewhere, such as Asia and the Middle East. Some of these have simply highlighted the different path of nationalist evolution in such cases, with the model having limited value in respect of Sikh nationalism (Deol, 2000) and Sindhi and Baloch nationalism (Siddiqi, 2010). The model has also been applied to Latin America, Syria and South Africa, as well as to Taiwan and India (Maxwell, 2010: 870), and also to Mexico (Hoyo, 2010). But structural similarities with Hroch's very distinctive model are hard to find outside Europe; he has himself rightly indicated that, for example, the new nationalism of central and eastern Europe of the post-communist period bears little similarity to its nineteenth-century predecessor (Hroch, 1993), and he queries the applicability of his own model in contemporary Asia, Africa and Latin America (Hroch, 2010: 889).

Anti-colonial nationalism

Research on nationalism outside Europe emphasizes a quite different dynamic. Nationalism in Asia was substantially political, encouraged particularly by the Japanese victory over Russia in 1905 – an outcome which showed that even great European empires were not invincible. Nationalism in such countries as the Philippines, India, Indonesia, Vietnam and Malaya took some time to mature. It was notably elite-dominated, though there existed also a strong communist movement – a particular target of European colonial powers. The experience of these cases began to diverge after the Second World War, during which Japanese military victories once again illustrated the vulnerability of European powers (Low, 1981). While the nationalist movements overtly resembled a revolt against the West, they also shared with nationalism in Europe an emphasis on the national past, especially in its pre-colonial form (Kennedy, 1968: 13). This form of nationalism contrasted with that in Europe in the modest role of the cultural (and especially linguistic) dimension: although the national language and national education system were supported and the ancient polity was glorified, the primary target was European racial hierarchy and the need for radical modernization, but boundaries established by the European imperial powers were substantially accepted (Reid, 2010: 7–10).

Nationalism in Africa was facilitated by the steady erosion of European commitment to maintenance of empire after the Second World War. Imperial rule left challenging legacies for the new nation-building elites. It has been argued that there were significant differences in the heritage of the two main European powers, Britain and France (Mazrui and Tidy, 1984: 373–84). The British tended to rely on a strategy of indirect rule, building up or even creating local ruling elites, tolerating a wide measure of cultural diversity, and promoting a high degree of colonial autonomy. The outcome was the emergence of a relatively strong state, but the survival or even intensification of big cultural differences within this. The French, by contrast, pursued policies of macro- and micro-integration: on the one hand, the political integration of African colonies into France; on the other, the assimilation of local populations to French culture, with an educational system 'designed to produce as rapidly as possible black Frenchmen and Frenchwomen' (Mazrui and Tidy, 1984: 377). The outcome after independence was a much weaker state with strong patterns of economic, cultural and political dependence on France, but a population that was more unified in its acceptance of French language and culture, and offering a less formidable nation-building challenge.

The tripartite structure described above formed a key part of the anti-colonial nationalist process. Although the conflict between the European metropolitan areas and their colonies has attracted most attention, the regional centre was always at least symbolically present, and its role was sometimes crucial. As we have seen, in South Africa and Southern Rhodesia it was able to temporarily halt the path to power of the majority, the regional periphery. In some cases, this group was tiny. Already in the early nineteenth century the historian Thomas Babington Macaulay (1866 [1833]: 122) speculated with amazement on how 'a handful of adventures from an island in the Atlantic should have subjugated a vast country divided from the place of their birth by half the globe' – the enormous sub-continent of India. The British achievement was all the more remarkable for its modest personnel costs: in the 1930s, the ratio of British rulers to ruled in India was 1:28,000, and it was 1:54,000 in Nigeria (Sharkey, 2003: 2–3). One Indian nationalist attributed this to the empire's capacity for cultural persuasion, successfully presenting itself as symbol of power and prestige of a level about which local leaders could only dream (Pal, 1971 [1910]). This has been described as 'one great confidence-trick, a huge game of white man's bluff' (Kirk-Greene, 1980: 44). It depended on compliant allies, recruited from the regional periphery. These were trained in a network of colleges, such as Makerere College in Uganda and Gordon College in Pakistan; other imperial powers used similar mechanisms (Sharkey, 2003: 7). These colleges proved, however, to be a double-edged sword, producing not only agents of empire, but also a new nationalist elite (Sharkey, 2003: 119). This imperial formula did not work everywhere else. In the Philippines in the nineteenth century, for example, the Chinese *mestizo* population was an obvious potential ally. Spanish policymakers there believed that 'the brains and money of the *mestizos* must not be allowed to become allied to the numerical strength of the *indios* [indigenous population]' (Wickberg, 1964: 88) – but they ultimately failed in this policy goal.

Important though anti-colonial nationalism is, it too was potentially faced by nationalist challenges of a nested type: Tibet in China, Punjab in India, Aceh in Indonesia and Mindanao in the Philippines are but a few examples (see Christie, 1996: 192–4; Kratoska and Batson, 1999: 299–305; Kingsbury, 2011). These resembled the forms of substate nationalism that were to emerge in Ethiopia (Ottaway, 1994: 20–3), Nigeria (Onuoha, 2011), South Africa (Settler, 2010) and elsewhere in Africa.

The Creole issue

Victory for peripheral or anti-colonial nationalism did not necessarily result in resolution of tensions with the Creole population. There were, of course, cases where this group was never large, and it disappeared after independence, as in many African and Asian countries. Elsewhere, where the Creole community was more substantial, considerable numbers returned to the 'mother country' after independence (the *Pieds-Noirs* in Algeria, the Anglo-Indians and many Irish Protestants, for example), leaving the remainder in a politically marginalized position. In yet other cases, 'repatriation' (as in the case of the Baltic Germans in 1939–40) or expulsion (as in the case of the Germans of Czechoslovakia and Poland in 1945) resulted in the disappearance of this group.

There were, however, also circumstances where a substantial Creole population remained. This might lead us to expect continuing problems in the relationship between majority and minority; but in general minorities of this type have been politically docile. Typically enjoying high social status and an economically privileged position, they stand to lose more than they are likely to gain in any confrontation with the majority, and their leaders consequently tend to play a relatively passive role. Thus, whites in South Africa and in Zimbabwe came to terms quickly with the implications of majority rule. The expropriation of many European-owned farms in Zimbabwe as part of a land reform programme showed the potential consequences of majority radicalism, as it had done in the early twentieth century in the Baltic republics (in respect of German landowners) and in Ireland (in respect of mainly Protestant landlords).

Indigenous divisions

Finally, the nationalism of the regional periphery is not always unproblematic itself. Competition over cultural norms is a common feature of the early stage of nationalist movements: over the language which should be cultivated as the language of the community, over the dialect of this language which should become the norm if an unstandardized 'national' language rather than a metropolitan one is chosen, over the relationship between the nation and particular religious belief systems, and over the content of the national historical myth. The central question concerns the manner in which the nation finds cultural expression.

Particularly in Africa, nationalist leaders deeply opposed to European rule have often favoured a European language as the medium for wider communication, and this is for a very pragmatic reason: as an 'outside' language, it is seen as politically neutral, and does not carry the risk of giving one community an advantage over another. Elsewhere, though, metropolitan languages have been embraced even though there is an indigenous language that may well be fit for purpose. In Ireland, Brittany and the Basque Country, for example, the indigenous language has been strongly challenged by a metropolitan one (English, French and Castilian Spanish respectively), leading to a conflict over issues of authenticity: traditional nationalists insist that the indigenous language represents the 'soul' of the nation, and should thus play a central role.

Occasionally, the kind of dispute over language standardization that was characteristic of phase B of the national movement (in Hroch's model) remains unresolved, resulting in continuing disputes over matters of authenticity. In Norway, competition between two 'national' standard languages has been discussed in Chapter 3; each claims authenticity as

'Norwegian'. Greece experienced a parallel form of competition between the more conservative Katharevusa, close to classical Greek, and the more popular Demotic, or colloquial language, but the distinction between these lacked a clearly defined geographical basis. Notwithstanding the association of Katharevusa with the politics of the right and the adoption of Demotic as the standard, the former retains an appeal to Greek nationalists because of its closeness to the ancient Greek language (Frangoudaki, 1992).

In cases where national identity has been defined in relation to religion, particular issues may arise in respect of those who abandon or do not adhere to the 'true faith'. The subtleties of the link between religion and nationalism, and the ambiguous status of those who belong to an unfavoured denomination, have already been discussed in Chapter 4. But what happens where, as is common, there is a drift to other denominations, or altogether away from any church, in a national community where a link with a particular religion has been established? There appear to be broadly two options. First, national identity can be redefined so that it no longer rests on a particular form of religious affiliation. This seems to have been the pattern in the United States, where the long-standing 'WASP' formula has been replaced by a more inclusive definition of American identity, and may perforce be the outcome in Latin America, where national identity was traditionally linked to Catholicism, in the face of large-scale conversions to Protestantism. In the second pattern, the challenge of secularism may well result in a redefinition of the traditional religion as an ancestral one rather than as a vibrant, contemporary form of collective worship: Russians and Serbs appear to have adopted this approach in relation to their traditional links with Orthodoxy, and the Irish and Poles may be in the process of adopting a similar perspective on Catholicism.

CONCLUSION

The process of nationalist mobilization is, then, a complex one. Seeking to identify a potential triangular relationship rather than a straightforward bilateral conflict complicates efforts to generalize about this process, but it offers a more fruitful account of what might otherwise be dismissed as a set of *sui-generis* developments. Seeing integrationist nationalism through the eyes of a metropolitan centre, colonial nationalism through the eyes of a regional centre (or a Creole or settler population) and separatist nationalism through the eyes of a marginalized, peripheral population draws attention to important dynamics that might otherwise be difficult to detect.

There is another lens that might be used to view these processes. It may be possible to generalize from Hroch's three-phase schema, which was designed to illuminate just one distinctive type of nationalism. Its three phases are explored further in Table 8.2, where an attempt is made to shoe-horn each of the five main variants of nationalism that have been discussed above into it. This has to start from the reality that elites enjoyed very limited success in forging any sense of national identity in pre-industrial Latin America, as in Gran Colombia (Brown, 2006). But otherwise there is a case for using the Hroch model as a framework, and even for extending it to a fourth phase. Incorporation of a 'phase D'

Table 8.2 Potential phases in nationalist movements

Type of nationalism	Phase A: cultural exploration	Phase B: elite organization	Phase C: mass mobilization	Phase D: national consolidation
Territorial unification	.	+	.	+
Cultural integration	–	–	–	+
Irredentism	.	+	.	+
Creole nationalism	.	+	.	+
Peripheral nationalism	+	+	+	+
Anti-colonial nationalism	.	+	+	+

Note: A plus sign indicates the presence and a minus sign the absence of a feature.

to coincide with post-independence nation building has been suggested on the basis of the study of the formation of nation-states in central Europe (Kamusella, 2001: 241), the Soviet Union (Martin, 2001: 15) and the Balkans (Stefanovic, 2005: 484). Hroch himself (2010: 888) explicitly rejects this approach on the grounds that national movements end with independence, adding that 'it is difficult to imagine a national movement existing inside a national state: against whom would this movement be directed?' Hroch may well be correct, depending on matters of definition; but it is not at all difficult to visualize the imagined enemies of a nationalist movement which has successfully established its statehood, and interwar Europe supplied abundant examples. This fourth phase matches the process characterized by Rogers Brubaker (1996: 4–5) as 'nationalizing nationalism': the core nation in the new state undertakes 'remedial' or 'compensatory' measures to promote its interests.

To complicate matters further, it must be pointed out that the patterns of nationalism just discussed are not mutually exclusive: they can and commonly do coexist. Thus American nationalism brings together themes of colonial separatism, territorial unification, cultural integration and irredentism. In the former Soviet Union, the view from Moscow was that of a metropolitan centre seeking to maintain territorial unity, but the view from certain of the capitals of the non-Russian Soviet republics was a regional nationalist one, committed to defending and expanding regional autonomy.

Separatist nationalism may show aspects of a 'domino effect'; indeed, the term 'sequential secession' has been coined to describe the common process where one national movement spurs a parallel one, while the term 'recursive secession' describes a process by which a further secession takes place within a seceding territory, as described above (Pavković, 2011: 297; see also Pavković and Radan, 2007). In the latter case, the secessionist movements are nested, like Russian *matrioshka* dolls (Taras, 1993). If we find a doll representing the United Kingdom, for instance, we may open it to explore the conflict inside; this reveals a smaller doll, Ireland. Opening the Irish doll reveals a yet smaller doll, Ulster; and opening the Ulster doll introduces a yet smaller one, the Northern Ireland Catholic community (Coakley, 2009). Many other such examples could be cited. Thus, in the mid-nineteenth century Vienna represented a metropolitan centre, German-speaking Budapest a regional centre and Magyar Hungary a regional periphery; but after 1867 Budapest also itself became a metropolitan centre in relation to Pressburg (Bratislava) as a regional centre and the Slovak counties as a regional periphery. But in many other cases, too, a nationalist elite fighting a struggle for 'freedom' against an external power was itself seen as an 'oppressor' by another nationalist elite at a lower tier, where the triangular relationship was potentially replicated. Indonesia fought for independence against the Dutch, but the Acinese fought for independence against the Indonesians, in a cycle that was to be repeated many times across the continents – and one which did not necessarily stop at just two levels.

9

EXPLAINING NATIONALISM

INTRODUCTION

Biographies of nationalist leaders very often report a 'Pauline moment': a conversion from indifference to fervent nationalism, on the model of the biblical account of Paul's sudden conversion to Christianity on the road to Damascus. Thus for Mahatma Gandhi, founding father of Indian nationalism, consciousness of his membership of a disadvantaged group was sparked off when, as a non-white, he was removed from a train in Pietermaritzburg during a visit to South Africa in 1893. A 1799 tour of the Rhine, with its ruined fortifications, is said to have stimulated the anti-French sentiment of Ernst Moritz Arndt, one of the key figures in the early stages of German nationalism. Discovery of the indigenous language and culture has also pushed many others into a new sense of their identity, often reflected by a name change from the metropolitan to the peripheral language. To mention just a few prominent examples (from the hundreds that could be cited), the Lithuanian historian Szymon Dowkont became Simonas Daukantas, the Finnish politician Johan Gustav Helstén became Juho Kusti Paasikivi, and the Irish school teacher Patrick Pearse became Pádraic Mac Piarais – abandoning respectively the Polish, Swedish and English forms of their names.

Anecdotal accounts of these kinds fail to offer robust evidence as to how nationalists are made. Psychological approaches, such as the 'relational' theory which sees ethnicity as a response to the need to simplify options for group identification in a complex world (Hale, 2008), may offer some insights. But in many cases nationalist leaders seem to have had their positions thrust on them by virtue of the offices they held, or by more general life conditions, rather than having deliberately chosen the path of nationalist revolt. For Creole nationalist elites in the Americas or for the leaders of anti-colonial movements in Africa and Asia (often newly returned from the metropolitan capital, and sometimes victims of rejection there), participation in the nationalist movement was scarcely a matter of choice: it was either that, or retirement into private life. But are there more systematic ways of approaching the explanation of nationalism as a collective phenomenon? The large volume of theoretical literature suggests that progress has been made (see Smith, A., 1971, 1998; Hall, 1998; Özkırımlı, 2000, 2005; Delanty and O'Mahony, 2002; Day and Thompson, 2004; and Atsuko and Uzelac, 2005).

Many researchers in the area are, however, rather pessimistic. Having reviewed the dominant approaches, John Breuilly (1982: 35–6) concluded that they either rested on an excessively vague conceptual basis or were incompatible with available evidence, and that 'it is therefore impossible to construct any acceptable theory of nationalism'. John Hall (1993a: 1) suggested that, in view of the diversity of the phenomenon, 'no single, universal theory of nationalism is possible'. Craig Calhoun (1997: 8) echoed this, arguing that the multiplicity of forms taken by nationalism requires multiple theories, and that nationalism is 'a rhetoric for speaking about too many different things for a single theory to explain it'. Nicos Mouzelis (1998: 163), similarly, concludes that 'I do not think that a theory of nationalism both *general* (that is, applying to all types of nationalism) and *substantive* (that is, telling us non-trivial things) is possible'. Anthony Smith (1998: 223) shares in this consensus: while a general theory is desirable for both intellectual and sociopolitical reasons, basic disagreements and rival approaches are such that 'a unified approach must seem quite unrealistic and any general theory merely utopian'.

Nevertheless, more optimistic voices are to be found. Christophe Jaffrelot, for example, suggested making a distinction that reduces this near-impossible task to two less unmanageable ones: explaining the emergence of nations, and accounting for the rise of nationalism (Jaffrelot, 2005: 10–11). Even that is, of course, a considerable challenge: how are we to find an explanation for the rise, say, of movements as diverse as French, German, Estonian, Kenyan and Mexican nationalism? This big question can, in fact, be divided into three smaller – but still immensely challenging – ones: trying to explain the manner in which a transition takes place from one nationalist phase to another, as these phases have been described in Chapter 8 (an agenda already recognized by Miroslav Hroch, 1998: 98). The possible paths are illustrated in Figure 9.1. First, how did cultural exploration lead to the appearance of nationalist elites (the transition from phase A to phase B, from cultural exploration to elite organization), or how did such elites appear through another route? Second, how were elites able to mobilize mass support, the transition from phase B to phase C (mass mobilization)? Third, which factors determined the success of the nationalist movement, the transition from phase C to phase D (national consolidation)? The following sections look at these three transitions, but in each case it will be necessary to explain not just 'successful' outcomes (A_1, B_1, C_1), but also 'unsuccessful' ones – the paths of cultural absorption, political assimilation and defeat of territorial demands (A_0, B_0, C_0).

THE BIRTH OF NATIONALISM

One of the recurring themes in recent overviews of explanations for the rise of nationalism is the notion that there are at least two distinctive sets of approaches: those which seek to explain nationalism by reference to its roots in distant history (the so-called 'primordialist' approach) and those which argue that nationalism is essentially a phenomenon that dates

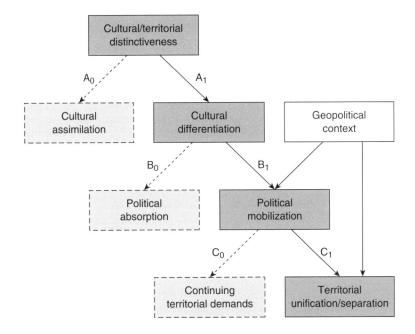

Figure 9.1 Potential phases in the evolution of nationalism

from the late eighteenth century at the earliest (the so-called 'modernist' approach). This is not a particularly fruitful dichotomy, but its ubiquity makes it necessary to discuss it here. After this, we consider the cluster of explanations that hold centre-stage: those which rest on the notion that nationalism is a relatively modern phenomenon, associated with large-scale economic dislocation and social mobilization.

The debate on the origins of nations

The identification of 'primordialism' as an analytical position in the study of nationalism is associated in particular with the work of Anthony Smith. Although Smith's initial overview of theories of nationalism (1971) did not identify any such perspective, the preface to the second edition of the same book introduced the notion of the 'primordialist' interpretation, associated with a small cluster of scholars (Smith, A., 1983: xxix–xxx). On the other side to the primordialists were what Smith (1991: 43–51) described as the 'modernists'. In a later discussion of 'the modernist fallacy', he identified not just a 'primordialist' alternative, but also a 'perennialist' one (Smith, A., 1995: 29–50). Later still, he argued for a compromise position, 'ethnosymbolism' (Smith, A., 1998: 190–8). Smith's later work maintained this form of terminology (Smith, A., 2001), though the perennialist position was later replaced by a 'neo-perennialist' one (Smith, A., 2009: 9–11). Smith's key exposition of these positions (Smith, A., 1998) concluded, then, that most approaches to the study of nationalism can be seen as falling under the heading of one of five major paradigms:

- Primordialism: nations are comprised of members whose commitment and willingness to make sacrifices are based on primordial (primeval) ties in such areas as language, religion and territory, and especially kinship.
- Perennialism: nations have existed over a long time-span, or are resuscitations of nations that have existed in the past, or derive from fundamental ethnic ties.
- Ethnosymbolism: nations are linked to a form of nationalism that is based on the rediscovery and reinterpretation of ethnic symbols, myths, memories, values and traditions.
- Modernism: nations have appeared only in the modern period in response to fundamental social and political changes and with variable interventions by elites.
- Postmodernism: nations are contemporary expressions of new patterns of identity, which are shifting and fragmented (Smith, A., 1998: 223–5).

Care needs to be taken when using this typology. Even as ideal types, the various positions appear not to be mutually exclusive. 'Primordialism' and 'perennialism' may be seen simply as two mutually reinforcing ways of explaining why nations have existed for centuries – the former by proposing a type of quasi-genetic permanence, the latter by arguing historical continuity. 'Ethnosymbolism', similarly, is entirely compatible with the broad grouping here labelled 'modernism': there is no inconsistency in seeing the nation as essentially a modern phenomenon *and* as one where leaders are prepared to exploit the potential of genuine or fabricated images and symbols from the past. The 'postmodernist' position is a residual one and not centrally concerned with historical explanation. The typology is even more problematic if it is seen not as a set of ideal types, but as a range of discrete analytical categories within which individual scholars may be located. Pigeon-holing researchers in this way – all too common in nationalism studies – is normally both perilous and pointless, resulting in oversimplification and sometimes distortion of certain scholars' perspectives without serving any particularly valuable end.

It is a tribute to the remarkable impact of Anthony Smith that the 'primordialism–modernism' debate finds a central if not dominant place in many important overviews of theories of nationalism. The core of one valuable survey focuses on primordialism, modernism and ethnosymbolism (Özkırımlı, 2000: 64–189), and the author later revisits the debate (2005: 34–62, 2007), though he rightly acknowledges that primordialism is 'an approach, not a theory' (Özkırımlı, 2000: 64). Another similar work focuses mainly on 'primordialism' and 'modernism' (Hearn, 2006: 20–116), while also acknowledging that 'as a school of theory, "primordialism" barely exists – it is more a broad tendency than a unified perspective' (Hearn, 2006: 230). To mention just a few of the many other works that discuss this issue, it is addressed explicitly in Fishman (2002), Conversi (2007), Penrose and Mole (2008), and Jackson-Preece (2010); and the primordialist position is assessed at length in Brown (2000: 6–13), Horowitz (2002), Joireman (2003: 19–34), and Atsuko and Uzelac (2005: 51–88).

The primordialist approach was subject to a forthright attack at an early stage (Eller and Coughlan, 1993: 183, 199, 200), and Rogers Brubaker described it as 'a long-dead horse that writers on ethnicity and nationalism continue to flog'. He continued:

No serious scholar today holds the view that is routinely attributed to primordialists in straw-man setups, namely that nations or ethnic groups are primordial, unchanging entities. Everyone agrees that nations are historically formed constructs, although there is disagreement about the relative weight of premodern traditions and modern transformations, of ancient memories and recent mobilizations, of 'authentic' and 'artificial' group feeling (Brubaker, 1996: 15, n. 4).

Nevertheless, the 'primordialist' position has its apologists. These are much easier to find in the early stages of social research than in contemporary writing, and include the social psychologist William McDougall (1920: 141, 282) and the British naturalist Ernest Hanbury Hankin (1937: 27–41). More recently, several historians seem to have occupied the primordialist position. Steven Grosby (2005: 7–26) sees nations as existing over the centuries; he cites as examples historical continuity over one or two millennia in the case of the Israeli, Sinhalese, Japanese and Polish nations (Grosby, 2005: 59–64, 2007). Adrian Hastings (1997: 1–34) offers a robust, historically informed attack on the notion of nations as exclusively modern, arguing that English nationhood, in particular, has medieval roots. It is by no means clear, however, that all historians who trace the origins of nations back over the centuries could themselves be classified as 'primordialists'. John Armstrong's monumental study of 'nations before nationalism' looks at the emergence of ethnic collectivities in the environs of Europe over many centuries, but carefully draws a distinction between this phenomenon and nationalism, which he sees as dating mainly from the late eighteenth century (Armstrong, 1982: 4). Hugh Seton-Watson (1977: 8–9), similarly, distinguishes between 'old nations' such as the English or French, which he dates from the early seventeenth century, and 'new nations' that appeared after the French revolution; but he generally reserves the term 'nationalism' for the modern period. Even sociologists who profess themselves more open on the issue do not offer primordialism a ringing endorsement, though they acknowledge its value in highlighting the deep roots of ethnicity (McKay, 1982: 397; Cohen, 1999: 10).

It is not clear that the four scholars cited as examples by Anthony Smith (1983: xxix–xxx) are indeed 'primordialists'. The article he cites by Edward Shils (1957) does not tackle the issue of nations or nationalism; Clifford Geertz (1963) goes no further than exploring the basis of substate identities; and Joshua Fishman acknowledged that he had occasionally been labelled a 'primordialist', but saw this as a misrepresentation, arising 'because of my being too successful at conveying the primordialist viewpoint, rather than for espousing it' (Fishman, 2002: 90, n. 2; see also Fishman, 1972). All three make clear their understanding of the subjective nature of primordial ties. Indeed Pierre van den Berghe (1981a: 15–36) stresses the significance of 'primordial' ethnic ties, but explicitly presents his own 'sociobiological' perspective as a rejection alike of exclusively cultural and exclusively primordialist approaches, dismissing as misleading 'such crudely dichotomous ways of characterising intellectual positions' (van den Berghe, 1978: 401).

The debate on primordialism as a theory of nationalism has not been particularly productive. Ernest Gellner described the disagreement 'between what I now call primordialists and modernists' as one

> where one side says that nations were there all the time or some of them were anyway, and that the past matters a great deal; and where the modernists like myself believe that the world was created round about the end of the eighteenth century, and nothing before that makes the slightest difference to the issues we face. This is a clear dividing line which is important (Gellner, 1996b: 366).

The problem is that, as thus defined, the dividing line is simply not sustainable, and Gellner's self-proclaimed position should be seen as a rhetorical flourish during a debate rather than as a serious dismissal of pre-eighteenth-century history – a dismissal to which Gellner himself in any event did not subscribe (see, for example, Gellner, 1994: 20–33). Much (but certainly not all) of the scholarly disagreement in this area may be put down to the old enemy noted in Chapter 1, terminological confusion, with different understandings of 'nation', 'nationalism' and 'primordialism'. Some argue that nations are ancient and nationalism is modern, others that nationalism is ancient and nations are modern, and yet others that both phenomena are modern. Indeed, James McKay has stated that the 'primordialist' approach may be synthesized with a 'mobilizationist' one in explaining such militant movements as the Basque, Quebecois and Breton secessionists (McKay, 1982: 401–8). But the key to much of the disagreement lies in the judgement of Dominique Schnapper (2003 [1994]: 50) that if by 'nation' one means essentially 'ethnic group', then nations have always existed, but if one means that distinctive political form to which the label is now applied, then nations are recent constructions.

In any case, whatever its shortcomings as a theory, it cannot be doubted that primordialism plays a central role in everyday nationalism. As we have seen in Chapter 5, nationalist history invariably links the contemporary nation to an ancient past, however flimsy the evidence for this. Primordialism, it could be argued, is as central a feature in nationalist ideology (and, therefore, demanding serious attention by analysts) as it is inappropriate as an approach to the analysis of nationalism.

Social mobilization

Much of the traditional literature on nationalism saw this as a modern phenomenon and sought to account for developments within particular countries, or to generalize across countries in an inductive way. Attempts to approach explanation in a deductive way, by deriving generalizations from broader social theories, were largely confined to two approaches, each of which was more successful in accounting for the disappearance of cultural distinctiveness than in explaining why such characteristics were sometimes used as a basis for nationalist mobilization. The first, and oldest, was Marxism, whose ideological commitment to internationalism nevertheless permitted extensive analysis of the 'national question' (for overviews, see, *inter alia*, Connor, 1984b; Munck, 1986), and this sometimes extended to the more specific problem of the mobilization of nations with an incomplete social structure

(Herod, 1976; Rosdolsky, 1986; Bauer, 2000 [1924]). The second is the 'political development' approach which in the 1960s sought to offer an alternative to Marxism, but which at least implicitly saw 'nation building' as a state-centred exercise designed to ensure the cultural and political dominance of the majority ethnic group; see Pye (1965) for an example of this approach; Wiarda (1989) for an overview; and Connor (1972) for a celebrated critique.

It has been pointed out that, notwithstanding its long-term contribution, classic sociological theory was a field in which the study of ethnic relations could find 'no place, patience or understanding' (Malešević, 2004: 13). From the 1970s onwards, however, the explosion in writing on nationalism was accompanied by further attempts to formulate theoretical explanations. As argued already, neither the primordialist–modernist dichotomy nor its extensions are particularly useful starting points in grouping such theories. Antoine Roger (2001: 3–6) has, however, devised an elegant two-dimensional classification of theories of nationalism. The first dimension has to do with the underlying determinants of nationalism: the extent to which explanations lie in the domain of socioeconomic transformation, or focus on specific choices by political actors. The second concerns the forces believed to hold nations together: the degree to which they rest on practices of sociopolitical domination, or comprise forms of social cohesion. Roger correctly sees each of these axes as a continuum, but they are simplified in Table 9.1, which presents them as dichotomies. This table includes only those theories which Roger regards as being open to accommodation with each other, in that they may be applicable simultaneously to the same movement (rather than being exclusive). Broadly speaking, the theories on the left-hand side refer to the more profound, earlier processes characteristic of the transition from Hroch's phase A to B; these shape the options for political elites in the transition from phase B to C (on the right-hand side). There is therefore a case for considering the 'social change' theories first, before going on to look at the more 'political' theories in the next section.

Early Marxist explanations. The most sustained attempt to explain nationalism by reference to underlying social forces has come from the Marxist camp. As is well known, Karl Marx (1818–83) and Friedrich Engels (1820–95) themselves largely ignored nationalism

Table 9.1 Classification of theories of nationalism

Fundamental principle	Underlying determinants	
	Structural change	*Political competition*
Socio-political domination	Social emancipation (Hroch) Recycling of identity (Hobsbawm)	Political demand (Breuilly, Brass) Political legitimation (Hermet, Greenfeld)
Social cohesion	Social communication (Deutsch) Cultural homogenization (Gellner)	Cultural interaction (Dumont) Cultural recasting (Smith)

Note: Roger also identifies a set of 'exclusivist' theories associated with these four categories: clockwise from the top left category, Marxist theories (e.g. Nairn, Hechter); interest and identity competition theories (e.g. Glazer and Moynihan, Banton); identity conflict and diffusion theories (e.g. Connor, Seton-Watson, Kohn); and primordialist and sociobiological theories (e.g. Kiernan, van den Berghe).

Source: Based on Roger (2001: 3–6)

as a theoretical challenge. Their voluminous works have been said not to contain 'a single (i.e. "scientific") and detailed study devoted to the national question', but rather a few 'newspaper articles, proclamations, historical "excursions" and correspondence' (Fišera and Minnerup, 1978: 5). For them, nationalism in general constituted an impediment to revolution, though they welcomed the 'progressive' nationalism associated with the German unification drive, Polish insurrectionary activity and, later, Irish separatist agitation, on the grounds that these would reinforce proletarian consciousness and organization. But they were particularly dismissive, as we have seen in Chapter 7, of what Hegel had called the 'historyless peoples':

> These relics of a nation … always become fanatical standard-bearers of counter-revolution and remain so until their complete extirpation or loss of their general character, just as their whole existence in general is itself a protest against a great historical revolution. Such, in Scotland, are the Gaels, the sup-porters of the Stuarts from 1640 to 1715. Such, in France, are the Bretons, the supporters of the Bourbons from 1792 to 1800. Such, in Spain, are the Basques, the supporters of Don Carlos. Such, in Austria, are the pan-Slavist Southern Slavs, who are nothing but the residual fragments of peoples (Engels, 1977 [1849]: 234–5).

This difficulty of Marxists in coming to terms with the vitality of nationalism led Tom Nairn (1975: 3) to the conclusion that 'the theory of nationalism represents Marxism's great historical failure'. Marxism's faith in the ultimate triumph of class over other forms of identity was derided by Gellner, who accused Marxists of resorting to a 'wrong address' theory of nationalism:

> The spirit of history or human consciousness made a terrible boob. The awakening message was intended for classes, but by some terrible postal error was delivered to nations. It is now necessary for revolutionary activists to persuade the wrongful recipient to hand over the message, and the zeal it engenders, to the rightful and intended recipient (Gellner, 1983: 129).

The perspective in mid-nineteenth-century Europe had, however, shifted dramatically by the end of the century, and it was clear that expressions of nationalism were no mere counter-revolutionary deviations that could be swept aside or ignored. The heartlands of Marxist social thought in central and eastern Europe coincided with areas of major cultural divisions, and Marxist intellectuals and activists such as the Austrian German Karl Kautsky (1854–1938), the Polish Jewish Rosa Luxemburg (1871–1919) and the future Russian leader Vladimir Lenin (1870–1924) presented differing analyses of nationalism and conflicting pre-scriptions as to how it should be handled. From this was descended a long line of research into the 'national question' in the communist world, and especially in the Soviet Union, heir to the multinational Russian empire and therefore itself contending with numerous prob-lems relating to a wide range of types of nationalism. The rich corpus of empirical research into nations, nationalities and ethnic groups conducted by Soviet scholars was, however, capped by a theoretical orthodoxy that refused to move far from what could be read into the collected works of Marx, Engels and Lenin. In one standard formulation, this distinguished four types of nationalism, each associated with a particular phase in historical evolution and related class structure: pre-bourgeois nationalism, characteristic of the feudal period; bourgeois nationalism of the capitalist period; nationalism of the 'national liberation' type, linked to a programme of social and national emancipation; and nationalist 'deviations' within communist-run countries (Rudenko et al., 1975: 52–68). One of the deviants was Yugoslavia, though here the constitutional acknowledgement of national diversity was also far-reaching and ultimately contributed to state break-up (Malešević, 2006: 157–226).

This approach to nationalism extended in large measure to western Marxists, whose research led them independently to similar conclusions. One of the most influential, Eric Hobsbawm (1990: 9–11), stresses the manufactured character of the nation, which he sees as the product of a form of social engineering designed to divert people from their real interests (namely class-based ones). But alternative interpretations are possible, and these emerged in particular as a by-product of studies of imperialism and neo-colonialism that could be reapplied in the domestic political context of certain large states. Thus, for Tom Nairn (1975), nationalism was an expression of uneven development, with excluded elites promoting a counter-culture which would offer the prospect of progress to a peripheral population left behind by the path of capitalism.

The most obvious precursor of contemporary materialist theories of nationalism was, however, a figure of whom his Marxist contemporaries (such as Luxemburg and Lenin) were critical: the Austrian Social Democratic activist Otto Bauer (1881–1938). As indicated in Chapter 7, Bauer was intensely conscious of the social roots of nationalist mobilization. He saw this as occurring in the context of advancing capitalism, which drew peasants and workers from the countryside into the towns. Thus, in Austria-Hungary, rural speakers of marginal languages (Ukrainians, Czechs, Slovaks, Slovenes and Romanians) were brought into more intense interaction with the two dominant groups, the Germans and, to an increasing extent, the Magyars. The picture of limited group consciousness in the countryside at this stage was vividly described by the perceptive Ukrainian Marxist Roman Rosdolsky. He argued that the coincidence between class difference and language in rural eastern Galicia (now western Ukraine), with its predominantly Greek Catholic (Uniate) Ruthenian (Ukrainian) peasant population and Polish upper class, resulted in an emerging but limited form of collective consciousness:

> What … were the Ruthenians of 1848? Nothing more than 'shadows of their forgotten ancestors', a mass of illiterate, semi-bonded serfs, who spoke a different language and went to a different church than the lords of the manor, but who were still submerged in the deepest 'nonhistoricity' and who only in their Greek Catholic clergy possessed the forerunners of a national intelligentsia. … In contrast to the clergy, the popular masses, the peasants, were hardly touched by the national idea in 1848. Certainly they felt Ruthenian, but only because the landlords and their creatures were Poles, because the

landlords, in their ostentatious contempt for the 'peasant language' and 'plebeian clergy' daily inculcated the difference between themselves and their subjects (Rosdolsky, 1986: 56–7).

Such relationships are likely to have been repeated, with some variation, in other areas where rural populations came into contact with dominant groups speaking a different language. As we have seen in Chapter 7, Bauer offered a set of 'laws' to determine what would happen as the dislocation brought about by capitalist development proceeded: rural populations of non-German backgrounds would either be absorbed into the culture of the German-speaking towns, or would, if the pace of urbanization exceeded a particular threshold and their class structure was sufficiently different from that of the towns, form the embryo of the leadership of an emerging nation (Bauer, 2000 [1924]). As Bauer vividly described the consequences of industrialization, it was 'as if the thundering din of the steam-driven engines, of the spinning machines and the mechanical looms, of the sugar factories and steam saws, of the railways had awakened the slumbering people' (2000 [1924]: 186). This had a major impact on Czech workers, so that 'they spoke without inhibition the language of the people where once only the language of the rulers had resounded ... no slogan was more frequently employed than that one should "not be ashamed" of one's mother tongue' (2000 [1924]: 187). But the onset of capitalism had an even bigger impact on the emerging Czech intelligentsia, made up of teachers, clergy, medical doctors and low-ranking civil servants and officials, who up to now would have been assimilated into German culture:

> They hated the [Austrian] German state, which gagged the freedom of thought; they hated the landed noble who looked down from his proud mansion with such contempt upon the poor country physician and the badly paid petty official; they hated the capitalist with that feeling of envy with which the poor intellectual so often confronts the pompous lack of education. … They now began to feel a solidarity with the popular masses, which were pervaded by the same hatred; they began to recall their origins among these masses, to recall their nationality. The use of the German language in the school and the administrative authority now appeared to them as an irksome constraint in which was manifested the domination of the detested social forces under which they suffered. It was they who – an extraordinary audacity – began to speak demonstratively in Czech at the 'society' balls, thereby declaring their support for the scorned, exploited masses of the people (Bauer, 2000 [1924]: 188).

The growth of a Czech petty bourgeoisie as a consequence of urbanization completed the process by providing a 'public' to whom the new intelligentsia could address their thoughts. The outcome was that 'a people of oppressed peasants and servants, which regarded its language with shame, had become a nation with a considerably broad stratum of intellectuals and prosperous petty bourgeois members who had become conscious of their nationality and were pervaded by a lively national sentiment' (Bauer, 2000 [1924]: 190).

Classical explanations. The importance of social mobilization was taken up from a non-Marxist perspective by Karl Deutsch, as we have seen in Chapter 7, in looking at factors determining the assimilation or differentiation of peripheral cultures. Echoing Bauer, he argued that the outcome depended on the relationship between two processes of change. First, he identified the rate of assimilation to a new language as a critical process: language communities were characterized by intense patterns of communication that erased barriers between members of the community and erected them against members of other communities. Expansion of the frontiers of the linguistic community thus meant an extension of the borders of a community held together by shared symbols and systems of understanding. The second process was the rate of mobilization: the pace at which people moved into more intense contexts of interaction, as measured, for instance, by the rate of urbanization or the rate of industrialization. The relationship between these two processes is critical. If the mobilized population is a subset of or is coextensive with the assimilated population, the peripheral language is in course of disappearance and the prospects for peripheral nationalism are weak. But if this relationship is reversed – in other words, the mobilized population has expanded outside the borders of the assimilated population – there exists a mobilized population which is unassimilated, and which may act as the base of a nationalist movement (Deutsch, 1966 [1953]: 107–30). Deutsch uses four examples to illustrate different paths. The rise of the Finnish- and Czech-speaking population in Finland and Bohemia respectively illustrated the challenges facing the traditionally dominant Swedish- and German-speaking populations in those two countries; developments in India indicated a growing challenge to English from regional languages; and Scotland showed a quite different pattern, with Gaelic melting away in the face of pressure from the powerful English language (Deutsch, 1966 [1953]: 130–7).

This approach evokes comparison with the work of two other influential authors. For Ernest Gellner (1983: 8–52), nationalism is inevitably linked to the transition from agrarian to industrial society. In the former, local peasant communities coexist in isolation from each other, ruled over by strata of cosmopolitan military, administrative, clerical and sometimes commercial elites. In industrial society, economic and social mobility ensures a breakdown of the barriers that kept local communities apart, thrusting individuals into new forms of society with quite different patterns of functional differentiation. In the new society, occupational and industrial interdependence entail the development of broad systems of communication, requiring education and the attainment of literacy. But literacy is inseparably linked to language, and schooling helps not just to disseminate the capacity to read but also to spread knowledge of a standardized language, and to create a new sense of community. As Gellner put it in respect of 'Ruritania' (an anonymous representative territory that we may equate with, say, Gellner's native Bohemia, or Slovakia, or Estonia), industrialization had distinctive consequences:

> Ruritanians had previously thought and felt in terms of family unit and village, at most in terms of a valley, and perhaps on occasion in terms of religion. But now, swept into the melting pot of an early industrial development,

they had no valley and no village: and sometimes no family. But there were other exploited and impoverished individuals, and a lot of them spoke dialects recognizably similar, while most of the better-off spoke something quite alien; and so the new concept of the Ruritanian nation was born of this contrast, with some encouragement from those journalists and teachers (Gellner, 1983: 62).

Gellner emphasizes that there is nothing inevitable about the transition from language category to proto-nation: in most cases, the language simply disappeared under pressure from a more powerful neighbour, or is currently disappearing, though he does not identify the reason for such an outcome (Gellner, 1983: 44–5). Indeed, the looseness of the causal connection has been the subject of comment by other analysts, who have sought ways to bolster the theory (Mouzelis, 1998; O'Leary, 1998).

The work of Miroslav Hroch offers a further insight into the options faced by such groups in the different phases of the national movement that he identified. In its pre-industrial phase (phase A, 'cultural exploration'), the emerging national movement is sparked off by members of the dominant classes, who promote historical and linguistic research and cultivate regional patriotism as a counterweight to pressure from the centre, which shows an increasing disposition to centralize the state and bring local autonomy to an end. In phase B ('elite organization'), with the transition to capitalist society, the traditional ruling group begins to generate the elements of a bourgeoisie, but a newly mobilized peasant class and a new bourgeoise emerging from its ranks form the vanguard of efforts to develop a counter-culture based on their own language and traditions. In phase C ('mass mobilization') this becomes a mass movement, with characteristic demands for rights for the emerging nation (Hroch, 1985: 177–83). But even though there were areas where this was the course run by the national movement – Norway, Finland, Bohemia, Slovakia, Estonia and Lithuania, for example – there were other culturally distinct areas, such as Polesia (now in Belarus), Masuria (now in Poland), Wales and Brittany, where no such mobilization took place (see Gellner (1996a) and Hroch (1998) for an assessment by each author of his intellectual relationship with the other).

Broader perspectives.   There is something rather geographically specific about the perspectives of the scholars so far discussed; these are at their most persuasive in the context of nineteenth-century central and eastern Europe. This is not surprising, given the background of the authors in question, rooted in the history of the Habsburg monarchy: the Viennese upbringing of Bauer and Hobsbawm and the Bohemian background of Deutsch, Gellner and Hroch endowed them with an intuitive understanding of peripheral nationalism in this complex area. Their approaches are particularly valuable in tackling one of the five types of nationalist mobilization already discussed, peripheral nationalism – at least in Europe. But to what extent might it be possible to generalize from these cases?

As it happens, a historian whose early focus was on Indonesia and South Asia has arrived at a similar position. For Benedict Anderson, the rise of nationalism was linked to the rise of 'print capitalism'. The printing revolution combined with the rise of capitalism to create new types of 'imagined community' (a term described as having 'an extraordinary appeal, as if people had been waiting for such a description to be coined'; Llobera, 1994: 103). Printing required linguistic standardization, a process that both slowed the pace of language change and broadened the extent over which standard languages stretched (Anderson, 1983: 41-9). This has obvious value in explaining the growth of peripheral nationalism, but it has implications also for other types of nationalism. Thus, the spread of Creole nationalism in the Americas was assisted by the process by which administrative borders acquired greater significance in a world of enhanced mobility of officials and growing circulation of region-specific newspapers and print media. So, too, was the 'official nationalism' of such countries as Russia, Britain and Japan helped by print capitalism – an important ally in advancing the cause of linguistic and cultural homogenization. But Anderson argues that this also helps to explain more recent anti-colonial nationalism in Indonesia, Indo-China, Africa and elsewhere. The spread of education created new communities, in some of which new indigenous languages ousted the colonial language; but, even where this displacement did not happen, technological progress ensured that printed media were partly superseded by media which no longer required literacy in the official language.

There is also something time-specific about the explanations so far discussed: it stresses the 'modern' character of nationalism. But even if, as we have seen, the kinds of perennialist or primordialist arguments that nationalist ideologists themselves make are rejected, we can still accept that in many cases the pre-modern inheritance carried some weight. Thus Seton-Watson (1977: 8–9) traced some nations (such as the English and the French) back to the seventeenth century, and Liah Greenfeld (1992: 14–17) came to a similar conclusion regarding the English and the Dutch. John Armstrong's analysis of 'nations before nationalism' traced the emergence of ethnic collectivities long before the modern period (Armstrong, 1982: 4); Josep Llobera (1994: 81–5) identified abundant evidence of pre-modern patterns of national identity and ethnic consciousness; and Aviel Roshwald (2006: 8–44) analyzed a form of 'pre-modern' nationalism. Arguments of this kind convinced Anthony Smith (1986, 1991: 19–42, 2009) of the importance of the pre-modern ethnic factor in the creation of the modern nation. Such evidence need not, however, encourage acceptance of arguments of historical determinism: ethnic heritage offers a rich mine of material from which new patterns of national identity may be constructed, but the shape of this pattern is not predetermined (Day and Thompson, 2004: 63–83).

THE GROWTH OF NATIONALISM

There are important respects in which the above discussion offers an incomplete explanation of nationalist mobilization. Sociological explanations typically focus on the impact of broad, long-term social changes, but they do not always indicate why it is that in some circumstances where these changes occur we encounter strong patterns of nationalist mobilization, while in others such patterns are weak or non-existent. In this section we consider more explicitly political factors, in a discussion which overlaps with that in the last section.

We begin by considering a long-standing debate on the character of nationalist mobilization, one which distinguishes narrow, exclusive, 'ethnic' forms of mobilization from broad, inclusive 'civic' ones. Having considered this dichotomy, we go on to look at explanations of the rise of nationalism that build on the features already considered but incorporate also a strong political dimension.

The debate on 'ethnic' and 'civic' nations

A great deal of the literature on nationalism is constructed around a very simple 'civic–ethnic' typology. The typology itself is largely descriptive, but it incorporates, at least implicitly, a sketch of an explanation for different paths in the evolution of nationalism. Some recent research attributes the authorship of this typology to Anthony Smith (for example, Popson, 2001: 326). Smith, A. (1995: 181, n. 4, 2000a: 6–7) attributes it to Hans Kohn, referring to it as 'the Kohn dichotomy', a label apparently coined by Louis Snyder (1968: 53–7) which has attracted a great deal of scholarly attention (Liebich, 2006). Kohn himself (1944), however, was familiar with a literature in which this distinction was commonplace, and like many who came later (such as Shulman, 2002: 555; Clark, 2010: 45), he cited the work of the celebrated German historian Friedrich Meinecke. Meinecke (1970 [1928]: 10), in turn, attributed the dichotomy to Julius Neumann, a distinguished German economics professor. Neumann (1888: 1–9) acknowledged the distinction as one already made by several scholars, and it is true that a number of earlier examples may be found. One of the earliest was produced by the remarkable Belgian economist and academic, Émile de Laveleye (1868). We may begin with his elaboration of the distinction, as it already possesses the analytical and normative features that were later to be associated with it.

According to Laveleye, a particular type of nationalism develops with the establishment of schools in which peasants and artisans acquire basic literacy skills and knowledge about the state:

> Alongside these, certain enthusiasts become enamoured of their despised dialect, study its origins, polish it, cultivate it and use it to write poetry or publish a newspaper. The newspaper is read, the winged song penetrates everywhere, the delighted people hear it with joy, as it emerges from their own insides and is no longer the hated language of their masters; it speaks to them of their sufferings, their past, of the glory of their ancestors, of their power of yesterday, of the future greatness which awaits them. They learn that they belong to a race which numbers 10, 20 or 30 million souls. United, they would be strong, free, rich, formidable; why would not they, too, have their place in the sun and their independent land? The writer, the priest, emerging from the crowd, sustain and stir up these aspirations, and thus stands up a nationality which must be either satisfied or wiped out – there is no middle way (Laveleye, 1868: 517).

This type of phenomenon is, however, associated with backward, ill-governed, oppressed peoples; especially in the West, an alternative and broader source of community identification was more likely:

Above the ethnographic nationalities are political nationalities, *elective* ones, one might say, having their roots in love of freedom, in the worship of a glorious past, in harmony of interests, in similarity of customs, ideas and all that makes up intellectual life. … Elective nationalities are more worthy of respect, as they rely on the intellect, while the others have as their justification only affinities of blood and origin (Laveleye, 1868: 518).

Here already, not in embryo but in fully-fledged maturity, is the distinction between *Kulturnation* and *Staatsnation* that was later to acquire such prominence in the analysis of nationalism in Germany, and to spread from there to the English-speaking world, where it was ultimately recycled as the 'Kohn dichotomy'.

This dichotomy, as we have seen, has attracted great interest. Before discussing its implications further, it is worth reviewing its main features as they have been expounded by other authors. Table 9.2 presents a free interpretation of one summary of the position (Cabanel, 1997: 9–10, based on Schnapper, 2003 [1994]: 223–39). Here, the gap has been narrowed to a simple dichotomy between the 'French' and 'German' conceptions of the nation, with their roots respectively in the French Enlightenment and Revolution, and German romanticism. On one side is the more 'open', inclusive, individualistic form, where affiliation is based on territory and free choice; on the other is the more 'closed', exclusive, holistic form, based on ethnic affiliation and perceived ancestry. This dichotomy is more generally labelled a 'civic–ethnic' one, and in this guise is to be found in many analytical works on nationalism, and it may be hidden behind other labels, such as the distinction between 'demotic' and 'ethnic' nationalism made by E.K. Francis (1976). It also coincides with a mainstream sociological distinction, that between *Gesellschaft* and *Gemeinschaft* (Liebich, 2006). Although it can be presented as a valuable analytical perspective, this distinction has also been dismissed as hopelessly biased – as a form of ethnocentric indulgence characterizing western nationalism as rational, voluntary and 'good', and eastern nationalism as emotive, inherited and 'bad' (Yack, 1999 [1996]: 105). As one set of authors concluded, theorists now emphatically take sides: 'the only acceptable conception is the civic one. The ethnic conception is the view held by the bad guys' (Seymour, Couture and Nielsen, 1996: 9).

Here, we are interested not in the normative content of this dichotomy but in its analytical capacity. If seen as categorical alternatives for the classification of nations or nationalism, the two halves of the 'Kohn dichotomy' are potentially misleading (Clark, 2010). Elements of both types will be found in many, if not all, nationalist movements (Smith, A., 1991: 13; Zimmer, 2003a; Kaufmann and Zimmer, 2004). Different approaches to the analysis of nationalism in Poland (Zubrycki, 2001), the Czech Republic (Vlachová and Řeháková, 2009), Russia (Rabow-Edling, 2008) and Belarus (Buhr, Shadurski and Hoffman, 2011), similarly, see both of these tendencies as being present, though in different levels of strength at different points in time. A comparative analysis of survey data from the 1995–96 period in 15 countries found little empirical support for the view that these two stereotypes could be geographically segregated (Shulman, 2002). It clearly makes more sense to regard these as ideal types; they then become a valuable framework for the analysis of nationalism (Smith, A., 1991: 81–3; Kuzio, 2002).

Table 9.2 Two conceptions of the nation

Area	French conception	German conception
Source	Enlightenment, French revolution	German romanticism
Type	'civic-territorial'	'ethnic-genealogical'
Label	state nation (*Staatsnation*)	cultural nation (*Kulturnation*)
Normative basis	contract (elective)	fundamental character (ethnic)
Social basis	civil society (*Gesellschaft*)	community (*Gemeinschaft*)
Collective basis	individualistic	holistic
Membership criterion	voluntaristic	organic
Definition of membership	subjective data	(quasi-)objective criteria
Orientation	structure open to future	tradition rooted in the past
Philosophical principle	freedom	determinism
Origin of people	citizenship	ancestry
Political affiliation	'daily plebiscite'	blood and language
Legal affiliation	*jus soli*	*jus sanguinis*
Characteristic formulation	Renan, 'What is a nation?' (1882)	Fichte, 'Discourses to the German nation' (1807–08)

Source: Derived loosely from the summary by Cabanel (1997: 10) of the overview of these types by Schnapper (2003 [1994]: 223–39)

The implications of this dicholomy for explanations of nationalism are mainly indirect. In Kohn's view (1944: 329–34), western-style nationalism was a project of the state, aiming to disseminate a sense of nationality that was essentially political, and coextensive with the state; elsewhere, nationalism was a protest against existing state forms, expressed initially largely in cultural terms, and was 'a venture in education and propaganda rather than in policy shaping and government' (Kohn, 1944: 330). This may well overstate the implications of the two types, especially since nationalism everywhere may be seen as containing different mixes of the two conceptions of the nation. What, then, determines the path taken by nationalist moblization?

Democratization and nationalism

As indicated in the last section, nationalism is closely linked to processes of social change. But the great eras of social change throughout the world were not characterized by socio-economic transformation alone; they were generally accompanied by radical processes of political modernization (and, frequently, democratization). The critical concern here is the extent to which this process led to nationalist mobilization, and the circumstances in which it did so (Laitin, 2007). The relevant literature addresses this question from two directions: first, the literature on political mobilization that addresses also the question of nationalism, and, second, analyses of nationalism that explore the role of political mobilization.

Political mobilization. We may begin with a geographically specific analysis of political mobilization. The dominant paradigm describing the emergence of mass politics in western Europe is associated with the model developed by Seymour Martin Lipset and

Stein Rokkan (1967; Rokkan, 1970). This was based on the notion of a bidimensional framework. First, a '*cleavage*' model identified four fundamental cleavages that became politically relevant as a consequence of the democratic and industrial revolutions (centre–periphery, church–state, urban–rural, and owner–worker). These cleavage structures were transformed into enduring party systems, depending on the alliance options available to and selected by nation-building elites, producing secular conservative, religious, liberal and socialist parties, with the occasional presence of parties representing specifically peripheral regional interests. Second, an '*institutional*' model interpreted the politicization of these cleavages as depending on four decisive steps in the democratization process (*legitimation* of the right to protest and organize politically, *incorporation* of the population through franchise extension, reform of the principle of *representation* through introduction of proportional electoral arrangements, and securing of *majority power* through the principle of parliamentary control of the government). This was later developed by Rokkan and his colleagues to look at the more general implications of changing patterns of centre–periphery relations in Europe (Rokkan and Urwin, 1982, 1983).

The implications of this model for nationalist mobilization, at least in western Europe, are twofold. First, in the typical west European state, political modernization stirred up underlying tensions that may have had a centre–periphery dimension, but that found expression mainly in the form of party systems concerned with *anything but* the rights of peripheral language, cultural or national groups – conflicts based on class, urban–rural and, even in unidenominational societies, religion-dominated public discourse, and groups seeking to articulate other interests had great difficulty breaking into the party system. Second, however, not all west European states had well-established geographical identities; in some (such as the United Kingdom, Spain, Belgium and to some degree Italy) the very territorial shape of the state was an issue. This left space for the emergence of the centre–periphery cleavage, and the rise of regionalist or nationalist parties. In general, though, the model is more effective in showing how west European peripheries were integrated than in explaining regionalist revolt.

Reframing nationalism. The logic of the Rokkan approach may, however, be generalized, so that it offers an insight into developments outside Europe. We may equate Rokkan's centre–periphery distinction with the metropolitan–regional dichotomy already extensively discussed here, and also note the evolution of divisions within the region. An effort is made in Table 9.3 to illustrate the chronological path taken by this process, based in particular on the European experience, but to varying degrees generalizable outside that continent. With a view to forcibly bringing out similarities between alternative accounts, three phases corresponding to those of Hroch are identified.

In each phase, the contending groups tend to adopt predictable positions. Michael Mann describes the initial position: he sees a 'militarist' period kicking off a process of nation building. Beginning in the late eighteenth century, the state increasingly intruded on a population on which it relied for military manpower, and either managed to extend its own reach or stirred up opposition among regional elites threatened by the growing power of the

Table 9.3   Nationalist mobilization: ideal types

Domain/perspective	Phase A	Phase B	Phase C
Infrastructural conditions			
Socioeconomic level:	Agrarian/feudal relations	Transitional society	Industrial/capitalist society
Political institutional level:	Authoritarian rule	Limited democracy	Mass mobilization
Collective features			
Metropolitan centre:	Dynastic government; military dominance	Embryonic political party system (traditional parties)	Fully-fledged party system (including socialists) OR mass authoritarian party; possible communist party
Regional centre:	Territorial patriotism; political resistance; cultural exploration	Party system of centre; possible regional party	Military and political alignment with centre; OR regional separatism
Regional periphery:	Political quiescence; possible peasant revolts, insurrectionary activity	Party system of centre; possible regional party	Party system of centre OR separate party system OR mass nationalist party; possible communist party

centre (Mann, 1995: 46–53). Paul Brass, whose main area of interest is India, has summarized the response of regional elites and political actors in such circumstances, identifying four options that interlock with the Rokkan approach (Brass, 1991: 26–9). First, the local aristocracy fights to preserve its autonomy against the metropolitan area by stressing the distinctiveness of its region, as in the case of the Magyar nobility in nineteenth-century Hungary (this is a common development that we may equate with *Landespatriotismus* or territorial patriotism in the 'cultural exploration' phase discussed by Hroch). Second, local religious elites mobilize the population against the influence of religious forces in the metropolitan centre, as in several East European and Asian cases. The third and fourth options resemble each other: local religious elites mobilize the population against the local aristocracy, which has aligned itself culturally with the metropolitan centre (as in Wales) or is itself of alien origin (as in Serbia and Bulgaria). More commonly, though, this phase is marked by resistance to the metropolitan centre on the part of the regional centre, as regional secular or religious elites seek to maximize their power; the regional periphery is largely politically irrelevant at this point.

The second phase is a critical one in the path of nationalist evolution. In an era of limited political freedom, organized political dissent begins to appear within the metropolitan centre and finds expression in an embryonic party system, typically a bipolar one that pits a conservative tendency against a reformist, 'liberal' one. In certain circumstances, this set of cleavages extends also to the region, with established regional interests and peripheral dissidents seeking out allies in the metropolitan centre. In such cases, the development of organized dissent within the metropolitan centre *assists in the integration of the periphery*. In Scotland

and Wales, for instance, peripheral dissent was channelled into support for the (state-wide) Liberal Party initially, and later for the Labour Party. But two other types of outcome are possible. If its capacity to control the regional periphery is secure, the regional centre may itself protest against the centralizing tendencies of the state, and mobilize against them. Alternatively, if the regional periphery is sufficiently powerful and is led by an elite whose interests are threatened by the process of centralization, we are likely to witness the emergence of a regionalist, nationalist or anti-colonial movement.

In the third phase, the state expands its reach over wider aspects of society, confirming the need for popular political participation and the concept of popular sovereignty as mechanisms for promoting democratic control, and therefore establishing a link between nationalism and democracy (Mann, 1995: 53–63). A fully-developed party system with mass parties develops in the metropolitan centre, and this may further assist the process of regional integration. But if, following the pathways charted in the second phase, the regional centre or the regional periphery respond autonomously to these developments, we get a different outcome. In one scenario, where the regional periphery is politically irrelevant, Creole nationalism finds expression in an entirely separate set of political organizations and parties. In an alternative scenario, we witness the birth of a mass nationalist party representing the interests of the regional periphery (such as the Irish Nationalist Party up to 1918), or of an entirely separate party system (as in pre-1918 Finland), or, more typically, of a party system that is largely autonomous of the centre, but with metropolitan parties also represented there (as in pre-1918 Bohemia, or contemporary Catalonia or the Basque Country). Anti-colonial movements commonly followed the model of the mass party, as in the case of the Congress Party in India and the African National Congress in South Africa. In such cases, a powerful communist party worked in close association with (if not as part of) the broad nationalist movement, though elsewhere, especially where the threat from the metropolitan centre was weaker (as in China), the nationalist party was more conservative and had a more confrontational relationship with communism.

Explaining these pathways offers a bigger challenge than describing them. But we may at least point to the ingredients in an explanation: the conflicting interests of the contending groups, and especially of elites within these groups. Thus, as Brass points out, elites within economically deprived groups may lead a struggle for equality against the dominant group, which is presented as an exploiter. Even in the case of privileged groups, there may be a similar form of mobilization in an effort to protect the material interests of this group in circumstances of competition over resources. In all cases, the availability of political resources is crucial. Examples of such resources include the capacity of the regional centre or the regional periphery to mobilize behind a single national movement, the capacity of established political forces to resist these, and the relative costs associated with particular political choices (Brass, 1991: 41–62). The extent to which territorial demands arise in such circumstances will of course depend on the spatial distribution of the population, as discussed in Chapter 8: political separatism requires attachment to a territory which is viable in respect both of its absolute size and population and the concentration there of the population of the 'nation' (Toft, 2003).

THE VICTORY OF NATIONALISM

The two perspectives discussed so far – the impact of profound social change on the structure of linguistically or culturally divided societies (often with a pronounced 'ethnic division of labour'), and the role of elite groups in promoting particular forms of political mobilization – are useful in helping us to understand the process of mobilization in peripheral nationalist movements, and may offer valuable insights into understanding anti-colonial nationalism. But their value diminishes in accounting for the two other main forms of nationalism examined in Chapter 8: colonial or Creole nationalism, and integrationist nationalism. In considering these, and in reflecting on the circumstances that account for the success of some forms of peripheral and anti-colonial nationalism but not others, it is necessary to look at two further factors: the process of state formation, and the implications of statehood for the advancement of the nationalist project.

The debate on the origins of states

The process of state formation is a good deal more concrete than that of nation formation, at least to the extent that we can recognize the end product more easily, and therefore have a better chance of identifying the factors that lie behind this process. The literature is rich, multidisciplinary, varied and venerable, and tends to fall into two clusters as regards explanation. First, 'voluntaristic' theories stress the role of individual actors or small collectivities in ceding sovereignty to a large political unit with a view to protecting collective interests, typically with an implicit 'social contract' between ruler and ruled. Second, 'coercive' theories rest on the notion that force rather than enlightened self-interest has been responsible for the path of political evolution that resulted in the creation of the state (Carneiro, 1970: 733–4). A variant of the first approach is illustrated by John Hall (1993b: 880), who describes the state as being born as a consequence of two factors: the development of irrigation agriculture (which implies fixed investment and facilitates taxation) and the 'service of a demanding god' (with early states commonly centred around temples and based on worship of the divine). The work of Charles Tilly lies closer to the second approach: in analyzing the emergence of the modern state in Europe, he compares governments to racketeers, offering their subjects 'protection' against a threat which they themselves have created, establishing a monopoly of the use of force, and supporting this by a tax-raising arrangement (Tilly, 1985: 171–2).

State formation and nationalism.   While there is a conflict between these approaches if they are seen as exclusive and general explanations, they may be seen as complementary to the extent that they apply to different phenomena (the early, pristine state, and the modern bureaucratic state, respectively). But what are their implications for our understanding of a central goal of nationalism: the establishment of a new state? We may start by looking at the universe of new states. One overview of the period 1816–2000 identified 191 new states as coming into existence (this includes some cases of the re-establishment of a state that had disappeared earlier). By far the most common category was that of division of states,

Table 9.4   Nationalist demands and statehood: examples

		Intensity of demand for statehood	
		Low	*High*
Independent state as outcome	*No*	Wales	Tamil Eelam
	Yes	Belarus	Poland

accounting for 180 cases in all: 118 post-colonial states (including 21 microstates), 50 post-secession states, six rump states and six post-occupation states (such as North and South Korea). A second category was that of unification of existing states, five in all (including, for example, Germany in 1871, and again in 1990). The third category is that of newly incorporated territories, of which there were six, including Liberia in 1847 and Transvaal in 1852 (Roeder, 2007: 5–9).

At first sight, it is difficult to relate these data and the cases to which they refer to either the 'voluntaristic' or the 'coercive' explanations for the emergence of states; and the centrality of nationalism is not immediately clear. But it is worth considering this big group further. The relationship between nationalist demands and political outcomes in such cases is presented in Table 9.4, which simplifies the nature of nationalist demands by distinguishing between those where there was a clear demand for independence and those where there was not. The second dimension distinguishes nationalist movements whose efforts were seen as resulting in independence from those where they were not.

While it is not possible to measure precisely whether or not a particular nationalist movement fell into or outside the 'pro-independence' category, extreme positions are clearly distinguishable, and Table 9.4 seeks only to give examples rather than to indicate how all cases can be accommodated in each of the quadrants that result from cross-classifying the two dimensions. When nationalist demands are modest, it is not surprising that independent statehood fails to materialize. Among Welsh nationalists, there does exist a pro-independence tendency, but public opinion is in general cautious (though it should be recalled that a large proportion of Welsh residents – 25% in 2001 – were born outside Wales). In the first referendum on devolution for Wales in 1979 only 20.3% supported the proposal; in the second referendum, in 1998, this had increased to 50.3%, though the level of devolution proposed was very modest; and in a third referendum, in 2011, 63.5% voted for new law-making powers for the National Assembly. Many other minorities are in a similar position, their demands falling well short of independence. Such very different groups as the Catalans, Bretons and Sardinians fall into this category.

Very commonly, however, groups like those just mentioned end up with independent states (Roeder, 2007: 24). In fact, this category is a very well-populated one. It could be argued that most of the Creole nationalist movements in Latin America in the early nineteenth century were not separatist, but in effect had independence imposed by the collapse of their

European imperial parents. The nationalist movements of the Estonians, Latvians, Czechs, Slovaks and other peoples of the early twentieth century were directed mainly at winning autonomy for their territories, but the collapse of the Romanov and Habsburg empires thrust independence on them. There was little evidence of a popular demand for Belarusian independence of the Soviet Union, for Slovak independence of Czechoslovakia or for Bosnian independence of Yugoslavia, but in the 1990s these peoples nevertheless found themselves inhabiting independent territories. There were other cases, such as the creation of Danzig in 1920, where there was virtually no domestic demand for this outcome at all.

In sharp contrast, there are cases where a strong, pro-independence nationalist movement has failed to win its objective. The bitter struggle of the Tamil Tigers to establish an independent state of Tamil Eelam is an example: it was decisively defeated in early 2009 by the Sri Lankan army. The Kurds, similarly, have not thus far succeeded in establishing a united, independent Kurdistan – a formidable challenge, given the fact that their territory extends over parts of Iran, Iraq, Turkey and Syria. Strong nationalist demands in the Basque Country and in Quebec, similarly, have not resulted in the appearance of independent states. These two cases point to the difficulty in identifying clear-cut examples of this type, since public opinion and electoral data suggest that while there is a strong separatist strand in each case, more moderate nationalism is predominant. It is clear, though, that there are many cases where an active nationalist movement has existed, but its efforts have met with little success in respect of its ultimate goals. Examples of such movements will be found in Europe (Keating, 1988), the western world more generally (Guibernau, 1999), Africa (Forrest, 2004), Southeast Asia (Reid, 2010) and, in the form of 'mininationalism', across the globe (Snyder, 1982).

The final case is that where separate statehood has been won by a strong nationalist movement. The re-establishment of Poland and the appearance of certain other independent states in Europe after 1918 illustrate this category, and more recent examples may also be cited, such as Eritrea (1993), Timor Leste (2002) and Kosovo (2008). In very many other cases, though, where the demand for independence was traditionally weak, there was a last-minute conversion to separatism, when it became clear that this was not just possible but, indeed, inevitable. Many of the successor states of the Ottoman, Habsburg and Russian empires, or, later, of the Soviet Union and Yugoslavia, are examples.

The success of nationalism.   In accounting for the success or failure of nationalist movements, we need to consider at least three sets of factors. Two of these are obvious: the character and intensity of the nationalist movement itself and the resources it is capable of deploying, and the capacity and willingness of its opponents to resist these. But the contest between these two sides does not take place in a vacuum: we need to consider also the international environment within which the relationship between these two sets of forces contend.

We have already discussed the potential resources available to regionalist movements in earlier chapters and considered the extent to which regionalist elites have managed to mobilize voters behind a party or set of parties. Such movements are to varying degrees ambitious by reference to their ultimate goals (which may extend as far as the attainment of independence), and in the ruthlessness with which they are prepared to pursue them (including their willingness to engage in unconventional forms of behaviour, such as civil disobedience, reliance on anti-state structures or even armed resistance). They also vary in the extent to which they are forced to confront domestic resistance (from the regional centre, as discussed in the last chapter) and in their success in overcoming or circumventing this.

The second set of factors relates to the standing of the region's main rival. In any bilateral confrontation between a regionalist movement and a metropolitan centre in 'normal' times, the cards are stacked strongly against separatism nationalism. The metropolitan centre is likely to be dominant demographically, economically, politically and militarily, and to possess resources that the regional periphery simply cannot match. Furthermore, it has a strong motivation to resist regional demands lest these spread to other regions (Walter, 2009). Nevertheless, it may be the case that the costs of defeating a mobilized periphery are greater from the perspective of the centre than the benefits (political, economic and symbolic) of retaining control, and the region may be allowed to leave, especially if its commitment and determination trumps that of the metropolitan centre. The secession of the Irish Free State from the United Kingdom following a two-year guerrilla war and the Anglo-Irish treaty of 1921 is a rare example. As it was put by one of the activists in the conflict, Terence MacSwiney, Lord Mayor of Cork, who died on hunger strike in 1920, 'it is not those who can inflict the most, but those that can suffer the most who will prevail' – a sentiment to be echoed in other unequal contests between nationalist militants and their much more powerful opponents. The struggle for American independence that began in 1776 was less unequal, and the secession of the Balkan countries from the Ottoman empire – Greece (1830), Romania (1878), Serbia (1878) and Bulgaria (1905) – took place in the context of a steadily weakening metropolitan centre.

But it is when times are not 'normal' that separatist nationalism is likely to be most successful. It was the French revolutionary wars that weakened Spain and Portugal sufficiently to facilitate independence in Latin America; the First World War dealt a death blow to the Habsburg and Russian empires, and to what was left of the Ottoman empire; and the collapse of communism removed the glue that had held together the multinational Soviet, Yugoslav and Czechoslovak federations (Ottaway, 1994: 32–3). The impact of the Second World War was less direct. In Europe, the territorial identity of most states survived; there was an emphasis in the postwar settlements on consolidation, reconstruction, boundary change and population transfer. But the war led quickly to a process of imperial disintegration, beginning with the vast British empire, and extending eventually to the French, Spanish, Dutch and (much later) Portuguese empires. In these cases, while the vigour of particular nationalist movements was also a key consideration, it was the decay in the economic, political and military power of the metropolitan centre that was to prove crucial.

We thus need also to consider a third set of factors. Conflicts between the metropolitan and peripheral areas are rarely confined to the domestic sphere. The 'Concert of Europe' system put in place in 1815 by the Congress of Europe sought to provide an international framework for the recognition of states in Europe, and was succeeded in this role by the

League of Nations and the United Nations (Watson, 1992). In an important sense, though, the international system reflected the global power balance rather than shaping it, and great power rivalry defined the context within which the metropolitan–regional relationship evolved. A further significant international factor is the international political cultural environment. Distinctive episodes of revolt seem to have a virus-like effect in spreading rapidly from country to country, creating new mass perceptions of what is politically possible and ideologically desirable, as in the 1790s, 1848, 1917–18, the late 1940s and 1968. Sometimes, such 'infections' seem to be regional rather than global in reach, as in 1989 in central and eastern Europe and 2011 in the Middle East.

Yet the international environment may have an impact at a second level. Many nationalist movements appeal for assistance to kin states (for example, the reliance of many smaller Slav groups on Russian support in the nineteenth century), or to diaspora populations in external states (very many nationalist movements sought support within emigrant communities abroad, notably in the USA). In the case of China, for example. the relatively activist path of Uyghur nationalism in Xinjiang may be related to the availability of external allies (such as the USSR initially, and certain Islamic states later), while the more passive pattern of the Mongols in Inner Mongolia is attributable to the absence of such allies, apart from support from Japan in the interwar period (Han, 2011). This factor often had a big impact on the outcome of the struggle between regional and metropolitan leaders, helping to tilt the balance in favour of the former.

Nationalism after statehood

Establishing a state represents a crucial victory for the nationalist project; consolidating this victory represents a continuing challenge. For many, the structures of the liberal democratic state are adequate; especially if the model of the Jacobin state is followed, minorities are seen as assimilable, and they are also conceded a full measure of individual rights. For others, authoritarian government is the answer. Thus, many nationalist intellectuals in interwar states such as Latvia saw authoritarianism as the only way of achieving 'a perfect statehood of national culture' (Zake, 2005: 97). Nationalism itself can also be an important prop for authoritarianism, as has been argued in respect of contemporary Belarus (Leshchenko, 2004: 340–8). The frequent interdependence of nationalism and authoritarianism makes each an attractive partner for the other; and radical nationalism also became a central ingredient in fascism (Zimmer, 2003b: 80–106). As we have seen, once the nationalist project has matured with the attainment of statehood, the issue of nationalism (understood, as defined in Chapter 1, as referring to the relationship between the boundaries of the state and the boundaries of the nation) may not simply disappear. There is a state to be maintained, and perhaps a nation to be further 'fulfilled'. In particular, nationalist elites may continue to highlight threats from remnants of the former regional centre, or from other 'alien' elements. Several types of explanation have emerged for this tendency, but two stand out: a type of rational calculus that rests on ethnic realities, and a sense of social psychological insecurity that is shaped by the existence of real or imaginary enemies.

The first type of explanation has to do with processes of ethnic competition within a state with established borders. Of the options available to the dominant group (as discussed in Chapter 10), why should the path of elimination, exclusion or assimilation rather than the course of accommodation be chosen? Michael Banton's 'theory of ethnic and racial competition' suggests that when ethnic groups compete intensely in the market, the boundary between them is strengthened (Banton, 1983: 100–36). This has implications for earlier stages in the evolution of nationalism, but it is particularly crucial when a new majority is competing with a new minority in a new state. The majority has just emerged from a successful struggle for statehood, and relations with other groups are likely to be inflamed. Indeed, such majorities normally enjoy a head start: Roeder (2007: 10–11) calculates that of 177 new states that appeared in the twentieth century, 153 (86%) were 'administrative upgrades of segment states', that is of an existing state-like institution, and he argues that strong nationalism was more likely to develop within these entities than elsewhere. In these conditions, ethnic competition is likely to highlight differences between majority and minority groups, and to further marginalize the latter. In circumstances of intense competition for resources, the temptation to demonize the minority is likely to be strong, and this may well convey material advantages on the dominant group.

The second type of explanation for the rise of militant (and often authoritarian) nationalism in independent states overlaps with the literature on the rise of fascism, and stresses the social psychological dimension (see Nolte, 1965; Hayes, 1973; Paxton, 2004). Of course, this is not to argue that a calculus of self-interest is lacking; the cultivation of an ideology of exclusivist nationalism may serve the interests of the leaders of the state well. The whipping up of nationalist sentiment may be an experiment in psychological manipulation for instrumental ends, with a focus on the 'threat' presented by minorities, and a stress on the need for 'national unity', providing a welcome diversion from other policy failings. By playing on suspicions of the disloyalty of minorities, in other words, the leaders of the dominant group further consolidate their own position. This was a distinctive feature of the authoritarian nationalist and especially fascist movements of the interwar period, with their cultivation of the myth of the nation and the race, and their veneration of its past (Carsten, 1982: 230–1). While the authoritarian movements of interwar Europe varied greatly, their emergence, and the distance that they progressed down the path towards fascism, seem to have been conditioned by distinctive historical developments: particular forms of class conflict fuelled by late capitalist development, the shock of military defeat that promoted the emergence of paramilitarism and rearmament, the weakness of the tradition of competitive politics, and the attractiveness and ease of transmission of an ideology that appealed to an emerging educated class of young males of military or religious predispositions (Mann, 2004: 48–91).

CONCLUSION

This chapter began by noting the scepticism of many analysts of nationalism as to the likelihood that an effective explanatory theory would ever emerge. Here, we have tried to do no more than to explore a set of partial explanations, directed at particular aspects of nationalist mobilization and with a more pronounced focus on separatist than on integrationist nationalism. These aspects are quite different, and we expect to find explanations of quite different kinds for them. Broadly speaking, the following are the kinds of questions we have asked and the kinds of answers that have emerged (they correspond to the four phases of nationalism already discussed).

- Why are some cultural collectivities transformed into ethnic groups, while others remain at the level of linguistic, religious or racial categories? We have sought the answer in theories relating to the interaction between underlying cultural patterns and the process of social modernization (that is, the transition to advanced capitalist society).
- Why are some ethnic groups mobilized politically into nationalist movements that make demands for institutional reform and/or a territorial restructuring of the state, while others remain politically passive? Here, the answer seems to lie in part in the circumstances associated with the answer to the first question, but also in political choices made by elites in the course of the process of political modernization or democratization.
- Why do some nationalist movements succeed in their goal of winning statehood, while others remain content with forms of autonomy or institutional reform, or continue to struggle for independence? The answers to the first two questions help in answering this, but of even greater importance is the relationship between the nationalist movement and the metropolitan centre (and in particular the balance of resources available to either), and the realities of the international system.
- Why do some nationalist movements which have succeeded in winning statehood insist on the need for cultural and especially linguistic uniformity, while others are prepared to accept pluralist realities? Here, the answer lies in part in the trajectory of the nationalist movement itself (including the answers to the three earlier questions), but also in mass social psychology and in perceptions (however insecurely founded) of communal vulnerability and self-interest.

The last of these questions takes us into a new aspect of the study of nationalism, inviting consideration of the manner in which states respond to national minorities within their borders. This is the issue to which we turn in the next chapter.

10

NATIONALISM AND STATE STRUCTURE

INTRODUCTION

The nineteenth-century Czech nationalist leader František Palacký once remarked that 'if the Austrian Empire did not exist, it would have to be invented': nothing but a complex set of institutional structures could cope with the mixture of nationalities that made up the Habsburg dominions. So far, our focus has been primarily on the nation: on the circumstances associated with its origin and development, and on the patterns in accordance with which it has been organized politically. This exploration has also, necessarily, taken us into the area of relations between nation and state: a demand for political self-expression, usually in the form of a state, is one of the most characteristic features of nationalism. But the relationship between nation and state needs also to be reviewed from the perspective of the state. It is this perspective that is explored in the present chapter, where we look at the options open to the modern state in responding to challenges from minority nations, or from ethnic diversity more generally. Indeed, the subordinate group sometimes constitutes a majority of the population, and the references to 'minorities' that follow should be seen as sometimes referring to numerical majorities.

In fact, there are very many possible state responses, and this is reflected in the writing of those who seek to generalize about them (Coakley, 2010; Guelke, 2012). For some, the options range from complete elimination of minorities, by means of such policies as genocide, to concession of relatively generous rights to them, such as power sharing or territorial autonomy (see for example, Horowitz, 1990; Coakley, 1992a; McGarry and O'Leary, 1993; Schneckener and Senghaas, 2003: 166–7; McGarry, O'Leary and Simeon, 2008). Others exclude the barbaric extreme and confine themselves to essentially political approaches, whether these seek to marginalize minorities or incorporate them in the political process (see for example, Zartman, 1990; Smooha and Hanf, 1992; Cohen, 1997; Peleg, 2007: 78–83). So great is the variety of competing classifications that we need to see if there is any more general way of categorizing state approaches to minorities. An attempt is made in Table 10.1 to do precisely this. This rests on the assumption that there are two key dimensions

Table 10.1 Approaches to national minorities

		Recognition of group identity	
		Low	High
Protection of individual rights	Low	1. Elimination: ethnic monopoly	2. Exclusion: ethnic hegemony
	High	3. Integration: ethnic homogeneity	4. Accommodation: ethnic coexistence

that we need to consider in classifying minority management strategies: the extent to which they are grounded in acceptance of basic principles of individual rights, and their openness to recognition of the coexistence of socially defined groups. Each of these is of course a continuum, but the position in Table 10.1 is simplified by treating each as a dichotomy with two values, 'high' and 'low'

The first (individual rights) dimension is a familiar one; it refers to the package of rights that has been taken for granted in democratic societies since the French revolution, as incorporated also in the bill of rights that became part of the American constitution, and as summarized by the United Nations in the Universal Declaration of Human Rights (1948). Adoption of this package represented huge progress in political modernization, with the displacement of earlier forms of political organization based on the separate rights and privileges of such groups as the nobility, clergy and urban bourgeois populations. There is a tension between this principle and the second one, recognition of group identity: this refers to the extent to which, quite apart from their perspective on acknowledging the principle of individual rights, regimes are disposed to accept differentiated groups (such as ethnic, linguistic or religious minorities) within the broader society. The poles of this dimension are defined by more complex positions than the 'individual rights' one. At one end is a rejection of pluralism, implying policies of either 'ethnic cleansing' or 'ethnic blindness'. At the opposite end is acceptance of the long-term reality of intergroup boundaries, whether these are used to facilitate discrimination against minorities or their incorporation in political structures.

It will be seen that when we cross-classify these two dimensions, as in Table 10.1, we get four sets of approaches, and these form the basis of the remaining sections of this chapter. Where the level of individual rights is low, there are two approaches: first, elimination of minorities (which refers to their physical eradication and results in a regime of *ethnic monopoly*), and, second, exclusion of minorities from political life (the outcome of which is a system of *ethnic hegemony*). The remaining approaches are based on acceptance of individual rights. The third is premised on the political integration and, typically, cultural assimilation of minorities (with no formal recognition of the existence of ethnic or other minority groups, commonly resulting in a regime of *ethnic homogeneity*). The fourth rests on the incorporation of these minorities (whose separate existence is formally acknowledged in a system of *ethnic coexistence*). The three approaches that eliminate or neutralize minorities are considered in the first part of this chapter; the second part considers the institutional options associated with the fourth approach.

SUPRESSING MINORITIES

The first two sets of strategies are based on ridding the state of minorities: physically through such devices as genocide or expulsion, or politically, by finding mechanisms for excluding members of the minority from political power (O'Leary, 2001). Of course, there are often other ways of ridding the state of its minorities: boundary change, for instance. However, states generally prefer to maximize control over their territories; they wish to part with the minority, but not with its territory. Thus, the secession of most of Ireland from the United Kingdom in 1922 left a 'more British' United Kingdom, but the British themselves had resisted this process. Sometimes, however, the dominant group is prepared to pay the price of territorial break-up: the withdrawal of 14 smaller national republics from the Soviet Union in 1991 left a 'more Russian' core territory, and was facilitated by the Russian government itself. We focus here, however, on two particularly brutal forms of 'ethnic cleansing', genocide and population expulsion. We go on to consider policies of political exclusion, and conclude with a discussion of the remaining (third) strategy, based on the principle of non-recognition of minorities in the context of a regime of full civil and political rights.

Genocide

The slaughter of one's enemies has had its advocates from ancient times. It has been pointed out that the Bible itself (and particularly the Old Testament) contains passages apparently endorsing what would now be called genocide, and that 'tales of war and assassination pervade the four books of Samuel and Kings, where it is hard to avoid verses justifying the destruction of God's enemies' (Jenkins, 2009). Medieval Europe offered many examples of mass killings, and European colonization of other continents (and, in particular, the Americas) provide more (Kuper, 1981: 11–19). The twentieth century, however, is the one that offers the most terrible evidence.

Identifying cases of genocide of course entails defining what we mean by the term. In international law, a definition formulated by the United Nations as part of its *Convention on the prevention and punishment of the crime of genocide* in 1948 offers a guideline:

> In the present Convention, genocide means any of the following acts committed with intent to destroy, in whole or in part, a national, ethnical, racial or religious group, as such:
>
> (a) Killing members of the group;
> (b) Causing serious bodily or mental harm to members of the group;
> (c) Deliberately inflicting on the group conditions of life calculated to bring about its physical destruction in whole or in part;
> (d) Imposing measures intended to prevent births within the group;
> (e) Forcibly transferring children of the group to another group (United Nations, 1951).

This definition has come in for a good deal of criticism, mainly directed at the fact that it represented a political compromise rather than a detached judgement (Horowitz, 1980:

9–20; Kuper, 1981: 19–39). Chalk and Jonassohn (1990: 10–11) argue that it is 'of little use to scholars': it fails to distinguish adequately between killing and non-lethal violence, and it excludes the annihilation of political and social groups. Indeed, an alternative term has sought to describe the process by which a group continues to exist physically but its culture is destroyed: 'ethnocide', which was defined in 1981 by another United Nations group as follows: 'ethnocide means that an ethnic group is denied the right to enjoy, develop and transmit its own culture and its own language, whether individually or collectively' (cited in Shaw, 2007: 65). In this chapter, a distinction between ethnocide and genocide is maintained, and we consider the former later.[1]

Kuper (1985: 150–6) distinguishes four types of 'domestic' genocide. The first is perpetrated against indigenous peoples, as in the case of colonization processes in the Americas, Africa and Australia. Although US policy on the native American population in the nineteenth century rested mainly on ethnocide, it has been argued that 'the federal government stood ready to engage in genocide as a means of coercing tribes when they resisted ethnocide or resorted to armed resistance' (Chalk and Jonassohn, 1990: 203). The second, most notorious, category is directed against 'hostage groups', such as Jews and Roma in Nazi Germany, and is considered further below. The third category is associated with colonial withdrawal, which removes external constraints on an unequal domestic power structure, allowing for retaliatory acts of mass killings. There are unfortunately abundant examples: the Burundi genocide of 1993 and the Rwanda genocide of 1994, for example, mainly perpetrated by the majority Hutu group against the powerful Tutsi minority. The fourth category has to do with the struggle of groups for power, secession, autonomy or equality, as in the case of the actions of the West Pakistanis in massacring Hindus and Bengalis during the process of establishing Bangladeshi independence. The massacre of Bosnian Muslims by Serbs in Srebrenica in 1995 is another example.

The extermination of 'hostage groups' offers the most terrible examples of genocide. The Armenian case is one: in 1915, hundreds of thousands of Armenians in Turkey were killed, some (including women, children and the elderly) in forced marches from their homeland to Syria, others (mainly men) by shooting (Hovannisian, 1986). But it is the Holocaust, the destruction of most of Europe's Jewish population during the Second World War, which offers what is now the archetypal example. This followed from the sustained marginalization of Jews in Germany during Nazi rule, as described in Chapter 2; but this was itself an expression of a wider form of anti-Semitism, as part of which Jews had been discriminated against over the centuries in European countries generally (Dawidowicz, 1975; Rubenstein et al., 2002). Conditions for Jews in Germany deteriorated further following that country's annexation of Austria and the Sudetenland in 1938, and in particular after the conquest of Poland in 1939. This, together with later German advances into the Soviet Union and elsewhere, resulted in German control over a huge Jewish population. In the occupied eastern

---

1 The term 'ethnocide' is also used in three other quite different senses: first, as equivalent to genocide, as suggested by Raphaël Lemkin (2005 [1944]: 79), who in fact coined the term 'genocide'; second, essentially, a subcategory of this, where the group that is destroyed is ethnically defined (Stein, 2004); and, third, it may refer to the unintended, or, in other words, not premeditated, wiping out of a group and its culture (Mann, 2005: 16).

Table 10.2 Jewish population of selected European states, *c.* 1920–48

	c. 1920		c. 1939		c. 1948		Change 1939–48	
	000s	*(%)*	*000s*	*(%)*	*000s*	*(%)*	*000s*	*(%)*
Poland	3,500	(12.9)	3,114	(9.0)	88	(0.4)	−3,026	(−97.2)
USSR	2,933	(2.9)	2,524	(2.0)	2,000	(1.1)	−524	(−20.8)
Romania	950	(5.5)	900	(4.5)	380	(2.3)	−520	(−57.8)
Germany	615	(1.0)	174	(0.2)	153	(0.2)	−21	(−11.9)
Hungary	499	(6.3)	445	(4.1)	174	(1.9)	−271	(−60.9)
Czechoslovakia	354	(2.6)	357	(3.6)	42	(0.3)	−315	(−88.2)
Austria	350	(5.4)	66	(0.9)	31	(0.4)	−35	(−53.3)
Other states	1,326	(0.6)	1,360	(0.6)	911	(0.3)	−449	(−33.0)
Total	10,527	(2.3)	8,940	(1.7)	3,779	(0.6)	−5,161	(−57.7)

Note: Austrian and German data for 1939 (when Austria formed part of Germany) are based on assigning the Jewish population to the two countries in proportion to their Jewish populations in 1933–34. The German total for 1948 includes a displaced Jewish population. The territorial borders of certain of these countries (in particular, Poland, the USSR and Germany) changed considerably as a consequence of the Second World War. Figures in brackets refer to Jews as a percentage of the total population, except in the last column.

Source: Computed from *American Jewish yearbook*, vols 27 (1925–26), 36 (1934–35), 42 (1940–41), 50 (1948–49)

lands, Jews were initially forced into urban ghettos, and many were massacred. A change in Nazi policy in late 1941 and early 1942 saw the adoption of a much more systematic programme designed to eradicate the Jewish population. Six major extermination camps were constructed in Poland, and Jews were shipped there to be murdered in gas chambers (many Poles, Roma and others perished in this way too).

An impression of the impact of these policies on the Jewish population is given in Table 10.2, which shows a decline of more than five million in the estimated Jewish population of Europe between 1939 and 1948. Most estimates suggest a higher number of Jewish deaths during the Holocaust: approximately six million, with about half dying in gas chambers and the remainder by other forms of violence, exhaustion, malnutrition or disease, and some in grotesque medical experiments.[2] Emigration also took a heavy toll: in Germany and Austria, hundreds of thousands of Jews had been able to emigrate to the United States and elsewhere before escape became possible during the war, and many surviving Jews in other countries left after the end of the war. The impact of the Holocaust was most extreme in Poland and territories to its east where there were large Jewish settlements in the interwar period; by the end of the war, these had virtually disappeared (Hilberg, 1985). But statistics do not tell the full story. Jews were victims not just of mass murder, but of countless acts of individual cruelty and both systematic and random confiscations of fixed and moveable property. The transformation of the ethnic structure (especially in cities) led to an impoverishment of the arts and sciences (in which Jews had traditionally been prominent) and a

---

2 The gap between the two figures may be explained in part by under-enumeration of the Jewish population in the interwar period, and also by natural population increase.

legacy of guilt that has been experienced particularly intensely in the country under whose rule these atrocities were committed.

Unlike other instruments for dealing with minorities, genocide requires particular explanation. As Michael Mann (2005: 26) put it, 'how can apparently ordinary people perpetrate murderous cleansing?' Some of the answer no doubt lies in psychological factors, and the variable disposition of people towards involvement in acts of brutality; part of the reason for the use by the Nazis of gas chambers rather than firing squads had to with the fact that this was less psychologically demanding on the perpetrators. Mann (2005: 2–10, 502–4) offers a set of eight persuasive theses on the circumstances in which genocide is likely to take place, highlighting those where there are rival claims to sovereignty over the same territory, and the weaker side is assisted by an external ally. Structural considerations clearly matter. Melson (1986: 79–81) identified four factors that help to explain genocide, and that have particular resonance in respect of the Holocaust: the status of the victimized group as a persecuted and despised minority; paradoxically, a successful adaptation of the group to modern challenges in the social, economic, cultural and political spheres in the years before the genocide, perceived as menacing by the majority; a real or imaginary link between the victimized group and enemies of the state (including in particular external ones); and a series of major military and political disasters for the state that undermine the security and worldview of the majority.

Expulsion

Like the extermination of ethnic minorities, the expulsion of minorities has deep historical roots, and has also been carried out with varying degrees of formality. It has been a feature of intergroup relations since ancient times: many national myths are based on a perceived history of migration, whether on the basis of attraction to a new homeland or banishment from an old one. As well as expulsion from the state, we need also to consider two variants, policies of colonization, and expulsion *within* the state, or deportation from one area to another (McGarry, 1998).

Examples of population expulsion as a mechanism for 'ethnic cleansing' may be drawn, then, from the same types of context as genocide: the ancient and medieval worlds, the European-driven imperial enterprise, and, once again, the twentieth century, which offers the most vivid examples. In Europe, the outstanding case in respect of scale is the expulsion of Germans from central and eastern Europe after the Second World War. The war itself had been responsible for massive population dislocation, affecting not least the Germans in its closing months; but the postwar settlement saw a major transfer of Germans in outlying lands to occupied Germany. Overall, it has been estimated that about 20 million people were transferred in Europe in the period 1945–55. Of these, 13 million were Germans, whether fleeing before the advancing Soviet army, driven from their localities towards the end of the war, or formally transferred as part of a planned process of expulsion, with the result that 'almost all German enclaves in European countries were practically eliminated' (Schechtman, 1962: 363). During their Potsdam conference in 1945, the British, American and Soviet governments agreed to the transfer of the remaining German populations in Poland and Czechoslovakia (and Hungary, where the numbers were much lower) to occupied Germany – a decision apparently influenced in part by a desire to inflict 'collective punishment' in response to Nazi excesses (De Zayas, 1977: 13–16, 80–102). The outcome in Czechoslovakia was the expulsion of three million Germans from the Sudetenland and elsewhere. In Poland the scale of the expulsion was even greater because of the manner in which the Polish borders were redrawn: Poland lost its eastern lands (with large Ukrainian and Belarusian populations, and smaller German and Lithuanian groups) to the Soviet Union, but acquired large territories with solid German populations to the west and in East Prussia. Expulsions from these various areas amounted to approximately six million people (Hayden, 1996: 728).

Many governments prefer the term 'transfer' to 'expulsion', but it is worth noting two related processes whose formal dynamics are different, and which hide behind a similarly euphemistic label. An example of the first is the 'resettlement' of several hundred thousand Germans living in outlying areas, 'splinters of German nationality, whose existence cannot be maintained' in the words of Hitler, to Germany or to German-occupied areas in the early years of the Second World War (Schechtman, 1962: 23). The implication was that they were being 'repatriated', and the initiative for this lay in Nazi policy. Thus, for example, in 1939–40 Estonian and Latvia lost their small but historically and politically significant German minorities. A second euphemism is 'exchange', designed to reduce the size of minorities in adjacent states, as in the case of Greece, Turkey and Bulgaria, which 'exchanged' minorities in the 1920s (see Ladas, 1932; Schechtman, 1971 [1946]: 16–22).

The expulsion of populations may also be associated with processes of colonization. This may take place in colonial frontier areas (as in American colonization resulting in the successive expulsion of indigenous tribes from the richer and more fertile areas of the United States), but moving populations around may also be a matter of domestic policy, perhaps designed to reinforce an ethnic frontier. Great Britain sought to pacify Ireland in the seventeenth century by 'planting' English and Scottish colonists in the northern province of Ulster. During the 1920s, similarly, the Polish government attempted rather unsuccessfully to polonize its eastern regions through a colonization policy (Kulisher, 1948: 126–31); but, as in Czechoslovakia, this proved easier in the areas vacated by German expellees after 1945. The ethnic composition of the newly-formed state of Israel was transformed by the expulsion of over 700,000 Palestinians in 1948. In yet another form, as part of a process of internal transfer, eight Soviet nationalities were deported eastwards during the Second World War on the grounds that they were potential collaborators with Germany (the Soviet Germans, Balkars, Chechens, Crimean Tartars, Ingushi, Karachi, Kalmyks and Meskhetians), though many were allowed to return after 1956 (Mann, 2005: 328–9).

Political exclusion

In some circumstances, rather than pursuing ethnic monopoly, states are satisfied with ethnic hegemony, achieved by, in effect, excluding minorities from political life, or, at least, greatly reducing their influence. In the traditional state, there was usually little difficulty in achieving this by simply relying on the conservative character of traditional institutions controlled by the ruling group – councils, diets or parliaments, for instance, or the monarchy itself. As the state modernized, though, the advent of democracy posed a challenge: minorities would now have to be sidelined in a more explicit way, or by means of some more indirect technique. We may consider examples from the traditional state, the modern state that discriminates explicitly, and the modern state that uses a surrogate criterion of discrimination.

In the traditional state, as we have seen, medieval principles of representation commonly survived into the nineteenth century. One of the most crucial of these was the notion of estate-based government, with power allocated to particular social groups. Thus, the houses of the nobility and of the bourgeoisie in the nineteenth-century Finnish diet were dominated by Swedish speakers (see Chapter 7). In Bohemia, similarly, the German-speaking aristocracy and urban elites enjoyed power out of all proportion to their numbers through the system of representation in the diet, and this pattern was repeated elsewhere within and outside the Habsburg monarchy. In Russia's Baltic provinces, for example, the provincial diets were controlled by a single social group, the German-speaking nobility. Quite apart from formally representative bodies, though, the reality of traditional monarchy gave enormous power to the hereditary ruler and his (or occasionally her) associated circle – and *ipso facto* to the ethnic group with which they were associated.

Second, there are circumstances where there is explicit exclusion of an ethnic minority from political rights. This was generally the case with European Jews until the nineteenth century, when most countries extended political rights (Baron, 1938). In the United States, many southern states excluded blacks from voting rights until the late nineteenth century; a form of emancipation of the black population took place in 1868–70, with the extension of citizenship and a constitutional prohibition on any racial restriction on voting rights, though this proved to be imperfectly effective in practice (Lawson, 1976: 3–4). The best-known twentieth-century case is that of South Africa. The South Africa Act of 1909, which established the state as a British dominion, confined the right of sitting in parliament to whites, and non-whites were in general deprived of voting rights, though enjoying limited rights in one province; but even there blacks lost the right to vote in 1936, as did coloureds in 1951 (Thompson and Prior, 1982: 77–9). It was only in 1994 that the position changed, with the election of the first multiracial parliament marking the end of white minority rule.

Third, even if direct discrimination against minorities is impossible or impractical, surrogate methods may be devised. The existence of income or wealth qualifications commonly has the effect of giving an advantage to the (wealthier) dominant group. At local elections in Northern Ireland until 1973, for instance, restriction of the electoral franchise to householders and their spouses had a disproportionately negative impact on Catholics, while the existence of multiple 'business votes' disproportionately helped Protestants. With the outlawing of race-based criteria for withholding the franchise in the United States in 1870, many states resorted to an alternative strategy, introducing a literacy requirement. This had a much bigger impact on black than on white voters, and was ended only by the Voting Rights Act of 1965. On independence in 1991, the Baltic states of Estonia and Latvia restricted voting rights to citizens, and confined citizenship to the descendants of those who had been citizens of the pre-1940 states, though allowing for naturalization in certain circumstances (Pettai, 1996: 42–4; Tsilevich, 1996: 52–3). In Estonia, ethnic Estonians made up 62.5% of the population in 1989, but about 90% of citizens; in Latvia, ethnic Latvians made up 52.5% of the population 1989, but 78.5% of citizens.

Policies of ethnic exclusion may also hide behind reforms that appear more generous. Later in this chapter, we consider the question of territorial autonomy, commonly a response to demands for self-rule on the part of ethnic minorities. But such autonomy may also form part of a quite different state strategy: it may have the effect of quarantining the minority, allowing its members to be excluded from participation in mainstream affairs of state. Examples include the 'homeland' or 'Bantustan' policy of South Africa under apartheid (where the political rights of specific African groups were restricted to their supposed ancestral homelands), or, if 'Israel' is defined as the set of territories under the *de facto* control of the Israeli government since 1967, the status of the Palestinian territories (to which the political rights of most Palestinians are confined).

Political integration

The strategy of integrating minority groups within the state is designed to secure the compliance of minorities in a different way: not by repressing them, but by offering them full citizenship rights and the capacity to participate in political life on a basis of individual equality. As indicated already, this represents a sharp break with earlier periods when premodern notions of corporate representation were dominant: instead of a privileged nobility and clergy, a collectivity of individual citizens would rule. This approach has been strongly defended as a civilized path towards ethnic peace (Horowitz, 2000: 563–680). Its much discussed alternative, installation of a regime of group rights, has been criticized as clashing with classic formulations of individual rights, with the 'non-recognition of ethnicity' seen as an appropriate response (van den Berghe, 1981b).

In practice, however, rule by popular majorities tends to have two less visible consequences. First, to the extent that groups survive in a sociological (but no longer legal) sense, dominant ones (such as the ethnic majority) will continue to exercise political hegemony. Second, for the same reason, it is likely that in the absence of any specific measures to the contrary, minorities will be assimilated within the culture of the *de facto* majority. Formal policies of ethnic neutrality may, in other words, disguise a reality of ethnic hegemony and an overwhelming pressure towards ethnic homogeneity. We shall consider these political and cultural dimensions in turn.

The principle underlying the integrationist approach was articulated clearly at the time of the French revolution. As the great historian of the revolution, Georges Lefebvre (2005 [1939]: 169) put it, the most profoundly important document of the time, the *Declaration of the rights of man and of the citizen* (1789), is 'so to speak only an exposition and commentary' on its first article: 'Men are born and remain free and equal in rights. Social distinctions may be founded only upon the general good'. The implications are not immediately obvious;

'men' might later have been interpreted as referring to 'people', but at the time meant pre-cisely that, to the exclusion of women; and 'social distinctions' obviously referred in the first place to those based on class. But the principle that 'all sovereignty resides essentially in the nation' was taken subsequently to refer to a conception of the collectivity as based on free and equal citizens. In addition, the first constitution (1791) set the tone for those that were to follow, by proclaiming France to be 'one and indivisible'; its successor (1793), as well as repeating this, explicitly endorsed representative government based on universal adult male suffrage and the majority principle in decision making.

This strong emphasis on the unmediated relationship between the individual citizen and the state precludes the recognition of groups, whether these are territorially defined or based on cultural characteristics such as language. Indeed, the French revolution implicitly endorsed the French language as the exclusive medium of communication in the state. However, this endorsement was not just implicit: the revolutionary regime sought actively to extend knowledge of French, and in 1794 the National Convention endorsed a report from the Abbé Henri Grégoire which lamented the fact that only a small minority spoke French and that 'with 30 different patois we are still, as regards language, at the Tower of Babel, while, as regards liberty, we are in the vanguard of the nations'. Grégoire suggested that in addition to the efforts of officially appointed teachers,

> The soft voice of persuasion can hasten the time when these feudal dialects will have disappeared. One of the most effective means to electrify citizens is perhaps to prove to them that knowledge and usage of the national lan-guage are important for the preservation of liberty. … No-one has been more conscious of the value of [certain areas of knowledge] than our American brothers, in whose country everyone can write, read and speak the national language (Convention Nationale, 1794).

French policy continued subsequently along these lines. The *Lois Ferry* of 1881–82 (called after education minister Jules Ferry) provided for a system of universal, secular elementary education designed to reinforce the French language and French identity. This system, as we have seen, enjoyed considerable success. But its significance lay not just in its impact in France: this model proved extraordinarily attractive elsewhere, and, in fact, became the dominant approach to minority management. Its American counterpart, identified already in the late eighteenth century by the Abbé Grégoire, was the 'melting pot' approach. As the dramatist Israel Zangwill famously summarized the position in his play *The melting pot*:

> America is God's Crucible, the great Melting-Pot where all the races of Europe are melting and re-forming! Here you stand, good folk, think I, when I see them at Ellis Island, here you stand in your fifty groups, with your fifty languages and histories, and your fifty blood hatreds and rivalries. But you won't be long like that, brothers, for these are the fires of God you've come to – these are the fires of God. A fig for your feuds and vendettas! Germans and Frenchmen, Irishmen and Englishmen, Jews and Russians – into the Cru-cible with you all! God is making the American (Zangwill, 2006 [1909]: 288).

The close link between integration and assimilation is, then, clear. Variants on the expression 'one state, one nation, one language', emphasizing the unity of the nation, will be found in many cultures: 'one faith, one King, one law' in eighteenth-century France, 'one Tsar, one faith, one nation' in mid-nineteenth-century Russia, 'one fatherland, one nation, one language', the catch-cry of Indonesian nationalist students in the 1920s, and 'Ein Volk, ein Reich, ein Führer' in Nazi Germany. Many examples could be cited of the pressures that were brought to bear on subordinate populations to conform to the dominant culture. In some cases, this took the form of encouraging conversion to the dominant religion (to Orthodoxy in the Russian empire, for example, or to Catholicism in Austria-Hungary). But the drive for linguistic assimilation was even more powerful, given effect mainly through the medium of the public school, but also through military service (Krulic, 1999: 85–96). Such policies of assimilation were pursued vigorously in France, as we have seen, and in Britain, Russia and other long-established states. But they were followed with even more vigour in cases where a newly independent state found itself confronted by sizeable national minorities, as in Hungary after 1867 (Jászi, 1961 [1929]). 'Assimilation' can of course have a less negative meaning, implying a minority becoming more similar to the majority, rather than being absorbed by it (Brubaker, 2004: 118–20), and it has been argued that following a relaxation of the earlier phase of traditional assimilationist policies, there has been a reversion to the milder, broader form of assimilation, at least in France, Germany and the USA (Brubaker, 2004: 120–8).

Commonly, the process of steady disappearance of cultural distinctiveness continues even when legal and political incentives for this are removed. Unforced assimilation may be the terminal stage of a process that in earlier stages had an explicitly assimilative form. Thus, in Scotland and Wales the proportion of speakers of Gaelic and Welsh continues to decline despite a new benevolence on the part of the state; and in Ireland the Irish language continues to disappear despite an even more strongly supportive official attitude. In other circumstances, certain subordinate groups may seek their integration in the dominant community in contexts where that community had once sought to exclude them by formal or *de facto* discrimination. Examples here are blacks in the USA, especially during the period of the civil rights movement, and immigrant minorities in most western societies.

INCORPORATING MINORITIES

The last set of strategies is based on the principle of formally recognizing minorities with a view to incorporating them definitively in the political structure – strategies based on the principle of the coexistence of multiple groups. Broadly speaking, these strategies rest on two approaches to political accommodation. The first is the sharing of power at the centre, where group leaders collaborate, especially in the form of the constitutional device labelled 'consociation'. The second rests not on the sharing of power at the centre, but on the division of power between the political centre and the leadership of the various groups into which the state is divided. In some cases, where minorities are territorially dispersed, this takes the form of non-territorial autonomy; but it finds its most characteristic expression in federal government or in some form of territorial autonomy. Before considering these approaches in the following subsections, however, we must examine a residual category: in some circumstances the strategy is non-political, but is still associated with a measure of formal recognition of groups through policies labelled 'multicultural'.

Multiculturalism

There are circumstances where states are prepared to formally recognize diversity and to concede certain group rights in the non-political domain, on the basis of distinctive ethnic or cultural characteristics of groups within the state. Limited provision for group rights is said to have been registered initially by the Congress of Vienna (1814–15), which placed an obligation on Austria, Prussia and Russia to respect the rights of their Polish subjects (Claude, 1955: 6–16). In the domain of religious freedom, it also required the United Netherlands, which had just incorporated Belgium, to respect the rights of its Catholic subjects (Mair, 1928: 30–1). This approach was more fully developed under the League of Nations minorities treaties in the interwar period: the League's treaty with Poland (1919) was used as the model for similar treaties elsewhere, with a focus on the protection of the rights of linguistic minorities in particular (see Mair, 1928; Laponce, 1960; Galántai, 1992). After the Second World War, the emphasis shifted to individual rights, in the context of allegations that the group rights regimes of the interwar period had encouraged certain minorities (notably the Germans) to challenge the authority of their host states. Following the shake-up of territorial structures that took place in Europe after the fall of communism in 1989, however, there was a new interest in group rights, especially on the part of such bodies as the Council of Europe and the Organization for Security and Cooperation in Europe (see Malloy, 2005: 28–30, 53–77; also Gülalp, 2006).

Unlike individual rights, which have been codified in some detail, 'group rights' are much harder to define. While certain group rights are clearly distinguishable from individual rights, not all may be unambiguously assigned to one category rather than the other (for further discussion see Janowsky, 1945: 3–4; Laponce, 1987: 160–4). The initial efforts of the League of Nations through the minorities treaties were designed to secure for members of minorities rights to citizenship, full civil and political rights, and the right to education in their mother tongue, if necessary with support from the state. In some cases, the right to local autonomy was recognized. The Framework Convention for the Protection of National Minorities adopted by the Council of Europe in 1994 outlined these rights in a general way: members of national minorities were to be allowed rights to use their language in private and in public, to interact with the state through its medium, to be facilitated in providing education through that language, and to use surnames and forenames in that language (for the text, see Cumper and Wheatley, 1999: 347–57).

The most obvious expressions of this approach in the contemporary world are to be found in societies with a tradition of cultural coexistence (see Kivisto, 2010: 259–64). This may take the form of a regime of bilingualism which recognizes the mixed linguistic composition of the population. Finland and Canada are examples, with formally equal status for

Swedish with Finnish, and for French with English, in the respective cases. This refers to the position in theory; in practice, if there is a big difference in the size and resource base of the two groups, personal bilingualism is likely to be better developed among members of the minority than among members of the majority. But multicultural policies may also extend to other aspects of ethnic identity. The system of coexistence in such cases as Germany (where the state collects a 'church tax' on behalf of the major religious denominations) can be seen as an example (church taxes in countries with a single state church, such as Denmark, are obviously not an expression of multiculturalism). More telling examples are offered by circumstances where dominant communities begin to acknowledge the separate cultural status of immigrant minorities (as in the United Kingdom and the Netherlands) or of indigenous peoples (as in Australia and Canada).

There are also circumstances where institutional recognition is conferred on groups whose leaders, far from demanding this, are being assimilated to the dominant group. The former Soviet Union offers a number of examples. Many uncodified languages were standardized and given their own writing systems, rules of grammar and vocabulary; by the end of the 1930s, all union republics had their own writers' unions, theatres, opera companies and national academies specializing in national history, literature and language (Slezkine, 1996 [1994]: 226). This policy, known as *korenizatsiya* or 'indigenization', no doubt contributed to the growth of substate ethnic consciousness (see Bromley and Kozlov, 1974; Safran, 1992; Martin, 2001). In Yugoslavia similar policies were adopted, with the cultivation, for example, of a new Macedonian language and the formal recognition of the rights of the nations, nationalities and ethnic communities by the state (Adamson and Jović, 2004: 295–9). China followed the same model, recognizing 55 national minorities alongside the Han Chinese (Hirata, 1979; Zhao, 2000: 25). Such policies were not necessarily disinterested: in the Soviet Union they were designed ultimately to assist the dissemination of knowledge of a common language (Russian), while in Yugoslavia part of the motivation for the cultivation of Macedonian was to differentiate it from the adjacent Bulgarian language and culture.

Consociation

One very distinctive political approach to minority accommodation is the notion of incorporating minorities in central, power-sharing institutions. A highly developed variant of this has been labelled 'consociational democracy', and is associated in particular with the work of Dutch political scientist Arend Lijphart. He defined the term as 'government by elite cartel designed to turn a democracy with a fragmented political culture into a stable democracy' (Lijphart, 1969: 216). Fragmented political cultures are associated precisely with the kinds of divided societies we have been considering in this chapter, though they do not always rest on ethnonational divisions.

Indeed, in the cases that Lijphart used to illustrate his model ethnonational divisions were not particularly prominent – not at all in Austria and the Netherlands, while in Belgium and Switzerland his focus was mainly on divisions whose origins lay in conflicts over religious values. He identifies consociation with a highly developed system of power sharing between groups, and specifies four distinctive institutional features: (1) government by grand coalition, (2) mutual veto to protect vital minority interests, (3) proportionality as the principal standard of political representation, civil service appointment and allocation of public funds, and (4) a high degree of autonomy on the part of the coexisting groups (Lijphart, 1977: 25–44). We discuss the last of these features later, in looking at particular mechanisms for devolving power from the centre. To the extent that consociation is equated with elaborate power sharing, we may also group the first and third characteristics, to give us two defining features that contrast sharply with the more familiar 'Westminster'-style principles of government:

- the allocation of political and administrative positions and resources is proportional rather than competitive (or, in extreme cases, monopolistic): ministerial posts, civil service positions, public sector appointments and material resources at the disposal of the state are distributed proportionally between the groups.
- the basis of decision making is consensual rather than majoritarian (or, in extreme cases, hegemonic): each group has a veto on matters affecting its vital interests.

As defined above, consociational government is an ideal type – a standard that may be used to assess the characteristics of a particular state or political system (McRae, 1974). Yet it is also possible to find useful illustrations in practice: Malaysia, Lebanon and Cyprus have been commonly cited in the past, though this system was disrupted in Lebanon from 1975 to 1990, and the experiment in Cyprus was short-lived (1960–63). If we replace the expression 'consociational democracy' by the broader 'consociational government' (which has the advantage of side-stepping the debate as to just how democratic this elite-driven system of government is), the range of possible cases increases. We may thus find traces of this approach also in such cases as Yugoslavia in its latter years, where, notwithstanding the dominance of the Communist Party, there were important elements of power sharing in political structures.

Consociational government may be illustrated by two contemporary examples. In Belgium, the old cleavage between Catholics, socialists and liberals was displaced by one that had always cut across this: a division between Dutch speakers (about 58% of the population) and French speakers (about 41%). As this division deepened, a programme of constitutional reform designed to respond to it began in 1970. The constitution was amended to provide for equal representation of Dutch- and French-speaking ministers in the government, alongside other principles and practices based on proportionality or even parity between the two communities. The constitution also allows for special consideration of any legislation whose provisions, in the opinion of at least three-quarters of the members of one of the two major linguistic blocs, 'gravely damage relations between the communities' (Lijphart, 1981). Northern Ireland, divided between a 53% Protestant and a 44% Catholic group, is another good example. Under the provisions of the Good Friday agreement of 1998, members of the government are selected in exact proportion to their strength in the Assembly, and there is an 'alarm bell' procedure similar to the Belgian one: decisions in certain policy areas require cross-community endorsement, implying support by a qualified majority (60%), plus support from at least 40% of nationalist and of unionist members; Assembly members are invited to designate themselves as belonging to one group or the other (McGarry and O'Leary, 2004; Taylor, 2009; see also Finlay, 2011, for a critique).

Non-territorial autonomy

Sharing power between groups, where all participate in decision making at the centre, is one approach to political accommodation; dividing power between the centre and the leadership of the groups, so that each group controls decision making for itself in particular sectors, is a second. Sometimes, where ethnic minorities are dispersed rather than being geographically concentrated, they may be given devolved institutions whose jurisdiction is non-territorial, an arrangement originally termed 'national cultural autonomy' (see McRae, 1975). As in the case of territorial devolution, power is devolved from the central state, but this time to authorities whose jurisdiction is over individuals defined not because of where they live but in respect of some cultural or subjectively-defined characteristic. Affiliation to the devolved institutions is thus based either on such measurable features as language or religion, or on self-identification, where members of the community explicitly 'opt in' (Coakley, 1994a; Nimni, 2005). The pre-democratic world offers some examples, as in Jewish autonomy in the old Polish–Lithuanian Commonwealth until 1764, and in the recognition of 'national' groups in the Hungarian province of Transylvania up to 1867. The most commonly cited example is the *millet* system in the Ottoman empire, which allowed non-Islamic religious denominations (including the Greek Orthodox, Armenian Catholic and Jewish communities) to administer their own affairs in the domains of education, religion and family matters, including marriage, divorce and inheritance (Katsikas, 2009).

Modern thinking on the principle of non-territorial autonomy is associated in particular with the leading Austrian social democrat and future President of Austria, Karl Renner (it was supported also by his colleague Otto Bauer, whose theoretical writings have been discussed in Chapters 7 and 9). In an effort to solve the extraordinary challenge of governing multinational Austria under the Habsburg monarchy, Renner proposed a system of dual federalism. On the one hand, the historic crown lands or provinces (*Länder*) would be the basis of a system of territorial federalism. Parallel to this, power would also be devolved in such areas as education, culture, the arts, sciences and museums to the nations that made up the Austrian population. Each would have its own national council (*Nationalrath*) comprising representatives of the nation regardless of where they lived (Springer, 1902).

The first and best-known attempt to apply Renner's ideas in the modern state was in the Austrian province of Moravia, where the Czechs (72% of the population) and the Germans (28%) overlapped significantly in their territorial distribution. In 1905, the 'Moravian compromise' divided voters into separate Czech and German electoral registers, allocated membership of the diet to them in fixed proportions, and provided for separate education departments for Czechs and Germans. Later, in Estonia, the Cultural Autonomy Law of 1925 empowered any national group numbering at least 3,000 to establish for itself a separate legal identity and elect a cultural council. This would be empowered to levy taxes, and to control such areas as education, culture, libraries, theatres, museums, sports and youth affairs. The two principal non-territorial minorities, the Germans and the Jews, took advantage of this to establish their own cultural councils in 1926 (Smith and Hiden, 2012). Belgium is a contemporary example: cultural councils for the French- and Dutch-speaking communities were established as part of the constitutional reform process after 1970 (though the latter was eventually absorbed by the Flanders region). Indigenous peoples offer a final set of examples: the Saami in Norway, the Maori in New Zealand and the indigenous 'First Nations' in Canada have all been given certain rights of non-territorial representation and self-administration, of rather different kinds.

Non-territorial autonomy is a conflict management device that has not been widely used. In many contexts where populations are inextricably intermingled, such as Northern Ireland, the possibility of introducing it has never even been debated. This arises in part from the limited extent to which power can be devolved on non-territorial lines. Mere provision of separate electoral registers for two or more groups, or even concession of limited group control over schooling, does not constitute autonomy, and may have the effect only of hardening divisions. There are practical limits to the amount of power that may be devolved to a community that does not have a territory of its own; some kind of apparatus for securing compliance is necessary, and it is difficult to set up a structure of this kind (such as a police force) on a non-territorial basis. This principle has also acquired a negative image through its association with repressive regimes that have used non-territorial autonomy as a mechanism for avoiding 'contamination' by subordinate groups, while at the same time ensuring that such groups offer no territorial threat. South Africa's efforts during the apartheid era to confer non-territorial autonomy on the Asian and coloured populations are an example. Nevertheless, there have been success stories: the cases of Moravia and Estonia, at least, attracted widespread praise from minority and majority commentators alike.

Territorial autonomy and federation

Non-territorial autonomy is, then, an unusual phenomenon; more commonly, when power is divided between different tiers, this is done along territorial lines. We may explore this by reference to the division of power between centre and regions (Coakley, 2003). In seeking to define the terminology associated with this, we may again revert to the notion of ideal types. Figure 10.1 illustrates five notional points along a continuum from the position where all power resides in the centre (the centralization strategy) to that where none resides in the centre (separation). Close to the first of these points, the centre holds ultimate authority but has decided to devolve power to the regions (regionalization); crucially, the centre can withdraw this. Close to the other end of the continuum, the regions hold ultimate authority but have agreed to devolve power to the centre (confederation); the regions can reverse position on this, or depart individually from the confederation. Finally, in the middle, there is a formal, constitutionally guaranteed division and balance of power between the centre and the regions (federation). We may look at these positions in turn, and then consider an issue that cuts across them: the question of symmetry.

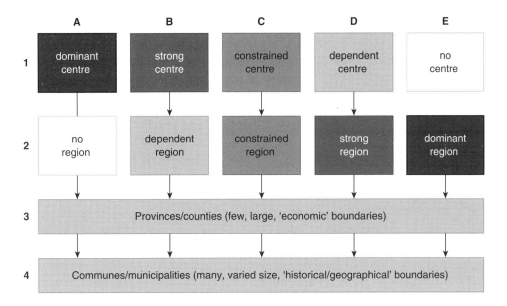

Figure 10.1   Notional approaches to territorial organization

Note: The four rows represent potential tiers of government. The five labelled positions refer to (A) centralized government, (B) regionalization, (C) federation, (D) confederation and (E) separate statehood.

Centralization.   Concentration of power in the centre and refusal to concede any kind of territorial recognition of ethnic diversity may arise for a number of reasons, and may be facilitated by a high level of intermingling of populations. This 'Jacobin' approach has been characteristic of certain European states (with France since the revolution as the prototype), and it was widely followed in the English-, French- and Spanish-dominated colonies and former colonies of the western hemisphere, and also in the African and Asian colonies of European powers. Of course, in reality complete centralization – the complete absence of any kind of local government – is impractical except, perhaps, in microstates. Instead, the typical Jacobin model is based on a two-tiered subcentral structure. There is usually an upper tier comprising a small number of large units (provinces or counties), with rationally defined boundaries that ignore traditional cultural borders, administered by a prefect or governor who is mainly an agent of the central government. The lower tier comprises a very large number of units of very unequal size (communes or municipalities), reflecting traditional historical and geographical realities, and with the rudiments of self-administration. Most of the states of continental Europe followed this model.

Regionalization.   The regionalist strategy is often based on the premise that ethnic protest can be undercut by the concession of at least a symbolic degree of regional autonomy. Arguments relating to economic planning and administrative rationality are also normally present, however, and regionalization is typically embarked on as a measure designed to resolve a number of problems (Keating, 1988: 167–244). Its essential principle is the devolution of authority from the centre to regional authorities; its essential weakness lies in the fact that the centre can limit or withdraw this autonomy, subject only to the political feasibility of this course of action.

Regional government varies both in the extent to which it recognizes substate ethnic boundaries and in the degree of power devolved. Three large west European states, France, Italy and Spain, began to follow their own distinctive paths in this direction in the 1970s (Mény, 1987; Khatami, 1991). In Italy and in Spain a great deal of power was devolved, and early recognition was given to units where there were elements of ethnic distinctness – in Italy, to Sicily and Sardinia already in the 1940s, and in Spain to Catalonia and the Basque Country in 1980 (Diaz Lopez, 1985; Leonardi, 1992; Douence, 1995; Conversi, 2000). In fact, Spain ultimately became in effect a federal-type state, with the powers of the regions (called autonomous communities) being constitutionally copper-fastened (see below). In France, by contrast, fewer powers were devolved (Loughlin, 1985a, 1985b). Examples of two types of what some nationalists saw as a sleight of hand by central governments in their regionalization experiments are afforded by these cases, both calculated to undercut regional ethnic distinctiveness. On the one hand, in Italy the concession of autonomy to the region of Trentino-Alto Adige in 1948 represented the creation of a new region, in which overwhelmingly Italian-speaking territory was added to the German-speaking province of South Tyrol to dilute the German character of the new 'oversized' entity (though these two components later became effectively separate). In Spain, in a rather different approach, Valencia was not included in the new region of Catalonia, while Navarre was excluded from the Basque Country; and in France the *département* of Nantes, historically part of Brittany, was excluded from the new region of Brittany – now an 'undersized' entity.

Federation. While federation bears some similarity to regionalization, there is an essential difference. Powers are not merely devolved by the centre; instead, a division of powers between the two levels (together with a definition of concurrent powers) is formally written into the constitution (Wheare, 1963; Friedrich, 1968; Duchacek, 1970; King, 1982; Forsyth, 1989; Burgess and Gagnon, 1993; de Filliers, 1994). Federation is not necessarily a response to ethnic diversity, and, indeed, many of the best-known examples of federal government are in states where there is little anti-state ethnic moblization. To take them in descending order of size, the examples of the United States, Brazil, Mexico, Germany, Argentina, Venezuela and Australia illustrate this. In other cases, such as Austria, the state is now virtually mono-ethnic, even though the multinational nature of pre-1918 Austria was one of the reasons for institutionalization of this form of government.

In other cases, a federal arrangement was either adopted initially or was retained to deal with problems of ethnic diversity (Gagnon, 1993; Smith, G., 1995; O'Leary, 2002). We may detect three patterns of relationship between ethnic territories and federal territorial units. In the first, the ethnic divisions cut across the boundaries of the federal units; there is little correspondence between ethnic and political boundaries. Malaysia is an example: the principal ethnic groups (Malays, Chinese and Indians) are dispersed over the 12 states. India and

Pakistan might at one time have been additional examples, but both have been moving in the direction of the third category described below.

In the second type, minority ethnic groups are given autonomy but they may be divided among several federal units, and the dominant ethnic group is also so divided. Spain, to the degree that it may legitimately be described as 'federal', is one example: it has 17 regions (as regards language, 12 Castilian, two Catalan and one Galician, with two other areas, Valencia with a 49% Catalan-speaking population and the Basque Country, approximately 25% Basque speaking, but with a higher proportion of Basque identifiers). Canada is another example: its 13 provinces and territories are mainly English-speaking but one, Quebec, is French speaking (another, New Brunswick, has a large French-speaking minority), and the new territory of Nunavut, created in 1999, has an Inuit majority. Similarly, Switzerland, though formally a confederation, is in reality a federation of 26 cantons and half-cantons; of these, 19 are German speaking, six French speaking and one predominantly Italian speaking, though four cantons have bilingual status.

Third, in a few cases the boundaries of the ethnic groups correspond with those of the federal units. The former Soviet Union, with its 15 union republics, offers such an example. The former Yugoslavia is a more ambiguous case: most of its six republics (Slovenia, Croatia, Montenegro, Serbia and Macedonia) corresponded with varying degrees of accuracy to the territories of ethnic nationalities (though the distinction between Montenegrins and Serbs is not clear-cut). The ethnic Muslims were a minority of 40% in their 'own' republic, Bosnia and Hercegovina. The former Czechoslovakia, with a clearly defined federal division between Slovakia and the Czech lands, is a better example; and, apart from the issue of control of the capital territory of Brussels, the partition of Belgium between Flanders and Wallonia is yet another case. These last examples draw attention to the exceptional difficulties that arise in dyadic federations, where there are only two territorial units, often of similar size and power, and therefore more likely to be engaged in a polarized struggle than in the case of federations made up of larger numbers of units (Duchacek, 1988).

Confederation.   The crucial difference between federation and confederation as these terms are used here is not just the greater power of component units in a confederation; it is the fact that they have ultimate power, sufficient individually to exit from the confederation, and sufficient collectively to bring it to an end. In practice, confederation appears to be an intermediate stage between federation and decomposition into independent states. The fact that 'pure' examples are so difficult to find points to the essential instability of this strategy of dealing with ethnic tensions: confederations appear to be short-term half-way houses from federation to independence, or, in the opposite direction, from international organization to federation.

There are three recent examples of the first of these types of confederation: the former Soviet Union, the former Yugoslavia and the former Czechoslovakia. In each case, efforts were made to halt a slide from federation to disintegration by devising a looser form of association. The Commonwealth of Independent States, linking most of the former Soviet republics, was the longest lasting of these, but its impact has been limited.

There are several obvious examples of movement in the opposite direction. The Swiss 'Confederation' may, indeed, once have lived up to its name, but in recent years (and, perhaps, since 1848) it has in effect been a federation. German unity in 1871 was preceded by several confederal experiments, with the German Confederation (1815–66) as the longest-lasting of these. In the western hemisphere, the Confederacy of the United States of America (1781–89) was an important predecessor of the United States as we know that entity today, but even after the latter had come into existence in 1789 the real source of power – whether this lay in Washington, DC, or in state capitols – continued to be a matter of dispute. It was only after the civil war of 1861–65, as significant for the definition of the character of the political system as the Swiss *Sonderbund* war of 1847, that it became clear that ultimate power lay in the centre, and that the political system was federal rather than confederal (Forsyth, 1981). Confederation may also have been a stage in the rapid evolution of the European Economic Community into the European Community and then into the European Union.

Disintegration. This last type more accurately represents the failure to accommodate minorities than a plan to accommodate them. It is hardly possible to go further in yielding to ethnic minority demands than the actual concession of the minority's right to sovereign statehood. The process of European withdrawal from colonial territories overseas was one illustration of this, especially in the middle of the twentieth century. Rather more traumatic was the disintegration of empires made up of adjacent territories and built up over a long time-frame, as in the case of the dissolution of the Habsburg monarchy in 1918, of the Ottoman empire even earlier than this, and of the Soviet Union in 1991. In such cases, the traces of old boundaries of the multinational parent state quickly cease to have real significance.

Territorial symmetry. So far, the approaches discussed have implicitly assumed a symmetrical shape: states are either centralized, or are organized along federal lines, or follow one of the other models discussed earlier. Indeed, there is usually at least formal symmetry in respect of the lower tiers of government, such as counties and municipalities, even though there may be great variation in the population (and therefore substantive importance) of the latter. In reality, however, it would be more accurate to think of states as following *predominant* rather than *pure* patterns. In the case of federal states, certain regions are commonly federally administered: the capital district, for example, or certain outlying territories, often poor and sparsely populated. Thus, Australia comprises six provinces, but also the Australian Capital Territory (containing the national capital, Canberra) and the Northern Territory, which do not have the status of equal membership of the federation. In the USA, similarly, the District of Columbia (containing the national capital, Washington) and such US possessions as Puerto Rico are not numbered among the 50 states. But this asymmetry may occur in other patterns too. The number of variations is enormous, but we may conclude with one example: the United Kingdom. Here, government institutions in Westminster relate to England as they would in any centralized state, to Scotland, Wales and Northern Ireland as they would in any regionalized state in theory and any federal state in practice, and to Isle of Man, Jersey and Guernsey as they would in a confederation.

CONCLUSION

The discussion in this chapter of mechanisms open to states in their relations with minorities has of necessity oversimplified the position. It has identified a set of ideal types, but everyday political life is more complex, and can rarely be accommodated neatly within a set of such ideal types. The difficulty lies not just in categorizing particular policy instruments, such as the British Labour government's devolution policy at the end of the twentieth century. A bigger challenge lies in generalizing about the broad thrust of state strategy. This is because of an important point about the classification system presented in this chapter: its categories are not mutually exclusive. In other words, states can simultaneously pursue a range of policies in respect of the same minority, they can adopt different policies in respect of different minorities, and all of these policy positions may shift fundamentally over time. In Belgium, for example, the most obvious change has been the transition from a centralized state to a regionalized one, followed by a further transition to federation (with three component units, Flanders, Wallonia and Brussels); but this has been accompanied by a form of non-territorial autonomy (between Dutch- and French-speaking communities); and it has been capped by a classic system of consociational government (with power sharing between Dutch- and French-speaking politicians).

The types of policy discussed in this chapter fall into two broad clusters – those based on procuring the disappearance of minorities, and those resting essentially on a strategy of co-opting them into the life of the state. What determines the probability that the state will opt for one of these clusters, or for a particular approach within either cluster? One obvious factor is state tradition – the extent to which elite and mass political culture is conditioned to a particular view of individual and group rights. States vary in the extent to which protection of individual rights is embedded in constitutional and societal norms, and they also vary in their level of tolerance of groups other than the national majority. A second consideration is the cultural distance between the majority and other groups, whether this is based on 'objective' factors, such as language distance, or 'subjective' ones, such as perceptions of different (overlapping or conflicting) historical experiences. Third, the resources available to the minority matter: relative and absolute population size, access to economic resources, capacity for political mobilization, and links to external allies. The greater these are, the stronger the bargaining power of the minority, in general. Certain physical facts will also constrain the state's options. If a minority is territorially dispersed and intermingled with the dominant group, then territorial strategies such as federation or autonomy will have to be ruled out.

To conclude, it should be pointed out that the great difficulty faced by states in seeking to accommodate minorities is that a programme designed to resolve one problem may create another. Non-territorial autonomy may satisfy one group, but it is likely also to reinforce the boundary between it and the rest of society. Territorial devolution may be compatible with the aspirations of those who receive new institutions of government, but it may also create new minorities within the borders of the autonomous territory. Consociation may enhance the standing of the groups in power, but it is likely also to remove smaller groups even further from access to power. Nationalism, in other words, has bequeathed to the modern state a powerful challenge that is exceptionally demanding on its political leaders.

CONCLUSION

11

NATION AND STATE IN PERSPECTIVE

INTRODUCTION

This book has sought to present a comparative historical perspective on nationalism, understood as an attempt to redefine relations between states and nations. One set of approaches to resolving this tension has been discussed in Chapter 10, which looked at strategies available to the state in dealing with what the dominant group typically sees as the problem of national minorities. Overall, though, the book has looked at the tension between state and nation from the opposite perspective – from that of the nation, with the state as an object it has been trying to influence.

If we start with the national community rather than state, two broad types of question arise on the basis of the discussion in this book. The first has to do with the lessons that emerge from the earlier chapters – with the extent to which our understanding of this phenomenon has been advanced. The second concerns the future, focusing on the extent to which nationalism has been associated with a particular historical epoch, or is likely to be with us for the foreseeable future. These issues are addressed in the two sections that follow.

REASSEMBLING THE ARGUMENT

Two broad sets of arguments have been made in the discussion of the phenomenon of nationalism in this book. The first has to do with the ingredients that shape people's sense of national identity, ingredients that are open in varying degrees to manipulation by elites, as discussed in Part One. The second, presented in Part Two, has to do with the character of nationalist mobilization: the socio-economic and political factors with which it is associated, the range of paths that it follows, explanations for its birth, rise and success or failure, and the resources available to the state in combating it.

In the analysis of the emergence of nationalism, it has for long been recognized that there is a link between national identity and certain background factors. These factors vary in their significance and in the ease with which they may be exploited by nation-building elites. They include the following:

- *Racial background.* Phenotypical pointers to ethnic and geographical descent are commonly emphasized by nationalist elites, and used in social boundary formation processes. This is despite the objective reality that modern nations are based on varying degrees of racial mixing (Chapter 2).
- *Language.* There is a natural tendency for those who share speech and writing forms to constitute a community, and for the border between this community and other speech communities to become increasingly clearly defined. This arises because of the extent to which community depends on communication, which has language at its heart; and particular circumstances may cause the borders of a linguistic community to be invested also with other forms of social significance (Chapter 3).
- *Religion.* Especially in the past, when religion played a more central public role, religious affiliation helped to define a community of belief. To the extent that religious affiliation is transferred from generation to generation, it may also act as pointer to a type of community of descent, and thus acquire ethnic significance. But the very content of religious belief, and its social implications, may also help to shape the direction taken by nationalist movements (Chapter 4).
- *Historical consciousness.* While the historical roots of all peoples may be investigated, there is a great deal of variation in the quantity and quality of documentary material available to assist in the production of narrative histories. Where particular peoples were linked to a state structure, the production of an historical myth was facilitated; but even where they were not, this was still possible. Such myths played a central role in shaping patterns of popular consciousness (Chapter 5).
- *Public culture.* In varying degrees, aspects of public culture (such as sports, culinary habits, housing styles, folklore, music and the arts) reflect traditions associated with particular peoples. They, too, may be held up as having particular value in defining the distinctiveness of such peoples (Chapter 6).

In many cases, nationalist mobilization is facilitated by a cultural division of labour: people sharing certain cultural characteristics are clustered into particular positions in the labour market, and this is often translated into a form of social stratification that highlights the distinctive status of the various groups (Chapter 7). In these circumstances, class or economically based conflict can sharpen culturally based conflict, and heighten sense of identity. The cultural infrastructure is to varying degrees open to manipulation by elites. Some features, such as language, are very hard to alter, though it is not impossible to do so. Others, such as public culture, are more easily manipulated: new forms of 'national dress' or other symbols may easily be created, and, depending on other circumstances, may be widely adopted. Indeed, the ethnic structure of whole states may be transformed in the long term by government policy (Chapter 10).

Three general themes run through the analysis of nationalism in this book. The first is that nationalism may be looked at from two perspectives – from that of the elites who promote a particular nationalist movement, and from that of their rivals (who, though they may deny it, advance an alternative nationalist agenda). There are times when nationalism may clash with cross-cutting forces, such as socialism, feminism or other expressions of global organization; but its most intense conflict is with other forms of nationalism. In most cases where nationalism finds violent expression, the opponents of nationalist insurgents are likely themselves to be bearers of the flag of other nationalist interests – whether they define themselves as peace-makers, counter-terrorists, political integrationists, or defenders of the state. Interpretations of particular forms of nationalism will vary, in other words, according to the perspective of the observer.

The second general theme in this book has been the character of the nationalist project. Nationalism tends to appear when groups that had previously been set apart from each other eventually came into contact within the same political structure, as in the case of encounters between Europeans and indigenous peoples, or when groups that had for long coexisted were mobilized into new forms of activity by the process of industrialization. But in such cases there were rarely just two groups; geography and identity tended to cut across each other. On the one hand, a metropolitan centre sought to preserve its own imperial-type interests; but the outlying territory that was the target of a nationalist movement was typically divided between one group linked to the metropolitan centre (the regional centre), and another which saw itself as indigenous to the region (the regional periphery). The nationalist project thus tended to be anything but a straightforward struggle for autonomy or unity. In some cases, such as settler or 'Creole' nationalism, the struggle of the regional centre could proceed only to the extent that the regional periphery (the indigenous population) was marginalized. In others, such as anti-colonial or European peripheral nationalism, the agenda of the regional periphery was often compromised by resistance from the regional centre. In integrationist nationalism, where a metropolitan centre is engaged in a state-building or unification process, the distinction between regional centre and regional periphery is less relevant (for example, in the case of Germany or Italy, where the regions were culturally similar to the centre), though it need not be altogether absent (as in the case of the nation-building processes in Britain and France).

It is important to point out that the three groups discussed in the last paragraph, however culturally and socially distinctive they may have been, were populations, not functionally defined interests. In each of the three, we can make a further distinction between the elite and the masses, and it was the elites which tended to dictate the pattern of political development. Indeed, the absence of effective elites among a potential regional periphery often had the effect of nullifying the nationalist project there, though in such cases members of the regional centre 'disloyal' to their own group sometimes met this need. Another particularly vital aspect of nationalist mobilization is the gender dimension. The elites referred to above were almost entirely male. While this reflected the generally subordinate or near-non-existent role of women in the political process before the twentieth century, it had an additional significance in nationalist movements. Although nationalist movements generally marginalized women, apart from certain exceptional cases (as where women played an active role in guerrilla movements), they typically acknowledged two areas where women had a particular role to play. The first was in ensuring the continued vitality of the nation, by producing children and inducting them into the national culture. Second, in very many cases the nation itself was presented in a feminized image – that of either a mother or of a maiden, for whom men would fight and, if necessary, die (Chapter 2).

The third general theme has to do with the manner in which the nationalist movement grew into maturity, and the circumstances determining whether it succeeded or failed. In analyzing that, this book has sought to adapt the approach of Miroslav Hroch (1985) in accounting for the rise of national movements in smaller Europe countries (Chapters 8 and 9). These began with an initial cultural phase (A, cultural exploration), where historical, archaeological and linguistic research helped to stimulate consciousness of the past of a potential nation, moved through an initial political phase (B, elite organization), where the beginnings of a political nationalist movement were launched, to a final phase (C, mass mobilization), where this movement secured mass support in the context of political modernization. It has been suggested that a fourth phase (D, national consolidation), a post-independence one where the state now tries to reinforce the nation, could be added to Hroch's schema. Furthermore, just as Hroch saw considerable variation in the relationship between these phases even in the small group of cases he examined, it is possible to see the schema as applying potentially to all nationalist movements. In some cases, of course, the movement never gets as far as phase D (as in the case of unsuccessful but highly mobilized movements); in others, it does not reach phase C (nationalist objectives remain an elite concern); in some, it never even gets as far as phase B (the potential of cultural distinctiveness is never developed); and in some (such as Creole nationalism) phase A is missing (though in certain cases it may appear *after* the later phases).

In seeking to explain the path from phase to phase, the most useful account also comes from a specific European context. The theory of Otto Bauer (2000 [1924]), based on his efforts to explain national processes in the Habsburg monarchy in its final decades, highlights the role played by the onset of capitalism in raising collective consciousness, as migrants from rural areas began to settle in linguistically alien cities. Although the outcome was sometimes their absorption by the 'high' culture of the cities, when the volume of migration exceeded a certain level the peripheral language was able to achieve a critical mass of speakers and develop as an alternative standard language. Similar but broader arguments were made later by Karl Deutsch (1966 [1953]), Ernest Gellner (1983) and Benedict Anderson (1983). If this type of approach helps to explain the emergence of a sense of identity where none existed earlier (partly represented by the transition from phase A to B), more explicitly political explanations are needed to account for the transition to phase C. These cannot be separated from the general process of political modernization, which had implications for the mobilization of political nationalist movements – a process analyzed in detail for Europe in a study which highlighted the importance of alliance choices made by the main political actors (Rokkan and Urwin, 1983). Finally, in the transition to phase D domestic considerations continued to be significant, but the international order and centre–periphery power balances were crucial (Chapter 9).

SPECULATING ABOUT THE FUTURE

Given the focus in this book on the past, there is yet another question that needs to be asked: what of the future? Since nationalism has been linked here to specific social and political processes, many of which were associated with distinctive historical phases, it might appear that it has exhausted or nearly exhausted its potential. Two questions therefore arise. First, are there indeed potential nationalist projects that have yet to flower by making a transition along the path from phase A to phase D? Second, are there other changes, perhaps less visible ones, that make it likely that we will see new, quite different forms of nationalism emerge, or will nationalism fade away in a 'globalizing' world?

As indicated earlier, nationalist movements can be seen as following a characteristic path, moving from cultural stirrings through early tentative political activity and mass mobilization to the attainment of independence. In Europe, the first of these phases was associated with the transition to modern, industrialized or capitalist society. Since this transition has already taken place, might it not be the case that we have seen the last of 'new' cultural revival movements – if a movement has not appeared by now, is there any reason to expect it to appear in the future? We need to be cautious in answering this in the negative: there may still be groups within Europe whose cultural distinctiveness remains to be 'discovered', and there are many such potential groups in Asia and Africa, where interest in unstandardized but demographically vibrant languages, though currently limited, might develop in the future. Such groups may also appear as part of a process of international migration, though in these circumstances they are not likely to be linked to a particular territory, with implications for the prospects of the development of nationalist-type demands. Furthermore, we should not ignore the continued vibrancy of 'banal' nationalism; Billig (1995: 128–53) argues that notwithstanding assessments that nationalism is being sidelined in a globalized world, its banal character means that it is simply rendered invisible in circumstances where it is still powerfully present, as in the USA.

Sometimes, however, as we have seen, phases B and C may occur in the absence of any initial phase A. A new nationalist movement may appear almost out of nowhere, as in the case of 'Padanian' nationalism in Northern Italy. But it may also result from profound political-territorial changes that have taken place suddenly. The creation of new states in response to demands from powerful nationalist groups, or as a consequence of imperial disintegration, does not only rid the parent state of a demanding minority; it also creates new minorities, and has the potential to stimulate the mobilization of groups which would otherwise be quiescent. Thus, in the successor states of the former Soviet Union and the former Yugoslavia, new minorities (such as Chechens and Crimean Russians in the former, and Albanians in Macedonia in the latter) suddenly appeared in the 1990s, just as the successor states of the Habsburg monarchy all found themselves with large and politically demanding national minorities in the 1920s. Furthermore, it is likely that some of these newly mobilized minorities may some day achieve independent statehood, notwithstanding a reluctance on the part of the international community to welcome such developments. Quite apart from the potential of separatism in Asia and Africa, the eventual prospects of an independent Flanders, Wallonia, Scotland and Quebec should not be ruled out.

Could it be the case, however, that in a world where communication patterns are much more intense than ever before, as a consequence of such visual media as television and such interactive facilities as the internet and mobile communications technology, boundaries between peoples will be further eroded, and humankind will move closer together, counteracting the more negative consequences of nationalism? Could there, in other words, be a kind of 'phase E' in nationalist movements, one where parochial nationalism is being replaced by cosmopolitan or internationalist values? Ernest Gellner (1994: 25–8), for example, in reformulating E.H. Carr's (1945) stages of nationalism, hinted that a fifth quasi-post-national phase might indeed exist (one other projection of a possible 'phase E', or even 'phase F', saw this essentially as a consolidation of nationalism; Stefanovic, 2005: 484). There are two reasons for suspecting that such a development is unlikely: the fact that confident previous predictions to this effect have proved misplaced, and contemporary evidence of trends in quite a different direction.

First, there were countries and movements which indeed proclaimed that a type of 'phase E' lay around the corner and had even been partly attained. The international communist movement, for instance, shared this ideology: a great universal proletarian brotherhood was being created behind the venerable Marxist slogan 'workers of all countries, unite!', and would lead ultimately to the disappearance of tensions between peoples. In this view, states would wither away, and international solidarity would replace narrow nationalism. Indeed, Soviet ideologists claimed that this had already been achieved over a substantial portion of the globe, in the Soviet Union itself. The Soviet constitution of 1977 attributed this status to Soviet society:

> It is a society of mature socialist social relations, in which, on the basis of the drawing together of all classes and social strata and of the juridical and factual equality of all its nations and nationalities and their fraternal co-operation, a new historical community of people has been formed – the Soviet people (USSR, 1977: preamble).

This was essentially a claim that a new 'Soviet' form of identity had been created to span the cultural identities of the various peoples of the country, and that this was marked by 'a new level of patriotic and internationalist awareness' (Semyonov, 1979: 237).

It was easy for western critics to deride the naïve articulation of belief in the inevitability of a certain form of progress, the apparently uncritical commitment to a narrow ideology, and the unconvincing and stilted (but politically necessary) citation of quasi-scriptular texts of Marx, Engels, Lenin and the current general secretary of the Communist Party. It was also easy – and appropriate – to deplore the fate of internally deported peoples such as the Crimean Tatars and of potential victims of Russian immigration such as Estonia and Latvia (whose absorption in the Soviet Union in 1940, like that of Lithuania, had never been recognized by the international community). It was even easier to gloat over the failure of the Soviet experiment in the creation of a new community and to welcome the break-up of this 'prison of peoples' (a term the Soviet authorities had earlier used in respect of the tsarist empire). But even a leading Russian ethnologist, Valery Tishkov (2008), probably understates the distinctiveness of the Soviet experience when he describes the Soviet people as a 'civic nation', and of the Soviet Union as being 'no different than other large and ethnically heterogeneous states'. In fact, by the standards of many large and ethnically mixed western states, Soviet concessions to non-dominant groups were extremely generous, if somewhat uneven. Western support for processes of 'nation building' as the route to progress were, as Walker Connor (1972) pointed out, in reality prescriptions for 'nation destroying', with non-dominant groups seen much as Engels regarded the 'ethnic trash' in the more developed states of western Europe: fragments of peoples whose fate it was to disappear.

Optimism regarding the disappearance of nationalism in a new world where nationalist values would be transcended was not, then, confined to believers in the communist message; until the 1970s it was the view also of an important western school of 'modernization theory'. But there are reasons for pessimism. In a world where competition over resources is likely to increase (with western military and political might matched by the growing economic strength of China, and oil resources in the Middle East as a major prize), nationalism is a readymade instrument for manipulating populations. It may be that discussion of a 'clash of civilizations' (Huntington, 1993, 1996), with its prediction of global competition between western, Islamic, Sinic and other great cultural-political blocs, becomes a self-fulfilling prophecy; but whether it does or not, the reality of increased population intermingling is likely to bring members of these blocs into closer contact with each other than ever before. The rise of new forms of nationalism is therefore not unlikely, even if they hide behind a superficially attractive form of cosmopolitanism, which, as Yeğenoğlu (2005) argues, may serve the interests of the global north better than it does excluded groups in the global south.

Evidence of some of these forms of nationalism is already visible. It is true that various forms of 'pan-nationalism' (such as pan-Slavism and pan-Arabism), like more recent variants (such as the pan-Thai and pan-Chinese movements; Kratoska and Batson, 1999: 305–9) failed to take root outside the elites who promoted them. But where cultural similarity was insufficient to drive integration, shared political and economic interest may be more successful. The experiment in European unification is a type of cautious state-building exercise, though contending with a set of powerful existing state structures. Furthermore, unlike the process of German unification in the nineteenth century, European unification is faced with much more culturally diverse populations. While the similarity between the two unification processes should not be exaggerated, it would be a serious misinterpretation to dismiss the European unification process as designed solely to counter nationalism. It is itself a nationalist-type experiment, designed to overcome Spanish and Italian particularism, just as German nationalism sought to overcome Bavarian and Saxon particularism. But it is faced with a much bigger challenge – the reality that, as Deutsch et al. (1957) pointed out long ago, and as Walker Connor (1994a) argued more recently, its component parts already have powerfully embedded national identities. Indeed, the scholarly consensus seems to be that nationalism is likely to be with us for the indefinite future (Smith, A., 1991: 143–60; Hechter, 2000: 135–6; Zuelow, Young and Sturm, 2007: 11; Breen and O'Neill, 2010: 4–7).

CONCLUSION

This book has set itself an ambitious goal – not to describe the evolution of nationalism in a particular, closely defined context using detailed historical evidence, as in the case of Miroslav Hroch (1985), nor to examine nationalism from the perspective of a general theory, as in the case of Ernest Gellner (1983), but from the intermediate perspective of pursuing explanations for different varieties of nationalism in different countries. In this, the risk is one of falling between two stools. On the one hand, the diversity of cases is so great that maintaining standards of empirical accuracy is a challenge. On the other hand, the range of theoretical perspectives is so great, and some rest on such high levels of generality, that any effort to synthesize them risks being meaningless. The ambitious goal of this book is therefore likely to be no more than partly met in these pages.

For this reason, both the type of illustrative data presented and the set of theoretical perspectives discussed tend to focus particularly on one continent, Europe. Their relevance for our understanding of nationalism outside this small area is, therefore, limited. Nevertheless, it seems likely that many of the themes outlined in the preceding chapters will have a resonance in other continents, even if the significance of, say, the African or Asian experience requires radical revision of the framework presented here. It is to be hoped that the familiar, underlying uniformities in the nationalist experience are likely to ensure that comparative studies of this kind will indeed evoke reactions of recognition even in the most diverse of circumstances.

This book began by citing the judgement of the great physicist, Albert Einstein, to the effect that nationalism is 'the measles of the human race', an illness now seen as an infectious but minor disease of childhood. Measles, however, can kill; and measles epidemics created havoc among the peoples of the 'new world', their immune systems vulnerable to this deadly virus brought in by European conquerors. The effects of nationalism, as this book has shown, are similar: sometimes relatively harmless, on other occasions devastating. The disease metaphor lets us down, though, in that nationalism, unlike an illness, changes shape depending on the lens through which it is viewed – the same force that is a disruptive scourge to some is a liberating blessing to others. This book has sought to side-step such normative perspectives, and to confine itself to the descriptive and analytical domains in seeking to make another contribution to the study of this vital topic. But ultimately, like other works in the area, it has been able to do little more than scratch the surface of this complex phenomenon.

REFERENCES

Abell, Jackie, Susan Condor, Robert D. Lowe, Stephen Gibson and Clifford Stevenson (2007) 'Who ate all the pride? Patriotic sentiment and English national football support', *Nations and Nationalism* 13 (1): 97–116.

Abelson, Raziel (1967) 'Definition', pp. 314–24 in *The encyclopedia of philosophy* (vol. 2). London: Collier-Macmillan.

Aberbach, David (2003) 'The poetry of nationalism', *Nations and Nationalism* 9 (2): 255–75.

Aberbach, David (2010) 'The British Empire and revolutionary national poetry', *Nations and Nationalism* 16 (2): 220–39.

Acton, Lord [John Dalberg-Acton] (1907 [1862]) 'Nationality', pp. 270–300 in *The history of freedom and other essays*. Freeport, NY: Books for Libraries Press.

Adamson, Kevin and Dejan Jović (2004) 'The Macedonian–Albanian political frontier: the re-articulation of post-Yugoslav political identities', *Nations and Nationalism* 10 (3): 293–311.

Ahmed, Ishtiaq (1996) 'Religious nationalism and Sikhism', pp. 259–85 in David Westerlund (ed.), *Questioning the secular state: the worldwide resurgence of religion in politics*. London: Hurst.

Aitken, Adam J. (1981) 'The good old Scots tongue: does Scots have an identity?', pp. 72–90 in Einar Haugen, J. Derrick McClure and Derick Thomson (eds), *Minority languages today*. Edinburgh: Edinburgh University Press.

Akenson, Donald Harman (1992) *God's peoples: covenant and land in South Africa, Israel, and Ulster*. Ithaca, NY: Cornell University Press.

Al Faruqi, Ismail Ragi and David E. Sopher (eds) (1974) *Historical atlas of the religions of the world*. New York: Macmillan.

Aldridge, Alan (2000) *Religion in the contemporary world: a sociological introduction*. Cambridge: Polity Press.

Alkan, Necati (2008) 'Youth and terrorism: example of PKK', pp. 159–69 in M Demet Ulusoy (ed.), *Political violence, organized crimes, terrorism and youth*. Amsterdam: IOS Press [NATO Science for Peace and Security Series: E, Human and societal dynamics vol. 46].

Allison, Lincoln (2000) 'Sport and nationalism', pp. 344–55 in Jay Coakley and Eric Dunning (eds), *Handbook of sports studies*. London: Sage.

Alter, Peter (1989) *Nationalism*. Trans. Stuart McKinnon-Evans. London: Edward Arnold.

Alter, Peter (1994) *Nationalism* (2nd edn). London: Edward Arnold.

American Sociological Association (2002) *Statement of the American Sociological Association on the importance of collecting data and doing social scientific research on race*. Washington, DC: American Sociological Association.

Andersen, Chris (2008) 'From nation to population: the racialisation of "Métis" in the Canadian census', *Nations and Nationalism* 14 (2): 347–68.

Anderson, Benedict (1983) *Imagined communities: reflections on the origin and spread of nationalism.* London: Verso.

Anderson, Benedict (1997) 'Recensement et politique en Asie du Sud-Est: représentations nationales et pouvoirs d'Etat', *Genèse* 26: 55–76.

Anderson, Benedict (1998) *The spectre of comparisons: nationalism, Southeast Asia, and the world.* London: Verso.

Anderson, Benedict (2006) *Imagined communities: reflections on the origin and spread of nationalism* (Rev. edn). London: Verso.

Anderson, Christopher (1828) *Historical sketches of the ancient native Irish and their descendants.* Edinburgh: Oliver and Boyd.

Andrews, George Reid (1985) 'Spanish American independence: a structural analysis', *Latin American Perspectives* 12 (1): 105–32.

Andrieux, Jean-Yves (2006) 'L'architecture et les figures du temps à l'âge des nations en Europe (1860–1919)', pp. 13–28 in Jean-Yves Andrieux, Fabienne Chevallier and Anja Kervanto Nevanlinna (eds), *Idée nationale et architecture en Europe, 1860–1919: Finlande, Hongrie, Roumanie, Catalogne.* Rennes: Presses Universitaires de Rennes.

Angress, Werner T. (1980) 'The German Jews, 1933–1939', pp. 69–82 in Henry Friedlander and Sybil Milton (eds), *The Holocaust: ideology, bureaucracy, and genocide.* Millwood, NY: Kraus International.

Anthias, Floya and Nira Yuval-Davis (1989) 'Introduction', pp. 1–15 in Nira Yuval-Davis and Floya Anthias (eds), *Woman – nation – state.* London: Macmillan.

Apostolov, Mario (1996) 'The Pomaks: a religious minority in the Balkans', *Nationalities Papers* 24 (4): 727–42.

Apostolov, Mario (2001) *Religious minorities, nation states and security: five cases from the Balkans and the eastern Mediterranean.* Aldershot: Ashgate.

Appadurai, Arjun (1988) 'How to make a national cuisine: cookbooks in contemporary India', *Comparative Studies in Society and History* 30 (1): 3–24.

Appleby, Ian (2010) 'Uninvited guests in the communal apartment: nation-formation processes among unrecognized Soviet nationalities', *Nationalities Papers* 38 (6): 847–64.

Armstrong, John A. (1982) *Nations before nationalism.* Chapel Hill, NC: University of North Carolina Press.

Armstrong, John A. (1995) 'Towards a theory of nationalism: consensus and dissensus', pp. 34–43 in Sukumar Periwal (ed.), *Notions of nationalism.* Budapest: Central European University Press.

Arnaud, Nicole (1980) 'Colonialisme intérieur et centralisme d'Etat: le cas de l'Occitanie', pp. 29–49 in Jacques Dofny and Akinsola Akiwowo (eds), *National and ethnic movements.* London: Sage.

Artz, Frederick B. (1962) *From the renaissance to romanticism: trends in style in art, literature, and music, 1300–1830.* Chicago, IL: University of Chicago Press.

Atsuko, Ichijo and Gordana Uzelac (eds) (2005) *When is the nation? Towards an understanding of theories of nationalism.* London: Routledge.

Attwater, Donald (1961) *The Christian churches of the East.* Vol. 2: *Churches not in communion with Rome.* London: Geoffrey Chapman.

Auer, Stefan (2004) *Liberal nationalism in Central Europe.* London: Routledge Curzon.

Babuna, Aydin (2000) 'The Albanians of Kosovo and Macedonia: ethnic identity superseding religion', *Nationalities Papers* 28 (1): 67–92.

Babuna, Aydin (2004) 'The Bosnian Muslims and Albanians: Islam and nationalism', *Nationalities Papers* 32 (2): 287–321.

Baggioni, Daniel (1997) *Langues et nations en Europe.* Paris: Payot.

Bairner, Alan (2001) *Sport, nationalism and globalization.* Albany, NY: State University of New York Press.

Balakrishnan, Gopal (ed.) (1996) *Mapping the nation.* London: Verso.

Baldacchino, Godfrey (2009) 'Pangs of nascent nationalism from the nationless state? Euro coins and undocumented migrants in Malta since 2004', *Nations and Nationalism* 15 (1): 148–65.

Banton, Michael (1983) *Racial and ethnic competition*. Cambridge: Cambridge University Press.

Banton, Michael (1997) *Ethnic and racial consciousness* (2nd edn). London: Longman.

Banton, Michael (1998) *Racial theories* (2nd edn). Cambridge: Cambridge University Press.

Banton, Michael and Robert Miles (1994) 'Racism', pp. 276–9 in Ellis Cashmore (ed.), *Dictionary of race and ethnic relations* (3rd edn). London: Routledge.

Barany, George (1968) *Stephen Széchenyi and the awakening of Hungarian nationalism, 1791–1841*. Princeton, NJ: Princeton University Press.

Barber, Richard (1991) *Pilgrimages*. Woodbridge, Suffolk: Boydell Press.

Barker, Ernest (1927) *National character and the factors in its formation*. London: Methuen.

Barker, Philip W. (2009) *Religious nationalism in modern Europe: if God be for us*. London: Routledge.

Baron, Sola W. (1938) 'The Jewish question in the nineteenth century', *Journal of Modern History* 10 (1): 51–65.

Barrett, David B. (ed.) (1982) *World Christian encyclopedia*. Oxford: Oxford University Press.

Barton, Jonathan R. (1997) *A political geography of Latin America*. London: Routledge.

Batt, Judy (2002a) 'Reinventing Banat', pp. 178–202 in Judy Batt and Kataryna Wolczuk (eds), *Region, state and identity in central and eastern Europe*. London: Frank Cass.

Batt, Judy (2002b) 'Transcarpathia: peripheral region at the "centre of Europe"', pp. 154–77 in Judy Batt and Kataryna Wolczuk (eds), *Region, state and identity in central and eastern Europe*. London: Frank Cass.

Battarbee, Keith (2007) 'The forest writes back: the *Ausbau* of Finnish from peasant vernacular to modernity', pp. 71–96 in Andrew Wawn, with Graham Johnson and John Walter (eds), *Constructing nations, reconstructing myth: essays in honour of T.A. Shippey*. Turnhout: Brepols.

Bauer, Otto (1979 [1912]) 'Der Separatismus in Wien', pp. 1003–15 in Otto Bauer, *Werkausgabe* (vol. 7). Ed. Hugo Pepper. Vienna: Europaverlag.

Bauer, Otto (1980 [1911]) 'Schlusswort zur Minoritätenfrage', pp. 476–90 in Otto Bauer, *Werkausgabe* (vol. 8). Ed. Hugo Pepper. Vienna: Europaverlag.

Bauer, Otto (1980 [1912]) 'Die Bedingungen der nationalen Assimilation', pp. 596–624 in Otto Bauer, *Werkausgabe* (vol. 8). Ed. Hugo Pepper. Vienna: Europaverlag.

Bauer, Otto (2000 [1924]) *The question of nationalities and social democracy*. Trans. Joseph O'Donnell. Minneapolis, MN: University of Minnesota Press.

Baycroft, Timothy (1998) *Nationalism in Europe, 1789–1945*. Cambridge: Cambridge University Press.

Beck, Jan Mansvelt (1991) 'Basque and Catalan nationalism in comparative perspective', pp. 153–70 in Hans van Amersfoort and Hans Knippenberg (eds), *States and nations: the rebirth of the 'nationalities question' in Europe*. Amsterdam: Koninklijk Nederlands Aardrijkskundig Genootschap, Instituut voor Sociale Geografie, Universiteit van Amsterdam.

Beiner, Ronald (ed.) (1999) *Theorizing nationalism*. Albany, NY: State University of New York Press.

Bekus, Nelly (2010) 'Nationalism and socialism: "phase D" in the Belarusian nation-building', *Nationalities Papers* 38 (6): 829–46.

Belgium (1949–54) *Recensement général de la population, de l'industrie et du commerce au 31 décembre 1947* (vol. 1). Brussels: Institut National de Statistique [and supplementary reports by province in *Moniteur Belge*, 1954].

Benedict, Ruth (1942) *Race and racism*. London: Routledge and Kegan Paul.

Benner, Erica (2001) 'Is there a core nationalist doctrine?', *Nations and Nationalism* 7 (2): 155–74.

Berger, Peter (1967) *The sacred canopy: elements of a sociological theory of religion*. Garden City, NY: Doubleday.

Berger, Stefan (2007) 'Introduction: towards a global history of national historiographies', pp. 1–29 in Stefan Berger (ed.), *Writing the nation: a global perspective*. Basingstoke: Palgrave Macmillan.

253

Berger, Stefan (2009) 'The comparative history of national historiographies in Europe: some methodological reflections and preliminary results', pp. 29–45 in Susana Carvalho and François Gemenne (eds), *Nations and their histories: constructions and representations*. Basingstoke: Palgrave Macmillan.

Berkoff, Giovanna Brogi (2002) 'Le mythe du baptême: Pologne, Ukraine et le respect de la diversité', pp. 65–81 in Chantal Delsol, Michel Masłowski and Joanna Nowicki (eds), *Mythes et symboles politiques en Europe centrale*. Paris: Presses Universitaires de France.

Bestor, Theodore C. (2005 [2000]) 'How sushi went global', pp. 13–20 in James L. Watson and Melissa L. Caldwell (eds), *The cultural politics of food and eating: a reader*. Oxford: Blackwell.

Bialasiewicz, Luiza (2002) 'Upper Silesia: rebirth of a regional identity in Poland', pp. 111–32 in Judy Batt and Kataryna Wolczuk (eds), *Region, state and identity in central and eastern Europe*. London: Frank Cass.

Bieber, Florian (2000) 'Muslim identity in the Balkans before the establishment of nation states', *Nationalities Papers* 28 (1): 13–28.

Billiet, Jaak and Hans de Witte (2008) 'Everyday racism as predictor of political racism in Flemish Belgium', *Journal of Social Issues* 64 (2): 253–67.

Billig, Michael (1995) *Banal nationalism*. London: Sage.

Blakkisrud, Helge and Shahnoza Nozimova (2010) 'History writing and nation building in post-independence Tajikistan', *Nationalities Papers* 38 (2): 173–89.

Blanke, Richard (1999) '"Polish-speaking Germans?" Language and national identity among the Masurians', *Nationalities Papers* 27 (3): 429–53.

Blinkhorn, Martin (2000) *Fascism and the right in Europe, 1919–1945*. Harlow: Longman.

Blom, Ida (2000) 'Gender and nation in international comparison', pp. 3–26 in Ida Blom, Karen Hagemann and Katherine Hall (eds), *Gendered nations: nationalisms and gender order in the long nineteenth century*. Oxford: Berg.

Bohlman, Philip V. (2004) *The music of European nationalism: cultural identity and modern history*. Santa Barbara, CA: ABC–Clio.

Boia, Lucian (2001) *History and myth in Romanian consciousness*. Trans. James Christian Brown. Budapest: Central European University Press.

Bonacich, Edna (1973) 'A theory of middleman minorities', *American Sociological Review* 38 (5): 583–94.

Boomgaard, M.C. (2008) 'The rise of militant Bretonité', *National Identities* 10 (3): 281–93.

Bose, Sugata (1998) 'Nation as mother: representations and contestations of "India" in Bengali literature and culture', pp. 50–75 in Sugata Bose and Ayesha Jalal (eds), *Nationalism, democracy and development: state and politics in India*. New Delhi: Oxford University Press.

Bosworth, R.J.B. (2007) *Nationalism*. London: Pearson Longman.

Bouchard, Gérard (2000) *Genèse des nations et cultures du nouveau monde*. Montréal: Boréal.

Boyd, Carolyn P. (1997) *Historia patria: politics, history and national identity in Spain, 1875–1975*. Princeton, NJ: Princeton University Press.

Bracewell, Wendy (2000) 'Rape in Kosovo: masculinity and Serbian nationalism', *Nations and Nationalism* 6 (4): 563–90.

Brady, Ciarán (ed.) (1994) *Interpreting Irish history: the debate on historical revisionism, 1938–1994*. Dublin: Irish Academic Press.

Brass, Paul R. (1985) 'Ethnic groups and the state', pp. 1–56 in Paul R. Brass (ed.), *Ethnic groups and the state*. London and Sydney: Croom Helm.

Brass, Paul R. (1991) *Ethnicity and nationalism: theory and comparison*. New Delhi: Sage.

Breen, Keith and Shane O'Neill (2010) 'Introduction: a postnationalist era?', pp. 1–18 in Keith Breen and Shane O'Neill (eds), *After the nation? Critical reflections on nationalism and postnationalism*. Basingstoke: Palgrave Macmillan.

Breuilly, John (1982) *Nationalism and the state*. Manchester: Manchester University Press.

Breuilly, John (1993) *Nationalism and the state* (2nd edn). Manchester: Manchester University Press.

Breuilly, John (2009) 'Nationalism and the making of national pasts', pp. 7–28 in Susana Carvalho and François Gemenne (eds), *Nations and their histories: constructions and representations*. Basingstoke: Palgrave Macmillan.

Brillat-Savarin, Jean Anthelme (2007 [1825]) *The physiology of taste, or, transcendental gastronomy*. Trans. Fayette Robinson. Adelaide: eBooks@Adelaide, University of Adelaide Library. Available at: http://ebooks. adelaide.edu.au/b/brillat/savarin/b85p/.

Brincker, Benedikte (2008) 'The role of classical music in the construction of nationalism: an analysis of Danish consensus nationalism and the reception of Carl Nielsen', *Nations and Nationalism* 14 (4): 684–99.

Bromley, Y.V. (1974) 'The term "ethnos" and its definition', in I.R. Grigulevich and S.Y. Kozlov (eds), *Races and peoples: contemporary ethnic and racial problems*. Moscow: Progress Publishers.

Bromley, Y.V. (ed.) (1988) *Narody mira: istoriko-etnograficheskii spravochnik* [*Peoples of the world: a historical-ethnographic handbook*]. Moscow: Sovetskaya Entsiklopediya.

Bromley, Y.V. and V.I. Kozlov (1974) 'National process in the USSR', pp. 116–38 in I.R. Grigorevich and S.Y. Kozlov (eds), *Races and peoples: contemporary ethnic and racial problems*. Moscow: Progress Publishers.

Brown, David (2000) *Contemporary nationalism: civic, ethnocultural, and multicultural politics*. London: Routledge.

Brown, Delmer M. (1955) *Nationalism in Japan: an introductory historical analysis*. New York: Russell & Russell.

Brown, Matthew (2006) 'Not forging nations but foraging for them: uncertain collective identities in Gran Colombia', *Nations and Nationalism* 12 (2): 223–40.

Brubaker, Rogers (1996) *Nationalism reframed: nationhood and the national question in the new Europe*. Cambridge: Cambridge University Press.

Brubaker, Rogers (2004) *Ethnicity without groups*. Cambridge, MA: Harvard University Press.

Brubaker, Rogers (2011) 'Nationalizing states revisited: projects and processes of nationalization in post-Soviet states', *Ethnic and Racial Studies* 34 (11): 1785–1814.

Brubaker, Rogers (2012) 'Religion and nationalism: four approaches', *Nations and Nationalism* 18 (1): 2–20.

Brubaker, Rogers, Margit Feischmidt, Jon Fox and Liana Grancea (2006) *Nationalist politics and everyday life in a Transylvanian town*. Princeton, NJ: Princeton University Press.

Bruce, Steve (1996) *Religion in the modern world: from cathedrals to cults*. Oxford: Oxford University Press.

Bruce, Steve (2002) *God is dead: secularisation in the West*. Oxford: Blackwell.

Bruce, Steve (2003) *Politics and religion*. Cambridge: Polity Press.

Bruk, S.I. and V.S. Apenchenko (1964) *Atlas narodov mira* [*Atlas of the peoples of the world*]. Moscow: Institut Etnografii im. NN Miklukho-Maklaya Akademii Nauk SSSR.

Brunn, Gerhard (1992a) 'The Catalans within the Spanish monarchy from the middle of the nineteenth to the beginning of the twentieth century', pp. 133–59 in Andreas Kappeler, with Fikret Adanir and Alan O'Day (eds), *Comparative studies on governments and non-dominant ethnic groups in Europe, 1850–1940*. Vol. VI: *The formation of national elites*. Aldershot: Dartmouth, for European Science Foundation.

Brunn, Gerhard (1992b) 'Historical consciousness and historical myths', pp. 327–38 in Andreas Kappeler, with Fikret Adanir and Alan O'Day (eds), *Comparative studies on governments and non-dominant ethnic groups in Europe, 1850–1940*. Vol. VI: *The formation of national elites*. Aldershot: Dartmouth, for European Science Foundation.

Brunnbauer, Ulf (2004) 'Fertility, families and ethnic conflict: Macedonians and Albanians in the Republic of Macedonia, 1944–2002', *Nationalities Papers* 32 (3): 565–98.

Buchanan, Allen (1991) *Secession: the morality of political divorce from Fort Sumter to Lithuania and Quebec*. Boulder, CO: Westview Press.

Buckley, Anthony (1989) '"We're trying to find our identity": uses of history among Ulster Protestants', pp. 183–97 in Elisabeth Tonkin, Maryon McDonald and Malcolm Chapman (eds), *History and ethnicity*. London: Routledge.

Buhr, Renee L., Victor Shadurski and Steven Hoffman (2011) 'Belarus: an emerging civic nation?', *Nationalities Papers* 39 (3): 425–40.

Burgess, Michael and Alain-G. Gagnon (eds) (1993) *Comparative federalism and federation: competing traditions and future directions*. London: Harvester Wheatsheaf.

Burke, T. Patrick (1996) *The major religions: an introduction with texts*. Oxford: Blackwell.

Burleigh, Michael and Wolfgang Wippermann (1991) *The racial state: Germany 1933–1946*. Cambridge: Cambridge University Press.

Buse, Ionel (2002) 'Mythes roumains des origines', pp. 81–94 in Chantal Delsol, Michel Masłowski and Joanna Nowicki (eds), *Mythes et symboles politiques en Europe centrale*. Paris: Presses Universitaires de France.

Butterfield, H. (1931) *The Whig interpretation of history*. London: G. Bell.

Cabanel, Patrick (1997) *La question nationale au XIXe siècle*. Paris: Editions La Découverture.

Cable, Vincent (1969) 'The "football war" and the Central American Common Market', *International Affairs* 45 (4): 658–71.

Caine, Barbara and Glenda Sluga (2000) *Gendering European history 1780–1920*. London: Leicester University Press.

Calhoun, Craig (1997) *Nationalism*. Buckingham: Open University Press.

Cannadine, David (1983) 'The context, performance and meaning of ritual: the British monarchy and the "invention of tradition", *c.* 1820–1977', pp. 101–64 in Eric Hobsbawm and Terence Ranger (eds), *The invention of tradition*. Cambridge: Cambridge University Press.

Canovan, Margaret (1996) *Nationhood and political theory*. Aldershot: Edward Elgar.

Cardinal, Linda, Claude Couture and Claude Denis (1999) 'La révolution tranquille à l'épreuve de la "nouvelle" historiographie et de l'approche post-coloniale: une démarche exploratoire', *Globe: revue internationale d'études québecoises* 2 (1): 75–95.

Carneiro, Robert L. (1970) 'A theory of the origin of the state', *Science* 169 (3947): 733–8.

Carr, E.H. (1945) *Nationalism and after*. London: Macmillan.

Carr, E.H. (1986) *What is history?* (2nd edn). London: Macmillan.

Carsten, F.L. (1982) *The rise of fascism* (2nd edn). Berkeley, CA: University of California Press.

Casanova, José (1994) *Public religions in the modern world*. Chicago, IL: University of Chicago Press.

Chalk, Frank and Kurt Jonassohn (1990) *The history and sociology of genocide*. New Haven, CT: Yale University Press.

Chamberlain, Houston Stewart (1911 [1899]) *The foundations of the nineteenth century* (2 vols). Trans. John Lees. London: John Lane/The Bodley Head.

Chanes, Jerome A. (2004) 'Review essay: what's "new" – and what's not – about the new antisemitism?', *Jewish Political Studies Review* 16 (1–2). Available at: www.jcpa.org/JCPA/.

Chapman, Malcolm (1995) '"Freezing the frame": dress and ethnicity in Brittany and Gaelic Scotland', pp. 7–28 in Joanne B. Eicher (ed.), *Dress and ethnicity: change across space and time*. Oxford: Berg.

Chatterjee, Partha (1986) *Nationalist thought and the colonial world: a derivative discourse*. London: Zed Books.

Chazan, Naomi (1991) 'Approaches to the study of irredentism', pp. 1–8 in Naomi Chazan (ed.), *Irredentism and international politics*. Boulder, CO: Lynne Rienner.

Cheboksarov, N.N. (1973) 'Races of man', pp. 376–9 in *Great Soviet encyclopedia* (vol. 21). New York: Macmillan.

Chilosi, David (2007) 'Old wine in new bottles: civic nation-building and ethnic nationalism in schooling in Piedmont, c. 1700–1861', *Nations and Nationalism* 13 (3): 417–36.

Chollet, Antoine (2011) 'Switzerland as a "fractured nation"', *Nations and Nationalism* 17 (4): 738–55.

Christie, Clive J. (1996) *A modern history of Southeast Asia: decolonisation, nationalism and separatism*. London: IB Tauris.

CIS Stat (1996) *Results of the 1989 USSR population census*. Minneapolis, MN: East View Publications [electronic resource].

Clanché, François (2002) *Langues régionales, langues étrangères: de l'héritage à la pratique* [INSEE Première 830]. Paris: INSEE.

Clark, Colin (2010) 'The nation-state: civic and ethnic dimensions', pp. 44–54 in Karl Cordell and Stefan Wolff (eds), *Routledge handbook of ethnic conflict*. London: Routledge.

Clark, Martin (1998) *The Italian Risorgimento*. Harlow: Longman.

Claude, I.L., Jr. (1955) *National minorities: an international problem*. Cambridge, MA: Harvard University Press.

Clayton, Tony and Ian McBride (1998) 'The trials of the chosen peoples: recent interpretations of protestantism and national identity in Britain and Ireland', pp. 3–29 in Tony Clayton and Ian McBride (eds), *Protestantism and national identity: Britain and Ireland, c. 1650 – c. 1850*. Cambridge: Cambridge University Press.

Coakley, John (1980) 'Independence movements and national minorities: some parallels in the European experience', *European Journal of Political Research* 8 (2): 215–47.

Coakley, John (1982) 'El estado, el sistema educativo y los problemas de identidad nacional: el caso de Irlanda, 1831–1971', *Universidad y Sociedad* 4: 29–54.

Coakley, John (1983) 'National territories and cultural frontiers: conflicts of principle in the formation of states in Europe', pp. 34–49 in Malcolm Anderson (ed.), *Frontier regions in western Europe*. London: Frank Cass.

Coakley, John (1990) 'National minorities and the government of divided societies: a comparative analysis of some European evidence', *European Journal of Political Research* 18 (4): 437–56.

Coakley, John (1992a) 'The resolution of ethnic conflict: towards a typology', *International Political Science Review* 13 (4): 343–58

Coakley, John (ed.) (1992b) *The social origins of nationalist movements*. London: Sage.

Coakley, John (1994a) 'Approaches to the resolution of ethnic conflict: the strategy of non-territorial autonomy', *International Political Sience Review* 15 (3): 309–26.

Coakley, John (1994b) 'The northern conflict in southern Irish school textbooks', pp. 119–41 in Adrian Guelke (ed.), *New perspectives on the Northern Ireland conflict*. Aldershot: Avebury.

Coakley, John (1998) 'Religion, ethnic identity and the Protestant minority in the Republic', pp. 86–106 in William Crotty and David Schmitt (eds), *Ireland and the politics of change*. London: Addison Wesley Longman.

Coakley, John (2002) 'Religion and nationalism in the first world', pp. 206–25 in Daniele Conversi (ed.), *Ethnonationalism in the contemporary world: Walker Connor and the study of nationalism*. London: Routledge.

Coakley, John (2003) 'Conclusion: towards a solution?', pp. 293–316 in John Coakley (ed.), *The territorial management of ethnic conflict* (2nd edn). London: Frank Cass.

Coakley, John (2004) 'Mobilising the past: nationalist images of history', *Nationalism and Ethnic Politics* 10 (4): 531–60.

Coakley, John (2008) 'Langage, identité et État moderne', pp. 181–99 in Guy Lachapelle (ed.), *Diversité culturelle, identités et mondialisation*. Sainte-Foy: Presses de l'Université Laval.

Coakley, John (2009) 'A political profile of Protestant minorities in Europe', *National Identities* 11 (1): 9–30.

Coakley, John (2010) 'Ethnic conflict resolution: routes towards settlement', in John Coakley (ed.), *Pathways from ethnic conflict: institutional redesign in divided societies*. London: Routledge.

Coates, Ken S. (2004) *A global history of indigenous peoples: struggle and survival*. Basingstoke: Palgrave Macmillan.

Cobban, Alfred (1969) *The nation-state and national self-determination*. London: Collins.

Cockburn, Cynthia (1998) *The space between us: negotiating gender and national identities in conflict*. London: Zed Books.

Cohen, Frank S. (1997) 'Proportional versus majoritarian ethnic conflict management in democracies', *Comparative Political Studies* 30 (5): 607–30.

Cohen, Mitchell (1987) *Zion and the state: nation, class and the shaping of modern Israel*. Oxford: Blackwell.

Cohen, Robin (1999) 'The making of ethnicity: a modest defence of primordialism', pp. 3–11 in Edward Mortimer and Robert Fine (eds), *People, nation and state: the meaning of ethnicity and nationalism*. London: IB Tauris.

Cole, Laurence (ed.) (2007) *Different paths to the nation: regional and national identities in Central Europe and Italy, 1830–70*. Basingstoke: Palgrave Macmillan.

Colley, Linda (1992) *Britons: forging the nation, 1707–1837*. New Haven, CT: Yale University Press.

Collingwood, R.G. (1946) *The idea of history*. Oxford: Clarendon Press.

Connor, Walker (1972) 'Nation building or nation destroying?', *World Politics* 24 (3): 319–55.

Connor, Walker (1978) 'A nation is a nation, is a state, is an ethnic group, is a ...', *Ethnic and Racial Studies* 1 (4): 377–400.

Connor, Walker (1979) 'An overview of the ethnic composition and problems of non-Arab Asia', pp. 11–27 in Tai S. Kang (ed.), *Nationalism and the crises of ethnic minorities in Asia*. Westport, CT: Greenwood Press.

Connor, Walker (1984a) 'Eco-nationalism or ethno-nationalism?', *Ethnic and Racial Studies* 7 (3): 342–59.

Connor, Walker (1984b) *The national question in Marxist-Leninist theory and strategy*. Princeton, NJ: Princeton University Press.

Connor, Walker (1992) 'The nation and its myth', *International Journal of Comparative Sociology* 33 (1–2): 48–57.

Connor, Walker (1994a) 'Elites and ethnonationalism: the case of western Europe', pp. 349–61 (vol. 2) in Justo G. Beramendi, Ramón Máiz and Xosé M. Núñez (eds), *Nationalism in Europe past and present: actas do Congreso Internacional os Nacionalismos en Europa pasado e presente, Santiago de Compostela, 27–29 de Setembro de 1993* (2 vols). Santiago de Compostela: Universidade de Santiago de Compostela.

Connor, Walker (1994b) *Ethnonationalism: the quest for understanding*. Princeton, NJ: Princeton University Press.

Convention Nationale (1794) *Instruction publique. Rapport sur la nécessité et les moyens d'anéantir les patois et d'universaliser l'usage de la langue française*. Par [l'Abbé Henri] Grégoire. 16 prairial an II. Available at: fr.wikisource.org/wiki/Rapport_Grégoire.

Conversi, Daniele (1994) 'Violence as an ethnic border: the consequences of a lack of distinctive elements in Croatian, Kurdish and Basque nationalism', pp. 167–98 (vol. 1) in Justo G. Beramendi, Ramón Máiz and Xosé M. Núñez (eds), *Nationalism in Europe past and present: actas do Congreso Internacional os Nacionalismos en Europa pasado e presente, Santiago de Compostela, 27–29 de Setembro de 1993* (2 vols). Santiago de Compostela: Universidade de Santiago de Compostela.

Conversi, Daniele (2000) 'Autonomous communities and ethnic settlement in Spain', in Yash Ghai (ed.), *Autonomy and ethnicity: negotiating competing claims in multi-ethnic states*. Cambridge: Cambridge University Press.

Conversi, Daniele (2007) 'Mapping the field: theories of nationalism and the ethnosymbolic approach', pp. 15–30 in Athena S. Leoussi and Steven Grosby (eds), *Nationalism and ethnosymbolism: history, culture and ethnicity in the formation of nations*. Edinburgh: Edinburgh University Press.

Cordell, Karl and Stefan Wolff (eds) (2011) *Routledge handbook of ethnic conflict*. London: Routledge.

Cornell, Stephen and Douglas Hartmann (1998) *Ethnicity and race: making identities in a changing world*. Thousand Oaks, CA: Pine Forge Press.

Coulmas, Florian (1989) *The writing systems of the world*. Oxford: Basil Blackwell.

Couture, Jocelyne, Kai Nielsen and Michel Seymour (eds) (1996) *Rethinking nationalism*. Calgary: University of Calgary Press.

Crampton, R.J. (1997) *A concise history of Bulgaria*. Cambridge: Cambridge University Press.

Cronin, Mike (1999) *Sport and nationalism in Ireland: Gaelic games, soccer and Irish identity since 1884*. Dublin: Four Courts Press.

Crystal, David (2002) *The English language* (2nd edn). London: Penguin.

Csikszentmihalyi, Mark (2003) 'Confucianism', pp. 213–32 in Jacob Neusner (ed.), *The politics of world religions*. Washington, DC: Georgetown University Press.

Cumper, Peter and Steven Wheatley (1999) *Minority rights in the 'new' Europe*. The Hague: Martinus Nijhoff.

Curtis, Edmond and R.B. McDowell (eds) (1943) *Irish historical documents 1172–1922*. London: Methuen.

Curtis, L. Perry, Jr. (1997) *Apes and angels: the Irishman in Victorian caricature* (Rev edn). Washington, DC: Smithsonian Institution Press.

Cusack, Igor (2003) 'Pots, pens and "eating out the body": cuisine and the gendering of African nations', *Nations and Nationalism* 9 (2): 277–96.

Cusack, Igor (2005) 'Tiny transmitters of nationalist and colonial ideology: the postage stamps of Portugal and its Empire', *Nations and Nationalism* 11 (4): 591–612.

Cusack, Tricia (2000) 'Janus and gender: women and the nation's backward look', *Nations and Nationalism* 6 (4): 541–61.

Cyprus (1962) *Census of population and agriculture, 1960* (Vol. 1). Nicosia: Government Printing Office.

Dahbour, Omar and Micheline R. Ishay (eds) (1995) *The nationalism reader*. Atlantic Highlands, NJ: Humanities Press.

Daniels, Peter T. and William Bright (eds) (1996) *The world's writing systems*. Oxford: Oxford University Press.

Darwin, John (2010) 'Empire and ethnicity', *Nations and Nationalism* 16 (3): 383–401.

Dave, Bhavna (2004) 'Entitlement through numbers: nationality and language categories in the first post-Soviet census of Kazakhstan', *Nations and Nationalism* 10 (4): 439–59.

Dawidowicz, L.S. (1975) *The war against the Jews 1933–1945*. London: Weidenfeld and Nicolson.

Day, Graham and Andrew Thompson (2004) *Theorising nationalism*. Basingstoke: Palgrave Macmillan.

Day, Mark (2008) *The philosophy of history*. London: Continuum.

de Filliers, Bertus (ed.) (1994) *Evaluating federal systems*. Cape Town: Juta and Co.

de Jong, Jutta (1982) *Der nationale Kern des makedonischen Problems: Ansätze und Grundlagen einer makedonischen Nationalbewegung (1890–1903): ein Beitrag zur komparativen Nationalismusforschung*. Frankfurt-am-Main: Peter Lang.

de Mel, Neloufer (2001) *Women and the nation's narrative: gender and nationalism in twentieth century Sri Lanka*. Lanham, MD: Rowman and Littlefield.

De Zayas, Alfred M. (1977) *Nemesis at Potsdam: the Anglo-Americans and the expulsion of the Germans: background, execution, consequences*. London: Routledge and Kegan Paul.

Deane, Phyllis (1953) 'Regional variations in United Kingdom incomes from employment, 1948', *Journal of the Royal Statistical Society, Series A* 116 (2): 123–39.

DeFrancis, John (1989) *Visible speech: the diverse oneness of writing systems*. Honolulu, HI: University of Hawaii Press.

Delanty, Gerard and Krishan Kumar (eds) (2006) *The Sage handbook of nations and nationalism*. London: Sage.

Delanty, Gerard and Patrick O'Mahony (2002) *Nationalism and social theory: modernity and the recalcitrance of the nation*. London: Sage.

Deol, Harnki (2000) *Religion and nationalism in India: the case of the Punjab*. London: Routledge.

DeSoucey, Michaela (2010) 'Gastronationalism: food traditions and authenticity politics in the European Union', *American Sociological Review* 75 (3): 432–55.

Deutsch, Karl W. (1966 [1953]) *Nationalism and social communication*. Cambridge, MA: MIT Press.

Deutsch, Karl, et al. (1957) *Political community in the North Atlantic area*. Princeton, NJ: Princeton University Press.

Díaz-Andreu, Margarita (2001) 'Nationalism and archaeology', *Nations and Nationalism* 7 (4): 429–40.

Díaz-Andreu, Margarita and Timothy Champion (1996) 'Nationalism and archaeology in Europe: an introduction', pp. 1–23 in Margarita Díaz-Andreu and Timothy Champion (eds), *Nationalism and archaeology in Europe*. London: UCL Press.

Diaz Lopez, Cezar (1985) 'Centre–periphery structures in Spain: from historical conflict to territorial-consociational accommodation', pp. 236–72 in Yves Mény and Vincent Wright (eds), *Centre–periphery relations in Western Europe*. London: Allen & Unwin.

Dietler, Michael (1994) '"Our ancestors the Gauls": archaeology, ethnic nationalism, and the manipulation of Celtic identity in modern Europe', *American Anthropologist*, ns, 96 (3): 584–605.

Dillon, Michele (2002) 'Catholicism, politics, and culture in the Republic of Ireland', pp. 47–67 in Ted Gerard Jelen and Clyde Wilcox (eds), *Religion and politics in comparative perspective: the one, the few, and the many*. Cambridge: Cambridge University Press.

Domínguez, Jorge I. (1980) *Insurrection or loyalty: the breakdown of the Spanish American empire*. Cambridge, MA: Harvard University Press.

Doob, Leonard (1964) *Patriotism and nationalism: their psychological foundations*. New Haven, CT: Yale University Press.

Dostál, Petr (1991) 'Accommodating post-communist national aspirations: secession or (con)federation?', pp. 100–29 in Hans van Amersfoort and Hans Knippenberg (eds), *States and nations: the rebirth of the 'nationalities question' in Europe*. Amsterdam: Koninklijk Nederlands Aardrijkskundig Genootschap, Instituut voor Sociale Geografie, Universiteit van Amsterdam.

Douence, Jean-Claude (1995) 'The evolution of the 1982 regional reforms: an overview', pp. 10–24 in John Loughlin and Sonia Mazey (eds), *The end of the French unitary state? Ten years of regionalism in France (1982–1992)*. London: Frank Cass.

Dubow, Saul (1992) 'Afrikaner nationalism, apartheid and the conceptualization of "race"', *Journal of African History* 33 (2): 209–37.

Dubow, Saul (1995) *Scientific racism in modern South Africa*. Cambridge: Cambridge University Press.

Duchacek, Ivo D. (1970) *Comparative federalism: the territorial dimension of politics*. New York: Holt, Rinehart and Winston.

Duchacek, Ivo D. (1988) 'Dyadic federations and confederations', *Publius: The Journal of Federalism* 18 (2), pp. 5–31.

Düding, Dieter (1987) 'The nineteenth-century German nationalist movement as a movement of societies', pp. 19–49 in Hagen Schulze (ed.), *National-building in Central Europe*. Leamington Spa: Berg.

Dukas, Helen and Banesh Hoffman (1979) *Albert Einstein – the human side: new glimpses from his archives*. Princeton, NJ: Princeton University Press.

Dunn, John (1999 [1979]) 'Nationalism', pp. 27–50 in Ronald Beiner (ed.), *Theorizing nationalism*. Albany, NY: State University of New York Press.

Dunning, Eric (1999) *Sport matters: sociological studies of sport, violence and civilisation*. London: Routledge.

Durkheim, Emile (1915) *The elementary forms of religious life*. Trans. Joseph Ward Swain. London: George Allen and Unwin.

Dwyer, Arienne M. (1998) 'The texture of tongues: languages and power in China', *Nationalism and Ethnic Politics* 4 (1–2): 68–85.

Ebbutt, M.I. (1920) *Hero-myths and legends of the British race*. London: George G. Harrap.

Echeverria, Begoña (2001) 'Privileging masculinity in the social construction of Basque identity', *Nations and Nationalism* 7 (3): 339–63.

Edmondson, Linda (2003) 'Putting Mother Russia in a European context', pp. 53–64 in Tricia Cusack and Síghle Bhreathnach-Lynch (eds), *Art, nation and gender: ethnic landscapes, myths and mother-figures*. Aldershot: Ashgate.

Edwards, John (1994) *Multilingualism*. London: Routledge.

Edwards, John (2009) *Language and identity*. Cambridge: Cambridge University Press.

Eicher, Joanne B. and Tonye E. Erekosima (1995) 'Why do they call it Kalabari? Cultural authentication and the demarcation of ethnic identity', pp. 139–64 in Joanne B. Eicher (ed.), *Dress and ethnicity: change across space and time*. Oxford: Berg.

Eicher, Joanne B. and Barbara Sumberg (1995) 'World fashion, ethnic, and national dress', pp. 295–306 in Joanne B. Eicher (ed.), *Dress and ethnicity: change across space and time*. Oxford: Berg.

Eile, Stanisław (2000) *Literature and nationalism in partitioned Poland, 1795–1918*. Basingstoke: Macmillan.

Ekeh, Peter P. (1990) 'Social anthropology and two contrasting uses of tribalism in Africa', *Comparative Studies in Society and History* 32 (4): 660–700.

Elekes, Desiderius (1940) 'Probleme der Nationalitäten-Terminologie und der Nationalitäten-Statistik', *Journal de la Société Hongroise de Statistique* 4: 302–18.

Eley, Geoff and Ronald Grigor Suny (eds) (1996) *Becoming national: a reader*. Oxford: Oxford University Press.

Elgenius, Gabriella (2007) 'The appeal of nationhood: national celebrations and commemorations', pp. 77–92 in Eric Zuelow, Mitchell Young and Andreas Sturm (eds), *Nationalism in a global era: the persistence of nations*. London: Routledge.

Elias, Norbert (2008a [1986]) 'An essay on sport and violence', pp. 150–73 in Norbert Elias and Eric Dunning, *Quest for excitement: sport and leisure in the civilising process*. Dublin: UCD Press [Collected works, vol. 7].

Elias, Norbert (2008b [1971]) 'The genesis of sport as a sociological problem, part 1', pp. 107–33 in Norbert Elias and Eric Dunning, *Quest for excitement: sport and leisure in the civilising process*. Dublin: UCD Press [Collected works, vol. 7].

Elias, Norbert (2012 [1939]) *On the process of civilisation*. Trans. Edmund Jephcott. Dublin: UCD Press [Collected works, vol. 3].

Eller, Jack David and Reed M. Coughlan (1993) 'The poverty of primordialism: the demystification of ethnic attachments', *Ethnic and Racial Studies* 16 (2): 183–202.

Engels, Friedrich (1977 [1849]) 'The Magyar struggle', pp. 227–38 in Karl Marx and Frederick Engels, *Collected works* (vol. 8). London: Lawrence and Wishart.

Engels, Friedrich (1979 [1852]) 'Poles, Tschechs and Germans', pp. 43–6 in Karl Marx and Frederick Engels, *Collected works* (vol. 11). London: Lawrence and Wishart.

English, Richard (2006) *Irish freedom: the history of nationalism in Ireland*. London: Macmillan.

Enloe, Cynthia H. (1975) "Ethnic factors in the evolution of the South African military", *Issue: A Journal of Opinion* 5 (4): 21–8.

Enloe, Cynthia H. (1978) "The issue saliency of the military-ethnic connection: some thoughts on Malaysia", *Comparative Politics* 10 (2): 267–85.

Enloe, Cynthia H. (1980) 'Religion and ethnicity', pp. 347–71 in Peter F. Sugar (ed.), *Ethnic diversity and conflict in Eastern Europe*. Santa Barbara, CA: ABC-Clio.

Enloe, Cynthia H. (1993) *The morning after: sexual politics at the end of the Cold War*. Berkeley, CA: University of California Press.

Enloe, Cynthia H. (2004 [1998]) 'All the men are in the militias, all the women are victims: the politics of masculinity and femininity in nationalist wars', pp. 99–118 in *The curious feminist: searching for women in a new wave of empire*. Berkeley, CA: University of California Press.

Erk, Jan (2005) 'Sub-state nationalism and the left-right divide: critical junctures in the formation of nationalist labour movements in Belgium', *Nations and Nationalism* 11 (4): 551–70.

Erk, Jan (2010) 'Is nationalism left or right? Critical junctures in Québécois nationalism', *Nations and Nationalism* 16 (3): 423–41.

Esposito, John L. (1998) *Islam and politics* (4th edn). Syracuse, NY: Syracuse University Press.

Ethnologue (2002) *Ethnologue: languages of the world*. Available at: www.ethnologue.com [2002-11-05 and later dates].

Eyck, F. Gunther (1995) *The voices of nations: European national anthems and their authors*. Westport, CT: Greenwood Press.

Facos, Michelle and Sharon L. Hirsh (2003) 'Introduction', pp. 16–38 in Michelle Facos and Sharon L. Hirsh, *Art, culture, and national identity in fin-de-siècle Europe*. Cambridge: Cambridge University Press.

Fair Employment Commission for Northern Ireland (1998) *Profile of the monitored workforce in Northern Ireland: summary of the 1998 monitoring results*. Belfast: Fair Employment Commission for Northern Ireland.

Falola, Toyin (2001) *Nationalism and African intellectuals*. Rochester, NY: University of Rochester Press.

Fedoseyev, P.N. et al. (1977) *Leninism and the national question*. Moscow: Progress Publishers.

Feitsma, Antonia (1981) 'Why and how do the Frisian language and identity continue?', pp. 163–75 in Einar Haugen, J. Derrick McClure and Derick Thomson (eds), *Minority languages today*. Edinburgh: Edinburgh University Press.

Ferguson, C.A. (1972 [1959]) 'Diglossia', pp. 232–51 in Pier Paolo Giglioli (ed.), *Language and social context: selected readings*. Harmondsworth: Penguin.

Ferguson, Priscilla Parkhurst (1998) 'A cultural field in the making: gastronomy in 19th-century France', *American Journal of Sociology* 104 (3): 597–641.

Fichte, Johann Gottlieb (1922 [1808]) *Addresses to the German nation*. Trans. R.F. Jones and G.H. Turnbull. Chicago and London: Open Court Publishing Co.

Fiji (1977) *Report on the census of the population 1976* (vol. 1). Suva: Parliament of Fiji.

Finlay, Andrew (2011) *Governing ethnic conflict: consociation, identity and the price of peace*. London: Routledge.

Fišera, V.C. and G. Minnerup (1978) 'Marx, Engels and the national question', pp. 5–19 in Eric Cahm and Vladimir Claude Fišera (eds), *Socialism and nationalism* (vol. 1). Nottingham: Spokesman.

Fishman, Joshua A. (ed.) (1970) *Readings in the sociology of language*. The Hague: Mouton.

Fishman, Joshua A. (ed.) (1971–72) *Advances in the sociology of language* (2 vols). The Hague: Mouton.

Fishman, Joshua A. (1972) *Language and nationalism: two integrative essays*. Rowley, MA: Newbury House.

Fishman, Joshua A. (ed.) (1978) *Advances in the study of societal multilingualism*. The Hague: Mouton.

Fishman, Joshua A. (1980) 'Bilingualism and biculturalism as individual and societal phenomena', *Journal of Multilingual and Multicultural Development* 1: 3–17.

Fishman, Joshua A. (2002) 'The primordialist–constructivist debate today: the language–ethnicity link in academic and in everyday-life perspective', pp. 83–91 in Daniele Conversi (ed.), *Ethnonationalism in the contemporary world: Walker Connor and the study of nationalism*. London: Routledge.

Fleming, Michael (2006) 'Nation and state in the immediate aftermath of war: the experience of the Belarussian minority in Poland 1944–1950', pp. 7–29 in Sakrat Yanovich (ed.), *Annus Albaruthenicus 2006*. Krynki: Villa Sokrates.

Forrest, Joshua B. (2004) *Subnationalism in Africa: ethnicity, alliances, and politics*. Boulder, CO: Lynne Rienner.

Forsyth, Murray (1981) *Unions of states: the theory and practice of confederation*. London: Leicester University Press.

Forsyth, Murray (ed.) (1989) *Federalism and nationalism*. London: Leicester University Press.

FRA: European Union Agency for Human Rights (2010) *Racism, ethnic discrimination and exclusion of migrants and minorities in sport: a comparative overview of the situation in the European Union*. Vienna: European Union Agency for Human Rights.

Francis, E.K. (1976) *Interethnic relations: an essay in sociological theory*. New York: Elsevier.

Frangoudaki, Anna (1992) 'Diglossia and the present language situation in Greece: a sociological approach to the interpretation of diglossia and some hypotheses on today's linguistic reality', *Language in Society* 21 (3): 365–81.

Fredrickson, George M. (1987) *The black image in the white mind: the debate on Afro-American character and destiny, 1817–1914* (new edn). Middletown, CT: Wesleyan University Press.

Freeze, Gregory L. (1986) 'The *soslovie* (estate) paradigm and Russian social history', *American Historical Review* 91 (1): 11–36.

Freud, Sigmund (1963 [1930]) *Civilisation and its discontents* (Rev. edn). Trans. Joan Riviere. London: Hogarth Press.

Fridell, Wilbur M. (1983) 'Modern Japanese nationalism: State Shinto, the religion that was "not a religion"', pp. 155–69 in Peter H. Merkl and Ninian Smart (eds), *Religion and politics in the modern world*. New York: New York University Press.

Friedrich, Carl J. (1966) 'Nation-building?', in Karl W. Deutsch and William J. Foltz (eds), *Nation-building*. New York: Atherton Press.

Friedrich, Carl J. (1968) *Trends of federalism in theory and practice*. London: Pall Mall Press.

Froese, Paul (2005) 'Secular Czechs and devout Slovaks: explaining religious differences', *Review of Religious Research* 46 (3): 269–83.

Gagnon, Alain-G. (1993) 'The political uses of federalism', pp. 15–44 in Michael Burgess and Alain-G. Gagnon (eds), *Comparative federalism and federation: competing traditions and future directions*. London: Harvester Wheatsheaf.

Galántai, Jószef (1992) *Trianon and the protection of minorities*. Boulder, CO: Social Science Monographs.

Galtung, Johan (1971) 'A structural theory of imperialism', *Journal of Peace Research* 8 (2): 81–117.

Ganguly, Rajat (ed.) (2009) *Ethnic conflict* (4 vols). London: Sage.

Garry, Jane and Carl Rubino (eds) (2001) *Facts about the world's languages: an encyclopedia of the world's major languages, past and present*. New York: H.W. Wilson.

Garvin, Tom (1981) *The evolution of Irish nationalist politics*. Dublin: Gill and Macmillan.

Geertz, Clifford (1963) 'The integrative revolution: primordial sentiments and civil politics in the new state', pp. 105–57 in Clifford Geertz (ed.), *Old societies and new states: the quest for modernity in Asia and Africa*. New York: The Free Press.

Geiss, Imanuel (1997) *The question of German unification 1806–1996*. Trans. Fred Bridgham. London: Routledge.

Gellner, Ernest (1983) *Nations and nationalism*. Oxford: Basil Blackwell.

Gellner, Ernest (1994) *Encounters with nationalism*. Oxford: Basil Blackwell.

Gellner, Ernest (1996a) 'The coming of nationalism and its interpretation: the myths of nation and class', pp. 98–145 in Gopal Balakrishnan (ed.), *Mapping the nation*. London: Verso.

Gellner, Ernest (1996b) 'Do nations have navels?', *Nations and Nationalism* 2 (3): 366–70.

Gellner, Ernest (2006) *Nations and nationalism* (2nd edn). Oxford: Basil Blackwell.

Germán Zubero, Luis (2006) 'Especialización sectorial y trayectorias económicas de las regions en Espana durante el siglo XX', pp. 859–84 in Augustín González Enciso and Juan Manuel Matés Barco (eds), *Historia economic de Espana*. Barcelona: Ariel.

Gerner, Kristian (1999) 'Regions in Central Europe under communism: a palimpsest', pp. 30–52 in Sven Tägil (ed.), *Regions in Central Europe: the legacy of history*. London: Hurst.

Giglioli, Pier Paolo (ed.) (1972) *Language and social context: selected readings*. Harmondsworth: Penguin.

Gilbert, Paul (1998) *The philosophy of nationalism*. Boulder, CO: Westview Press.

Gillespie, Joan (1960) *Algeria: rebellion and revolution*. London: Ernest Benn.

Gilligan, Chris (2010) 'Race and ethnicity', pp. 79–88 in Karl Cordell and Stefan Wolff (eds), *Routledge handbook of ethnic conflict*. London: Routledge.

Gillis, John R. (1994) 'Memory and identity: the history of a relationship', pp. 3–24 in John R. Gillis (ed.), *Commemorations: the politics of national identity*. Princeton, NJ: Princeton University Press.

Giordano, Benito and Elisa Roller (2001) 'A comparison of Catalan and "Padanian" nationalism: more similarities than differences?', *Journal of Southern Europe and the Balkans* 3 (2): 111–30.

Girardet, Raoul (1996) *Nationalismes et nation*. Brussels: Editions Complex.

Glatz, Ferenc (1983) 'Backwardness, nationalism, historiography', *East European Quarterly* 17 (1): 31–40.

Gobineau, Compte de (1970 [1853]) 'The three basic races', pp. 134–45 in Michael D. Biddiss (ed.), *Gobineau: selected political writings*. London: Jonathan Cape.

Golan, Daphna (1994) *Inventing Shaka: using history in the contruction of Zulu nationalism*. Boulder, CO: Lynne Rienner.

Goody, Jack (1982) *Cooking, cuisine and class: a study in comparative sociology*. Cambridge: Cambridge University Press.

Graham, Richard (1994) *Independence in Latin America: a comparative perspective* (2nd edn). New York: McGraw-Hill.

Grand'maison, Jacques (1970) *Nationalisme et religion*. Vol. I: *Nationalisme et révolution culturelle*. Montréal: Beauchemin.

Green, William Scott (2003) 'Introduction: religion and politics: a volatile mix', pp. 1–10 in Jacob Neusner (ed.), *The politics of world religions*. Washington, DC: Georgetown University Press.

Greenfeld, Liah (1992) *Nationalism: five roads to modernity*. Cambridge, MA: Harvard University Press.

Greenwood, Davydd J. (1985) 'Castilians, Basques, and Andalusians: an historical comparison of nationalism, "true" ethnicity, and "false" ethnicity', pp. 202–27 in Paul R. Brass (ed.), *Ethnic groups and the state*. London and Sydney: Croom Helm.

Griebel, Helen Bradley (1995) 'The West African origin of the African American headwrap', pp. 207–26 in Joanne B. Eicher (ed.), *Dress and ethnicity: change across space and time*. Oxford: Berg.

Grimes, Barbara F. (2000) *Ethnologue* (14th edn) (2 vols). Dallas, TX: Summer Institute of Linguistics.

Grosby, Steven (2005) *Nationalism: a very short introduction*. Oxford: Oxford University Press.

Guelke, Adrian (2005) *Rethinking the rise and fall of apartheid: South Africa and world politics*. Basingstoke: Palgrave Macmillan.

Guelke, Adrian (2012) *Politics in deeply divided societies*. Cambridge: Polity Press.

Guglielmo, Jennifer and Salvatore Salerno (eds) (2003) *Are Italians white? How race is made in America*. London: Routledge.

Guiberneau, Montserrat (1996) *Nationalisms: the nation state and nationalism in the twentieth century*. Cambridge: Polity Press.

Guibernau, Montserrat (1999) *Nations without states: political communities in a global age*. Cambridge: Polity Press.

Guibernau, Montserrat and John Rex (eds) (1997) *The ethnicity reader: nationalism, multiculturalism and migration*. Oxford: Polity Press.

Guindon, Hubert (1988) 'The crown, the Catholic church, and the French-Canadian people: the historical roots of Quebec nationalism', pp. 94–111 in Roberta Hamilton and John L. McMullan (eds), *Quebec society: tradition, modernity and nationhood*. Toronto: University of Toronto Press.

Gülalp, Haldun (2006) *Citizenship and ethnic conflict: challenging the nation-state*. London: Routledge.

Gullberg, Tom (1999) 'The primacy of the nation and regional identity: Carinthia, Burgenland and state-formation after the dissolution of the dynastic system', pp. 147–77 in Sven Tägil (ed.), *Regions in Central Europe: the legacy of history*. London: Hurst.

Gutiérrez Chong, Natividad (2006) 'Patriotic thoughts or intuition: roles of women in Mexican nationalisms', *Nations and Nationalism* 12 (2): 339–58.

Gutiérrez Chong, Natividad (2007) 'Ethnic origins and indigenous peoples: an approach from Latin America', pp. 312–24 in Athena S. Leoussi and Steven Grosby (eds), *Nationalism and ethnosymbolism: history, culture and ethnicity in the formation of nations*. Edinburgh: Edinburgh University Press.

Hale, Henry E. (2008) *Foundations of ethnic politics: separatism of states and nations in Eurasia and the world*. Cambridge: Cambridge University Press.

Hall, John A. (1993a) 'Nationalisms: classified and explained', *Daedalus* 122 (3): 1–28.

Hall, John A. (1993b) 'State', pp. 878–83 in Joel Krieger (ed.), *The Oxford companion to politics of the world*. Oxford: Oxford University Press.

Hall, John A. (ed.) (1998) *The state of the nation: Ernest Gellner and the theory of nationalism*. Cambridge: Cambridge University Press.

Hamilton, Carrie (2007) *Women and ETA: the gender politics of radical Basque nationalism*. Manchester: Manchester University Press.

Han, Enze (2011) 'From domestic to international: the politics of ethnic identity in Xinjiang and Inner Mongolia', *Nationalities Papers* 39 (6): 941–62.

Handman, Max Silvius (1921) 'The sentiment of nationalism', *Political Science Quarterly* 36 (1): 104–21.

Hankin, E. Hanbury (1937) *Nationalism and the communal mind*. London: Watts.

Hann, Chris (1993) 'Religion and nationality in central Europe: the case of the Uniates', *Ethnic Groups* 10 (1–3): 201–13.

Hann, Chris (1995) 'Intellectuals, ethnic groups and nations: two late-twentieth-century cases', pp. 106–28 in Sukumar Periwal (ed.), *Notions of nationalism*. Budapest: Central European University Press.

Harbottle, Lynne (1997) 'Fast food/spoiled identity: Iranian migrants in the British catering trade', pp. 87–110 in Pat Caplan (ed.), *Food, health and identity*. London: Routledge.

Harris, Marvin (1997 [1985]) 'The abominable pig', pp. 67–79 in Carole Counihan and Penny Van Esterik (eds), *Food and culture: a reader*. London: Routledge.

Hasenclever, Andreas and Volker Rittberger (2000) 'Does religion make a difference? Theoretical approaches to the impact of faith on political conflict', *Millennium* 29 (3): 641–74.

Hastings, Adrian (1997) *The construction of nationhood: ethnicity, religion, and nationalism*. Cambridge: Cambridge University Press.

Hastings, Adrian (1999) 'Special peoples', *Nations and Nationalism* 5 (3): 381–96.

Haugen, Einar (1966a) 'Dialect, language, nation', *American Anthropologist* 68 (4): 922–35.

Haugen, Einar (1966b) *Language conflict and language planning: the case of modern Norwegian*. Cambridge, MA: Harvard University Press.

Haugen, Einar (1968) 'The Scandinavian languages as cultural artifacts', pp. 267–84 in Joshua A. Fishman, Charles A. Ferguson and Jyotirindra Das Gupta (eds), *Language problems of developing nations*. New York: John Wiley.

Haugen, Einar (1983) 'The implementation of corpus planning: theory and practice', pp. 269–89 in Juan Cobarrubia and Joshua Fishman (eds), *Progress in language planning: international perspectives*. Berlin: Mouton.

Hautala, Juoko (1969) *Finnish folklore research 1828–1918*. Helsinki: Societas Scientiarum Fennica.

Hay, Colin and Michael Lister (2006) 'Introduction: theories of the state', pp. 1–20 in Colin Hay, Michael Lister and David Marsh (eds), *The state: theories and issues*. Basingstoke: Palgrave Macmillan.

Hayden, Robert M. (1996) 'Schindler's fate: genocide, ethnic cleansing, and population transfers', *Slavic Review* 55 (4): 727–48.

Hayes, Carlton J.H. (1926) *Essays on nationalism*. New York: Macmillan.

Hayes, Carlton J.H. (1931) *The historical evolution of modern nationalism*. New York: Russell & Russell.

Hayes, Carlton J.H. (1960) *Nationalism: a religion*. New York: Macmillan.

Hayes, Paul M. (1973) *Fascism*. London: George Allen & Unwin.

Hearn, Jonathan (2006) *Rethinking nationalism: a critical introduction*. Basingstoke: Palgrave Macmillan.

Heater, Derek (1998) *The theory of nationhood: a platonic symposium*. Basingstoke: Macmillan.

Hechter, Michael (1975) *Internal colonialism: the Celtic fringe in British national development, 1536–1966*. London: Routledge and Kegan Paul.

Hechter, Michael (2000) *Containing nationalism*. Oxford: Oxford University Press.

Hemenway, Elizabeth Jones (1997) 'Mother Russia and the crisis of the Russian national family: the puzzle of gender in revolutionary Russia', *Nationalities Papers* 25 (1): 103–21.

Heng, Geraldine (1997) '"A great way to fly": nationalism, the state, and the varieties of third-world feminism', pp. 30–45 in M. Jacqui Alexander and Chandra Mohanty (eds), *Feminist genealogies, colonial legacies, democratic futures*. London: Routledge.

Hensel, Leszek (2002) 'Le mythe sarmate et le mythe scythe: une tentative de comparaison', pp. 41–51 in Chantal Delsol, Michel Masłowski and Joanna Nowicki (eds) (2002) *Mythes et symboles politiques en Europe centrale*. Paris: Presses Universitaires de France.

Héran, François, Alexandra Filhon and Christine Deprez (2002) *La dynamique des langues en France au fil du XXe siècle* [Population et Sociétés, 376]. Paris: INED.

Herod, Charles C. (1976) *The nation in the history of Marxian thought: the concept of nations with history and nations without history*. The Hague: Martinus Nijhoff.

Herrity, Peter (1973) 'The role of the Matica and similar societies in the development of the Slavonic literary languages', *Slavonic and East European Review* 51 (124): 368–86.

Hertz, Frederick (1944) *Nationality in history and politics: a psychology and sociology of national sentiment and character*. London: Routledge and Kegan Paul.

Hilberg, Raul (1980) 'The anatomy of the Holocaust', pp. 85–94 in Henry Friedlander and Sybil Milton (eds), *The Holocaust: ideology, bureaucracy, and genocide*. Millwood, NY: Kraus International.

Hilberg, Raul (1985) *The destruction of the European Jews*. London: Holmes and Meier.

Hill, Christopher R. (1993) 'The politics of the Olympic movement', pp. 84–104 in Lincoln Allison (ed.), *The changing politics of sport*. Manchester: Manchester University Press.

Hill, Emmeline W., Mark A. Jobling and Daniel G. Bradley (2000) 'Y-chromosome variation and Irish origins', *Nature* 404 (6776) (23 March): 351–2.

Hirata, Lucie Cheng (1979) 'Leadership in China's minority nationalities, autonomous regions – continuity and change', pp. 41–7 in Tai S. Kang (ed.), *Nationalism and the crises of ethnic minorities in Asia*. Westport, CT: Greenwood Press.

Hirsch, Francine (2005) *Empire of nations: ethnographic knowledge and the making of the Soviet Union*. Ithaca, NY: Cornell University Press.

Hobsbawm, Eric (1983) 'Mass-producing traditions: Europe, 1870–1914', pp. 263–307 in Eric Hobsbawm and Terence Ranger (eds), *The invention of tradition*. Cambridge: Cambridge University Press.

Hobsbawm, Eric (1990) *Nations and nationalism since 1780: programme, myth, reality*. Cambridge: Cambridge University Press.

Hobsbawm, Eric (1992) *Nations and nationalism since 1780: programme, myth, reality* (2nd edn). Cambridge: Cambridge University Press.

Hobsbawm, Eric (1995) 'Foreword', pp. 11–15 in Dawn Ades, Tim Benton, David Elliott and Iain Boyd Whyte, *Art and power: Europe under the dictators 1930–45*. London: Thames and Hudson.

Hoddie, Matthew (1998) 'Ethnic identity change in the People's Republic of China: an explanation using data from the 1982 and 1990 census enumerations', *Nationalism and Ethnic Politics* 4 (1–2): 119–41.

Hoffmann, Charlotte (1991) *An introduction to bilingualism*. London: Longman.

Hoffmann, Fernant (1981) 'Triglossia in Luxemburg', pp. 201–7 in Einar Haugen, J. Derrick McClure and Derick Thomson (eds), *Minority languages today*. Edinburgh: Edinburgh University Press.

Holland, Henry (1815) *Travels in the Ionian Isles, Albania, Thessaly, Macedonia etc. during the years 1812 and 1813*. London: Longman, Hurst, Rees, Orme, and Brown.

Holmans, A.E. (1965) 'Inter-regional differences in levels of income: are there "two nations" or one?', *Journal of Industrial Economics* 13 (supplement): 1–19.

Holmes, Janet (1992) *An introduction to sociolonguistics*. London: Longman.

Holmes, Michael and David Storey (2011) 'Transferring national allegiance: cultural affinity or flag of convenience', *Sport in Society* 14 (2): 253–71.

Holt, Richard (1989) *Sport and the British: a modern history.* Oxford: Clarendon Press.

Horn, D.B. and Mary Ransome (eds) (1957) *English historical documents 1714–1783.* London: Eyre and Spottiswoode.

Horowitz, Donald L. (1990) 'Ethnic conflict management for policymakers', pp. 115–30 in Joseph V. Montville (ed.), *Conflict and peacemaking in multiethnic societies.* Lexington, MA: Lexington Books.

Horowitz, Donald L. (2000) *Ethnic groups in conflict.* Berkeley, CA: University of California Press [first edition 1985].

Horowitz, Donald L. (2002) 'The primordialists', pp. 72–82 in Daniele Conversi (ed.), *Ethnonationalism in the contemporary world: Walker Connor and the study of nationalism.* London: Routledge.

Horowitz, Irving Louis (1980) *Taking lives: genocide and state power.* New Brunswick, NJ: Transaction Books.

Hovannisian, Richard G. (ed.) (1986) *The Armenian genocide in perspective.* New Brunswick, NJ: Transaction Books.

Hoxie, Frederick E. (2008) 'Retrieving the Red Continent: settler colonialism and the history of American Indians in the US', *Ethnic and Racial Studies* 31 (6): 1153–67.

Hoyo, Henio (2010) 'Transplant or graft? Hroch and the Mexican patriotic movements', *Nationalities Papers* 38 (6): 793–812.

Hroch, Miroslav (1968) *Die Vorkämpfer der nationalen Bewegungen bei den kleinen Völkern Europas: eine vergleichende Analyse zur gesellschaftlichen Schichtung der patriotischen Gruppen.* Prague: Universita Karlova.

Hroch, Miroslav (1985) *Social preconditions of national revival in Europe: a comparative analysis of the social composition of patriotic groups among the smaller European nations.* Cambridge: Cambridge University Press.

Hroch, Miroslav (1986) *Evropská národní hnutí v 19. století: společenské předpoklady vzniku novodobých národů* [European national movements in the 19th century: social preconditions for the rise of modern nations]. Praha: Nakladatelství Svoboda.

Hroch, Miroslav (1993) 'From national movement to the fully-formed nation: the nation-building process in Europe', *New Left Review* 168: 18–45.

Hroch, Miroslav (1995) 'National self-determination from a historical perspective', pp. 65–82 in Sukumar Periwal (ed.), *Notions of nationalism.* Budapest: Central European University Press.

Hroch, Miroslav (1998) 'Real and constructed: the nature of the nation', pp. 91–106 in John A. Hall (ed.), *The state of the nation: Ernest Gellner and the theory of nationalism.* Cambridge: Cambridge University Press.

Hroch, Miroslav (2000) *In the national interest: demands and goals of European national movements of the nineteenth century: a comparative perspective.* Trans. Robin Cassling. Prague: Faculty of Philosophy, Charles University.

Hroch, Miroslav (2010) 'Comments', *Nationalities Papers* 38 (6): 881–90.

Hunt, Alan (1996) 'The governance of consumption: sumptuary laws and shifting forms of regulation', *Economy and Society* 25 (3): 410–26.

Huntington, Samuel P. (1993) 'The clash of civilizations?', *Foreign Affairs* 72 (3): 22–49.

Huntington, Samuel P. (1996) *The clash of civilizations and the remaking of world order.* New York: Simon & Schuster.

Hurt, J. (1904) *Über die pleskauer Esten oder die sogennanten Setukesen.* Helsingfors: Drückerei der Finnischen Litteratur-Gesellschaft.

Hussain, Athar (2000) 'Peregrinations of Pakistani nationalism', pp. 126–53 in Michael Leifer (ed.), *Asian Nationalism.* London: Routledge.

Hutchins, Rachel D. (2011) 'Heroes and the renegotiation of national identity in American history textbooks: representations of George Washington and Abraham Lincoln, 1982–2003', *Nations and Nationalism* 17 (3): 649–68.

Hutchinson, John (1987) *The dynamics of cultural nationalism: the Gaelic revival and the creation of the Irish nation state.* London: Allen and Unwin.

Hutchinson, John (1994) *Modern nationalism*. London: Fontana.

Hutchinson, John (2005) *Nations as zones of conflict*. London: Sage.

Hutchinson, John and Anthony D. Smith (eds) (1994) *Nationalism*. Oxford: Oxford University Press [Oxford Readers].

Hutchinson, John and Anthony D. Smith (eds) (1996) *Ethnicity*. Oxford: Oxford University Press [Oxford Readers].

Hutchinson, John and Anthony D. Smith (eds) (2000) *Nationalism: critical concepts in political science* (5 vols). London: Routledge.

Huysseune, Michel (2010) 'Landscapes as a symbol of nationhood: the Alps in the rhetoric of the Lega Nord', *Nations and Nationalism* 16 (2): 354–73.

Igartua, José E. (2006) *The other quiet revolutions: national identities in English Canada, 1945–71*. Vancouver: UBC Press.

Ignatieff, Michael (1999) 'Nationalism and the narcissism of minor differences', pp. 91–102 in Ronald Beiner (ed.), *Theorizing nationalism*. Albany, NY: State University of New York Press.

Ignatiev, Noel (1995) *How the Irish became white*. London: Routledge.

Ignazi, Piero (1997) 'The extreme right in Europe: a survey', pp. 47–64 in Peter H. Merkl and Leonard Weinberg (eds), *The revival of right-wing extremism in the nineties*. London: Frank Cass.

Ileto, Reynaldo (1999) 'Religion and anti-colonial movements', pp. 193–244 in Nicholas Tarling (ed.), *The Cambridge history of Southeast Asia* (vol. 3) (New edn). Cambridge: Cambridge University Press.

Ireland (1856) *Census of Ireland, 1851, part 4: report on ages and education*. Dublin: HMSO.

Ireland (1863) *Census of Ireland, 1861, part 4: report and tables relating to the religious professions, education, and occupations of the people*. Dublin: HMSO.

Ireland (1882) *Census of Ireland, 1881: general report*. Dublin: HMSO.

Ireland (1912) *Census of Ireland, 1911: general report*. Dublin: HMSO.

Isayev, M.I. (1977) *National languages in the USSR: problems and solutions*. Moscow: Progress Publishers.

Israel (2003) *The land of promise*. Available at: www.mfa.gov.il/MFA/MFAArchive/2000_2009/2003/3/The+Land+of+Promise.htm [2010-03-19].

Iurchenkov, Valerii (2001) 'The Mordvins: dilemmas of mobilization in a biethnic community', *Nationalities Papers* 29 (1): 85–95.

Jääts, Indrek (2000) 'Ethnic identity of the Setus and the Estonian–Russian border dispute', *Nationalities Papers* 28 (4): 651–70.

Jackson-Preece, Jennifer (2010) 'Origins of nations: contested beginnings, contested futures', pp. 15–25 in Karl Cordell and Stefan Wolff (eds), *Routledge handbook of ethnic conflict*. London: Routledge.

Jaffrelot, Christophe (2005) 'For a theory of nationalism', pp. 10–61 in Alain Dieckhoff and Christophe Jaffrelot (eds), *Revisiting nationalism: theories and processes*. London: Hurst.

James, Allison (1997) 'How British is British food?', pp. 71–86 in Pat Caplan (ed.), *Food, health and identity*. London: Routledge.

Janowsky, O.I. (1945) *Nationalities and national minorities (with special reference to East-Central Europe)*. New York: Macmillan.

Jászi, Oscar (1961 [1929]) *The dissolution of the Habsburg monarchy*. Chicago, IL: University of Chicago Press.

Jayawardena, Kumari (1986) *Feminism and nationalism in the third world*. London: Zed Books.

Jelavich, Charles (1990) *South Slav nationalisms: textbooks and Yugoslav union before 1914*. Columbus, OH: Ohio State University Press.

Jelavich, Charles and Barbara Jelavich (1977) *The establishment of the Balkan national states, 1804–1920*. Seattle, WA: University of Washington Press.

Jenkins, Philip (2009) 'Dark passages: does the harsh language in the Koran explain Islamic violence? Don't answer till you've taken a look inside the Bible', *Boston Globe*, 8 March. Available at: www.boston.com/bostonglobe/ideas/articles/2009/03/08/dark_passages/ [2010-11-21].

Jenkins, Richard (1997) *Rethinking ethnicity: arguments and explorations*. London: Sage.

Jennings, Sir Ivor (1956) *The approach to self-government*. Cambridge: Cambridge University Press.

Jha, Hetukar (1980) 'Stages of nationalism: some hypothetical considerations', pp. 193–200 in Jacques Dofny and Akinsola Akiwowo (eds), *National and ethnic movements*. London: Sage.

Johansson, Rune (1999) 'The impact of imagination: history, territoriality and perceived affinity', pp. 1–29 in Sven Tägil (ed.), *Regions in Central Europe: the legacy of history*. London: Hurst.

Johnston, Hank (1992) 'Religious nationalism: six propositions from eastern Europe and the former Soviet Union', pp. 67–79 in Bronislaw Misztal and Anson Shupe (eds), *Religion and politics in comparative perspective: revival of religious fundamentalism in East and West*. Wesport, CT: Praeger.

Joireman, Sandra Fullerton (2003) *Nationalism and political identity*. London: Continuum.

Jones, Ernest (1964 [1922]) 'The island of Ireland: a psycho-analytical contribution to political psychology', pp. 95–112 in *Essays in Applied Psycho-analysis* (Vol. 1). London: Hogarth Press.

Joseph, Bernard (1929) *Nationality: its nature and problems*. London: Allen and Unwin.

Joseph, John E. (2004) *Language and identity: national, ethnic, religious*. Basingstoke: Palgrave Macmillan.

Joseph, Nathan (1986) *Uniforms and nonuniforms: communication through clothing*. Westport, CT: Greenwood Press.

Kamusella, Tomasz D.I. (2001) 'Language as an instrument of nationalism in Central Europe', *Nations and Nationalism* 7 (2): 235–51.

Kamusella, Tomasz D.I. (2011) 'Silesian in the nineteenth and twentieth centuries: a language caught in the net of conflicting nationalisms, politics, and identities', *Nationalities Papers* 39 (5): 769–89.

Karnes, Kevin C. (2005) 'A garland of songs for a nation of singers: an episode in the history of Russia, the Herderian tradition and the rise of Baltic nationalism', *Journal of the Royal Musical Association* 130 (2): 197–235.

Karolewski, Ireneusz Pawel, and Andrzej Marcin Suszycki (2011) *The nation and nationalism in Europe: an introduction*. Edinburgh: Edinburgh University Press.

Katsikas, Stefanos (2009) '*Millets* in nation-states: the case of Greek and Bulgarian Muslims, 1912–1923', *Nationalities Papers* 37 (2): 177–201.

Kaufmann, Eric and Oded Haklai (2008) 'Dominant ethnicity: from minority to majority', *Nations and Nationalism* 14 (4): 743–67.

Kaufmann, Eric and Oliver Zimmer (2004) '"Dominant ethnicity" and the "ethnic–civic" dichotomy in the work of A.D. Smith', *Nations and Nationalism* 10 (1/2): 63–78.

Keane, A.H. (1896) *Ethnology*. Cambridge: Cambridge University Press.

Kearney, Hugh (1989) *The British Isles: a history of four nations*. Cambridge: Cambridge University Press.

Keating, Michael (1988) *State and regional nationalism: territorial politics and the European state*. London: Harvester Wheatsheaf.

Keating, Michael (1998a) 'Is there a regional level of government in Europe?', pp. 11–29 in Patrick Le Galès and Christian Lequesne (eds), *Regions in Europe*. London: Routledge.

Keating, Michael (1998b) *The new regionalism in western Europe: territorial restructuring and political change*. Cheltenham: Edward Elgar.

Kedourie, Elie (1993) *Nationalism* (4th edn). Oxford: Blackwell.

Kellas, James E. (1998) *The politics of nationalism and ethnicity* (2nd edn). Basingstoke: Macmillan Education.

Kemiläinen, Aira (1964) *Nationalism: problems concerning the word, the concept and classification*. Jyväskyla: Jyväskylan Kasvatusopillinen Korkeakoulu.

Kennedy, J. (1968) *Asian nationalism in the twentieth century*. London: Macmillan.

Khatami, Siamak (1991) 'Decentralization: a comparative study of France and Spain since the 1970s', *Regional Politics and Policy* 1 (2): 161–81.

Kimball, Stanley B. (1964) *Czech nationalism: a study of the national theatre movement, 1845–83*. Urbana, IL: University of Illinois Press.

Kimball, Stanley B. (1969) 'The Serbian 'Matica' – prototype of Austro-Slav literary foundations: the first fifty years 1826–76', *East European Quarterly* 3 (3): 348–70.

King, Preston (1982) *Federalism and federation*. London: Croom Helm.

Kingsbury, Damien (2011) 'Post-colonial states, ethnic minorities and separatist conflicts: case studies from Southeast and South Asia', *Ethnic and Racial Studies* 34 (5): 762–78.

Kipling, Rudyard (1912) *Rudyard Kipling's verse: definitive edition*. London: Hodder and Stoughton.

Kirk-Greene, A.H.M. (1980) 'The thin white line: the size of the British colonial service in Africa', *African Affairs* 79 (314): 25–44.

Kivisto, Peter (2010) 'Multiculturalism and racial democracy: state policies and social practices', pp. 253–74 in Patricia Hill Collins and John Solomos (eds), *The Sage handbook of race and ethnic studies*. London: Sage.

Kligman, Gail (1998) *The politics of duplicity: controlling reproduction in Ceausescu's Romania*. Berkeley, CA: University of California Press.

Knowles, Caroline (2010) 'Theorising race and ethnicity: contemporary paradigms and perspectives', pp. 23–42 in Patricia Hill Collins and John Solomos (eds), *The Sage handbook of race and ethnic studies*. London: Sage.

Kohn, Hans (1944) *The idea of nationalism: a study in its origins and background*. New York: Macmillan.

Kohn, Hans (1946) *Prophets and peoples: studies in nineteenth-century nationalism*. New York: Macmillan.

Kolstø, Pål (2006) 'National symbols as signs of unity and division', *Ethnic and Racial Studies* 29 (4): 676–701.

Konstantinov, Yulian (1997) 'Strategies for sustaining a vulnerable identity: the case of the Bulgarian Pomaks', pp. 33–53 in Hugh Poulton and Suha Jahi-Farouki (eds), *Muslim identity and the Balkan state*. London: Hurst.

Kořalka, Jiří (1969) *Co je národ?* [*What is a nation?*] Prague: Svoboda.

Kossuth, Louis (1852) *The future of nations: in what consists its security*. New York: Fowlers and Wells.

Kpessa, Michael, Daniel Béland and André Lecours (2011) 'Nationalism, development, and social policy: the politics of nation-building in sub-Saharan Africa', *Ethnic and Racial Studies* 34 (12): 2115–33.

Kratoska, Paul and Ben Batson (1999) 'Nationalism and modernist reform', pp. 245–320 in Nicholas Tarling (ed.), *The Cambridge history of Southeast Asia* (vol. 3) (New edn). Cambridge: Cambridge University Press.

Krejčí, Jaroslav and Vítězslav Velímský (1981) *Ethnic and political nations in Europe*. London: Croom Helm.

Krueger, Rita (2009) *Czech, German and noble: status and national identity in Habsburg Bohemia*. Oxford: Oxford University Press.

Krulic, Brigitte (1999) *La nation: une idée moderne*. Paris: Ellipses.

Kulisher, E.M. (1948) *Europe on the move: war and population changes, 1917–47*. New York: Columbia University Press.

Kumar, Krishan (2010) 'Nation-states as empires, empires as nation-states: two principles, one practice?', *Theory and Society* 39 (2): 119–43.

Kuper, Leo (1981) *Genocide: its political use in the twentieth century*. New Haven, CT: Yale University Press.

Kuper, Leo (1985) *The prevention of genocide*. New Haven, CT: Yale University Press.

Kurtz, Lester R. (2007) *Gods in the global village: the world's religions in sociological perspective* (2nd edn). Thousand Oaks, CA: Pine Forge Press.

Kuzio, Taras (2002) 'The myth of the civic state: a critical survey of Hans Kohn's framework for understanding nationalism', *Ethnic and Racial Studies* 25 (1): 20–39.

Kuzio, Taras (2005) 'Nation building, history writing and competition over the legacy of Kyiv Rus in Ukraine', *Nationalities Papers* 33 (1): 29–58.

Kymlicka, Will (1995) *Multicultural citizenship: a liberal theory of minority rights*. Oxford: Clarendon Press.

Kymlicka, Will (2001) *Politics in the vernacular: nationalism, multiculturalism and citizenship*. Oxford: Oxford University Press.

Ladas, Stephen P. (1932) *The exchange of minorities: Bulgaria, Greece and Turkey*. New York: Macmillan.

Lafont, Robert (1967) *La révolution régionaliste*. Paris: Gallimard.

Laitin, David (2007) *Nations, states and violence*. Oxford: Oxford University Press

Lambert, John (2005) 'An identity threatened: White English-speaking South Africans, Britishness and Dominion South Africanism, 1934–1939', *African Historical Review* 37 (1): 50–70.

Lane, Christel (1981) *The rites of rulers: ritual in industrial society – the Soviet case*. Cambridge: Cambridge University Press.

Laponce, Jean (1960) *The protection of minorities*. Berkeley, CA: University of California Press.

Laponce, Jean (1987) *Languages and their territories*. Trans. Anthony Martin-Sperry. Toronto: University of Toronto Press.

Laponce, Jean (2003) 'Canada: the case for ethnolinguistic federalism in a multilingual society', pp. 23–44 in John Coakley (ed.), *The territorial management of ethnic conflict* (2nd edn). London: Frank Cass.

Laveleye, Émile de (1868) 'L'Allemagne depuis la guerre de 1866: VII: Les nationalités en Hongrie et les Slaves du Sud (Yougo-Slaves)', *Revue des deux mondes* 76 (1 August): 513–49.

Law, Ian (2010) *Racism and ethnicity: global debates, dilemmas, directions*. Harlow: Longman.

Lawrence, Paul (2005) *Nationalism: history and theory*. Harlow: Pearson Longman.

Lawson, Steven E. (1976) *Voting rights in the South, 1944–1969*. New York: Columbia University Press.

Leerssen, Joep (2006) 'Nationalism and the cultivation of culture', *Nations and Nationalism* 12 (4): 559–78.

Lefebvre, Georges (2005 [1939]) *The coming of the French revolution* (New edn). Trans. R.R. Palmer. Princeton, NJ: Princeton University Press.

Lemkin, Raphaël (2005 [1944]) *Axis rule in occupied Europe*. Clark, NJ: Lawbook Exchange.

Lentz, Carola (1995) 'Ethnic conflict and changing dress codes: a case study of an Indian migrant village in Highland Ecuador', pp. 269–94 in Joanne B. Eicher (ed.), *Dress and ethnicity: change across space and time*. Oxford: Berg.

Leonardi, Robert (1992) 'The regional reform in Italy: from centralized to regionalized state', *Regional Politics and Policy* 2 (1–2): 217–46.

Leoussi, Athena S. (ed.) (2001) *Encyclopaedia of nationalism*. New Brunswick, NJ: Transaction Books.

Leoussi, Athena S. (2004) 'The ethno-cultural roots of national art', *Nations and Nationalism* 10 (1–2): 143–59.

Leshchenko, Natalia (2004) 'A fine instrument: two nation-building strategies in post-Soviet Belarus', *Nations and Nationalism* 10 (3): 333–52.

Levinger, Matthew and Paula Franklin Lytle (2001) 'Myth and mobilisation: the triadic structure of nationalist rhetoric', *Nations and Nationalism* 7 (2): 175–94.

Lewis, Bernard (1975) *History – remembered, recovered, invented*. Princeton, NJ: Princeton University Press.

Lewis, Todd (2003) 'Buddhism: the politics of compassionate rule', pp. 233–56 in Jacob Neusner (ed.), *The politics of world religions*. Washington, DC: Georgetown University Press.

Liebich, Andre (2006) 'Searching for the perfect nation: the itinerary of Hans Kohn (1891–1971)', *Nations and Nationalism* 12 (4): 579–96.

Lijphart, Arend (1969) 'Consociational democracy', *World Politics* 21 (2): 207–25.

Lijphart, Arend (1977) *Democracy in plural societies: a comparative exploration*. New Haven, CT: Yale University Press.

Lijphart, Arend (ed.) (1981) *Conflict and coexistence in Belgium: the dynamics of a culturally divided society*. Berkeley, CA: Institute of International Studies, University of California at Berkeley.

Lindeborg, Lisbeth (1999) 'Regional deep structures in the German cultural space', pp. 53–113 in Sven Tägil (ed.), *Regions in Central Europe: the legacy of history*. London: Hurst.

Lipoński, Wojciech (1999) 'Sport in the Slavic world before communism: cultural traditions and national functions', pp. 203–49 in J.A. Mangan (ed.), *Sport in Europe: politics, class, gender*. London: Frank Cass.

Lipset, S.M. and Stein Rokkan (1967) 'Cleavage structures, party systems and voter alignments: an introduction', pp. 1–64 in S.M. Lipset and Stein Rokkan (eds), *Party systems and voter alignments*. New York: The Free Press.

Llobera, Josep R. (1994) *The god of modernity: the development of nationalism in modern Europe*. Oxford: Berg.

Lluch, Jaime (2011) 'Sovereigntists and associationists: explaining the origins of national movements' political orientation', *Nationalism and Ethnic Politics* 17 (2): 203–24.

Lodge, Tom (1983) *Black politics in South Africa since 1945*. London: Longmans.

Loewen, James W. (1996) *Lies my teacher told me: everything your American history textbook got wrong*. New York: Simon & Schuster.

Loftus, Belinda (1990) *Mirrors: William III and Mother Ireland*. Dundrum, Co. Down: Picture Press.

Loit, Aleksander (1994) 'Nation-building in the Baltic countries (1850–1918)', pp. 479–503 (vol. 1) in Justo G. Beramendi, Ramón Máiz and Xosé M. Núñez (eds), *Nationalism in Europe past and present: actas do Congreso Internacional os Nacionalismos en Europa pasado e presente, Santiago de Compostela, 27–29 de Setembro de 1993* (2 vols). Santiago de Compostela: Universidade de Santiago de Compostela.

Loughlin, John (1985a) 'A new deal for France's regions and linguistic minorities', *West European Politics* 8 (3): 101–13.

Loughlin, John (1985b) 'Regionalism and ethnic nationalism in France', pp. 207–35 in Yves Mény and Vincent Wright (eds), *Centre–periphery relations in Western Europe*. London: Allen & Unwin.

Low, D.A. (1981) 'Conclusion: sequence, crux and means: some Asian nationalisms compared', pp. 258–80 in Robin Jeffrey (ed.), *Asia: the winning of independence*. London: Macmillan.

Lucassen, Leo, David Feldman and Jochen Oltmer (2006) 'Drawing up the balance sheet', pp. 283–96 in Leo Lucassen, David Feldman and Jochen Oltmer (eds), *Paths of integration: migrants in western Europe (1880–2004)*. Amsterdam: Amsterdam University Press.

Lundskow, George (2008) *The sociology of religion: a substantive and transdisciplinary approach*. Thousand Oaks, CA: Pine Forge Press.

Lynch, Cecelia (2000) 'Dogma, praxis and religious perspectives on multiculturalism', *Millennium* 29 (3): 741–59.

Lynch, John (1973) *The Spanish American revolutions 1808–1826*. London: Weidenfeld and Nicolson.

Macaulay, Thomas Babington (1866 [1833]) 'The government of India', pp. 111–42 in *The works of Lord Macaulay complete* (vol. 8). Ed. Lady Trevelyan. London: Longmans, Green, and Co.

MacCormick, Neil (1999) 'Nation and nationalism', pp. 189–204 in Ronald Beiner (ed.), *Theorizing nationalism*. Albany, NY: State University of New York Press.

Mackey, William F. (1970 [1962]) 'The description of bilingualism', pp. 554–84 in Joshua A. Fishman (ed.), *Readings in the sociology of language*. The Hague: Mouton.

MacManus, Seumas (1944) *The story of the Irish race: a popular history of Ireland*. New York: Devin-Adair.

Magocsi, Paul R. (2002) *The roots of Ukrainian nationalism: Galicia as Ukraine's Piedmont*. Toronto: University of Toronto Press.

Mair, L.P. (1928) *The protection of minorities: the working and scope of the minorities treaties under the League of Nations*. London: Christophers.

Malaysia (2008) *Yearbook of statistics, Malaysia, 2007*. Kuala Lumpur: Department of Statistics.

Malešević, Siniša (2004) *The sociology of ethnicity*. London: Sage.

Malešević, Siniša (2006) *Identity or ideology: understanding ethnicity and nationalism*. Basingstoke: Palgrave Macmillan.

Malešević, Siniša and Gordana Uzelac (2007) 'Nation-state without the nation? The trajectories of nation-formation in Montenegro', *Nations and Nationalism* 13 (4): 695–716.

Malinowski, Bronislaw (1954 [1925]) *Magic, science and religion and other essays*. Garden City, NY: Doubleday Anchor.

Malloy, Tove H. (2005) *National minority rights in Europe*. Oxford: Oxford University Press.

Manela, Erez (2007) *The Wilsonian moment: self-determination and the international origins of anticolonial nationalism*. Oxford: Oxford University Press.

Mann, Michael (1995) 'A political theory of nationalism and its excesses', pp. 44–64 in Sukumar Periwal (ed.), *Notions of nationalism*. Budapest: Central European University Press.

Mann, Michael (2004) *Fascists*. Cambridge: Cambridge University Press.

Mann, Michael (2005) *The dark side of democracy: explaining ethnic cleansing*. Cambridge: Cambridge University Press.

Mann, S.E. (1958) 'Vaclav Hanka's forgeries', *Slavonic and East European Review* 36 (87): 491–6.

Manor, Johanan (2003) *Les manuels scolaires palestiniens: une génération sacrifiée*. Paris: Berg International.

Markoff, John and Daniel Regan (1987) 'Religion, the state and political legitimacy in the world's constitutions', pp. 161–82 in Thomas Robbins and Roland Robinson (eds), *Church–state relations: tensions and transitions*. New Brunswick, NJ: Transaction Books.

Marsland, David (2001) 'National symbols', pp. 220–2 in Athena S. Leoussi (ed.), *Encyclopaedia of nationalism*. New Brunswick, NJ: Transaction Books.

Martin, Terry (2001) *The affirmative action empire: nations and nationalism in the Soviet Union, 1923–1939*. Ithaca, NY: Cornell University Press.

Marx, Anthony W. (2003) *Faith in nation: exclusionary origins of nationalism*. Oxford: Oxford University Press.

Maslow, A.H. (1943) 'A theory of human motivation', *Psychological Review* 50 (4): 370–96.

Maxwell, Alexander (2005) 'Multiple nationalism: national concepts in nineteenth-century Hungary and Benedict Anderson's "imagined communities"', *Nationalism and Ethnic Politics* 11 (3): 385–414.

Maxwell, Alexander (2010) 'Typologies and phases in nationalism studies: Hroch's A–B–C schema as a basis for comparative terminology', *Nationalities Papers* 38 (6): 865–80.

Mayer, Tamar (2000) 'Gender ironies of nationalism: setting the stage', pp. 1–22 in Tamar Mayer (ed.), *Gender ironies of nationalism: sexing the nation*. London: Routledge.

Mazrui, Ali A. and Michael Tidy (1984) *Nationalism and new states in Africa*. Nairobi: Heinemann.

Mazzini, Giuseppe (1887) *Essays: selected from the writings, literary, political, and religious, of Joseph Mazzini*. Ed. William Clarke. London: W. Scott.

McClintock, Ann (1997) '"No longer in a future heaven": gender, race and nationalism', pp. 89–112 in Anne McClintock, Aamir Mufti and Ella Shohat (eds), *Dangerous liaisons: gender, nation and postcolonial perspectives*. Minneapolis, MN: University of Minnesota Press.

McCrone, David (1998) *The sociology of nationalism: tomorrow's ancestors*. London: Routledge.

McDermid, Jane and Anna Hillyar (1999) *Midwives of the revolution: female Bolsheviks and women workers in 1917*. London: UCL Press.

McDougall, William (1920) *The group mind: a sketch of the principles of collective psychology with some attempt to apply them to the interpretation of national life and character*. New York: G.P. Putnam & Sons.

McGarry, John (1998) '"Demographic engineering": the state-directed movement of ethnic groups as a technique of conflict regulation', *Ethnic and Racial Studies* 21 (4): 613–38.

McGarry, John and Brendan O'Leary (1993) 'Introduction: the macro-political regulation of ethnic conflict', pp. 1–40 in John McGarry and Brendan O'Leary (eds), *The politics of ethnic conflict regulation: case studies of protracted ethnic conflict*. London: Routledge.

McGarry, John and Brendan O'Leary (2004) *The Northern Ireland conflict: consociational engagements*. Oxford: Oxford University Press.

McGarry, John, Brendan O'Leary and Richard Simeon (2008) 'Integration or accommodation? The enduring debate in conflict regulation', pp. 41–88 in S. Choudhry (ed.), *Constitutional design for divided societies: integration or accommodation?* Oxford: Oxford University Press.

McInnis, Marvin (1968) 'The trend of regional income differentials in Canada', *Canadian Journal of Economics* 1 (2): 440–70.

McKay, James (1982) 'An exploratory synthesis of the primordial and mobilizationist approaches to ethnic phenomena', *Ethnic and Racial Studies* 5 (4): 395–420.

McKay, James and Frank Lewins (1978) 'Ethnicity and the ethnic group: a conceptual analysis and reformulation', *Ethnic and Racial Studies* 1 (4): 412–27.

McKenna, Mark (1997) *Different perspectives on black armband history* [Research paper 5]. Canberra: Parliamentary Library, Parliament of Australia. Available at: www.aph.gov.au/Library/pubs/ rp/1997-98/98rp05.htm [2009-12-17].

McLeod, Hugh (1999) 'Protestantism and British national identity, 1815–1845', pp. 44–70 in Peter van der Veer and Hartmut Lehmann (eds), *Nation and religion: perspectives on Europe and Asia*. Princeton, NJ: Princeton University Press.

McRae, Kenneth (ed.) (1974) *Consociational democracy: political accommodation in divided societies*. Toronto: McClelland and Stuart.

McRae, Kenneth D. (1975) 'The principle of territoriality and the principle of personality in multilingual states', *Linguistics* 158: 33–54.

McRae, Kenneth D. (1983) *Conflict and compromise in multilingual societies*. Vol. 1: *Switzerland*. Waterloo: Wilfrid Laurier University Press.

McRae, Kenneth D. (1986) *Conflict and compromise in multilingual societies*. Vol. 2: *Belgium*. Waterloo: Wilfrid Laurier University Press.

McRae, Kenneth D. (1997) *Conflict and compromise in multilingual societies*. Vol. 3: *Finland*. Waterloo: Wilfrid Laurier University Press.

Meadwell, Hudson (1993) 'The politics of nationalism in Quebec', *World Politics* 45 (2): 203–41.

Meinecke, Friedrich (1970 [1928]) *Cosmopolitanism and the national state*. Trans. Robert B. Kimber. Princeton, NJ: Princeton University Press.

Mellor, Roy E.H. (1989) *Nation, state, and territory: a political geography*. London: Routledge.

Melman, Billie (1992) 'Claiming the nation's past: the invention of an Anglo-Saxon tradition', pp. 221–41 in Jehuda Reinharz and George L. Mosse (eds), *The impact of western nationalisms: essays dedicated to Walter Z. Laqueur on the occasion of his 70th birthday*. London: Sage.

Melson, Robert (1986) 'Provocation or nationalism: a critical enquiry into the Armenian genocide of 1995', pp. 61–84 in Richard G. Hovannisian (ed.), *The Armenian genocide in perspective*. New Brunswick, NJ: Transaction Books.

Mennell, Stephen (1985) *All manners of food: eating and taste in England and France from the middle ages to the present*. Oxford: Basil Blackwell.

Mennell, Stephen, Anne Murcott and Anneke H. van Otterloo (1992) *The sociology of food: eating, diet and culture*. London: Sage.

Mény, Yves (1987) 'The political dynamics of regionalism: Italy, France, Spain', pp. 1–28 in Roger Morgan (ed.), *Regionalism in European politics*. London: PSI.

Miles, Robert (1987) 'Recent Marxist theories of nationalism and the issue of racism', *British Journal of Sociology* 38 (1): 24–43.

Miles, Robert (1993) *Racism after 'race relations'*. London: Routledge.

Mill, John Stuart (1861) *Considerations on representative government.* London: Parker, Son and Bourn.

Miller, David (1995) *On nationality.* Oxford: Clarendon Press.

Milojkovic-Djuric, Jelena (1985) 'The role of choral societies in the 19th century among the South Slavs', pp. 475–82 in Aleksander Loit (ed.), *National movements in the Baltic countries during the 19th century: the 7th Conference on Baltic Studies in Scandinavia, Stockholm, June 10–13, 1983.* Stockholm: Almqvist and Wiksell.

Minogue, K.R. (1967) *Nationalism.* London: Batsford.

Misiunas, Romould J. (1968) 'Versailles and Memel', *Lituanus* 14 (1): 65–93.

Mitchell, Claire (2006) *Religion, identity and politics in Northern Ireland: boundaries of belonging and belief.* Aldershot: Ashgate.

Monmonier, Mark (1991) *How to lie with maps.* Chicago, IL: University of Chicago Press.

Montgomery, Martin (1995) *An introduction to language and society* (2nd edn). London: Routledge.

Moore, Margaret (2001) *The ethics of nationalism.* Oxford: Oxford University Press.

Moran, Anthony (2002) 'As Australia decolonizes: indigenizing settler nationalism and the challenges of settler/indigenous relations', *Ethnic and Racial Studies* 25 (6): 1013–42.

Morgan, Prys (1983) 'From a death to a view: the hunt for the Welsh past in the romantic period', pp. 43–100 in Eric Hobsbawm and Terence Ranger (eds), *The invention of tradition.* Cambridge: Cambridge University Press.

Motyl, Alexander (2001) *Encyclopedia of nationalism* (2 vols). London: Academic Press.

Mouzelis, Nicos (1998) 'Ernest Gellner's theory of nationalism: some definitional and methodological issues', pp. 158–65 in John Hall (ed.), *The state of the nation: Ernest Gellner and the theory of nationalism.* Cambridge: Cambridge University Press.

Mugglestone, Lynda (1995) *'Talking proper': the rise of accent as social symbol.* Oxford: Clarendon Press.

Muir, Ramsay (1917) *Nationalism and internationalism: the culmination of modern history.* London: Constable.

Munck, Ronaldo (1986) *The difficult dialogue: Marxism and nationalism.* London: Zed Books.

Murcott, Anne (1996) 'Food as an expression of identity', pp. 49–77 in Sverker Gustavsson and Leif Lewin (eds), *The future of the nation state: essays on cultural pluralism and political integration.* Abingdon: Routledge.

Murphy, Cliona (1997) 'A problematic relationship: European women and nationalism, 1870–1915', pp. 144–58 in Maryann Gialanella Valiulis and Mary O'Dowd (eds), *Women and Irish history: essays in honour of Margaret MacCurtain.* Dublin: Wolfhound Press.

Nagel, Joane (1998) 'Masculinity and nationalism: gender and sexuality in the making of nations', *Ethnic and Racial Studies* 21 (2): 242–69.

Nairn, Tom (1975) 'The modern Janus', *New Left Review* 94: 3–29.

Nettle, Daniel and Suzanne Romaine (2000) *Vanishing voices: the extinction of the world's languages.* Oxford: Oxford University Press.

Neuberger, Benyamin (1991) 'Irredentism and politics in Africa', pp. 97–109 in Naomi Chazan (ed.), *Irredentism and international politics.* Boulder, CO: Lynne Reider.

Neumann, Fr[iedrich] J[ulius] (1888) *Volk und Nation: eine Studie.* Leipzig: Duncker & Humblot.

Ngũgĩ wa Thiong'o (1977) *Petals of blood.* New York: Dutton.

Nielsen, Christian Axboe (2010) 'The goalposts of transition: football as a metaphor for Serbia's long journey to the rule of law', *Nationalities Papers* 38 (1): 87–103.

Nimni, Ephraim (ed.) (2005) *National cultural autonomy and its contemporary critics.* London: Routledge.

Nolte, Claire (2007) 'Voluntary associations and nation-building in nineteenth-century Prague', pp. 82–99 in Laurence Cole (ed.), *Different paths to the nation: regional and national identities in Central Europe and Italy, 1830–70.* Basingstoke: Palgrave Macmillan.

Nolte, Ernst (1965) *Three faces of fascism: Action Française, Italian fascism, national socialism.* Trans. Leila Vennewitz. London: Weidenfeld and Nicolson.

Norman, Wayne (1999) 'Theorizing nationalism (normatively): the first steps', pp. 51–65 in Ronald Beiner (ed.), *Theorizing Nationalism*. Albany, NY: State University of New York Press.

Northern Ireland: Equality Commission for Northern Ireland (2008) *Monitoring report no. 19, 2008*. Belfast: Equality Commission for Northern Ireland.

Nowicka-Ježova, Alina (2002) 'Le mythe des trois frères ou la communauté slave programmée dans l'historiographie du moyen âge et de la renaissance', pp. 51–65 in Chantal Delsol, Michel Masłowski and Joanna Nowicki (eds), *Mythes et symboles politiques en Europe centrale*. Paris: Presses Universitaires de France.

Nuessel, Frank (2006) 'Language: semiotics', pp. 665–79 in Keith Brown (ed.), *Encyclopedia of language and linguistics* (2nd edn). Amsterdam: Elsevier.

O'Connor, Kaori (2009) 'Cuisine, nationality and the making of a national meal: the English breakfast', pp. 157–71 in Susana Carvalho and François Gemenne (eds), *Nations and their histories: constructions and representations*. Basingstoke: Palgrave Macmillan.

O'Leary, Brendan (1998) 'Ernest Gellner's diagnoses of nationalism: a critical overview, or, what is living and what is dead in Ernest Gellner's philosophy of nationalism?', pp. 40–88 in John Hall (ed.), *The state of the nation: Ernest Gellner and the theory of nationalism*. Cambridge: Cambridge University Press.

O'Leary, Brendan (2001) 'The elements of right-sizing and right-peopling the state', pp. 15–73 in Brendan O'Leary, I.S. Lustick and T. Callaghy (eds), *Right-sizing the state: the politics of moving borders*. Oxford: Oxford University Press.

O'Leary, Brendan (2002) 'Federations and the management of nations: agreements and arguments with Walker Connor', pp. 153–83 in Daniele Conversi (ed.), *Ethnonationalism in the contemporary world: Walker Connor and the study of nationalism*. London: Routledge.

O'Shea, Helen (2009) 'Defining the nation and confining the musician: the case of Irish traditional music', *Music and Politics* 3 (2). Available at: www.music.ucsb.edu/projects/musicandpolitics/archive/2009-2/oshea.html.

Oftedal, Magne (1981) 'Is Nynorsk a minority language?', pp. 120–9 in Einar Haugen, J. Derrick McClure and Derick Thomson (eds), *Minority languages today*. Edinburgh: Edinburgh University Press.

Oldson, William (1992) 'Tradition and rite in Transylvania: historic tensions between East and West', pp. 161–79 in Richard Frucht (ed.), *Labyrinth of nationalism, complexities of diplomacy: essays in honor of Charles and Barbara Jelavich*. Colombus, OH: Slavica.

Onuoha, Godwin (2011) 'Contesting the space: the "New Biafra" and ethno-territorial separatism in South-Eastern Nigeria', *Nationalism and Ethnic Politics* 17 (4): 402–22.

Opoku, K. Asare (1985) 'Religion in Africa during the colonial era', pp. 508–38 in A. Adu Boahen (ed.), *General history of Africa* (vol. 7). Paris: UNESCO; London: Heinemann.

Orange, Claudia (1997) *The Treaty of Waitangi*. Wellington: Bridget Williams Books.

Østergård, Uffe (1996 [1992]) 'Peasants and Danes: the Danish national identity and political culture', pp. 179–201 in Geoff Eley and Ronald Grigor Suny (eds), *Becoming national: a reader*. Oxford: Oxford University Press.

Ottaway, Marina (1994) *Democratization and ethnic nationalism: African and Eastern European experiences*. Washington, DC: Overseas Development Council.

Özkırımlı, Umut (2000) *Theories of nationalism: a critical introduction*. Basingstoke: Palgrave.

Özkırımlı, Umut (2005) *Contemporary debates on nationalism: a critical engagement*. Basingstoke: Palgrave.

Özkırımlı, Umut (2007) 'The "perennial" question: nations in antiquity or the antique shop of history?', *Nations and Nationalism* 13 (3): 523–9.

Özkırımlı, Umut (2010) *Theories of nationalism: a critical introduction* (2nd edn). Basingstoke: Palgrave.

Paasi, Anssi (2009) 'The resurgence of the "region" and "regional identity": theoretical perspectives and empirical observations on regional dynamics in Europe', *Review of International Studies* 35 (1): 121–46.

Page, Edward (1978) 'Michael Hechter's internal colonial thesis: some theoretical and methodological problems', *European Journal of Political Research* 6 (3): 295–317.

Paine, Robert (1989) 'Israel: Jewish identity and competition over "tradition"', pp. 121–36 in Elisabeth Tonkin, Maryon McDonald and Malcolm Chapman (eds), *History and ethnicity*. London: Routledge.

Pal, Bipin Chandra (1971 [1910]) 'Hinduism and Indian nationalism', pp. 338–52 in Elie Kedourie (ed.), *Nationalism in Asia and Africa*. London: Weidenfeld and Nicolson.

Pan, Christoph and Beate Sibylle Pfeil (2003) *National minorities in Europe: handbook*. Vienna: Braumüller.

Parekh, Bhikhu (2000) *Rethinking multiculturalism: cultural diversity and political theory*. Basingstoke: Palgrave.

Park, Chis C. (1994) *Sacred worlds: an introduction to geography and religion*. London: Routledge.

Pavković, Aleksandar (2011) 'Recursive secession of trapped minorities: a comparative study of the Serb Krajina and Abkhazia', *Nationalism and Ethnic Politics* 17 (3): 297–318.

Pavković, Aleksandar and Peter Radan (2007) *Creating new states: theory and practice of secession*. Aldershot: Ashgate.

Paxton, Robert O. (2004) *The anatomy of fascism*. London: Allen Lane.

Payne, Stanley G. (1971) 'Catalan and Basque nationalism', *Journal of Contemporary History* 6 (1): 15–51.

Payne, Stanley G. (1980) *Fascism: comparison and definition*. Madison, WI: University of Wisconsin Press.

Payton, Philip (2004) *Cornwall: a history* (New edn). Fowey: Cornwall Editions.

Pearson, Raymond (1983) *National minorities in Eastern Europe 1848–1945*. London: Macmillan.

Pearson, Raymond (1994) *The Longman companion to European nationalism, 1789–1920*. London: Longman.

Pei, Mario (1965) *The story of language* (Rev. edn). Philadelphia, PA: J.B. Lippincott.

Peleg, Ilan (2007) *Democratising the hegemonic state: political transformation in the age of identity*. Cambridge: Cambridge University Press.

Penrose, Jan and Richard C.M. Mole (2008) 'Nation-states and national identity', pp. 271–83 in Kevin R. Cox, Murray Low and Jennifer Robinson (eds), *The Sage handbook of political geography*. London: Sage.

Pershai, Alexander (2008) 'Localness and mobility in Belarusian nationalism: the tactic of *tuteishasć*', *Nationalities Papers* 36 (1): 85–103.

Peterson, V. Spike and Anne Sisson Runyan (1993) *Global gender issues*. Boulder, CO: Westview Press.

Petráň, Josef and Lydia Petráňová (1998) 'The White Mountain as a symbol in modern Czech history', pp. 143–63 in Mikuláš Teich (ed.), *Bohemia in history*. Cambridge: Cambridge University Press.

Petrovich, Michael B. (1980) 'Religion and ethnicity in Eastern Europe', pp. 373–417 in Peter F. Sugar (ed.), *Ethnic diversity and conflict in Eastern Europe*. Santa Barbara, CA: ABC–Clio.

Pettai, Vello (1996) 'The situation of ethnic minorities in Estonia', pp. 41–50 in Magda Opalski and Piotr Dutkiewicz (eds), *Ethnic minority rights in Central Eastern Europe*. Ottawa: Canadian Human Rights Foundation Forum Eastern Europe.

Pfeffer, Leo (1958) *Creeds in competition: a creative force in American culture*. New York: Harper.

Pickering, W.S.F. (1984) *Durkheim's sociology of religion: themes and theories*. London: Routledge and Kegan Paul.

Pierson, Christopher (2004) *The modern state* (2nd edn). London: Routledge.

Piscatori, James P. (1986) *Islam in a world of nation-states*. Cambridge: Cambridge University Press.

Pittock, Murray G.H. (1991) *The invention of Scotland: the Stuart myth and the Scottish identity, 1638 to the present*. London: Routledge.

Plakans, Andrejs (2011) 'Regional identity in Latvia: the case of Latgale', pp. 49–70 in Martyn Housden and David J. Smyth (eds), *Forgotten pages in Baltic history: diversity and inclusion*. Amsterdam: Rodopi.

Pluvier, Jan (1974) *South-East Asia from colonialism to independence*. Kuala Lumpur: Oxford University Press.

Pohlsander, Hans A. (2008) *National monuments and nationalism in 19th century Germany*. Bern: Peter Lang.

Polakovič, Stefan (1985) 'Ethne, Nationes, Volker, Narody', *Europa Ethnica* 42 (2/3): 105–16.

Poole, Ross (1996) 'National identity, multiculturalism, and aboriginal rights: an Australian perspective', pp. 407–38 in Jocelyne Couture, Kai Neilson and Michel Seymour (eds), *Rethinking nationalism*. Calgary: University of Calgary Press.

Poole, Ross (1999) *Nation and identity*. London: Routledge.

Popson, Nancy (2001) 'The Ukrainian history textbook: introducing children to the "Ukrainian nation"', *Nationalities Papers* 29 (2): 325–50.

Porat, Dina and Roni Stauber (eds) (2010) *Antisemitism worldwide 2009: general analysis*. Tel Aviv: Stephen Roth Institute for the Study of Contemporary Antisemitism and Racism.

Przeworski, Adam and Henry Teune (1970) *The logic of comparative social enquiry*. New York: Wiley.

Pugh, A.K., G.J. Lee and J. Swann (eds) (1980) *Language and language use: a reader*. London: Heinemann Education, in association with the Open University Press.

Puhle, Hans Jürgen (1982) 'Baskischer Nationalismus im spanischen Kontext', pp. 51–81 in Heinrich August Winkler (ed.), *Nationalismus in der Welt von heute*. Göttingen: Vandenhoeck & Ruprecht.

Puri, Jyoti (2004) *Encountering nationalism*. Oxford: Blackwell.

Puzinas, J. (1935) 'Vorgeschichtsforschung und Nationalbewusstsein in Litauen' [Dissertation, Heidelberg]. Kaunas: n.p.

Pye, Lucian W. (1965) 'Introduction: political culture and political development', pp. 3–26 in Lucian W. Pye and Sidney Verba (eds), *Political culture and political development*. Princeton, NJ: Princeton University Press.

Qvortrup, Matt (2012) 'The history of ethno-national referendums 1791–2011', *Nationalism and Ethnic Politics* 18 (1): 129–50.

Rabow-Edling, Susanna (2008) 'The relevance of Kohn's dichotomy to the Russian nineteenth-century concept of nationalism', *Studies in Ethnicity and Nationalism* 8 (3): 560–78.

Rakic, Vojin (1998) 'Theories of nation formation and case selection: the meaning of an alternative model', *Nationalities Papers* 26 (4): 599–618.

Ram, Haggay (2000) 'The immemorial Iranian nation? School textbooks and historical memory in post-revolutionary Iran', *Nations and Nationalism* 6 (1): 67–90.

Ramet, Pedro (1984) *Nationalism and federalism in Yugoslavia, 1963–1983*. Bloomington, IN: Indiana University Press.

Ramet, Pedro (1989) 'Religion and nationalism in Yugoslavia', pp. 299–327 in Pedro Ramet (ed.), *Religion and nationalism in Soviet and East European politics* (New edn). Durham, NC: Duke University Press.

Ramos, Howard (2000) 'National recognition without a state: Cree nationalism within Canada', *Nationalism and Ethnic Politics* 6 (2): 95–115.

Randall, Vicky (1987) *Women and politics: an international perspective* (2nd edn). Basingstoke: Macmillan.

Ranger, Terence (2009) 'The politics of memorialisation in Zimbabwe', pp. 62–76 in Susana Carvalho and François Gemenne (eds), *Nations and their histories: constructions and representations*. Basingstoke: Palgrave Macmillan.

Raun, Toivo U. (1985) 'Die Rolle Finnlands für das nationale Erwachen der Esten', *Zeitschrift für Ostforschung* 34 (4): 568–78.

Raun, Toivo U. (2003) 'Nineteenth- and early twentieth-century Estonian nationalism revisited', *Nations and Nationalism* 9 (1): 129–47.

Reid, Anthony (2010) *Imperial alchemy: nationalism and political identity in Southeast Asia*. Cambridge: Cambridge University Press.

Rémi-Giraud, Sylvianne and Pierre Rétat (eds) (1996) *Les mots de la nation*. Lyon: Presses Universitaires de Lyon.

Rémond, René (1999) *Religion and society in modern Europe*. Trans. Antonia Nevill. Oxford: Blackwell.

Renan, Ernest (1896) 'What is a nation?', pp. 61–83 in *Poetry of the Celtic races and other essays*. London: W. Scott.

Reny, Marie-Eve (2009) 'The political salience of language and religion: patterns of ethnic mobilization among Uyghurs in Xinjiang and Sikhs in Punjab', *Ethnic and Racial Studies* 32 (3): 490–521.

Rerup, Lorenz (1992) 'Channels of communication', pp. 309–26 in Andreas Kappeler, with Fikret Adanir and Alan O'Day (eds), *Comparative studies on governments and non-dominant ethnic groups in Europe, 1850–1940.* Vol. VI: *The formation of national elites.* Aldershot: Dartmouth, for European Science Foundation.

Rex, John (1983) *Race relations in sociological theory* (2nd edn). London: Routledge and Kegan Paul.

Riall, Lucy (1994) *The Italian Risorgimento: state, society and national unification.* London: Routledge.

Ribeira, Aileen (1986) *Dress and morality.* Oxford: Berg.

Riggs, Fred (ed.) (1985) *Ethnicity: intercocta glossary: concepts and terms used in ethnicity research* (Pilot edn). Honolulu, HI: Committee on Conceptual and Terminological Analysis of the International Social Science Council.

Ripley, William Z. (1899) *The races of Europe: a sociological study.* London: Kegan Paul, Trench, Trubner & Co.

Robinson, Leland (1987) 'When will revolutionary movements use religion?', pp. 53–63 in Thomas Robbins and Roland Robinson (eds), *Church–state relations: tensions and transitions.* New Brunswick, NJ: Transaction Books.

Roces, Mina (2007) 'Gender, nation and the politics of dress in twentieth-century Philippines', pp. 19–41 in Mina Roces and Louise Edwards (eds), *The politics of dress in Asia and the Americas.* Eastbourne: Sussex Academic Press.

Roces, Mina and Louise Edwards (2007) 'Transnational flows and the politics of dress in Asia and the Americas', pp. 1–18 in Mina Roces and Louise Edwards (eds), *The politics of dress in Asia and the Americas.* Eastbourne: Sussex Academic Press.

Rodgers, Peter W. (2006) 'Contestation and negotiation: regionalism and the politics of school textbooks in Ukraine's eastern borderlands', *Nations and Nationalism* 12 (4): 681–97.

Roeder, Philip G. (2007) *Where nation states come from: institutional change in the age of nationalism.* Princeton, NJ: Princeton University Press.

Roger, Antoine (2001) *Les grandes théories du nationalisme.* Paris: Armand Colin.

Rokkan, Stein (1969) 'Models and methods in the comparative study of nation building', *Acta Sociologica* 12 (2): 53–73.

Rokkan, Stein (1970) 'Nation building, cleavage formation and the structuring of mass politics', pp. 72–144 in *Citizens, elections, parties: approaches to the comparative study of the processes of development.* Oslo: Universitetsforlaget.

Rokkan, Stein and Derek Urwin (eds) (1982) *The politics of territorial identity: studies in European regionalism.* London: Sage.

Rokkan, Stein and Derek Urwin (1983) *Economy, territory, identity: politics of West European peripheries.* London: Sage.

Romaine, Suzanne (1995) *Bilingualism* (2nd edn). Oxford: Blackwell.

Romania (2002) *Recensamantul populatiei și al locuintelor, 18–27 martie 2002.* Vol. IV: *Structura etnică și confesională* [*Census of population and housing, 18–27 March 2002.* Vol. IV: *Ethnic and confessional structure*]. Bucharest: Institutul National de Statistica.

Rosdolsky, Roman (1986) *Engels and the 'nonhistoric' peoples: the national question in the revolution of 1848.* Trans. and ed. John-Paul Himka. Glasgow: Critique Books [based on doctoral dissertation, Vienna, 1929].

Rosenberg, Alfred (1966 [1928]) 'The earth-centred Jew lacks a soul', pp. 75–8 in George L. Mosse (ed.), *Nazi culture: intellectual, cultural and social life in the Third Reich.* Madison, WI: University of Wisconsin Press.

Rosenberg, Scott (1999) 'Monuments, holidays, and remembering Moshoeshoe: the emergence of national identity in Lesotho, 1902–1966', *Africa Today* 46 (1): 49–72.

Roshwald, Aviel (2006) *The endurance of nationalism: ancient roots and modern dilemmas.* Cambridge: Cambridge University Press.

Ross, Allen P. (1980) 'The table of nations in Genesis 10: its content', *Bibliotheca Sacra* 138: 22–34.

Rosselli, John (2001) 'Music and nationalism in Italy', pp. 181–96 in Harry White and Michael Murphy (eds), *Musical constructions of nationalism: essays on the history and ideology of European musical culture 1800–1945*. Cork: Cork University Press.

Royal Institute of International Affairs (1939) *Nationalism: a report by a study group of members of the Royal Institute of International Affairs*. London: Oxford University Press.

Ruane, Joseph and Jennifer Todd (2010) 'Ethnicity and religion', pp. 67–78 in Karl Cordell and Stefan Wolff (eds), *Routledge handbook of ethnic conflict*. London: Routledge.

Rubin, Joan (1985) 'The special relationship of Guarani and Spanish in Paraguay', pp. 111–20 in Nessa Wolfson and Joan Manes (eds), *Language of inequality*. Berlin: Mouton.

Rubin, Joan, Björn H. Jernudd, Jyotirindra Das Gupta, Joshua A. Fishman and Charles A. Ferguson (eds) (1977) *Language planning processes*. The Hague: Mouton.

Rubinstein, Hilary L., Dan Cohen-Sherbok, Abraham J. Edelheit and William D. Rubinstein (2002) *The Jews in the modern world: a history since 1750*. London: Arnold.

Rubinstein, Ruth P. (1995) *Dress codes: meanings and messages in American culture*. Boulder, CO: Westview Press.

Rudenko, G.F., et al. (1975) *The revolutionary movement of our time and nationalism*. Trans. Vic Schneierson. Moscow: Progress Publishers.

Russia (1899–1905) *Pervaya vseobshchaya perepis' naseleniya Rossiiskoi Imperii 1897 g.* [*First general census of the population of the Russian Empire, 1897*] (vols 4, 5, 17, 19, 21, 49, 59) [gubernia reports for Baltic and Lithuanian areas] St Peterburg: Izdanie Tsentralnogo Statisticheskogo Komiteta Ministerstva Vnutrennikh Del.

Rustow, Dankwart A. (1967) *A world of nations: problems of political modernisation*. Washington, DC: Brookings Institution.

Rustow, Dankwart A. (1968) 'Nation', pp. 7–14 in David L. Sills (ed.), *International encyclopedia of the social sciences* (vol. 11). New York: Macmillan.

Sabourin, Paul (1996) *Les nationalismes européens*. Paris: Presses Universitaires de France.

Safran, William (1992) 'Language, ideology, and state-building: a comparison of policies in France, Israel, and the Soviet Union', *International Political Science Review* 13 (4): 397–414.

Safran, William (2008a) 'Language, ethnicity and religion: a complex and persistent linkage', *Nations and Nationalism* 14 (1): 171–90.

Safran, William (2008b) 'Names, labels, and identities: sociopolitical contexts and the question of ethnic categorization', *Identities* 15 (4): 437–61.

Sampson, Geoffrey (1985) *Writing systems*. London: Hutchinson.

Samson, Jim (2007) 'Music and nationalism: five historical moments', pp. 55–67 in Athena S. Leoussi and Steven Grosby (eds), *Nationalism end ethnosymbolism: history, culture and ethnicity in the formation of nations*. Edinburgh: Edinburgh University Press.

Sarkar, Tanika (1987) 'Nationalist iconography: image of women in 19th century Bengali literature', *Economic and Political Weekly* 22 (47): 2011–15.

Schaeffer, Richard T. (2006) *Racial and ethnic groups* (10th edn). Upper Saddle River, NJ: Pearson Education.

Schechtman, J.B. (1962) *Postwar population transfers in Europe, 1945–1955*. London: Oxford University Press.

Schechtman, J.B. (1971 [1946]) *European population transfers, 1939–1945*. New York: Russell & Russell.

Schermerhorn, R.A. (1970) *Comparative ethnic relations: a framework for theory and research*. New York: Random House.

Schjerve, Rosita Rindler (1981) 'Biligualism and language shift in Sardinia', pp. 208–17 in Einar Haugen, J. Derrick McClure and Derick Thomson (eds), *Minority languages today*. Edinburgh: Edinburgh University Press.

Schnapper, Dominique (2003 [1994]) *La communauté des citoyens: sur l'idée moderne de nation*. Paris: Gallimard.

Schneckener, Ulrich and Dieter Senghaas (2003) 'In quest of peaceful coexistence: strategies in regulating ethnic conflict', pp. 165–200 in Farimah Daftary and Stefan Troebst (eds), *Radical ethnic movements in contemporary Europe*. Oxford: Berghahn.

Schoenauer, Norbert (2000) *6,000 years of housing* (Rev edn). New York: W.W. Norton.

Schöpflin, George (1997) 'The functions of myth and a taxonomy of myth', pp. 19–35 in Geoffrey Hosking and George Schöpflin (eds), *Myths and nationhood*. London: Hurst.

Schöpflin, George (2001) 'Music and nationalism', pp. 194–7 in Athena S. Leoussi (ed.), *Encyclopaedia of nationalism*. New Brunswick, NJ: Transactions Books.

Schrad, Mark Lawrence (2004) 'Rag doll nations and the politics of differentiation on arbitrary borders: Karelia and Moldova', *Nationalities Papers* 32 (2): 457–96.

Schulze, Hagen (1987) 'The revolution of the European order and the rise of German nationalism', pp. 5–18 in Hagen Schulze (ed.), *Nation-building in Central Europe*. Leamington Spa: Berg.

Semyonov, V.S. (1979) *Nations and internationalism*. Trans. Lenina Hyitskaya. Moscow: Progress Publishers.

Seng, Yvonne J., and Betty Wass (1995) 'Traditional Palestinian wedding dress as a symbol of nationalism', pp. 227–54 in Joanne B. Eicher (ed.), *Dress and ethnicity: change across space and time*. Oxford: Berg.

Senn, Alfred Erich (1999) *Power, politics, and the Olympic Games*. Champaign, IL: Human Kinetics.

Seton-Watson, Christopher (1967) *Italy from liberalism to fascism 1870–1925*. London: Methuen.

Seton-Watson, Hugh (1965) *Nationalism old and new: ninth George Juday Cohen memorial lecture delivered in the University of Sydney, 14 September 1964*. Sydney: Sydney University Press.

Seton-Watson, Hugh (1977) *Nations and states: an enquiry into the origins of nations and the politics of nationalism*. London: Methuen.

Settler, Federico (2010) 'Indigenous authorities and the post-colonial state: the domestication of indigeneity and African nationalism in South Africa', *Social Dynamics* 36 (1): 52–64.

Seybolt, Peter J. and Gregory Kuei-ke Chiang (1979) 'Introduction', pp. 1–27 in Peter J. Seybolt and Gregory Kuei-ke Chiang (eds), *Language reform in China: documents and commentary*. White Plains, NY: ME Sharpe.

Seymour, Michel, with Jocelyne Couture and Kai Nielsen (1996) 'Introduction: questioning the ethnic/civic dichotomy', pp. 1–61 in Jocelyne Couture, Kai Nielsen and Michel Seymour (eds), *Rethinking nastionalism*. Calgary: University of Calgary Press.

Sharkey, Heather J. (2003) *Living with colonialism: nationalism and culture in the Anglo-Egyptian Sudan*. Berkeley, CA: University of California Press.

Shaw, Martin (2007) *What is genocide?* Cambridge: Polity Press.

Shaw, William (1780) *A Galic and English dictionary* (vol. 1). London: W. and A. Strahan.

Shils, Edward (1957) 'Primordial, personal, sacred and civil ties: some particular observations on the relationships of sociological research and theory', *British Journal of Sociology* 8 (2): 130–45.

Shulman, Stephen (2002) 'Challenging the civic/ethnic and West/East dichotomies in the study of nationalism', *Comparative Political Studies* 35 (5): 554–85.

Siddiqi, Farhan (2010) 'Nation-formation and national movement(s) in Pakistan: a critical estimation of Hroch's stage theory', *Nationalities Papers* 38 (6): 777–92.

Simonsen, Sven Gunnar (2005) 'Between minority rights and civil liberties: Russia's discourse over "nationality" registration and the internal passport', *Nationalities Papers* 33 (2): 211–29.

Skocpol, Theda (1979) *States and social revolutions: a comparative analysis of France, Russia, and China*. Cambridge: Cambridge University Press.

Slezkine, Yuri (1996 [1994]) 'The USSR as a communal apartment, or how the socialist state promoted ethnic particularlism', pp. 203–38 in Geoff Eley and Ronald Grigor Suny (eds), *Becoming national: a reader*. Oxford: Oxford University Press.

Smart, Ninian (ed.) (1999) *Atlas of the world's religions*. Oxford: Oxford University Press.

Smith, Anthony D. (1971) *Theories of nationalism*. London: Duckworth.

Smith, Anthony D. (1983) *Theories of nationalism* (2nd edn). London: Duckworth.

Smith, Anthony D. (1984) 'National identity and myths of ethnic descent', pp. 95–130 in *Research in social movements, conflict and change* (vol. 7). Greenwich, CT: JAI Press.

Smith, Anthony D. (1986) *The ethnic origins of nations*. Oxford: Basil Blackwell.

Smith, Anthony D. (1991) *National identity*. London: Penguin Books.

Smith, Anthony D. (1992) 'Chosen peoples: why ethnic groups survive', *Ethnic and Racial Studies* 15 (3): 436–56.

Smith, Anthony D. (1995) *Nations and nationalism in a global era*. Cambridge: Polity Press.

Smith, Anthony D. (1996) 'The resurgence of nationalism? Myth and memory in the renewal of nations', *British Journal of Sociology* 47 (4): 575–98.

Smith, Anthony D. (1998) *Nationalism and modernism: a critical survey of recent theories of nations and nationalism*. London: Routledge.

Smith, Anthony D. (1999) *Myths and memories of the nation*. Oxford: Oxford University Press.

Smith, Anthony D. (2000a) *The nation in history: historiographical debates about ethnicity and nationalism*. Cambridge: Polity Press.

Smith, Anthony D. (2000b) 'The "sacred" dimension of nationalism', *Millennium* 29 (3): 791–814.

Smith, Anthony D. (2001) *Nationalism: theory, ideology, history*. Cambridge: Polity Press.

Smith, Anthony D. (2003) *Chosen peoples*. Oxford: Oxford University Press.

Smith, Anthony D. (2009) *Ethno-symbolism and nationalism: a cultural approach*. London: Routledge.

Smith, Brian K. (2003) 'Hinduism', pp. 185–211 in Jacob Neusner (ed.), *The politics of world religions*. Washington, DC: Georgetown University Press.

Smith, David J. and John Hiden (2012) *Ethnic diversity and the nation state: national cultural autonomy revisited*. London: Routledge.

Smith, Graham (ed.) (1995) *Federalism: the multiethnic challenge*. London: Longman.

Smith, Huston (1991) *The world's religions: our great wisdom traditions* (New edn). New York: Harper San Francisco.

Smooha, Sammy and Theodor Hanf (1992) 'The diverse modes of conflict-regulation in deeply divided societies', *International Journal of Comparative Sociology* 33 (1–2): 26–47.

Smouts, Marie-Claude (1998) 'The region as the new imagined community?', pp. 30–38 in Patrick Le Galès and Christian Lequesne (eds), *Regions in Europe*. London: Routledge.

Snyder, Louis (1954) *The meaning of nationalism*. New Brunswick, NJ: Rutgers University Press.

Snyder, Louis (ed.) (1964) *The dynamics of nationalism: readings in its meaning and development*. Princeton, NJ: Van Nostrand.

Snyder, Louis (1968) *The new nationalism*. Ithaca, NY: Cornell University Press.

Snyder, Louis (1982) *Global mini-nationalisms: autonomy or independence*. Westport, CT: Greenwood Press.

Snyder, Louis (1990) *Encyclopedia of nationalism*. New York: Paragon House.

Sopher, David E. (1967) *Geography of religions*. Englewood Cliffs, NJ: Prentice-Hall.

South Africa (2001) *Census 2001: primary tables South Africa: census 1996 and 2001 compared*, Report No. 03-02-04. Pretoria: Statistics South Africa.

Sow, Alfa I. and Mohamed H. Abdulaziz (1993) 'Language and social change', pp. 522–52 in Ali A. Mazrui (ed.), *General history of Africa* (vol. 8). Paris: UNESCO; London: Heinemann.

Sparks, Cheryl Logan (2000) 'Citizen-soldiers or republican mothers: US citizenship and military obligation in an era of "choice"', pp. 181–95 in Sita Ranchod-Nilsson and Mary Ann Tétreault (eds), *Women, states, and nationalism: at home in the nation?* London: Routledge.

Spencer, Philip and Howard Wollman (2002) *Nationalism: a critical introduction*. London: Sage.

Spencer, Philip and Howard Wollman (eds) (2005) *Nations and nationalism: a reader*. Edinburgh: Edinburgh University Press.

Spira, Thomas (ed.) (1999) *Nationalism and ethnicity terminologies: an encyclopedic dictionary and research guide*. Gulf Breeze, FL: Academic International Press.

Springer, Rudolf [*pseud.* Karl Renner] (1902) *Der Kampf der oesterreichischen Nation um den Staat*. Leipzig and Vienna: Franz Deuticke.

Stackhouse, Max L. (1987) 'Politics and religion', pp. 408–23 in Mircea Eliade (ed.), *The encyclopedia of religion* (vol. 11). New York: Macmillan.

Stalin, J.V. (1953 [1913]) 'Marxism and the national question', pp. 300–81 in *Works* (vol. 2). Moscow: Foreign Languages Publishing House.

Stefanovic, Đorđe (2005) 'Seeing the Albanians through Serbian eyes: the inventors of the tradition of intolerance and their critics, 1804–1939', *European History Quarterly* 35 (3): 465–92.

Stein, Stuart (2004) 'Ethnocide', pp. 147–6 in Ellis Cashmore (ed.), *Encyclopedia of race and ethnic studies*. London: Routledge.

Stergios, James (2006) 'Language and nationalism in Italy', *Nations and Nationalism* 12 (1): 15–33.

Stevenson, Garth (2004) 'The politics of remembrance in Irish and Quebec nationalism', *Canadian Journal of Political Science* 37 (4): 903–25.

Stoddart, Brian (1988) 'Sport, cultural imperialism, and colonial response in the British Empire', *Comparative Studies in Society and History* 30 (4): 649–73.

Stone, John and Bhumika Piya (2007) 'Ethnic groups', in George Ritzer (ed.), *Blackwell encyclopedia of sociology*. Oxford: Blackwell.

Stone, Lawrence (1969) 'Literacy and education in England 1640–1900', *Past and Present* 42: 69–139.

Stooksbury, Kara E. and Lori Maxwell Edgemon (2003) 'The First Lady scholarship reconsidered: a review essay', *Women and Politics* 25 (3): 97–111.

Storm, Eric (2009) 'Painting regional identities: nationalism in the arts, France, Germany and Spain, 1890–1914', *European History Quarterly* 39 (4): 557–82.

Strauss, Gerald (1984) 'Lutheranism and literacy: a reassessment', pp. 109–23 in Kaspar von Greyerz (ed.), *Religion and society in early modern Europe 1500–1800*. London: George Allen and Unwin.

Super, John C. and Briane K. Turley (2006) *Religion in world history: the persistence of imperial communion*. London: Routledge.

Switzerland (1851) *Uebersichten der Bevölkerung der Schweiz, nach den Ergebnissen der letzten Eidgenössischen Volkszählung (vom 18. bis 23. März 1850)*. 1 Theil. Bern: gedruckt in der Stämpflischen Buchdruckerei.

Switzerland (1904) *Die Ergebnissen der Eidgenössischen Volkszählung (vom 1. Dezember 1900)*. Erster Band. Bern: Buchdruckerei Lack & Grunau.

Switzerland (1956) *Eidgenössische Volkszählung (1 Dezember 1950)*. Band 24. Bern: Eidgenossisches Statistisches Amt.

Tägil, Sven (1999) 'The roots of identity: territoriality in early Central European history', pp. 30–52 in Sven Tägil (ed.), *Regions in Central Europe: the legacy of history*. London: Hurst.

Tall, Johannes (1985) 'Estonian song festivals and nationalism in music towards the end of the nineteenth century', pp. 449–60 in Aleksander Loit (ed.), *National movements in the Baltic countries during the 19th century: the 7th Conference on Baltic Studies in Scandinavia, Stockholm, June 10–13, 1983*. Stockholm: Almqvist and Wiksell.

Tamir, Yael (1993) *Liberal nationalism*. Princeton, NJ: Princeton University Press.

Taras, Ray (1993) 'Making sense of matrioshka nationalism', pp. 513–38 in Ian Bremmer and Ray Taras (eds), *Nations and politics in the Soviet successor states*. Cambridge: Cambridge University Press.

Taylor, Charles (1994) 'The politics of recognition', pp. 25–73 in Amy Gutman (ed.), *Multiculturalism: examining the politics of recognition*. Princeton, NJ: Princeton University Press.

Taylor, Rupert (ed.) (2009) *Consociational theory: McGarry and O'Leary and the Northern Ireland conflict.* London: Routledge.

Tazbir, Janusz (2002) 'La Pologne: rempart de la chrétienté', pp. 97–107 in Chantal Delsol, Michel Masłowski and Joanna Nowicki (eds), *Mythes et symboles politiques en Europe centrale.* Paris: Presses Universitaires de France.

Teleki, Count Paul and Andrew Rónai (1937) *The different types of ethnic mixture of population.* Budapest: Athenaeum.

Thaler, Peter (2012) 'The discourse of historical legitimization: a comparative examination of Southern Jutland and the Slovenian language area', *Nationalities Papers* 40 (1): 1–22.

Thiesse, Anne-Marie (1999) *La création des identités nationales: Europe XVIIe – XXe siècle.* Paris: Éditions du Seuil.

Thomas, Dominic (2002) *Nation-building, propaganda, and literature in francophone Africa.* Bloomington, IN: Indiana University Press.

Thomas, Raju G.C. and Bharat Karnad (1991) 'The military and national integration in India', pp. 127–49 in Henry Dietz, Jerrold Elkin and Maurice Roumani (eds), *Ethnicity, integration, and the military.* Boulder, CO: Westview Press.

Thompson, Leonard and Andrew Prior (1982) *South African politics.* New Haven, CT: Yale University Press.

Thomson, Catherine Claire (2004) 'Nationalism', pp. 789–90 in Christopher John Murray (ed.), *Encyclopedia of the romantic era, 1760–1850* (vol. 2). London: Fitzroy Dearborn.

Thornton, Russell (2000) 'Population history of native North Americans', pp. 9–50 in Michael R. Haines and Richard H. Steckel (eds), *A population history of North America.* Cambridge: Cambridge University Press.

Tilly, Charles (1985) 'War making and state making as organised crime', pp. 169–91 in Peter B. Evans, Dietrich Rueschmeyer and Theda Skocpol (eds), *Bringing the state back in.* Cambridge: Cambridge University Press.

Tishkov, Valery A. (2000) 'Forget the "nation": postnationalist understanding of nationalism', *Ethnic and Racial Studies* 23 (4): 625–50.

Tishkov, Valery A. (2008) 'The Russian people and national identity', *Russia in Global Affairs* 3. Available at: http://eng.globalaffairs.ru/number/n_11287.

Todorova, Maria (1995) 'The course and discourses of Bulgarian nationalism', pp. 70–102 in Peter F. Sugar (ed.), *Eastern European nationalism in the twentieth century.* Washington, DC: American University Press.

Toft, Monica Duffy (2003) *The geography of ethnic violence: identity, interests and the indivisibility of territory.* Princeton, NJ: Princeton University Press.

Tomaszewski, Jerzy (1985) 'Belorussians in the eyes of the Poles, 1918–1939', *Acta Poloniae Historica* 51: 101–22.

Tomlinson, Janis A. (2003) 'State galleries and the formation of national artistic identity in Spain, England, and France 1814–1851', pp. 1–15 in Michelle Facos and Sharon L. Hirsh (eds), *Art, culture, and national identity in fin-de-siècle Europe.* Cambridge: Cambridge University Press.

Tortora, Phyllis (2005) 'Ancient world: history of dress', pp. 51–9 in Valerie Steele (ed.), *Encyclopedia of clothing and fashion* (vol. 1). Farmington Hills, MI: Thomson Gale.

Toyoda, Maria A. and Aiji Tanaka (2002) 'Religion and politics in Japan', pp. 269–86 in Ted Gerard Jelen and Clyde Wilcox (eds), *Religion and politics in comparative perspective: the one, the few, and the many.* Cambridge: Cambridge University Press.

Trask, Haunani-Kay (1997) 'Feminism and indigenous Hawaiian nationalism', pp. 187–98 in Lois A. West (ed.), *Feminist nationalism.* London: Routledge.

Trevor-Roper, Hugh (1965) *The rise of Christian Europe.* London: Thames and Hudson.

Trevor-Roper, Hugh (1983) 'The invention of tradition: the Highland tradition of Scotland', pp. 15–42 in Eric Hobsbawm and Terence Ranger (eds), *The invention of tradition*. Cambridge: Cambridge University Press.

Trewin, Dennis (2000) *Australian standard classification of cultural and ethnic groups*. Canberra: Australian Bureau of Statistics. Also available at: www.abs.gov.au.

Trudgill, Peter (1974) *Sociolinguistics: an introduction*. Harmondsworth: Penguin.

Trumpa, Vincent (1965) 'Simonas Daukantas, historian and pioneer of Lithuanian national rebirth', *Lituanus* 11 (1): 5–17.

Tshibangu, Tshishiku, with J.F. Ade Ajayi and Lemin Sanneh (1993) 'Religion and social evolution', pp. 501–21 in Ali A. Mazrui (ed.), *General history of Africa* (vol. 8). Paris: Unesco; London: Heinemann.

Tsilevich, Boris (1996) 'The situation of ethnic minorities in Latvia', pp. 51–60 in Magda Opalski and Piotr Dutievicz (eds), *Ethnic minority rights in Central Eastern Europe*. Ottawa: Canadian Human Rights Foundation Forum Eastern Europe.

Tully, James (1995) *Strange multiplicity: constitutionalism in an age of diversity*. Cambridge: Cambridge University Press.

Turnock, David (1991) 'The planning of rural settlement in Romania', *Geographical Journal* 157 (3): 251–64.

Turpin, John (2003) 'Visual marianism and national identity in Ireland 1920–1960', pp. 67–78 in Tricia Cusack and Síghle Bhreathnach-Lynch (eds), *Art, nation and gender: ethnic landscapes, myths and mother-figures*. Aldershot: Ashgate.

UK Cabinet Office (2008) *Helping to shape tomorrow: the 2011 census of population and housing in England and Wales*. Cm 7513. London: HMSO

Unesco (1950) 'The race question', *Unesco and its programme* 3: 1–11 [Unesco publication 791]. Paris: Unesco.

Unesco (1977) *Unesco Thesaurus*. Paris: Unesco. Current edition available at: www2.ulcc.ac.uk/unesco/.

Unesco (1981) *La définition d'une stratégie relative à la promotion des langues africaines. Documents de la reunion d'experts qui a lieu à Conakry (Guinée) 12–15 septembre 1981*. Doc CLT–/85/WS/72. Paris: Unesco. Available at: http://unesdoc.unesco.org/images/0008/000809/080934mo.pdf.

United Nations (1951) 'Convention on the prevention and punishment of the crime of genocide. Adopted by the General Assembly of the United Nations on 9 December 1948', *United Nations Treaty Series* 78 (1021): 277–322. Available at: http://treaties.un.org/doc/Publication/UNTS/Volume 78/volume-78-I-1021-English.pdf [2010-11-21].

United States Bureau of the Census (1975) *Historical statistics of the United States: colonial times to 1970* (Part I). Washington, DC: US Bureau of the Census.

USSR (1977) *Constitution (fundamental law) of the Union of Soviet Socialist Republics*. Moscow: Novosti Press Agency.

Uzelac, Gordana (2010) 'National ceremonies: the pursuit of authenticity', *Ethnic and Racial Studies* 33 (10): 1718–36.

van den Berghe, Pierre L. (1978) 'Race and ethnicity: a sociobiological perspective', *Ethnic and Racial Studies* 1 (4): 401–11.

van den Berghe, Pierre L. (1981a) *The ethnic phenomenon*. London: Elsevier.

van den Berghe, Pierre L. (1981b) 'Protection of ethnic minorities: a critical appraisal', pp. 343–55 in Robert G. Wirsing (ed.), *Protection of ethnic minorities: comparative perspectives*. Oxford: Pergamon.

van den Berghe, Pierre L. (1984) 'Ethnic cuisine: culture in nature', *Ethnic and Racial Studies* 7 (3): 387–97.

van der Veer, Peter (1994) *Religious nationalism: Hindus and Muslims in India*. Berkeley, CA: University of California Press.

Vermeulen, Hans (2010) 'Segmented assimilation and cross-national comparative research on the integration of immigrants and their children', *Ethnic and Racial Studies* 33 (7): 1214–30.

Viķe-Freiberga, Vaīra (1985) 'Andrejs Pumpurs' *Lāčplēsis* ('Bearslayer'): Latvian national epic or romantic creation?', pp. 449–60 in Alexander Loit (ed.), *National movements in the Baltic countries during the 19th century: the 7th Conference on Baltic Studies in Scandinavia, Stockholm, June 10–13, 1983*. Stockholm: Almqvist and Wiksell.

Vinski, Ivo (1961) 'National product and fixed assets in the territory of Yugoslavia 1909–1959', *Review of Income and Wealth* 9 (1): 206–33.

Vlachová, Klára and Blanka Řeháková (2009) 'Identity of non-self-evident nation: Czech national identity after the break-up of Czechoslovakia and before accession to the European Union', *Nations and Nationalism* 15 (2): 254–79.

von Busekist, Astrid (1998) *Nations et nationalismes: XIXᵉ et XXᵉ siècles*. Paris: Armand Colin.

von Treitschke, Heinrich (1916 [1897]) *Politics* (2 vols). New York: Macmillan.

Vovina, Olessia P. (2000) 'Building the road to the temple: religion and national revival in the Chuvash Republic', *Nationalities Papers* 28 (4): 695–706.

Wachtel, Andrew Baruch (1998) *Making a nation, breaking a nation: literature and cultural politics in Yugoslavia*. Stanford, CA: Stanford University Press.

Wald, Kenneth D. (2002) 'The religious dimension in Israeli political life', pp. 99–122 in Ted Gerard Jelen and Clyde Wilcox (eds), *Religion and politics in comparative perspective: the one, the few, and the many*. Cambridge: Cambridge University Press.

Wallace, Peter G. (2004) *The long European reformation: religion, political conflict and the search for conformity, 1350–1750*. Basingstoke: Palgrave Macmillan.

Wallis, Roy and Steve Bruce (1986) *Sociological theory, religion and collective action*. Belfast: Queen's University.

Walter, Barbara F. (2009) *Reputation and civil war: why separatist conflicts are so violent*. Cambridge: Cambridge University Press.

Wandycz, Piotr S. (1974) *The lands of partitioned Poland, 1795–1918*. Seattle, WA: University of Washington Press.

Watson, Adam (1992) *The evolution of international society: a comparative historical analysis*. London: Routledge.

Watson, G.J. (1994) *Irish identity and the literary revival: Synge, Yeats, Joyce and O'Casey* (2nd edn). Washington, DC: Catholic University of America Press.

Watson, James L. (2005 [2000]) 'China's Big Mac attack', pp. 70–79 in James L. Watson and Melissa L. Caldwell (eds), *The cultural politics of food and eating: a reader*. Oxford: Blackwell.

Watson, James L. and Melissa L. Caldwell (2005) 'Introduction', pp. 1–10 in James L. Watson and Melissa L. Caldwell (eds), *The cultural politics of food and eating: a reader*. Oxford: Blackwell.

Weber, Eugen (1976) *Peasants into Frenchmen: the modernisation of rural France 1870-1914*. Stanford, CA: Stanford University Press.

Weber, Eugen (1980) 'Modern anti-Semitism', pp. 37–52 in Henry Friedlander and Sybil Milton (eds), *The Holocaust: ideology, bureaucracy, and genocide*. Millwood, NY: Kraus International.

Weber, Max (1968 [1922]) *Economy and society: an outline of interpretive sociology* (2 vols). Ed. Guenther Roth and Claus Wittich. Berkeley, CA: University of California Press.

Welch, Claude E., Jr (1991) 'The military and social integration in Ethiopia', pp. 151–78 in Henry Dietz, Jerrold Elkin and Maurice Roumani (eds), *Ethnicity, integration, and the military*. Boulder, CO: Westview Press.

Wellings, Ben (2009) 'Nation, history, museum: the politics of the past at the National Museum of Australia', pp. 274–88 in Susana Carvalho and François Gemenne (eds), *Nations and their histories: constructions and representations*. Basingstoke: Palgrave Macmillan.

Welters, Linda (1995) 'Ethnicity in Greek dress', pp. 53–78 in Joanne B. Eicher (ed.), *Dress and ethnicity: changes across space and time*. Oxford: Berg.

West, Anson (1893) *A history of Methodism in Alabama*. Nashville, TN: Printed for the author. Methodist Episcopal Church, South.

Wheare, K.C. (1963) *Federal government* (4th edn). London: Oxford University Press.

Whyte, J. (1981) *Catholics in western democracies: a study in political behaviour*. Dublin: Gill and Macmillan.

Wiarda, Howard J. (1989) 'Rethinking political development: a look backward over thirty years, and a look ahead', *Comparative Studies in International Development* 24 (4): 65–82.

Wickberg, Edgar (1964) 'The Chinese *mestizo* in Philippine history', *Journal of Southeast Asian History* 5 (1): 62–100.

Wickberg, Edgar (2000 [1965]) *The Chinese in Philippine life 1850–1898*. Manila: Ateneo de Manila University Press.

Wilford, Rick (1998) 'Women, ethnicity and nationalism: surveying the ground', pp. 1–22 in Rick Wilford and Robert L. Miller (eds), *Women, ethnicity and nationalism: the politics of transition*. London: Routledge.

Williams, C.H. (ed.) (1967) *English historical documents 1485–1558*. London: Eyre and Spottiswoode.

Williams, Colin H. (1988) 'Minority nationalist historiography', pp. 203–21 in R.J. Johnston, David B. Knight and Eleonore Kofman (eds), *National self-determination and political geography*. London: Croom Helm.

Williams, Verna L. (2009) 'The first (black) lady', *Denver University Law Review* 86 (SI): 833–50.

Wilson, Andrew (1997) 'Myths of national history in Belarus and Ukraine', pp. 182–97 in Geoffrey Hosking and George Schöpflin (eds), *Myths and nationhood*. London: Hurst.

Wilson, Christopher S. (2007) 'The persistence of the Turkish nation in the mausoleum of Mustafa Kemal Atatürk', pp. 93–114 in Eric Zuelow, Mitchell Young and Andreas Sturm (eds), *Nationalism in a global era: the persistence of nations*. London: Routledge.

Wilson, William A. (1978) 'The Kalevala and Finnish politics', pp. 51–75 in Felix J. Oinas (ed.), *Folklore, nationalism, and politics*. Columbus, OH: Slavia Publishers.

Wimmer, Andreas (2002) *Nationalist exclusion and ethnic conflict: shadows of modernity*. Cambridge: Cambridge University Press.

Wimmer, Andreas (2008) 'Elementary strategies of ethnic boundary making', *Ethnic and Racial Studies* 31 (6): 1025–55.

Wimmer, Andreas (2011) 'A Swiss anomaly? A relational account of national boundary-making', *Nations and Nationalism* 17 (4): 718–37.

Woolf, Stuart (ed.) (1996) *Nationalism in Europe, 1815 to the present: a reader*. London: Routledge.

Wright, Quincy (1942) *A study of war* (2 vols). Chicago, IL: University of Chicago Press.

Wright, Stephen (1977) 'Are the Olympics games? The relationship of politics and sports', *Millennium* 6 (1): 30–44.

Wright, Stephen (1991) 'State-consolidation and social integration in Nigeria: the military's search for the elusive', pp. 209–27 in Henry Dietz, Jerrold Elkin and Maurice Roumani (eds), *Ethnicity, integration, and the military*. Boulder, CO: Westview Press.

Yack, Bernard (1999 [1996]) 'The myth of the civic nation', pp. 103–18 in Ronald Beiner (ed.), *Theorizing nationalism*. Albany, NY: State University of New York Press.

Yahuda, Michael (2000) 'The changing faces of Chinese nationalism: the dimensions of statehood', pp. 21–37 in Michael Leifer (ed.), *Asian nationalism*. London: Routledge.

Yeğenoğlu, Meyda (2005) 'Cosmopolitanism and nationalism in a globalized world', *Ethnic and Racial Studies* 28 (1): 103–31.

Yuval-Davis, Nira (1989) 'National reproduction and "the demographic race" in Israel', pp. 92–109 in Nira Yuval-Davis and Floya Anthias (eds), *Woman – nation – state*. London: Macmillan.

Yuval-Davis, Nira (1997) *Gender and nation*. London: Sage.

Zacek, Joseph F. (1964) 'Palacky and his history of the Czech nation', *Journal of Central European Affairs* 23 (4): 412–23.

Zake, Ieva (2005) 'Latvian nationalist intellectuals and the crisis of democracy in the inter-war period', *Nationalities Papers* 33 (1): 97–117.

Zangwill, Israel (2006 [1909]) 'The melting pot', pp. 265–364 in *From the ghetto to the melting pot: Israel Zangwill's Jewish plays: three playscripts*. Ed. Edna Nahshon. Detroit, MI: Wayne State University Press.

Zartman, I. William (1990) 'Negotiations and prenegotiations in ethnic conflict: the beginning, the middle, and the ends', pp. 511–33 in Joseph V. Montville (ed.), *Conflict and peacemaking in multiethnic societies*. Lexington, MA: Lexington Books.

Zhao, Suisheng (2000) 'Chinese nationalism and its international orientations', *Political Science Quarterly* 115 (1): 1–33.

Zimmer, Oliver (2003a) 'Boundary mechanisms and symbolic resources: towards a process-oriented approach to national identity', *Nations and Nationalism* 9 (2): 173–93.

Zimmer, Oliver (2003b) *Nationalism in Europe, 1890–1940*. Basingstoke: Palgrave Macmillan.

Znaniecki, Florian (1952) *Modern nationalities: a sociological study*. Urbana, IL: University of Illinois Press.

Zubrycki, Geneviève (2001) '"We the Polish nation": ethnic and civic visions of nationhood in post-communist constitutional debates', *Theory and Society* 30 (5): 629–68.

Zuelow, Eric, Mitchell Young and Andreas Sturm (2007) 'The owl's early flight: globalisation and nationalism, an introduction', pp. 1–13 in Eric Zuelow, Mitchell Young and Andreas Sturm (eds), *Nationalism in a global era: the persistence of nations*. London: Routledge.

INDEX